John Green

Greg Kallevig

Jeff Massicotte

Bill Melvin

Herbie Andrade

Warren Arrington

Lenny Bell

Mike Boswell

Steve Hill

Jerry LaPenta

Elvin Paulino

Marty Rivero

Rick Wilkins

Eddie Williams

THE BOYS WHO WOULD BE
CUBS

THE BOYS WHO WOULD BE
CUBS

*A Year in the Heart of Baseball's
Minor Leagues*

JOSEPH BOSCO

William Morrow and Company, Inc.
NEW YORK

Recognizing the importance of preserving what has been written, it is the policy
of William Morrow and Company, Inc., and its imprints and affiliates to have the books it
publishes printed on acid-free paper, and we exert our best efforts to that end.

Library of Congress Cataloging-in-Publication Data

Bosco, Joseph.
    The boys who would be Cubs : a year in the heart of baseball's minor leagues /
Joseph Bosco.
        p.   cm.
    ISBN 0-688-08261-0
    1. Baseball clubs—United States—History.   2. Chicago Cubs (Baseball team)—History,
I. Title.
GV875.A1B67   1990
796.357′64′0977311—dc20   90-34666
                                                                              CIP

Printed in the United States of America

First Edition

1 2 3 4 5 6 7 8 9 10

BOOK DESIGN BY CIRCA 86, INC.

FOR HIRAM AND FOR ZIGGY

"Come on, blue! Christ . . . this kid's painting black like a Rembrandt . . . he's gotta give 'im the corner."

"Why? Miller don't call corners on odd-numbered Tuesdays and Thursdays."

"Yeah. Well, if he makes 'im come across the plate with that *stuff, they're gonna be huntin' up balls in those ligustrums."*

"Uh-huh. Bring that dog back out in the yard, too."

"Jesus, umpsie! Gotta be a strike zone there somewheres, huh?"

"Kid oughta sue his mama for givin' 'im that arm. And he ain't got no kinda breaking ball."

"It ain't round, you know, Miller. Ain't your favorite . . . a dinner *plate! Hey, Hiram . . . tell me something."*

"What's that?"

"You know ol' Hoss could throw Vas'leen through a cypress stump . . . reckon how come he's selling shoes?"

"I dunno, man. Probably a woman or something."

Pii-thwack-iing! The sound of a Black Magic Easton aluminum bat meeting a Diamond Pro baseball hard. Very hard.

"That's yours, blue . . . told ya if you made 'im groove it."

"Dog's gonna play hell with that . . . that one's got the roof.*"*

"No arms this year, Big Man. Ain't no Hosses around for true, I'ma tell you that. Sumbitch had the livest arm I ever saw . . . personally, you understand?"

"Yepper. And he's working for Gryder's."

"Go figure it, huh? I mean, how good are *those dudes up there, anyway?"*

"I'm telling you . . . hadda be a broad. Or something."

—Not quite anonymous

A PROLOGUE

New Orleans, late September 1987

HOMETOWN HEROES. MOST every town gets one or two every now and again. Some towns, big and little, seem to get more than others; but just about every town has had, at one time or another, a high school or college phenom sign a professional baseball contract, buy an automobile—don't know why, but even when they sign for less than what a schoolteacher in Mississippi earns by Thanksgiving, which is the case as often as not, almost always they will go out and buy a car of some fashion—and pack it full of unaccustomed-to pots and pans, new socks and jock, old pillow and all of their wettest dreams and worst fears, and then head off toward small towns in Montana, or Idaho, or West Virginia, or Florida, or maybe upstate New York, where they'll join up with a couple dozen or so other phenoms-from-everywhere to play for pay a strange brand of baseball known as the "low minors" and where (just for instance) they will learn how to keep from swallowing a plug of Red Man while coming across the bag on the front end of a slowly developing 3-6-4 double play.

In short, they will begin to learn how to play "hard" ball the hard way, the "organization way," in front of unfamiliar people who never saw them strike out nineteen batters in a seven-inning game against overmatched non-phenoms; or two-hop the loading dock of the administration building some 150 feet beyond the chain-link fence in left center off a 76-mile-per-hour fastball delivered by a future veterinarian, welder, or mayor to win the district tournament with a three-run dinger; or go deep in the hole, backhand, and hose out a 7.4-in-the-60 would-be baserunner and soon-to-be Dixie Beer truck driver to preserve a state title.

While these young men will be burdened by an equipment-bagful of their own unanswered questions, so also will they leave one behind in the minds of all those good folks who've watched them play ball since that

9

time when their noses ran faster than they did and the bases were only sixty feet apart. This question will hang like vapor breath in the air of early morning on the opening day of deer season. Or it will ricochet lazily—almost visible against the green-and-yellow grass and red clay—through the heat and humidity, propelled onward by the small clusters of the old and not-yet-old who will, year in and year out, gather in the mostly empty "stands" at rickety prep-school ballparks everywhere and patiently wait and watch for the next Hoss.

The question? Do any of us know a goddam thing about the game we love? We—who'll sit through an American Legion doubleheader and then come home and switch on the Cubs (if they're on the road) or the Braves (what the hell, at least it's baseball); who'll lie to a boss, an editor, or a spouse in order to attend a meaningless nondistrict game in mid-February played by half-frozen teenagers almost all of whom will be playing beer league softball inside of three years? I mean, if Hoss wasn't good enough to cut it, what does that say about the baseball sophistication of all the downhome bleacher-squatters who used to marvel at his domination over his decidedly less than peers?

Just how good *are* those 624 ballplayers who at any fleeting, dizzying moment find themselves on the active rosters of one of the twenty-six major league teams? And why wasn't Hoss, Augie, Tommy, or Brian ever in that number? Was it simply just a matter of be-*very*-good-or-be-gone? Or *was* it as slice-of-gritty-tragicomic-life on the bush league trail and as mysteriously mythical as ball yard folklore has always held it to be?

"Coming home, Pop. These guys are throwing curves and change-ups when they're *behind* in the count . . . and they throw 'em for strikes!"

"What's it like to miss New Orleans? Riding seventeen hours on a bus only to end back up in a dry county? Bluefield, West Virginia, or Bourbon Street? You'd probably come home and work for Co-Cola too. Had too much city in that boy. Pat O'Brien's and Mardi Gras called his young ass home."

"She had 'im by the pecker. Can't play no baseball with a ring through his pecker. It was the nookie what got him. Yet if he coulda kept it in his pocket *then,* now he'd be knocking off *major league* twat."

"Sumbitch threw his arm out with all them crooked balls Firmin had 'im throwing when he was only fifteen. Wasn't anything left in the tank, man."

"Attitude. Hadda be attitude . . . get 'em every time. Ol' Hoss didn't want it enough."

Right. But really. How come? When say Ryne Sandberg goes down with an injury, and the Chicago Cubs reach down to Iowa, their Triple A club, and bring up Paul Noce for his day in the sun, why is it Noce? How come he's there, the next in line, and not some Smith or Jones or one of the many dozens of other middle infielders the Cubs have signed over the last decade?

Dammit! How come Hoss is home working for Gryder's?

After the universally lamented dearth of consistent umpiring, that question, in one form or another, is surely the most relished topic of conversation among that sun-crinkled, forever spring-hearted, yet strangely subterranean society of serious but small-time baseball junkies—and there really is no kinder and still accurate word or phrase to describe them unless we digress too far into the metaphysical, the religious, the poetic. Not that even the more casual fans haven't also wondered, because they have. Anyone who's ever watched schoolboy baseball and seen a big league game has. It is part of the lore and lure of the game: Christ! Do those guys on the tube come from some higher league someplace—like Mars? If Hoss wasn't cut from that cloth, where *do* those fellows come from?

Of course, if one lives in an area where more than a handful get the call every year, and one sees a lot of baseball, the question can often be as compelling as it is, paradoxically, even more stupefying. Because maybe a hundred Hosses came back.

But Will Clark didn't. He's hitting game-winning homers by the bunches for the Giants—each of which is more fun to watch *now* than when he was knocking shingles off the houses behind the fifty-foot-high centerfield fence of Skelley Field for the Jesuit High Blue Jays against *my* O. Perry Walker Chargers. And Randy Bush is still coming off the bench and jerking line drives down the right-field line for the Twins—which is pretty much the same thing he did at the University of New Orleans's Privateer Park; except then he was also a country fair everyday left fielder instead of only a left-hand-hitting DH and pinch hitter. The two of them might even be swapping favors and jambalaya recipes come October.

But Augie Schmidt won't. Last I heard he *was* playing beer league softball up north somewheres; and he won the Golden Spike Award (college baseball's Heisman Trophy) in 1982 playing shortstop for the University of New Orleans and was the second player drafted in that June's first round—he was taken ahead of Dwight Gooden, for chrissakes! Tommy Mathews came home, too. Likewise, Brian Migliore. But not yet Chito, or Webster, or Scott, or Sammy, David, Jan, Jimmy, Mike, Gregg, Mark . . .

In fact, when the *Times Picayune* runs its weekly sidebar "Hometown Heroes" every summer there are always from sixty to seventy-five minor leaguers with either a local high school or college connection whose updated stats are conveniently posted for the back-home faithful. And this Mississippi-born and -raised storyteller, now living in New Orleans, Louisiana, is more than grateful because he unashamedly confesses to being a sore-assed (those damn wooden benches) member of the true believers.

Therefore, when one sees a lot of young men play, leave, come back, or stick, our question soon evolves from "How good are those guys up there?" to *Just what do they want up there and How do they go about getting it?"*

Which is a better question. Because it can be asked and answered. It isn't nearly as subjective. I mean, is one "good" all that better than another? One man's "good" is somebody else's "Yeah, but not as good as . . ." Is Chivas Regal *better* than Johnny Walker Black? You got me, although I do have an opinion—and so does that guy over there waiting for a bus.

So, if we wanted some answers, we could go to one of the twenty-six major league farm systems and ask. Simple enough. Go to a source. Ask the right questions. Then hole up and spell the words right.

Since how the major leagues go about the daily business of managing their assets has been unalterably changed since the mid-'60s by the free-agent draft, expansion, double-digit inflation, television saturation, and the evolution of college baseball, all of which have had something to do with the National Association of Professional Baseball leagues shrinking from a postwar high of some 450 minor league teams to the current number of about 160 clubs with Player Development Contracts with one of the twenty-six parent organizations; and since rampant free agency has made the necessity of a sound farm system markedly obvious to all—watch the two-year-old logjam explode now that the arbitrator has ruled in favor of the players over the owners in the benchmark "collusion" decision—one would think it a particularly interesting question to ask and have answered. I would think this true even if one isn't really even a baseball fan—there *are* such creatures allowed to roam free among us, I'm told—and is only a little curious about exactly how one very real theory of supply and demand actually works. Talk about your supply-side economics? There ain't no unions in the "bush."

What will make the Chicago Cubs a stronger franchise? Or the Mets? The Brewers? The Dodgers? The Angels? A system-wide unity of goals, philosophy, and methodology? Or just a toss of the oracle bones and a little gris-gris? For instance, why did Wade Boggs and Don Mattingly have to knock around the farms for years hitting well over .300 at every stop before getting the opportunity to prove they could do even *better* against big league pitching; and why did Will Clark, fresh and green (and of course Olympian Red, White, and Blue) out of his junior year at Mississippi State, have to dally but three months or so in the bush before becoming young Will the Thrill on the best team to call Candlestick home since the days of long sideburns and the two Willies?

What's the deal?

A relatively compelling subject for a look-see, right?

In truth, and not at all coincidentally, I was well into plotting a novel which would've examined our question from the liberating but removed pedestal of fiction. I was, that is, until a hotter-than-hell-and-twice-as-humid day this past August when I was in "church" (a ballyard, any ballyard—and you wondered about our use of the word "religious"?) watching an American Legion doubleheader with Earl Winn, the Chicago Cubs scout, and damn right fine friend and fellow Mississippian through whose generosity of spirit I'd been assured of cooperation if the need for any on-the-road research occasioned itself.

But then along about the third inning of the first game, while I'm watching a six-three, 170-pound, sleek, chisel-faced sixteen-year-old black right-hander glide with the loping, arrogant stride of a panther from *his* mound back toward the third-base dugout after pitching out of a two-on, one-out jam some erratic fielding by his shortstop had gotten him into, Earl is scribbling in his ever-present ring binder and saying: "Got a body kind of like Strawberry, you think?"

"He's pretty . . . got a loosey-goosey arm. Like his kick. What's his name? Sylva?"

"Sylve . . . with a silent e. Oughta go out and get my gun."

"He's only a baby . . . catch 'im in February. Probably just a teaser anyway. I don't believe he's bustin' eighty-one, eighty-two miles an hour."

"Which is how come I've got the stopwatch and you're a writer. I like his extension. I'm going to write him up."

" 'Spect you should."

"And you should write a book about a *real* minor league team."

"What . . . a nonfiction book?"

"Uh-huh."

What the hey, I'm always game for a gag. "Right. And just who in the hell have you got in mind?"

He looks up from his notebook and straight into my laughing eyes and says as serious as a three-two count, "How about our organization?"

I almost choke on my Barq's root beer. "Jesus. You're serious!"

"Yep. What's the matter? You only up to writing make-believe?" Damned if I knew. But it *was* all I'd ever done. "Now, Peoria would be the place—"

"Earl. You're gonna make me mess my britches. You're really talking for true here?"

"—be perfect, as a matter of fact. It's just down the highway from Chicago, Wrigley Field, Harry and Steve and Dewayne. The romantic in you can really play connect-the-dots-with-the-dream. And Pete will love it—"

And without having to overpay a mortician, I am going to Heaven. Baseball Heaven.

Peoria, Illinois, Winter 1988

It doesn't just get cold but damn-yankee cold during late January in Peoria, Illinois. In that regard, Tuesday the 26th was not exceptional. Yet that evening something better than a thousand people plopped down ten bucks a head to go out through the snow and ice to eat two-star-cafeteria food and *talk baseball*. They did so even though that gimcrackery called a wind-chill factor was yet again so double-digit-below-zero that for this broiled-in-the Gulf son of deepest Dixie it was too godawful scary to even think about.

We even sang the National Anthem. Not as you would at some Republican flag, prayer, and bullets-for-the-Contras social. But as you would at a ballgame—fun, apolitical, a little raucous.

Of course, no sooner than the last warbling note of ". . . home of the brave" was still reverberating round from the rafters, more than just a few of the hundreds sang out with a better than halfhearted "Play ball!" and then gave that silly-fun laugh and not at all embarrassed shrug and catbird grin at their table neighbors.

Why were all of these seemingly otherwise normal men, women, and children gathered in the cavernous main hall of Peoria's Expo Center eating, drinking, and talking the Summer Game on that far-too-cold-for-even-football night?

Something called the Chicago Cubs Caravan had rolled into town for the last stop on its annual goodwill and show-the-flag-in-the-market-hinterlands bus expedition. Shawon Dunston and Les Lancaster were the ballplayers on display—and patiently available for finger-crippling, seemingly endless single-file lines of autograph seekers. The golden-tongued Dewayne Staats was the WGN broadcast celebrity representative and master of ceremonies. And it was interesting to note that his autograph line was every bit as long as those of Messrs. Dunston and Lancaster, which tells us something I'm sure about the marriage made in heaven and Madison Avenue between baseball and television.

Jim Frey himself was there, the first Cubs manager to win *anything* since the Japanese lost World War II—the National League East in '84— who was then fired by Dallas Green when he couldn't win again with a club whose casualty rate in '85 approached that of the Bataan Death March and was then relegated to the WGN radio booth as color man with Lou Boudreaux for a couple of seasons, but who was now the brand-new general manager and Executive Vice President for Baseball Operations.

"It's a damn funny game. What the hell, here I was just getting used to playing golf again. Had a real family life six months out of each year. And I'm not getting any younger. But they called. It's my life. It's what I do. It's the *game*. What could I say?" He also didn't say no to the just-as-long line streaming by for his "Jim Frey," as he too sat at one of the four tables in each corner of the great hall and signed his name for well over an hour—and no food would be served until everyone who desired any or all of the autograph worthies' signatures was satisfied.

Finally, mercifully, we then sang, ate, played "talkball," and then laughed and applauded through a brisk, well-oiled presentation of the program and found out that Mr. Staats is just as smooth and effortlessly sincere in person, on the rubber-chicken circuit, as he is on the air, and a great deal funnier.

In a "roast" humor vein, Dewayne had a little something funny to say about almost all of the people at the raised head table: Dewey Kalmer, the head baseball coach at Bradley University; Ray Picl, president of the Chicago Cubs Boosters of Central Illinois, mayor of Peoria Heights, and adman at the *Journal Star;* the three guest speakers for the evening, Frey, Dunston, and Lancaster; and, of course, sitting just to the right of the podium, Harold A. "Pete" Vonachen II, unquestionably Mr. Peoria, and quite arguably the most nationally known and publicized owner of a Single A baseball team, the Peoria Chiefs.

But then *everybody* said something either funny or solicitous about or at Pete Vonachen—Harry Caray's somewhat legendary friend and fellow elbow bender for four decades, renowned restaurateur, entrepreneur, and raconteur extraordinaire. And certainly everyone there would have preferred listening to one of his ad-lib "speech" performances than to one or two who did speak. However, ballplayers are asked to speak because they can hit, run, throw, and field—not talk. Plus Pete Vonachen makes so damn many speeches everybody there had heard or would hear him several times over. Ever the showman and people-person he is without betters, maybe only equals, Pete instinctively knew that it was his night just to sit and smile, laugh and snort and belly-chuckle with that little jerk and then shake of his head when he was gigged, look down in genuine embarrassment, shrug and hunch his shoulders as all ex-football players always will, and then rub a stubby hand over a balding crown while his Winston Churchill jowls jiggled and blushed.

In the winter mostly all you *can* do is talk baseball. It's such a part of the game it's long since been legitimized into our language with a name: the Hot Stove League. Just about everyone plays it to some degree or another. Even if one has but scant interest in baseball. Because surely even that stunted soul will be at a cocktail party or the laundromat and hear someone ask, "Who do you like for the American League East?" or "I wanna see Horner hit 'em out of there. Can you believe he turned down all that Japanese yen to play long-ball-out in Jack Rabbit Flats?"

However, for some benighted—or bedeviled—souls, talking baseball in January is as much business as it is winter-bound passion for this game of ours. And if you're in the business of minor league baseball—and you're not in it for the purposes of toys or tax write-offs—you'd better be able to play talkball like a Hall of Famer. Pete Vonachen is, he isn't, and he does.

In fact, within three weeks of that Cubs Caravan, he would be inducted into the Greater Peoria Sports Hall of Fame because of it. No less an authority on the dynamics of talkball than Jack Brickhouse would personally do the honors as his old friend was enshrined into that same locally august body he himself belongs to—of course, Mr. Brickhouse is also a member of that even more august hall alongside that lovely lake in Cooperstown, New York.

To be sure, and even though once when he was president of the Peoria Pacers of the Central Illinois Collegiate League he had the distinction and the placid temerity to trade Mike Schmidt for a pitcher who never showed up, Pete's honored baseball legerdemain has very little to do with the manipulation of ballplayers and strategies effecting any columns of wins and losses (although not for any lack of wanting or attempting to on his part, God knows!); but rather with putting record multitudes of Midwest butts into box seats and bleachers—with them (or a corporate sponsor) *paying* for the privilege. This in an industry insider-notorious for "papering the yard." In four years he had taken a once-storied yet long-defunct—but recently and briefly only moribund—baseball franchise and almost quadrupled its attendance while making it financially and organizationally one of the acknowledged showcases of the "new" minor leagues.

He had been named the *Sporting News* Class A Executive of the Year for 1985 when, in only his second year of ownership, the Peoria Chiefs had drawn 165,000 fans to Meinen Field. Only long-established Durham of the Carolina League and Greensboro of the South Atlantic League had outdrawn the Chiefs among the then fifty-one full-season A clubs in America. To put that into its proper perspective it must be noted that in 1983, when minor league baseball returned to Peoria after a twenty-seven-year absence, under the control of absentee ownership in the principal of Lou Eliopulos and his Baseball Enterprises, Inc., and amid a storm of controversy of bad debts papered around town, inflated attendance figures, and a brutally cavalier attitude toward public relations, the franchise had drawn somewhere in the neighborhood of 65,000 (?) with a team called the Suns and affiliated with the California Angels.

The city and the Midwest League were prepared to run them out of town on a barbed rail when Pete jumped in, hammered out a "sell now or be damned" deal from the beleaguered Mr. Eliopulos, bought the franchise, brought back the old Chiefs name for nostalgia, and with the same Angels affiliation in 1984, immediately doubled the gate. Then he maneuvered into an affiliation with the Chicago Cubs for the following season and started to make Midwest League history: over the three years the young Cubbies had been in residence, the Chiefs had *averaged* 179,766, culminating in 1987's 195,832 paid-for butts, which set the Midwest League attendance record.

Not only had the fans responded. It is a commonly shared sentiment among recent Cubs big league players and minor league management that, "If you're in the Cubs organization, there's really only one place other than Peoria to play ball—and that's Wrigley Field. Pete, that staff, and that town treat minor leaguers like they're major leaguers."

Visiting teams also love to come to Meinen Field because, "Hey, those five thousand screaming people? Those fireworks, the music, that crazy Pete? The Big Show atmosphere doesn't pump up just the home team. You try giving a shit when you're oh for seventeen, ya got a stone bruise the size of Texas on your ass, the guy ahead of you in the next league is hitting a ton, the manager's starting to look at the bench for someone to play while you sit, and there's only three hundred people in the seats—and that's counting the no-shows!"

Pete Vonachen had done this in a city with a magical, almost mythical name—the proverbial benchmark mid-America city—which had of late, however, fallen on hard recessionary times, and the accompanying symptoms of a lagging community self-image.

While it would be a gross oversimplification to link Peoria's quite recent and apparently successful resurgence with that of the singular fortunes of a minor league baseball team, Pete had at the very least provided his unabashedly beloved hometown with a banner to wave as it waited for Caterpillar, Inc., to get right with the Japanese and then charge back up the real-world mountain toward "Happy days are here again."

Those banners? Pete probably placed every one of them into the hands of his fellow citizens personally while remembering their first and last names, where they worked, the ages and disposition of their children, what their granddads liked to drink, and then selling them a season ticket, a book of twenty, a billboard sign on the outfield fences, or an ad in either the Chiefs souvenir program or the scorecard. Of course, he also might take the time to sell them on something else while he was at it. A spare restaurant? A motel or two perhaps? Office, apartment, or retail building possibly? Or how about a paved parking lot, or better yet a road or highway? And of two things you may be certain if you buy: Pete will make a profit, and you will get exactly what he bargained you for—that missing pitcher not withstanding.

While Pete Vonachen has and will sell (or buy) any and all of the above, since October of 1983, mostly what he's been selling is baseball: "My partners over at Peoria Blacktop are gonna change the locks on me, keep that stranger out. I was over there the other morning and was heading into my office and this new girl asked if I had an appointment!"

Most people, however, are more than happy with how Pete spends so much of his time now. Peoria's mayor, Jim Maloof, was smiling, but he wasn't joking when he said, "Good. Folks like you just keep on making sure Pete's having fun and doing so well with that ballclub. Otherwise he might want my job."

"I'd beat him, too. And he knows it. But what do I want that job for? You've got no control. If I'm gonna take the blame or the credit, I want the control. If something's wrong, I can fix it or find someone who will—now! But the mayor's good people. Wait'll you hear him sing out at the ballpark. Look, grab a handful of brochures and bumper stickers, gotta drop some by what's-his-name's place. We'll do it on our way to the talk. Wait. Jeanne? Where in the hell am I speaking today?" Then, "Well, are you coming or what? They're serving lunch."

Politics and any number of civilization's other more pedestrian pursuits would have to wait. Pete Vonachen had a mission. Nay, an obsession. And actually there were two of them. Although back then, in the cold and the eternal optimism of a baseball winter, to Pete and his driven staff, they were as yet inseparable—always spoken of in tandem: the 1988 Peoria Chiefs *must* surpass their own Midwest League attendance mark of the year before and they *must* win a championship. Nothing less would do.

Therefore, over the fall and winter, Pete had been talking baseball with all the righteous fervor of a stump and tent preacher—and whatever or whoever could, in some small or larger capacity, be useful toward those greater ends should be only too willing grist for his just and holy mill. So spake Peter of Peoria; the brand-new slick, four-color, four-fold brochure was his testament: "*It's not over* . . . until we get it right!" supered over a glinting design of a dazzling gold-and-diamond Midwest League Championship Ring.

"There's no secret to this business. If you want 'em in the seats come May and June, then you've gotta talk to 'em from October till March. You've gotta be a presence in the community year-round. No group too small. Church, club, school . . . a goddam coffee klatch. And always give 'em something. A souvenir they can raffle off. And good-quality promotional material. It's gotta be first-class because you're selling the mystique of professional baseball. It's the little things, that's all. You do all the little things right, then someone will take you seriously when you go to do business. . . .

"And don't you think the Cubs don't notice, either. You don't wanna pay a hundred and fifty grand to some first-round kid you're projecting as a major leaguer, and have to develop him someplace where the atmosphere isn't even *Little League*! Hell yes that enters into their thinking when they start assigning ballplayers. Or at least it should. And it has."

In truth, though, most of the time Pete is able to work with any discernible efficacy toward only half of his goal, that which he directly controls—promotion.

That is not the case, however, when the mountain comes to the prophet. That is a blessed, double-gospel opportunity. Particularly when the mountain has a brand-new chief; and even more so when the kingdom of the mountain has recently expanded its territorial boundaries, thereby for now surely diluting the strength of the whole.

So on the day of the Cubs Caravan, even though he would get a respite from speechifying, Pete Vonachen's talkball scorecard was full.

In 1988 the Chicago Cubs would be one of only six major league farm systems to field more than six teams. (All in the National League, incidentally, four from one division, the NL East: the Mets, Pirates, Cardinals, Cubs. The Dodgers would also have seven; the Braves, as incongruous as it is to ponder, would have eight!) Four of the twenty-six big league franchises would have only five (all in the American League: Orioles, Angels, Tigers and Twins).

Since each big league franchise has only one Triple A and one Double A affiliate, it is at the Single A and Rookie League levels that the differences in organizational economics and player development philosophies begin to appear in the individual structure of each organization's idiosyncratically tiered system.

Heretofore the Cubs' organizational chart had been:

AAA—Iowa Cubs (Des Moines), American Association
  AA—Pittsfield Cubs (Massachusetts), Eastern League
    A—Winston-Salem Spirits (North Carolina), Carolina League
    A—Peoria Chiefs
    A (Short Season)—Geneva Cubs (New York), New York–Penn League
    Rookie (Short Season)—Wytheville Cubs (Virginia), Appalachian League

That was the ladder not only compartmentally, but also vertically in both theory and practice. Of the two short-season clubs (seventy games), Geneva, playing in what baseball traditionally accepts as being a "faster" league, is a step "up" from Wytheville. Likewise, in full-season Class A, the Carolina League is considered by the Cubs and still most of baseball to be a more refined circuit than the Midwest League, leading to the industry-wide but unofficial distinction expressed as "high A" and "low A"—which are words to be used around Pete Vonachen only immediately prior to *ducking*.

It was then with a decidedly mixed bag of emotion and intellect that Pete viewed the addition of another full-season Class A club, the Charleston Wheelers (West Virginia) of the South Atlantic League, to the Cubs minor league family. On the one hand his Chiefs could no longer in fairness and accuracy be denoted as "low A"—he chafed so against that distinction, he'd successfully lobbied the Cubs to force Dennis Bastien (the previous Winston-Salem owner and now owner of the new Charleston team) to remove the emblazoned affectation "Chicago Cubs High Class A Team" from over the portals of Ernie Shore Stadium—when there was after all now another club beneath his playing in a league that was universally recognized as being the "slowest" of the full-season Class A circuits. However, ballplayers capable of competing at the full-season level are not produced as rapidly as, by a stroke of pen to a Player Development Contract, one produces a club for them to play on.

For the coming year and the next, until the pipeline had time to adjust and catch up, the available talent above Rookie ball and below Double A that had been drafted and developed to staff two competitive clubs would have to be distributed among three—while still maintaining the internal appearance of a pecking order.

Pete said he understood, and even agreed—in principle and surely only intellectually—that in the long run the expanded system could only be beneficial to the farm system as a whole and to the Peoria franchise individually. The end result being that the mean age and relative skill level of the players assigned to Peoria should perceptibly rise: that the Cubs could draft and sign more freely from both the high school and college ranks safe in the knowledge that there would be a level at which all could play and develop according to their talent and experience, mitigating the constant peril of "getting a kid in a situation where he can't succeed." By adding a buffer between Peoria and Geneva it would mean that fewer Chiefs would be facing their first full season of Class A ball. And the ones that did still come from Geneva (or Wytheville—this single-letter alphabet ladder business ain't an exact science) would have demonstrated ability and growth, not just that they had "graduated" and must be passed on (or released) to make room for each June's new crop of signees.

Of course, just by enlarging your net, some would say that the likelihood of landing a profitable catch is proportionately enhanced, and for that reason alone it makes sense. Then others will argue, as they have for millennia over similar theories toward venture and gain, that there is that point of diminishing returns, that more is not always better, and that good money after bad is just that. Branch Rickey, the father of baseball's farm system, who as late as the '50s, when he was operating the Brooklyn and later Pittsburgh franchises, fielded as many as two dozen or more minor league teams from which he not only stocked his ball club but those of his competition for value returned—thereby stocking the exchequer for good measure—was a champion and past master of the former theory. Marge Shott, currently the owner of the Cincinnati Reds, who has been quoted as questioning the propriety of even employing scouts since "all they do is get paid to watch baseball," and those Chisox wizards Reinsdorf and Einhorn, who not so long ago endeared themselves to few baseball people by suggesting the elimination of the minor leagues entirely because the returns didn't justify the expense and offered the symbiotic relationship between the National Football League and college football as a model for their argument (and envy), are extreme proponents of the latter axiom of asset acquisition and development.

Whatever your economic meat or poison might be, the recent trend back toward larger farm systems might also simply be due to the fact that some of baseball's more visionary executives are already preparing for the certainty of major league expansion. In fact, Gordon Goldsberry, the Cubs Vice President of Minor Leagues and Scouting, who along with Dallas Green had made the decision to go with the seventh team, had explained their true rationale—and not surprisingly it had little to do with any of the publicly stated obvious: "When expansion comes and all of the existing major league clubs have to contribute to the expansion pool, we want to be ready—every team will need a surplus of talent, and we'll have it."

In January of 1988, however, Pete Vonachen was finding it difficult to look that far ahead. In the past he'd not been unsuccessful in effecting some moderation of the status quo. At least so he felt. And whether it had been his special brand of lobbying or the luck of the draw, the rapid ascendancy of major leaguers Greg Maddux and Rafael Palmiero, and soon-expected-to-be Mark Grace, each of whom had bypassed Winston-Salem and springboarded good years at Peoria right into Double A and beyond without missing a beat, lent even more ammunition for him to fire in his running battle for:

". . . parity. That's all I'm asking. I don't think they should stack my team just because I'm Pete Vonachen, because of what we've done here. Just because we draw better than a lot of Triple A teams. Or because we have the best staff and work harder than anyone else. That's what we're supposed to do. That's only expected. Hell, I don't want favoritism. People think just because I'm Harry's friend I get or expect favors. They're fulla shit. *But,* we don't work this hard, or spend the extra money we do to do all of the little things the Cubs say they're so happy we're doing, just to be treated unequally! I don't want to take away from that man down in Winston-Salem. I just want our share. Parity. This staff and the Peoria fans deserve that at the very least. Plus the Cubs have got to realize that this league has changed. You can't be competitive anymore with basically rookies. They'd better wake up and see which way the wind is blowing!"

Then, as he would at the end of many such litanies he'll intone on this subject, Pete paused, fiddled with something on his massive desk, smiled like the altar boy he once was, and rubbed his head as he poured snake oil over the timber and contents of his latest harangue: "Of course, I'm not complaining, the Cubs have always been good to us. They've always been *sensitive* to our needs. When we've needed help, they've sent it."

But it never hurts to hedge your bets. Leaving things to chance is not Pete's style. Therefore, by his own admission, he had gone beyond his role of squeaking wheel for the coming season and as early as last fall had started his efforts to ensure that Peoria would not be short-sheeted in the new three-way split by going down to Arizona during the Instructional League to discuss the expansion with Dallas, Gordon, and Bill Harford, the Director of Minor League Operations. While everyone agreed that the system would necessarily be spread too thin, they had assured him that winning in Peoria was indeed important to them too and that he would get a fair shake. In fact, they said in his case there was even reason for optimism: the nucleus of his '88 squad would come from the '87 Geneva Cubs, who by winning the New York–Penn League had been the only Chicago Cubs farm team to win a championship that past season.

In early December, in Dallas, Texas, at the annual Baseball Winter Meetings, although Jim Frey had been at the helm only a fortnight or so, Pete had stated his case and left feeling that the new chief Cub was committed to a strong farm system and was not unaware of Peoria's unique place in this one.

Yet still Pete fretted. Two divided by three is less than one even if it is cut equally. And if not, if a leveraged system of division was applied, then numbers two and three would be at the shitty end of an emaciated trickle-down. And that just would not do. Not this year. For whatever reason, for Pete Vonachen the 1988 season just *had* to be bigger, better, and the very best of them all.

CHAPTER 1

"DAMN, AND BILLY Mel had been mowing, too," mused the utility infielder.

"Why don't you shut up," answered the star catcher.

But then Bill Melvin had been mowing. Pitching shutout ball through three. Of course, everything went to hell in a frozen hurry in the fourth and fifth innings and soon it's a quiet bus ride home. . . .

Home? The Amora Villa Motel in Appleton, Wisconsin?

Why not. It was the closest thing to home the 1988 Peoria Chiefs had as yet known since they left the desert and mountains of Arizona to open the Midwest League season with a loss against archrival Springfield and then immediately embarked on a fifteen-day road trip into a part of the world where spring wasn't even a rumor.

Home also implies family. And although we couldn't have bought a hit when it really counted if they'd been on sale at K-Mart, even so early on we did have that. A "family" besieged by doubt from within, certainly, yet alone on foreign soil, so therefore a family bonding together quickly. As in circling the wagons.

Home can also mean continuity. After the helter-skelter manic-depression of providing the dubious entertainment for three gala home openers in three different cities in as many days, the four games, four days, and three whole nights the Chiefs were scheduled to be in little Appleton, Wisconsin, had loomed as welcome and hospitable as a lazy visit to Maw Maw's house.

Home is also a place one goes to get well. And as we had rolled out of South Bend, Indiana, shortly after dawn of that Tuesday, April 12, making hard and fast for the northern shores of Lake Winnebago some 270 miles away, that's exactly what we'd had in mind. Whether we deserved it or not.

Because even though this team had, from the first days of spring training, carried on its young shoulders the burden of perhaps the highest expectations of all of the Chicago Cubs minor league teams for the 1988 season, we also knew the Gods of Baseball would have been aghast if somehow our play so far had *not* resulted in a record of 1 and 3 coming out of the getty-up.

I mean, it hadn't been pretty. Except for maybe the first eight and a third innings of Opening Day, Friday, April 8, when, in front of some six thousand screaming Peorians, Mike Aspray had finessed a three-hitter into the ninth of a 2-2 game. But then Ray Lankford, the Springfield Cardinals' center fielder, sent one of Mike's batting-practice fastballs—that he'd errantly left hanging up around the belt on a one-out, 1-2 pitch—over the double-board green wall in straightaway center of Meinen Field and the '88 Peoria Chiefs suffered loss number one. And even how pretty can that be when your offense manages only three hits scattered among twelve strikeouts? Notwithstanding the fact that Cardinals starter Bill Bivens had won fourteen games in this league the year before.

"Jesus, what's he doing back? Whaddaya gotta do to get promoted in that organization?" The Shooter had also said, "I'm not worried. I saw a lotta things I liked out there tonight. And I know these kids are gonna hit."

And Jim Tracy, the manager of the Peoria Chiefs, kept on saying that to every one of the front-running, first-skirmish doomsayers the gods must've liked so much because they made way too many of them, while smiling that big ol' goofy smile of his. He said it again the next day after we'd gone down to open up Lanphier Park in Springfield and Jeff Massicotte lasted only one and a third innings as some more untimely hitting was overshadowed by the 10-3 pasting the Chiefs had to stomach with their wolfed-down concession-stand food before having to jump back on that big bus and make the 250-mile trip up to South Bend.

Pete Vonachen, who along with his staff had made the first two days of the trip with us, had sent word down to cancel the order of steak sandwiches for everyone after the score went to 8-1 in the sixth.

The Shooter was still chirping that Mr. Optimist song on Sunday after we'd opened that brand-new ten-million-dollar *minor league* baseball palace, Stanley Coveleski Regional Stadium, by wasting another fine pitching performance by a starter and the bullpen, in a 2-1 loss to the White Sox. True, we'd hit some, as evidenced by ten safeties. But then we also struck out eleven times. Which goes a long way toward explaining how you score only one run on ten hits when four of them are for extra bases.

He might've still been saying it—and was, in fact, to anybody who would listen—the following day, again against the Sox, when finally we weren't playing in front of the mania of an opening-day crowd. But surely he wasn't *thinking* that way when, already down 3-0 in the third inning, just to get a run across the dish—any run—the Shooter had sent Rick "the Phenom" Wilkins tagging from third base on a little looping pop-up to the outfield grass just behind second. The harmless enough effort had been fielded nonchalantly by the South Bend shortstop. Nonchalantly, that is, until he—being just as surprised as everyone else in the ballyard that night—spotted the big Peoria Chiefs catcher thundering for home and, in his shock, threw a tad wide and nonetheless too late as Wilkins slid in safe in a cloud of cold, hard red brick dust. That was *not* Jim Tracy baseball.

The Shooter, who'd made it all the way to the big leagues only because *he* could hit a baseball—particularly with men on base—was for now obviously going to have to do some compromising of his baseball credos if he was going to start winning with the ballclub he'd brought north from spring training virtually promising its owner it would do more than its share of just that. But then so had almost everyone else in the Cubs organization. It was the party line.

However, at the moment he'd yelled "Go!" to the ex–Furman University football linebacker, but now twenty-year-old Big Bonus Baseball Baby, it wasn't only a run he was thinking about. Or another pitching performance deserving of a W but seemingly predestined for an L. Just as important, he also hadn't wanted to waste the first hit of the season, a ringing one-hop double off the right-center-field wall, by the full-blown "can't miss major league prospect." The intense yet young Mr. Wilkins had been purposely placed in Tracy's tutelage so that the left-handed-batting, sure-to-be-a-Cub slugger might more readily learn to do so against a curveball, and *any* lefthander, from one of the organization's acknowledged masters of that art. Going into that at bat Rick Wilkins had been 0 for 12.

"Jesus, Mary and Joseph . . . the Kid's gotta carry us. That's his role. Whether he can handle it or not, I don't know—but they sent him here to be the Man on this team. And if I've gotta nudge his confidence along a little bit so he'll stop sulking around here like his goddam puppy died or something, I'll do it. That's why I'm here. And there's nothing like scoring from third on a bang-bang play to get your dick hard. And if we get him going? Well, then maybe we've got something!"

If it sounded good, it worked even better. In the top of the ninth, facing a left-hander, "Wilkie" punched a curveball back where it came from to drive in the tying run. No matter that we had to go twelve innings late into a cold, blustery night (Mario Impemba, our radio play-by-play announcer, going into that frame, had said, "I don't know what's going to run out first, my scorecard or my piss") before we could win it somewhat ignominiously when the South Bender's center fielder misplayed short-stop Marty "Cap" Rivero's cinch-third-out line drive into a run-scoring three-base error.

It was a win. Number one. We'd take it. Perhaps now the frustrated and sullen Phenom would start pulling his much expected share of the lightnin' wagon. Up to then he'd been leaving it all up to third baseman Lenny "Ding Dong" Bell, who was much more of a suspect than a prospect; regardless of the fact he'd been the hottest hitter in spring training and then carried it right over into the first week of the season, albeit all by his lonesome.

"Get both of them hot? And those non-skilled athletes"—pitchers in Tracy's lexicon—"we've got? Look out—'cause somebody's gonna get hurt. Just maybe them Appletons. Lee? You got this thing gassed up and the shitter emptied?"

Lee Kline, the Peoria Charter Coach bus driver assigned to the Chiefs for the duration, had grinned back at this strange man and just said, "Ready to roll, Trace."

"You ain't gonna get us lost, are you? You get us lost while we're winning, and I'll make *you* stand out there in that third-base coaching box freezing your gonads off!"

"If it's on a map, I'll get us there."

"Yeah, but this is Wisconsin we're going in to. Anybody know—hey Kranny, they got maps in Cheesehead Country?"

Rick Kranitz, the Peoria Chiefs pitching coach, who, as was his custom after every game, had been intently studying the game charts and swearing to himself, looked up from his seat across the aisle and said in that sly, offhand way of his, "Hell if I know, Trace. When I was pitching in this league they didn't leave me here long enough to find out. 'Course, I was on a team that could score some runs."

"Shut up, Mule. Who asked you anything anyway? Hey! Youse guys hear what my Mule just said?" Catcalls and jeers from only thirteen of the twenty-three ballplayers on the bus. Then, "Let's hit it, Lee."

We were soon rolling away from the land of the Touchdown Jesus toward that north country close by the reliquary of another football legend, Vince Lombardi and Green Bay, hoping all to hell and back that at least some of those dozen-plus-one real athletes had indeed started to "hit it." Because, as the Shooter, basking finally in the ebullient glow of a win and the prospects for adventure and perhaps pillage in Wisconsin, had added with all of the conviction and logic necessary for making us believe it:

"Hey! Them Cheeseheads'll never get around on Mel's fastball. And then Aspray? With him painting the zone with that dancing pus of his? And wait'll they get a snootful of that knee-buckling yakker from the Panamanian Devil. I'm telling you guys, we've got 'em right where we want 'em. Herbie, tell Eduardo what I just said about him. Translato, Herberto. Sí? And fuck yourself while you're at it . . . no offense."

None was taken as he shrugged his right shoulder across his nose to complete the high-sign gesture and phrase which had been institutionally adopted as this family's trademark salutation for everything from "atta baby" to "Your ol' lady's uglier than you are—she must give the best head in baseball."

*   *   *

During the fourth and fifth innings, seven out of nine would-be Kansas City Royals hit safely—and not a bleeder in the bunch, we're talking *shots;* we would use the frozen-rope cliché, but when it's 27 degrees by the sixth inning, everyfuckingthing is frozen and if you had a rope you'd burn it to keep warm—off Bill Melvin, the tall, gangling, and gentle young fireballer from North Carolina. His heater wasn't the problem. It was his big, old-fashioned curveball that suddenly couldn't find the plate, which made his then behind-in-the-count, poop-chute fastball a gleam in the waiting eyes of the Appleton Foxes.

After perhaps coming to the understandable conclusion that if he didn't throw it anywhere near the plate ever again maybe they couldn't hit it at all, much less so hard, he walked a run in to make it 5-zip with only one out and bases still loaded in the fifth and Tracy mercifully went out and got him before he could do any more damage—to himself, to hell with the score!

That, plus an overall sloppily played game which included, among other atrocities, two crucial fielding errors more mental than physical and three scarcer-than-a-ray-of-sunshine base runners getting their sleeping-dumb asses picked clean (Wilkins twice—once off second!), led all too surely to a 6-3 loss in front of all of 174 hardy—or stone-cold crazy—souls. And of course a now 1-and-4 record as the Peoria Chiefs head back to the Amora Villa for their first night in sleepy (hell, they're still *hibernating*) little Appleton, Wisconsin, on a bus so quiet you can hear other folks breathing from across the aisle and two or three seats back. But mostly you don't because everybody is collectively holding his breath just knowing that the Trace Monster was going to have to rear its rumored-to-be-ferocious head sooner or later.

It almost does there for a moment after Lee pulls the bus to a stop just past the lobby of the motel and everyone sits there in the dark and the silence waiting for the explosion. Seconds tick by like minutes as those in the first few rows can definitely hear the Shooter breathing—and boiling. Then, finally, after a sharp sigh and disgusted jerk of the head, that Ohio twang barks out: "Lee, put on the light."

But by the time Jim Tracy unfolds that rawboned six-three body of his from out of those always too narrow seats and turns to face his ballclub in the pool of overhead light, most of the bite is gone. What is left is mostly a personal sense of failure and his puzzlement at it. Which of course the heart-as-big-as-a-fishing-lake father-confessor and baseball purist still tries his best to make sound as harsh as he thinks the moment calls for.

". . . the fact is, gentlemen, you stunk it up out there. Forget everything else—youse guys didn't even play fundamental baseball! And all of youse is capable of that. Else you wouldn't be here. That's expected by the time you get to this league. You think me and Richie, and Colbie, and Mick, and Tony and everybody else who's been through it, were just pulling our pudding and getting suntans down there in Arizona when we putcha through all them drills? Not me. I got better things to do. Like a wife and family I could be with instead of freezing my ass off watching this shit and trying to teach you something what just might getcha out of here and into higher baseball. You think you're struggling now? This is A ball! What the hell you think's gonna happen at the next level? If you're overmatched here, forget it. I'ma tell ya that. 'Cause it don't get any easier. Play this way and you'll be telling your grandchildren how you once played *Class A* ball for the Chicago Cubs—and that's all!"

Tracy pauses, sighs long and loud, and then pushes his glasses back further onto the bridge of that chiseled, wide nose and open-as-a-book Midwestern face which quickly gives way to a high sloping forehead under a crown of curly, close-cropped sandy hair. When he continues the voice is much quieter. The hurt and puzzlement now there alone without any of the feigned harshness that had been its mask.

"For the first time, guys, I saw you quit. Now, professional baseball is about getting beat. I can live with that. And you'll learn to. But it ain't about quitting. That's why there's no clock. Somebody's gotta *beat* you before you pack the equipment bag and go get ready to do it again tomorrow. That's the only way I ever learned to play this game. And by God it got me my two years in the big leagues and I was never no prospect. Just like most of you, I was a suspect all the way up. But I got there over people a lot better than me because I wanted it more than the other fellow. Youse can bet your ass on that."

Another pause, as he looks at each of them. Then, "You let me down tonight, guys. But so what? I got out of A ball. I've got nothing to prove in these game reports Kranny and I send in on you every day. So you let yourself down, didn't you? All right, be in your rooms by one. Bus leaves tomorrow at four o'clock. Lee?"

Lee Kline pushes the button which opens the automatic doors and very quietly we gather our gear and slowly file off the bus. But not before Jim Tracy. He is always the last to get on the bus and the first to get off. Those are the unwritten rules. And he never does anything in a hurry.

Indeed, before we make an end to this voyage of discovery perhaps you will come to some understanding of just how truly fortunate were those chance winds of fate which had already determined that James Edwin Tracy, at thirty-two years of age and only three years removed from an eight-year professional playing career highlighted by the eighty-seven games he played in the major leagues with the Chicago Cubs and the year he spent playing in Japan making the really big money, and now only a year and a half removed from a job "making damn good money selling boxes," would return for his sophomore season as a minor league manager and serve as skipper during an often tumultuous passage. Particularly on those certain days when, make no mistake about it, the infidels were *pouring* over the gunwales.

Because, Jim Tracy, while he is many other things, and most especially do those things fall within the province of that broad and perhaps most noble calling of them all, a teacher, he is also a real-life natural clown.

Even when he isn't trying to be. Perhaps especially then.

I mean that big ol' face with the wire-rimmed glasses, jutting, jaunty jaw, an always bobbing chin that could gouge granite, with the flat-out *goofiest* combination of mercurial grins, frowns, and pouts which are never more than a millisecond away from appearing in any random and rapid-fire sequence on a wide mouth with a full expanse of strong white teeth, is also never more than a millisecond away from making you laugh out loud no matter the circumstances.

In truth, the Shooter could make you laugh at your mother's funeral if you happened to look at him during the eulogy and he was, with a hound-dog glance, a nod or shrug, attempting to convey his condolences.

That rare gift, displayed at its very best even in the face of adversity, was, on balance and certainly in the end, worth far more than its weight in three-run homers.

One of the slowest things Jim Tracy does is shower and dress after a ballgame. He will sit for sometimes an hour or more still in his long johns, jock, and sanis, sitting on a stool or chair, in whatever cubbyhole is provided in the various Midwest League ballparks for managers, mulling over every facet of the game just played while everyone else is long ago dressed and dutifully waiting on him.

Which is why Kranny, Mario, and I have followed him off the bus and are standing there in that godawful cold watching the ballplayers straggle in dejected twos and threes toward their rooms while we bemoan the fact that the only nice restaurant close by the motel, which we, in anticipatory glee, had spied out earlier in the day, is by now closed.

Tracy, who had started across the parking lot toward his room, his head hanging and his shoulders drooping in his best Sad Sack imitation for the benefit of his young Cubbies, now turns around and ambles back to join us. With his back to the retreating Chiefs, he gives his best shit-eating grin.

"Aw . . . fuck it. Let's go eat."

Kranitz says, "Now that you mention it."

Mario, the only one of us who had traveled this same road with Trace the year before when they'd both been rookies at their jobs, has balls enough to say, "Where? Reflections? It closed down about twenty-five minutes ago."

"Oh," Trace says. A sheepish frown. Then, "Hey, that Shakey's is still open, I bet. I felt like pizza anyway."

Kranny isn't thrilled. But then Rick Kranitz hates to lose at least as much as the notoriously competitive Tracy. Particularly if one of his pitchers has a bad outing and loses, or worse yet if one has a good outing and still loses. Which of course means that as a pitching coach in the low minors he's unthrilled a goodly part of the time; so he just says, "What the hell. Pizza . . . and several pitchers of beer."

The only Southerner among us, teeth chattering, looks across the highway and sees what looks to be one very slow pizza parlor possibly on the verge of closing momentarily itself. "At least let's move this party *inside*."

After dashing the hundred yards or so through the bracing cold in the fashion of a gaggle of teenagers, we got inside, and although they were closing, we made it just under the wire and had the place to ourselves. "They probably roll the sidewalks up in this town, too," grumbled Kranny as he passed around the beer.

But Tracy wanted to get serious a minute. Now that is not always an easy task around the Shooter. *Particularly* when he adopts any one of several let's-get-serious looks on that face.

"Kranny, you don't think maybe I was too hard on 'em, do ya?"

The three of us stifle the involuntary reflex of an outright guffaw by putting a beer mug to our grins before the dark-haired, handsome, and laconic Arizonan was sufficiently composed enough to give a straight—and obvious—answer.

"Trace, they played horseshit baseball. What are you supposed to tell them?"

"They did, didn't they? Fuck 'em." A slap of the table and a big grin. "Better not let me catch one of 'em out tonight. My boat fund could use the money."

After the pizzas had arrived, Trace was feeling morose again and made a pronouncement with all of the sad gravity of the truly betrayed. "They did quit tonight. You know that, huh? And that's one thing I never thought I'd see from this ballclub."

Kranny just said, "Yep."

Mario, always the sanest of our "adult" group, even though at twenty-five he was the youngest, said, "Trace, they played a bad ballgame. But it's only April twelfth, it's freezing cold, they're in the middle of a fifteen-day road trip, and they've been living in motels now what, five weeks?"

"So? If they quit this early, what they gonna do come July and August when their dicks are dragging the dirt 'cause we're playing a gillian doubleheaders and it's so hot ya don't wanna spit your dip 'cause ya know it's gonna sizzle and burn holes in Vonachen's grass?"

The Southerner spit up beer on that one. Then offered, "Trace, seven out of nine batters hitting rockets in one stretch is enough to take the steam out of most ballclubs."

"Jesus, Mary, and Joseph . . . they hit him hard, didn't they? I covered my eyes on the ball that kid hit in the fourth. Thought sure I was gonna have to go out there with a body bag instead of the hook. Was already composing a letter to his momma. How that Ichabod Crane neck got that hillbilly head out of the way, I'll never know."

"American Legion curveball's back," Kranny said. "And we had it nice and tight back in Mesa."

"He's got a live arm though, don't he? Billy Mel's gonna pitch some higher baseball, or I'm an Ayrab." Just as swiftly as the moroseness had reappeared in Tracy, so had it vanished. "You know, even as horseshit as it was, I saw a lot of things out there I liked. That damn Lenny Bell just might be trying to prove to somebody that he's a prospect. He looked good on that scoop at first, huh? Am I right? You know, that just might be his best position. He looks comfortable over there, don't he? But this organization's looking for people to play third, so that's where they want him. But I had to sit Elvie down for a game. Only way to get that *coño*-head's attention."

It hadn't been a bad lineup hunch, either. Sergio Espinal, a twenty-four-year-old returnee from the '87 squad, who'd again been cast by the organization in a utility role for this season, had been given a start at third and answered with a 3-for-4 night at the plate. His third hit of the evening had been an RBI double pulled hard into the left-field corner with two out in the ninth. Now, in the fullness of Jim Tracy's resurgent good spirits, self-boostered by his increasingly animated litany on the "lotta things I saw I liked out there tonight," the Shooter even granted himself the full appreciation of one of the most deadly ironies of minor league baseball: a too-old-for-that-level "nonprospect" and role player who, in limited service, is making it cosmetically difficult to justify his sitting the bench while younger "prospects" fall on their face night after night. In only nine at bats on the young season, Sergio now had five hits, second on the team only to Lenny Bell with eight. That made for a rather robust average of .556. But the realities of this business prompted Tracy to wax philosophical on that feat instead of laudatory.

"Hey, I love the kid. I swear I do. But when he has a night like this and we don't win, all I can think about is how I'm gonna hear it recited back to me by Dana when he's not in the lineup! I'd rather face Nolan Ryan blindfolded than to try and explain the definition of utility infielder to that woman."

One by one a play or a player would come due for its nightly recap. "Hey. What about Gator [Warren Arrington, the Chiefs' five-eight, 150-pound leftfielder]? As long as it ain't bouncing, that peckerwood can run down and catch the wind. And up at the plate? He *hurt* that ball in the eighth. That peanut put it against the fence! Gator the power hitter and we are in trouble, huh, guys?" Or "And the Cap? They say he's just an organizational shortstop? You watch what I'm saying, Cap's gonna make them eat that someday."

Finally it was determined by this revisionist method that the only thing the Chiefs had come up short on was the score. And what was that against the fact that for the second time in the season the boys in travel Cubbie blue had hit for a double digit?

"We did get ten, didn't we? Hey, Mule . . . order us some more beer, will ya? Do something constructive if you can't give me a pitcher who can win with ten hits behind him."

"And what did your bullpen do? Answer me that."

"He's right, you know. I'll get the beer, Mule. You give good bullpen. Trouble is I can't give 'em the damn ball with a lead."

Inevitably, as would almost every other such discourse over the next four and a half months, this one began to focus on the pearls and perils of the Phenom. Aside from the fact that he'd gotten picked off base twice, Rick Wilkins, while only going 1 for 4, had hit the ball hard twice that night and again displayed the arm that should get him to the big leagues even if the ambitious projections upon his "quick bat" prove to be only that. "The Kid" had been shutting down base runners since day one.

"You'd think he'd proved his point, huh? But ain't nobody doing any advance scouting in this league. So they don't know."

"They're learning," Kranny said. "The hard way."

"I hope they stay stupid. Jesus . . . did he gun down that little center-fielder or what? Zip! And thanks for coming."

"Y'all know who that dude is, huh?"

"Who? Gainous?"

"That's Trey Gainous. Remember that tough little wide receiver for Auburn? He was Bo Jackson's roommate."

"That's him? He could catch a football . . . in traffic, too."

"Yepper."

"Fast for a white boy. But he'd better keep up his friendship with Bo, 'cause that's the only way he's gonna see the big leagues. On a pass left at the gate. No pop, and no swing to begin with. But he can run."

"Not tonight," Kranny summed up that issue succinctly enough.

Jim Tracy is by now positively beaming. "Wilkie sure enough hung him out to freeze, and that's a fact.

"The kid's got all the tools to get him there. And he's gonna hit. I believe that. His hands are sure quick enough, the bat speed's there. And I think he's gonna put it together up here." The Shooter taps his temple. "Figure out the adjustments. That was a bomb he hit in the eighth."

With everyone now inclined to look only for silver linings among the losses, the pizza, and the beer, in due course it was pointed out that with those ten hits the team batting average would now slip over .200 for the first time.

"We're gonna bust the Mendoza line, Shooter" is how it was said. But the look on Jim Tracy's face foretold that it probably shouldn't have been said at all—because he immediately wanted to know what the average had been coming in. When told, the storm clouds burst in those blue-green eyes and there wasn't any lining to be seen anywhere, silver or otherwise.

"One eighty-three! Mario weighs more than that."

"Afraid not, Trace," said the diminutive Michigan State grad with the golden voice.

But the Shooter goes right past it. "A team of mine hitting a buck-eighty! Whatcha trying to do, cheer me up or make me terminal?"

In an attempt at damage control of the Shooter's sinking-fast mood it was rationalized that what the hell do averages mean after only five ballgames? Plus there was the encouraging sign that the Chiefies had struck out only five times that night; whereas heretofore the baffling preponderance of whiffs had of course been the obvious cause of the offensive anemia. That only brought on another get-out-the-bailing-buckets question.

"How many strikeouts did we have coming in?"

The truth is that Jim Tracy can almost always accurately "guesstimate" team and individual stats within a margin of error give or take about the size of a gnat's hind leg, but he likes to pretend he doesn't have a clue and wants his ballplayers to also disdain statistics—it's an unwritten no-no for a ballplayer to be caught reading the daily updated Howe stats sheet. In this case the number is 38.

"So that's forty-three punchouts in five goddam ballgames?" Trace almost shrieked and his voice cracked like a puberty victim. Kranny reached for another slice of pizza. "And you slander my pitching staff?"

The Shooter took a small sip of beer and slammed his mug down on the table. "The trouble with these know-it-all no-swingers is they heard somewhere something about 'guess hitting' and so they go up there umpiring and waiting for that cock shot they saw *last* at bat but didn't swing at because they thought sure as hell there's gotta be something better yet coming! Whoever made up that dumb phrase oughta be sentenced to a lifetime of *guessing* who their wife's sleeping with! You don't 'guess' hit. You 'think' hit. What did that guy throw me or somebody else in this situation? What is this guy's pattern? All but just the very best of them nonathletes out there on that hill have a pattern and they're gonna fall back on it everytime. It's their security blanket."

It appeared as if that phrase had caught in his mind's eye, so he stopped and glared at it in a detached silence for a moment. Then he proved exactly how well he did keep up with certain statistics.

"Some 'Phenom,' huh? Nine of those forty-three K's belong to one particular third strike statue sonofabitch." And he was dead on. Rick Wilkins had nine strikeouts in twenty-one at bats—mostly looking. Though he'd had none that night. Which meant that Tracy's mind compressed those nine into an even more repugnant etching of nine no-contact outs out of seventeen in four ballgames! Now the Shooter looked like *his* puppy had just been run over by a beer truck, again, and he wasn't going to take it anymore.

"Why me? Huh? And then the dumdum gets his dead ass picked off. Twice! The Kid better stop calling home every night to ask his momma and daddy to pray for divine intervention and get on with business. How much they give that kid, anyway? Hundred and fifty grand or something. . . ?"

"About a hundred and a quarter."

"And he can't stay awake on base? That's the kid that's gotta carry us? To where? The shitter?"

"Can't, Trace. We're already there." Only from Kranny.

"And can you believe Cap booted that double-play ball? Jesus, we're horseshit. I oughta go back over there and get 'em all together and really give 'em a spitful!"

Rick Kranitz carefully wiped his hands on a napkin and said, "No you shouldn't."

"Why the hell not?" demanded Jim Tracy.

"Because we're throwing Aspray tomorrow night," Kranny explained simply and quietly.

"That's right!" A suddenly beaming Shooter thumped the table.

"And," further counseled the Kran-dog, "this isn't a bad ballclub, Trace. Not yet, anyway. They're just a ball club that's playing bad."

The Shooter thought about that for only a beat. Then, "Yeah, you're right, Mule. Saw a lotta things I liked out there tonight. And what are we? Three under? With the human paintbrush going tomorrow night? We got those Appletons right where we want 'em—they sure as hell can't beat us if they can't hit it either!"

"You sure about that, Trace?"

"Mario, I hope all your children grow up to have the same nose you've got. And I was starting to feel better."

Back at the Amora Villa, Trace thought it would be a good idea to stop in the lounge to see if any mischief had occurred in our absence.

We got in there about thirty minutes before the one o'clock bed call. Like the rest of Appleton, Wisconsin, it was decidedly on the quiet side. But not a bad bar. In fact the Amora Villa itself would in the end prove to be the best motel in the entirety of the Midwest League circuit, a big, rambling inn with all the creature comforts you need as a base camp for a ballclub on the road, including an indoor swimming pool.

It was just an empty bar—except for the skinniest barmaid any of us had ever seen leaning over the brass and hardwood bantering with about a half-dozen Chiefs.

"Aw shit, there goes the neighborhood," somebody said. But after a couple more good-natured needles, the grown-ups moved on down and laid squatter's claim to the short end of the L-shaped bar.

With players in earshot, the conversation was now forced to reach for a much more metaphysical level.

"Don't even think about it . . . it'd be like drilling bone."

"You know . . . that might be one of this ballclub's problems. These kids have been on the move so much the groupies can't catch up with 'em. Not a one of 'em's been laid since Arizona, I bet, and probably before for a lot of 'em."

"And I guess you have?"

That was about the gist of it as the clock ticked closer to one o'clock and, seemingly on five-minute intervals, one or two of the Chiefs would give a furtive look our way, a look back at the clock, and then take their leaves, always making sure to say a distinct good night to Tracy and Kranitz—with one more glance back at the clock to punctuate that they were indeed good citizens of the unit and were abiding by its rules.

At five minutes till, they were all gone except for one. Even Fernando Zarranz, the "Z Man" and late-inning stopper, and his inseparable soulmate, Gabby Rodriguez, the left-handed setup man, had finally made their flamboyant exit. But not John Green, the long, tall son of Dallas Green—who until just a short few months ago had been president and general manager of the Chicago Cubs.

The blue-eyed, very laid-back but bulldog right-handed reliever has every bit of his father's good looks, intelligence, imposing yet easygoing physicality, and aura of *presence;* a charmer and daredevil heartbreaker with a smile and twinkle to melt even Mata Hari's cold, cheating one.

If there is a line that says "Don't cross," John Green is going to lope right up to it, straddle it, and then, grinning to beat the band, look around and say, "Who, me?"

Right now he looked at the clock, then us, and called to the blade-thin barmaid who was standing back watching this little scene in bemusement, "Five shots of Wild Turkey, and set them up down there." His long legs got him down to our end of the bar in just a stride or three. "Come on. To change our luck, Skip? I'm buying. One for the pillow and a new day."

"She'd better get 'em here damn quick or that's going to be one of the most expensive rounds you ever bought. And you just be sure you're ready to go to war when I need you."

"Haven't I always?"

As the barmaid set down a tray of shot glasses and poured quickly, Jim Tracy gave the grinning youth, who was seeing his third tour of duty in the Midwest League, a long look. Then, "That you have, Greenie. That you have."

Three of us shot ours down. But the Shooter just took a sip. And Kranny was still staring at his brimful shot glass of bourbon when John slapped down what I later found out was his last twenty-dollar bill. "Keep the change," he said to the lady behind the bar. Then, "It *is* going to get better, Trace. Good night," and he was out the door heading for his room at one minute of.

"I loved his daddy, and I love him. You know, they say he's just wasting his time. Almost twenty-five and not out of A ball? That with what he knows about this game, having grown up with it, his education, and his connections, that he oughta just get on with what his life's work is gonna be, the front office of baseball. And hell, he probably will be a general manager one day. Maybe even give me a job. But he's not done yet. He can damn sure get people out in this league, and who knows? With that knuckle curve he's come up with, he might ride it all the way to Triple A, and then you're just a heartbeat away from the show. If Mr. Greenjeans ever got there, something tells me he'd figure out a way to stay awhile."

When Tracy finished his scouting report on the not-so-young Mr. Green, he polished off his whiskey almost daintily. But Kranitz just kept on staring at his until, finally, "You know . . . it's all kind of like a swimming pool," he said. "I mean, just about everything. You know it's cold. You don't want to dive in. But you do. And after you do you feel so *good.*" With that he shoots his Wild Turkey. Grimaces. Sighs. And then chuckles and adds, "Or bad. But at least it's over. For that day."

Then we head on out of the bar toward sleep and another "day" to the tune of Tracy's "Fuck those Appletons. We've got 'em right where we want 'em. They don't think we can play!"

Maybe a swim and then a gabfest breakfast that lasts until lunch, so you eat again before it's time to lay up back in the rooms and catch the big club on the cable, is mostly how you spend your mornings and early afternoons on the road. This is particularly true when you look out the window and see it is still a mean-looking Wisconsin winter day outside and chastise yourself for ever complaining about that hide-burning sun of Arizona.

Of course, on eleven-bucks-a-day meal money the talk around a table of minor league ballplayers on the road is always more plentiful than the actual food: it's truly amazing how long one can stretch the use of a table with refills of coffee, or iced tea, and a Danish here, or cup of soup there; and if it's a buffet breakfast or lunch? Forget it and put on extra kitchen help. The Amora Villa did.

One of the better tables to hang around was any table where the Z Man was holding court. Not only did his swarthy, Latin-lover good looks, always simmering sense of the Rebel Who Needed No Cause, styled, longish wavy black hair, and Adonis physique—which, no matter the weather, he always exposed to a point of actual beefcake with a unique wardrobe that can only be called Contemporary Z, South Florida style— inevitably mean that the stockings-and-lace scenery would be the best available, but his loose-cannon irreverence toward everything established or commonplace always held at least the promise for a vicarious glimpse of a life lived perpetually out in the passing lane of a *two-lane* highway!

He also at twenty-four years of age was back for his third tour at Peoria. He was the other old salt of the ballclub. Yet because of his style was more of an out-front rallying figure for some of the younger pitchers than John Green, who, although he could—and did—match if not surpass Z's worldly exploits in the fleshier and flashier aspects of professional baseball, didn't always feel the necessity of making a spectator sport of it.

That same do-not-cross line? Z would charge across it yelling "Look, Ma, no hands!" and then "Fuck you" to whoever put the line there to begin with.

He also was a hell of a closer in the Al "the Mad Hungarian" Hrabosky mold. And on this ballclub, he was the only pitcher with a W as yet in his column. He'd picked it up pitching shutout ball over the final two and two-thirds innings of the marathon in South Bend.

"This is ridiculous. It's Antarctica out there and they want us to play baseball. Whatcha think, ba'y? Should I subject this body to that abuse?"

The doll of a blond blue-eyed waitress with the incredible legs, traffic-stopping ass, come-hither-if-you're-man-enough sensuality, and shortest skirt we'd seen since Arizona absolutely purred as she answered the Miami-born and -raised Cuban-American heart throb who'd given her reason to come back to the table every excuse she could find.

"Maybe you fellows won't have to play tonight." It was an invitation if ever we'd heard one. Lee Kline looked embarrassed and stirred his coffee. Jeff Massicotte and Mike Aspray gulped, smiled, and rolled their eyes. Gabby Rodriguez winked and tried to think up a line himself. Steve "Esteban" Melendez, our trainer, raised his eyebrows but not his face from his plate of food (only another plate of food, or maybe Lola Falana, could get the Bronx Strutter to do that). And Z now ignored her pointedly.

"It's fucking stupid to send the Southern Division north this time of the year. I know this league. It doesn't have to be done this way. But the bastards don't care about us. We're just the hired help. You know what I mean?"

"They're predicting snow flurries tonight or tomorrow," blondie tried again. "Maybe they won't make you play?"

"Why? They make everything else hard on us. We'll play."

"But maybe they won't," she says with the simple logic of wanting it to be so.

"So what's to do around here if we don't?"

"Plenty . . . if you know where to look." She smiled that saucy smile again and shook that ass as she walked away.

"You're in, Z."

"Was last year."

"No shit?"

"Ah . . . she's nothing, you should see this girl she runs with."

"You know 'em all, huh Z?"

"I ought to. If they plan on making me die in this league."

As the bus pulled out of the motel parking lot and headed toward Goodland Field, Trace leaned back over his seat and said, "Pete called again today."

"Oh yeah?"

"He's sounding low. He's really starting to worry."

"I'll bet."

"I got him this time, though. As soon as he starts off, 'I'm really worried, Doc'"—Pete calls Trace Doc most of the time—"I said, 'Take two aspirin and call me in the morning,' and hung up!"

"Good for you."

While we laughed we also knew it was going to take more than aspirin and the flippant confidence of his manager to keep Pete Vonachen from going through the roof. Only some wins were going to do that.

"Back to reality" is how Mike Boswell had best summed it up the day before upon our first look at Goodland Field in Appleton, Wisconsin. The Boz, a utility infielder who'd started in right field the previous two nights because Fast Eddie Williams was still down from a hamstring strain he'd suffered in spring training and aggravated on Opening Day, like the fifteen other Peoria Chiefs in their second or third year of pro ball and seeing the Midwest League for the first time, had been spoiled by the first three parks we'd been to.

Peoria, with its wide-open flashiness and carnival atmosphere under the media glare, with its immaculate facilities on and off the field to rival Double A and Triple A accommodations; Springfield, not as splashy as Peoria, but more modern and in some ways more efficiently utilitarian in its gleaming aluminum even as it is sterile, but with all the accouterments of the Class AAA ballyard it had been until just a few years before; and then Stanley Coveleski Stadium in South Bend, which can only be characterized as a major league ballpark minus about 35,000 seats—which they can add whenever they choose to because it was so designed by the architects (the same who gave us Royals Stadium in Kansas City, which Coveleski is modeled after). Here we're talking skyboxes. *Elevators* down into clubhouses, managers' *and* coaches' offices more spacious than most big league facilities (we lost Trace and Kranny for a spell). A press box more luxurious and spacious than a good-size office complex. Enormous dugouts (too large, even by major league standards, with built-in TV camera positions; but great for hiding far from the wrath of a manager on a bad day) with wide tunnels leading directly into the clubhouse. And a beautifully landscaped grassy hill with gardens out beyond the outfield fences which serves as a fine hitting background and is also so pleasing to the eye.

Goodland Field is what a minor league ballpark is *supposed* to look like. As all of us have become accustomed to visualizing same from the pages of baseball literature and the tobacco-spitten lore of the old-timer spinning yarns about his days of young manhood spent playing "D ball, ya unnerstan'? Back when wad'n jist them three sissy class'fication's ya got today. We hadda start down on th' itty-bitty end a th' stick, ya follow what I'm sayin'?" Colorful, bittersweet tales about traveling circuits with such names as the Evangeline League, the Three I League, the Wisconsin State League.

Surely that elder diamond warrior could have seen some service in Goodland Field—since, over the course of a history of professional baseball in Appleton dating back to 1891, it had, at different times, played host to ballclubs from both the long-vanished Wisconsin State League (Class D) and Three I League (Illinois, Indiana, Iowa, Class B). And the same cramped, dingy locker rooms, and pillbox-sized, unattached, spike-worn and chaw-stained dugouts he'd dressed and spit in during those "good ol' days" were still there. Along with the same reinforced-concrete and wood-and-tin-covered "grandstand" his fans jeered or cheered him on from. Just another one of the dwindling, yet still dominant anachronisms in the era of the "new" minor leagues.

Bush? Undoubtedly. Nostalgic? Charming? Baseball for the pure and old of heart? I'm sure of it. Even that sheer drop-off from the second-base position into immediate right field does not detract from but rather only enhances the "color" of this decidedly no-cookie-cutter, somewhat gussied-up, but still only good high-school-equivalent ballyard.

However. Not in April. There is no romance to any of it when you can no longer feel your toes by the first round of batting practice, and the frozen pallor of the afternoon more readily brings to mind Grantland Rice ("Against a gray November sky . . .") than Ring Lardner.

"Now this is the kind of ballpark I'm supposed to be playing in," said the crew-cut, ruddy-faced Boz as he picked up his line of thought from the day before in that self-deprecating manner which he, like so many other utility "gamers," seems to wear as a mantle to shield the otherwise fiercely competitive pride in the abilities which had made him and all the others like him "stars" and "legends" back on the campuses and playgrounds of home.

"Tell it to the padre, Boz. You're in the lineup, huh?"

"Yeah, but the way I'm hitting they're liable to think Eddie's better on one leg than I am on two. Think I'll go trip him and fuck up his other leg. I know I'm better than a no-legged man."

"Aaa . . . you're gonna eat that Gordon dude up. They gotta be scratching the bottom of the barrel, these Royals. A five-nine skinny right-hander? Who's he gonna get out?"

Trace's cavalier dismissal of another of Pete's daily phone frets was evidently somewhat akin to whistling past a graveyard. Because out at the ballpark, once everyone was dressed, the Shooter locked the clubhouse door and while he said virtually the same words he'd said on the bus the night before, this time the dressing-down he gave his ballclub had very little of the sound of hurt and puzzlement. Rather it was loud, a great deal more profane, and accompanied by a pacing, arms-flailing body language which left no doubt that he was flat-out pissed off and they'd better do something about it. Like now!

But then, true to form, by the time he'd let the steam screech and hiss out of his boiling kettle and the Chiefs had gotten outside for batting practice, the harangue was yesterday's news and the real Jim Tracy was back having more fun than the law should allow—on this ballclub anyway—doing that which he was born to do.

Back in Mesa, during what was always the best part of any day, leaning on the piping of a cage during batting practice and lazily discussing, if not always solving, the more pressing issues of existence and our place in it with Richie Zisk, Trace, sometimes Colbie, Big Jim, or maybe the Killer, to the percussive, reassuring rhythm of thwack . . . a-thwack . . . a-thwack . . . a-thwunk . . . a-thwack, the metal would fry the flesh at a careless move. In Appleton in April, however, while the uniquely endemic pleasures of the game's most blessed ritual are likewise for the faithful not diminished by the elements, it is the freezer burn that gets you.

Thwack!

"I see you working, Wilkie. That's where you hit that pitch."

Ka-plunk.

"Hey, Fatso, throw strikes. We're working on something here."

"What's he want . . . me to hit it for him, too? I just threw it by him. I own him."

"Nobody asked you nothing, Mule. You don't own nobody. I wore your ass out in the Coast League. Now throw strikes."

"Here it comes, pussy."

Thwunk.

"Keep that shoulder in, dammit."

Thwunk.

"Can I read that paper when you're done hitting with it, Wilkie?"

"Throw it again . . . and watch your lips," snapped Wilkins.

Thwunk.

"Shoulder in. Hands back. You've got the time. Wait on it and trust your hands. They're good enough. *Then* the hips, okay, numbnuts?" Jim Tracy then sighs happy as a bullfrog on a lily pad and glances around at the sky and says to anyone in general but Mario and me in particular, "Great day for fishing, huh? I mean really, cold like this, overcast . . ."

Thwack!

". . . remember the hips. Hips are the trigger. But I see you working. Group two! Group two! One more and get outa there, Rick. Last round, Phil. . . . No, really. Them walleye'd be biting today."

"Trace? Answer me something."

"What's that?"

"How come you let Herbie hit last night in the ninth?" Herberto Andrade, our right-handed-hitting Venezuelan backup catcher, had gotten his first start, at DH, and had been obviously overmatched in his first three at bats, striking out badly twice and rolling out weakly to second the other time. In the ninth with Sergio on second after his double had brought the Chiefs within three, Herbie had K'd again, looking even more foolish than before, to end the game.

Tracy's answer tells us something of the man, and of managing at the Class A level where rosters are necessarily kept to the barest minimum; in this case twenty-three.

"It would've been a slap in his face. Got a lefty on the hill and only had left-handed hitters available on the bench? But I know your thought. And believe me I thought about it too. I mean all of the left-handed pinch hitters I had were more likely to have hit that guy last night than Herbie."

"So?"

"I wanted to give him a chance. At this time of the year, and particularly at this level, you wanna let these kids lay a pattern. Then later in the season when they come complaining how come they're not playing in certain situations, I can pull out the book and show 'em. Stops 'em cold every time. . . ."

Thwack!

". . . Atta baby, Ding Dong. Double Johnson . . . ? Yep! So how many you gonna get today . . . and whatcha been eating, anyway? Rocket fuel? Dammit, how can you cover the plate from there?"

Thwack!

Lenny Bell, the strapping, good-timin' gee-whiz-am-I-really-here kid out of the University of Texas, finished off his swing and drawled easily, along with that shit-kickin' grin, "I don't know. What's it look like?"

Tracy watches the flight of a screaming, arcing missile until it ends up banging high off the top of the left-center-field wall, then looks down at Lenny set up way off the plate, shakes his head, and says, "What the hell can I say to that? He's wearing it out from there. It's all wrong, but he's doing all right. Come on, Mulc, give him something good to swing at. This kid's hotter than a two-dollar whore on a submarine!" Then, out of the side of his mouth, into an icy wind that mutes his words, "But not for long with that stance. And *then* he'll be teachable."

Aspray put on a damn clinic. I mean he pitched his ass off for a complete game, three-hit thing of beauty.

Only one problem. That little right-hander, Gordon? First name of Tom. Age twenty. He pitched his and somebody else's off to boot! Go figure this: that five-nine right-hander, that had best not go walking on any piers lest he fall through, took a plus-90 fastball and a crackling curve, shoved them both up our ass at will, gave up a poop lead-off single to Phil Hannon to open the game, and then proceeded to strike out eleven of the next sixteen batters he faced. Seven of them consecutively. And four of those in one inning! That was in the third. His catcher couldn't corral one of those snap-dragon breaking balls for strike three on Jossy Rosario, who looked silly on the swing but got safely to first well enough for the only other base runner young Mr. Gordon allowed that evening. But not to worry, he simply blew Wilkins away on three straight pitches, again.

At that point, besides the freezing-our-ass-off question of who in the hell might score period that night, what with Mike Aspray matching out for out this truly awesome display of pure pitching dominance with pure pitching smarts, the only thought among us observers (and, unfortunately too many of the participants) was just how many *can* this little dude punch out and are we going to see some kind of record set?

Well, it seems the Kansas City Royals knew exactly what they had, and were taking no chances with getting this prodigy hurt in the cold of April in A Ball, so he was on a pitch count and didn't come out to take the hill in the sixth. (Little did we know at the time that before the summer was over that "skinny little right-hander" would blaze his way up through three whole levels, leading all of baseball in strikeouts for most of the season, and end the year in the big leagues and be named *Baseball America*'s 1988 Player of the Year for all of the minor leagues.)

So all right, he's out of there, the exhibition is over, we'd all been held spellbound by the once-in-maybe-a-decade brilliance of such an athlete, but now it was time to get on about winning a 0-0 ballgame. Nuh-uh. Tom-little-Terrific had so cowed the Chiefies that two merely mortal pitchers finished the K circus by collecting six more for seventeen! And that was an Appleton record.

But then "they can't beat us if they can't hit it either," right? Wrong. And all it took was one of the oldest tricks in the book. In the seventh, with one out, Aspray gets a slider in and nicked the third sacker. The DH then rolls a room-service double-play ball to Sergio, but Jossy flat drops a perfect flip at second when he lets the runner in too close on him, everybody safe. A fielder's choice by their first baseman, Don Wright (should've been another double play, but Jossy takes one look at another runner about to take his banjo legs out from under him and doesn't even try), leaves men at the corners with two outs. *Then!* The old walking steal off first, rundown, back and forth, runner breaks for the plate, Jossy breaks out of the rundown, wheels and throws a fraction too late, Wilkie fires it back to Sergio, who then tags no-wheels Wright going back to first for out three, but the run scores. No hits. One run. The only one they would get. The only one they would need as the Chiefs lost 1-0 and were now 1 and 5 on the young but getting-old-and-stale-in-a-hurry season.

The only consolation was that precious few folks had come out into the utter mean cold to watch it—134, to be precise. Boz, who'd struck out in all three at bats, said, "Is it still a hat trick if there's nobody there to see it?"

"Does a falling tree make a sound in the forest if there's no one to hear it?"

"Deep."

"Hell yes it does," said Wilkie, "and I got *my* two knocks tonight."

That he had. After two helpless whiffs had come two meaningless singles—after "Flash" Gordon had gone to defrost in a shower, of course. And to go with Phil's lead-off single that had made a total of three to match the Foxes output.

But they had the run. Aspray was calling his lawyer to institute a suit for nonsupport, and we had to ride back to the motel with the Trace Monster.

"Four-o'clock bus tomorrow. Be in your rooms by one."

That was it? Then when Kranny, Mario, and I followed him off the bus Jim Tracy surprised us even further. We had immediately started sidling away as inconspicuously as we thought we should, but he'd called after us as if nothing at all had happened and simply said, "Don't you wanna get something to eat? That restaurant's open."

So it was. One-to-nothing games with a grand total of only ten base runners of any fashion for *both* sides do not take long to play. And the upside of a decidedly downside night, we thought, was that at least we could have a real drink with a real dinner even if we had to cry in it.

But no. There were almost no histrionics that night. And certainly no crying of any kind. In fact, "That little sumbitch was pretty, wasn't he? He shoved it up our ass and made us like it. You just saw a big league arm, gentlemen."

"Undoubtedly. But fuck him anyway," grumbled the Kran-dog.

"Listen at my Mule here, takes this stuff personal, don't he?"

"If that isn't the pot calling the kettle black. Huh, big guy?"

But strangely enough, Tracy didn't see it that way. There was a logic to go along with the method of his un-madness which for the most part was the focus of his words and thoughts for the balance of that evening and the following morning: "That one you put in a special file and then you might just as well forget it. Like it never even happened."

A minor league baseball game such as that second one in Appleton proves little or nothing to anybody, felt Tracy. (The noted exception being Tom Gordon's agent—if he had one yet. If he didn't, "Where do you get in line?") When a truly phenomenal talent, particularly a pitcher, who, regardless of his chronological age, developmentally is already so obviously above the level he's playing at, his as-yet-less-than-peers on both sides would've been just as well served by taking the night off. Class A hitters are Class A hitters precisely because it is presumed that they are not yet ready to hit major league pitching. Therefore it can certainly be no indictment when they do not. If anything, the occurrence is but a reassuring endorsement of the always nebulous and so subjective—therefore always defensive—yet collective wisdom of the "system" and the "baseball judgment" of the men who sent them there. And the to-be-developed young men playing behind such a talent? When the ball is put into play but maybe ten times in an evening, the only thing that can be said of them is that they know how to play catch—since their game is spent mostly throwing the ball around the horn as overmatched not-yet sluggers slink back to the dugout after yet another humiliation. "We know they can do that! But can they play? We don't know because we haven't tested 'em."

On the other hand, Jim Tracy said he knew the Chiefs could play. They had proved that the year before and again in spring training. We were getting the generally solid, sometimes spectacular defense that had been expected. Ditto the pitching. Only one bad and one so-so performance by a starter out of six. The bullpen had been nothing short of brilliant. And hitting? Well, nobody can hit that badly for any length of time. The baseball law of averages has to come into play at some point.

"Doesn't it? Huh? Tell me it ain't always gonna be this way, Mule."

With all his intermittently repeated rationalizations, Trace did manage at times to reason himself right into a kind of whimsied melancholy.

"Jesus, Mary, and Joseph . . . seventeen strikeouts. Sixty punchouts in six games. Maybe I can't manage for shit, but I can count. What else I got to do over there in the coaching box? At least I'm not gonna get frostbite. All I do is keep my hands stuck down around my nuts—haven't got any traffic to direct. I swear I wouldn't know what to do if we had two base hits back to back. . . . I'm telling you, tonight I actually thought about activating myself. Really. You know when we had one on in the ninth? Just one lousy extra base hit in the clutch every now and then isn't asking too much, is it? I'm asking ya."

It had been at one of those low moments when Mario asked, "Really Trace, right now, what do you think you'd hit in this league?"

The veteran minor league slugger and major league overachiever gave the young broadcaster's question some thought. Then, "Well, even though this is A ball, the pitching's pretty good . . . and on my legs? I might hit .300 . . . but I'd drive in a lot of ribbies."

"Not with nobody on base you wouldn't," said one of us, picturing the Shooter on *this* ballclub.

"You know, he's telling the truth," Trace said, shaking his head slowly. Then, "Hey, I know! I'll hit 'em so far they'd have to count 'em as two each."

He mused silently for a moment on the remembered thrill of when he was driving in runs by the bunches. Then Kranny brought him back. "Trace, I think maybe it's time you sit Jossy down. If he doesn't do something different on the pivot we're going to bring him back to Peoria in pieces."

"That little Chico's gonna get killed out there the way he's going, I know that. I don't know whether it's because he's getting a late start to the bag. Or whether he's just not clearing himself right. You had him last year at Wytheville. Was he getting creamed like this then?"

"No. But I'll be damned if I see what he's doing different."

"I'm gonna put a call in to the Killer"—Mick Kelleher, Cubs roving infield instructor. "In the meantime I'm gonna work with him during BP tomorrow. Maybe I can see something. Maybe he's not using the bag to protect himself. But he's sure enough gonna end up dead doing what he's doing."

"If my pitchers don't kill him first. But sometimes just sitting down does the trick. Watching somebody else do it."

"Maybe so. But he's a bona fide prospect. They want him to play. 'Course, it's not like he's hitting, either. What is he hitting, anyway?"

"Counting tonight? Oh eighty-three."

The look that came over Jim Tracy's face was an awed incredulity of the sort one might get when suddenly face-on with the incomprehensible; his voice was a whisper as if he were a little boy in a museum of dinosaurs for the first time.

"Is he? Is he really?"

Then there was silence as the absurdly low number and Trace's reaction to it had crystallized for all of us the utter futility of trying to win ballgames with a club that had only one regular hitting over .300 (Bell, .333) and only one other regular hitting over .200 (Rivero, .208).

It was too damn early in the season to feel that way, and everyone knew it, but only Mario had the sense to do something about it. He changed the subject to one where the enemy was from without. "What the hell did Marty say for Rainforth to run him like that? I mean, come on, Marty!"

Just the image of the "Captain," the mature-beyond-his-years, soft-spoken art student and Errol Flynn look-a-like from Los Angeles, the quiet conscience and leader of the 1988 Peoria Chiefs, getting tossed for arguing balls and strikes had been enough to snap Tracy out of his brief torpor.

"Wasn't that something, huh? Cold day in hell before I thought I'd see that. And I guess it was at that. Jeez . . . I'm shocked, right? I can't even work up a good spit of dip before I get down there to him."

It had happened quickly. Almost politely. There had been a very questionable checked swing on a 2-2 count. But there wasn't the slightest hesitation in Vince Rainforth's right arm and voice as he immediately rang Marty up. There also wasn't a moment's hesitation when in almost the same breath came "You're outta here!" when Cap had turned and said something briefly before heading back to the dugout.

"I'm almost tongue-tied, I said, 'Jeez, Vince, what'd he say?' He goes, 'The kid said I'm brutal.' 'Yeah, but what'd he say?' 'He said, "You're brutal.'"' I go, 'That's it? Being a little soft here, aren't you?' 'They know what they can say and what they can't say,' that's his answer . . ."

"'Brutal' they can't say?"

"No. The no-no was 'you're,'" answered Kranny, who hates all umpires the way some folks hate snakes. "You can't personalize it. 'You' or 'you're' or 'you all.' Those sissy bastards are trying to take over the damn game and now they've got rabbit ears too!"

"Look at my Mule! He gets hot at those guys in blue, don't he? I'm gonna have to let him go after one of 'em one of these days. . . ."

Not only could we not beat those Cheeseheads on the field, apparently, likewise we couldn't win the argument.

Against Tracy's protestations, Larry Dawson, the Appleton general manager, "banged" Thursday's game because of cold and snow and scheduled an afternoon doubleheader for Friday. By midday, when the temperature was 36 degrees and falling, with snow flurries already evident and a promise of more, there had been telephone discussions on the subject, but Trace had argued against a final decision until everybody got out to the ballpark. "We're coming no matter what. My guys need the work."

Once there he'd told the Chiefs to get dressed quickly and get out onto the field. But Dawson, supported by Jim Cutler, vice president of the Midwest League (and on the board of directors for the Appleton Foxes), had made up his mind even though the forecast for Friday wasn't any better. But his logic wasn't bad. He reasoned that if we started at one o'clock when the temperature was maybe 40, we would be finishing up when it was about 30. As opposed to starting there and finishing up in the low 20s.

Trace knew it was cold but he wanted to play. His stated logic wasn't bad, either. "So sure it's cold. It's been cold. But my point is that right now it's playable. *You* say it's going to get that cold. So okay, what happens if later tonight we get some real snow, or the weather's even worse tomorrow, and you bang that? That means we're playing back-to-back doubleheaders down in Peoria in the heat of August." He turns to Vince Rainforth and Mike Pietro, the two umpires—who, until the lineups are exchanged and the game official, are only observers in any argument such as this. "You see what I'm saying, Vince? What assurance do I have we'll play tomorrow?"

"I can tell you this," Rainforth answered. "If it's not below twenty-five we won't bang it."

"Then I don't understand, because it's not twenty-five now."

"It's not our call yet, Trace. Tomorrow, once we start, it will be."

"I understand that, but—"

The Shooter was about to argue some more, but Dawson ended all discussion with a firm "Doubleheader tomorrow, one o'clock, gentlemen," and headed for the warmth of his office.

"Respectfully, sir . . . it's your ballpark and it's your decision. But I wantcha to know if we were in Peoria, we'd play!" Trace threw after him.

"You're not in Peoria, are you?" And that was that.

So that's how Elvin Paulino, Jossy Rosario, and Eduardo Caballero not only saw the first snow of their life, they also got to play, or at least practice, baseball in it.

"Let those wimps go home. We're gonna show 'em. Let's go!"

The Peoria Chiefs then went on to have what was if not their best-quality workout since spring training, certainly it was the most spirited. Watching Polly chasing down snowflakes and whooping as he tried to hit them with that big old bat of his was worth the bone-chilling cold we pretended wasn't there as some of the Foxes, bundled up like Eskimos, came out—briefly—to see if the Peoria Chiefs were indeed going to take batting practice and work infield situations in a Wisconsin deep freeze.

Herbie Andrade, whose father is a prominent government official in the city of Maracaibo, Venezuela, and who had traveled in the States on vacations and for amateur baseball tournaments, and spoke the best English—well, at first, pretty much the only English—of our four Latin American green-card Chicfics, was a little embarrassed for the naiveté of the other three.

"Sometimes they not know how to act so good? You understand, my friend?" Then he smiled as would maybe a young Desi Arnaz—who uncannily he resembles in not only looks but infectious persona—and pointed to himself. "But I teach. This is very different for them. But I know . . . a little. And Trace good, too . . . you know? The book . . . how I say? Happy ending? Yes, book have happy ending. We win. You see, my friend. This is fun. It's not so cold, no?"

Later that evening, and at innumerable times over the course of an evening when at least we got an early start on the food, the beverage, and mostly the baseball talk which is really the bread, wine, and breath of our existence, Jim Tracy gave his real reasons for having wanted to play even in that cold. In the minor leagues, from A ball to Triple AAA, doubleheaders are played as two seven-inning games. For the Shooter there is a special place in hell reserved for the person or persons responsible for that heresy.

"A seven-inning ballgame is an aberration. No place for it in real baseball. Hell, the way we're hitting, they get just a couple runs here or there and before we know it we're swept on getaway-day and gotta go to Wausau with our tails between our legs one and seven! Why me, Mule? Maybe I oughta stop swearing so much. Even God's on their side."

Maybe He was, but Peter of Peoria had been in Chicago that day for the unveiling of best friend Harry Caray's new soft drink, Holy Cow. The word from Peoria and Chicago was that "the Boss" was raising more

Cain with the Cubs management about his Chiefs than he was toasts to Harry's newest venture in self-aggrandizement.

John Butler, the Chiefs' general manager, had told us by phone from Peoria that the mood was "pretty grim" around the Meinen Field offices, but that at least with Pete up in Chicago for the day they would get a respite from his getting-fouler-by-the-day moods and maybe also get some unharassed work done. Peoria's gain was Wrigley Field's loss. "He's not too happy" was how Scott Nelson, the young, most capable, but so very droll prankster and Assistant Director of Scouting for the Chicago Cubs had put it during a phone conversation of that same afternoon. "He's been in meetings with Bill and Gordon most of the day. Frey too. I saw smoke coming out from under the door a little while ago. Anyway, I was right, wasn't I?"

"What's that?"

"That team can't hit." It was true, during spring training Scotty had been one of the very few in Cubs management to factor the .233 team batting average of the '87 Geneva Cubs with their glossy won-loss record of 48 and 28 somewhat differently than the professed and proffered dogma and had voiced more realistic expectations for the 1988 Peoria Chiefs.

One of the guys who was supposed to be hitting was big Bob "Strychnine" Strickland. In fact the almost twenty-four-year-old fourth-year player had, about halfway through spring training, been moved down from the Winston-Salem roster and ticketed for Peoria expressly for that purpose. At six-foot-three and 215 pounds, the left-handed-hitting DH/outfielder/catcher from Tonawanda, New York, had originally been signed as a pitcher. Now the much-traveled big-swing, no-field "fringe suspect" was being asked to deliver some veteran wallop to a lineup of younger, much shinier, albeit less experienced prospects. Prospects who were possessed of linedrive promise and speed, but as yet were untested at the full-season level. And who, in any case, except for Wilkins, weren't projected for longball power to begin with. Of course, that the big guy was afflicted by the same mysterious malaise as his teammates was evidenced by a .154 batting average, no homeruns, and 1 RBI.

Struggling? Yes. But then that "colded-out" night in Appleton, Wisconsin, he was the most *envied* member of the family—he had the company of a beautiful young lady whom he also loved. Jackie had arrived the day before just in time for her to sit in that cold and witness the seventeen-carat spanking (her man had been a three-time victim). Now most of the envy came not at the fact that she is as comely as she is witty and gracious, but that she was *no groupie*! (Or gold-digging, pushy baseball wife, for that matter.) Engaged to marry as soon as his career could afford it, the hometown sweethearts were as true a picture of youthful "married" bliss as you'll too seldom find in the world of minor league baseball.

"Have dream, will travel," she'd said with a smile too real and too pretty to be called rueful. But she was also too perceptive not to realize that that was the effect.

"His dream, we travel," she'd corrected herself, laughing. Then, pulling her wrap more snugly about her and glancing around at a frozen, sparsely peopled Goodland Field grandstand, she'd added, "Seeing America on the baseball plan."

Just the year before she and Bob had seen both Charleston, West Virginia, and Winston-Salem, North Carolina.

"We were hoping to be back in Winston-Salem. It's such a lovely area. There are so many nice things to see and do in that league." There was that smile again; and again she caught herself. "Of course, I should've said Pittsfield, right?"

Well, "The Pits" of Pittsfield, Massachusetts, being Double A, *was* closer to the dream. It was also closer to home and parents and school and jobs.

"We live with both families in the off-season. Back and forth. We're equal-opportunity moochers." During the winter Bob works when he can between trying to finish his college degree and working out. Jackie works.

"I don't mind. We're together. He has his dreams. I have the man I want to marry. A man who would be miserable all his life if he didn't follow his dream wherever it takes him. And I would be miserable if he did it alone while I waited for it to come true. Or for him to come home."

So for another five months out of another year she had again loaded up a U-Haul and made a long move alone—he was in spring training—so that she might already have seen to the setting up of yet another "home" for them, and also to finding yet another job for herself so that they could afford to "chase his dream together." With that done, she had then driven up to Wisconsin to be at his side during the cold miseries of an April slump and skid.

"We're happy. And all young couples struggle financially in the early years. At least there are dreams and romance to ours."

And if you think that didn't tug at more than just a few supposedly cold, hard, gotta-be-cynical-or-die male hearts, even as shamelessly enough it sent a stirring through a somewhat less noble part of the male anatomy, then you'd best not ever travel with a minor league baseball team.

"Broom Johnson."

Kranny mumbled in disgust over his Cheese Whopper and then didn't say anything else. He didn't have to. And no one else did much talking either as a strikingly strange red sun was setting on Appleton while we solemnly ate burgers we couldn't taste before having to get out on the highway for the now very long 103-mile drive even farther north into a Wisconsin bad dream.

A Johnson? In the ever-changing insider lingo of baseball, a Johnson can be anything. Good or bad. It is just something that is what it is when modified by the fore word or words.

A broom? Well, a broom sweeps. And now you know why the burgers went down like chalk and the conversation wasn't even of the gallows-humor type, but rather like the hushed tones of a wake. A 1-and-7 funereal repast.

The amazing thing was that it had all gone so closely to form. As if everything talked about just had to come true—except only in the worst-case scenario version.

In 1987, Jeff "Massacre" Massicotte, in only his first year of pro ball, had won the Rolaids Fireman of the Year trophy in the New York–Penn League. He'd led that short-season circuit in saves with fifteen, while sporting a gaudy record of 4-0 with an earned run average of 2.23 in thirty-five appearances all out of the bullpen for the Geneva Cubs. However, during spring training a not wholly illogical decision had been made to turn him at least temporarily into a starter. James Colborn, the Cubs' Coordinator of Minor League Instruction, had reasoned that although "Jeff's future might be as a reliever, and probably is, right now, at this stage of his career, he needs innings pitched. He looks like he's a major league prospect, and the more mound experience he gets can only get him there faster. The things he needs to work on, he can work on the most as a starter."

Jeff Massicotte thought it was "a very *bad* idea." He couldn't remember the last game he'd started. He had pitched only out of the bullpen during a successful junior college career which had seen him drafted by the Cubs in the eleventh round, somewhat unusual for a juco relief pitcher. He'd been "a reliever in high school, for chrissakes!" It was his identity. The man who comes in with the game on the line and the crowd hushed and on the edge of their seats. He said he needed that for his concentration. And he hadn't kept quiet about his feelings on the matter during spring training. He had, of course, been overruled. Therefore he wasn't a completely happy Cubbie upon leaving Mesa. And when he got shelled in one and a third down in Springfield the second game of the season he'd become one very frustrated and confused Chiefie.

Now, after the first game of the Frost Bowl doubleheader, Jeff Massicotte was just plain "bitter. I am. I've got no fucking business being a starter! They're messing with my head—and my career."

He had also been given a nickname by his pitching coach. And it really had somewhat resembled a massacre. In three and a third this time ("Longest I've been out there since Pony League!") he gave up seven hits, including two doubles and a triple, balked in a run, walked two, and left in the fourth down 5 to 1. Of course, John Green relieved and threw well, shutting the Foxes down until some tough luck cost two in the bottom of the sixth.

So, a bad outing by a starter—and what happens? We actually hit the ball a little. Even had the lead for half an inning when Rick Wilkins took Jesus Deleon deep over the right-field wall in the first (and how appropriate: the first homer of the season for the Peoria Chiefs, and it's a two-out solo Johnson). And we started to make a run in the sixth when Lenny Bell laid down another beautifully executed surprise bunt. Then, with Bell on second by virtue of a wild pitch, Paulino sent a liner hard into center to drive him in. Marty slammed a "seed" off the stabbing glove of one-eyed reliever Doug Nelson which resulted in a fluke 1-4-3 out instead of at least a double. Gator went long but out to right. Then "Strychnine" jumped all over a getting-beleaguered fastball and pulled it into the right-field corner. Out there the ball rattled around long enough for that big old *happy* body to keep on lumbering around the bases before finally belly-flopping into third very surprised, winded, and relieved with an RBI triple, to the sedate but oh so proud delight of his Jackie. That's hardly to mention the absolute delirium of Jim Tracy. He had gotten to wave those long gorilla arms around sending runners home *twice* in one inning! And the Chiefs actually might've ended up making a game of it; but when it's 7 to 3 and you've only got four outs left ("goddam seven-inning games"), the odds get long for even an offensive juggernaut, of which of course it could be said that we weren't even in the same species with.

Game two? Well, the Panamanian Devil did nothing to dispel the sense of adventure which always imbues one of his performances and which had led to his Trace-given moniker. Eduardo Caballero sizzled and crackled that "knee-buckling yakker" past the Foxes, with uncanny control for such a hard, sharp-breaking curveball, to the tune of ten strikeouts in five innings, while scattering five hits, three of them cheap, *three balks,* one walk, and a jillion gyrations and mound stompings, only to lose 3 to 2 on the "Phantom Passed Ball."

It took that glaring anomaly to do it because of course with this fine pitching by a Chief going on we couldn't hit it either. We did, however, have a 2-1 lead going into the bottom of the fifth courtesy of a one-out walk by Boswell, Andrade's first hit of the season, in his first start behind the plate, a perfectly placed hit-and-run through the right side putting Chiefies on the corners for Phil Hannon, our gentlemanly and rabbit-legged center fielder (who'd already driven in the first run in the third with a double), to then execute a flawless safety squeeze with Boz scoring and everybody safe. Ah ha! The makings of a big inning? And maybe getting to sneak out of town with one win, and it being the last at least the trip up to Wausau wouldn't have to be on a totally sour stomach. With Eduardo mowing, and our bullpen, another run or two should see us safely through the final six outs and then we're out of there. Right? Who, us? With runners at second and third, one out, Gator lofts a weak "can of bean shit" to short right field and for some ungodly reason Phil Hannon, the Chiefs' best base runner, decides out of the gray to tag up and haul ass to third base. That, however, is already occupied by one now very confused Herbie—he wasn't about to go anywhere on *that*—who in the ensuing Keystone Cops routine is eventually tagged out for an inning-ending double play!

But then they "can't fucking beat us if they can't fucking hit that fucking little thing in the fucking clutch either!"

They can if Vince Rainforth doesn't see the same foul tip off the bat of Foxes DH Don Wright that everybody else in the ballyard saw. Admittedly that wasn't many. Besides the participants there might've been a dozen or more in attendance; these would be the only ballgames that season where the National Anthem wasn't even played.

With two outs, the score then tied and a runner at third, Wright checks his swing on a fastball up and ticks it back to the wall, where it then dribbles down toward the Foxes' dugout. Foul ball, right? Herbie doesn't even give it chase. Instead he turns to Rainforth for a new baseball while the Appleton batboy runs the other one down and everybody else relaxes for one of those hundred little moments during a baseball game when one might smooth out the dirt, hitch up a glove, shift a cup to a more comfortable position on the genitals, or look up into the sky or stands in search of plumage or plunder . . . everybody, that is, except for the Fox on third. He, just as inconspicuously as he could, skips on across home and Rainforth starts pointing at the plate in the umpiring gesture of run scored.

All hell breaks loose in the brouhaha department. But although Vince gets his face and windbreaker splattered with quickly frozen tobacco spray from Tracy ("Hot damn, I'd just loaded up, too") as the Shooter, leading with that jackhammer chin stuck way out, that fishhook Adam's apple bobbing like a buoy in a squall, his back arched swayback, and his big, bony ass stuck up and out the other way, while keeping his twitching fists steadfastly glued to his hips, looking for all the world like an enraged chicken, gave him the devil in a cloud of dip and vapor breath, the inning ended without any further scoring and everybody still in the game. Not for long. When Mike Pietro called Lenny Ball out at first on a bang-bang play for the first out of the next inning, Kranny, who because of the cold had been wearing a white towel draped over his head and shoulders with his ballcap turned around and stuck on top, looking for all the world like some totally misplaced bedouin, shot out of the dugout as if from a cannon, a screaming, whirling dervish, and was tossed before he got within twenty feet of the cocky little pretty boy who'd been giving us shit for days with his floating strike zone and penchant for seeing balks under every mattress. It had all gotten to be just too much for the Kran-dog.

"Broom fucking Johnson!", and Kranny threw his partially eaten burger back on the table. We were sitting well away from the small group of players who'd been brave enough to follow the "adults" into Burger King instead of the majority who'd opted in their shame to hike over to a close-by McDonald's when Tracy had simply said, "Here," and Lee had stopped the bus on the way out of town. The Shooter, without another word, had gotten off the bus and, head down, but jaw twitching and veins popping, left us all behind as he'd stomped into the fast-food eatery oblivious to everything except that his ballclub was now 1 and 7.

"We didn't deserve to win it," he finally said. The doom and gloom in his voice for the first time sounded all too real.

"Of all the people on this ballclub, Phil Hannon would've been the last person I'd have thought could make that dumb of a base-running error . . . I don't know, guys. I just don't know." After more uncomfortable silence, only interrupted occasionally by the muttered cursing of Kranny, Trace asked of the cosmos, "Is it possible that we won't ever win again?" Then, "Really, Mule, is it possible?"

"If these umpires keep following us around the league like a goddam black cloud it just might be." Rainforth and Pietro had also been with us for the first two against Springfield. And of course Kranitz still swears that if Aspray hadn't been squeezed by Rainforth Opening Night he never would've grooved that fastball to Lankford which seemed to have been the start of all this horror that just kept getting worse. "We've had them six out of the first eight games. Enough's enough!"

"Uh . . . not yet."

"What?"

"They're going to Wausau, too."

"No. They couldn't be . . . nuh-uh. No way! Huh?" Soon the Kran-dog was reduced to sputtering. And that's when the Trace Monster cracked the only hint of a smile we would see on his face the rest of that evening and said, "Kranny, ya know why he ran you so quickly, huh? You scared him. You came out of there so hard you were putting dents in the grass. And you looked like one of them terrorists . . . ya know, one of them rock throwers from the Gaza Strip?"

"That's me," Kranny said. "Fuck, that's us."

While the heater works fine on the Peoria Charter bus, "That was the coldest ride I've ever made," Lee Kline said after we'd pulled into the Holiday Inn in Wausau. He was right. If anyone said anything it was only in a whisper that had better not be audible up at the front. Even after the bus had stopped and everyone was waiting for Steve Melendez to come back with the keys and room assignments, and some few voices were starting to be heard as gear was being gathered, Trace had snapped, "Shut up. You start talking when you start winning!"

"Congratulations on the dinger," I said to Rick Wilkins as we both trudged up the flight of stairs carrying the luggage we'd been living out of since the start of spring training almost two months before. "Thanks," said the Wheaties-box-handsome young man from Jacksonville, Florida. "I just wished it would've meant something."

"Yeah," I said as I paused for a moment at the opened door and watched him drop his bags and look around at yet another motel room.

"Home sweet home," he said in that God's Country accent and manner which reminded me so much of my own son just about his age and playing junior college ball some 1,200 miles and at least another world away.

Rick "the Phenom" "the Kid" "Wilkie" Wilkins. He had been the first of the 1988 Chiefs I had met. We had been together the longest. Now he looked at me and said, "Things are going to start changing here. This isn't us, you know that."

"Yeah."

"We're starting to get the red-ass. And that's all it's going to take. I mean, we're not used to losing!"

After unpacking and organizing another room into some kind of home and office yet again, I dialed Trace's number. "Going down for a beer. Wanna come?"

The voice I heard was one I'd thought I'd never hear from James Edwin Tracy. It was empty of everything. It was a monotone of nothingness. "Not tonight, pal. Look, I'll see you in the morning, all right?"

So it was by myself for the first time in some time that I went on down to a barroom alone. And it was empty. Just me and a bartender named Tess. A cold wind was howling outside and the weather forecaster on the TV above the bar was predicting more of the same.

Mesa, Arizona.

One of the ironies of organized baseball is that major leaguers get some six weeks in the Valley of the Sun—or that balmy, humid peninsula of eternal youth—in which to hone their skills for the championship season to come, yet their inevitable replacements when they age, falter, go lame, or stop hitting only get about three. That is, unless they happen to be one of the shiny young Hosses who get their cup of coffee *before* the fact as non-roster invitees to a big league camp, thereby adding bodies to an official forty-man roster already swollen by that year's crop of legitimate comers with a chance to stick, career minor leaguers, or "fringe" veterans in for a last look or to "push a starter," top prospects which an organization needs and chooses to protect that year and select others it wishes to reward or goose with a taste of the Promised Land.

Seeming incongruity or not, because at least one young man who would surely come within the scope of this inquiry was among those several categories composing the unofficial 1988 spring training roster of the forty-four Chicago Cubs who had been in camp since February 25 (pitchers and catchers reported the 21st), I had reason and blessed excuse to leave the snow and *hustle* of a Peoria winter and drive some 1,700 miles in search of sunshine and baseball. After almost two months in the bleak of a Midwest winter, it was definitely time!

Therefore I was already well tanned and nigh on to hog heaven up in the press box of HoHoKam Park, the Winter Home of the Chicago Cubs, already almost comfortable among the *real* McCoys and celebs who are allowed to sojourn there, that afternoon of Wednesday, March 9, when, under an endless blue sky rimmed by the burnt-umber-and-violet highlights of the craggy Superstitious Mountains, at approximately two-forty in the afternoon, Rick Wilkins bounced a sharp single to center off a fastball delivered by the veteran major leaguer Donnie Moore, that day pitching and losing in relief for the California Angels.

Why the drama? Less than ten months removed from facing juco pitching when he'd been the "Hoss" catcher for Florida Junior College in Jacksonville, in his first at bat against the Big Boys, the Kid got a hit. The Chicago Cubs had bet big dollars that there would be plenty more.

He was so cool about it. After rounding the bag at first and making sure center fielder Devon White made the play before settling back into a first base patrolled by Wally "World" Joyner, there was no jump of elation. Just a quick, sharp clap of the hands before he nonchalantly took off his batting gloves and looked for the signs soon to be flashed by third-base coach Chuck Cottier after he'd gotten them from Don Zimmer. Welcome to the show. Spring training exhibition version.

But why was he here? Surely the .251 batting average with eight home runs and forty-three runs batted in at Geneva during his first half-summer of professional baseball when he'd helped carry that ballclub to a pennant showed definite promise and was worthy of promotion, but an invitation to big league camp? As less than a third-year player he didn't need to be protected. And while he was certainly a major league prospect, he wasn't there to push any starter or even reserve; that was at least two to three years away. He wasn't there to make a team—in fact he'd already been assigned to a team, Peoria. He wasn't there for a look-see either, because with an entirely new regime in its early stages of transition from the Dallas Green reign, Jim Frey and Don Zimmer were hard pressed to evaluate what was in the major league cupboard, much less the minor league garage. And although you need at least five and better yet six catchers to get your pitchers ready during spring training, there were several catchers farther up the ladder and more deserving of a goose than Rick, so he wasn't there as a body.

But he *was* there because of a reward. An entirely different reward from the other starry-eyed would-be Cubs in big league camp for the first time. He was there because just maybe Mr. Ray Wilkins, his father, should be negotiating arms control with Gorbachev!

You see, Rick had been a pretty good linebacker. As a freshman attending Furman University on a football scholarship he'd been a starter on a ballclub that won an NCAA Championship in the fall of 1985. Then when the football coach reneged on a recruiting promise that he could also play baseball, he immediately transferred that very spring semester to Florida Junior College, where he promptly had a season of baseball good enough to be drafted in June of '86 by the Cubs in the twenty-third round.

However, upon consultation with the senior Mr. Wilkins, he eschewed that apparent insult, didn't sign, and went back for another fall and spring of juco baseball. There he performed well enough to stir the interest of a lot of other scouts and gave Ray Wilkins the leverage he needed to negotiate *first-round* money out of the Cubs only hours before his son was eligible to go back into the free-agent pool for the June '87 draft. One of the perks Mr. Wilkins negotiated for his son was that he be invited to big league camp the following spring. And on balance, perhaps it hadn't been such a good idea.

That is said even knowing that Rick performed well enough in his three weeks with the big club to in fact at least catch the eye of both Don Zimmer and Jim Frey. This being evidenced by a conversation in the VIP lunchroom of Hy Corbett Field down in Tuscon with Mr. Frey. We'd just played Alphonse and Gaston over the last three weiners on the rotisserie and were then enjoying them as we escaped the heat and waited for that afternoon's game against the Cleveland Indians in at least spartan comfort, it not being nearly as plush and bountiful as the gratis digs back at HoHoKam.

". . . Yeah, well, he certainly looks like he's got all the tools. He has the body you like to see in a catcher. And they say he might have some power. Looks like he has the swing for it."

"You think he's a major league prospect?"

Long pause. He shoves away his plate and reaches for a cigarette. "You mind?"

I pat the Camel Lights in my pocket and say, "No, sir. You just beat me to it."

"Yeah. Is he a big league prospect? Obviously our organization thinks he is. Wouldn't you say?"

"Yeah. But what do *you* see?"

A longer pause. Then, "He's young. And of course I haven't seen that much of him. But I'd have to say he has a pretty good chance of playing in the major leagues."

Now there certainly isn't any harm in having your general manager say nice things about you to a guy writing a book. There can be a problem, however, when Don Zimmer, the major league field manager, comes over to the minor league clubhouse some ten days later and singles a twenty-year-old Class A player out from the other 150-plus Cubs farm-hands who had been gathered together to hear a State of the Organization message and pep rally from "Popeye," the only one of the Boys of Summer who has a steel plate in his head:

". . . He's an example of the kind of talent we were hoping was in this organization when we took this job. Rick Wilkins is going to play major league baseball, gentlemen. And so can some of you if you put the same kind of hustle and desire into it as he does."

Those words made Rick Wilkins very proud. I'm afraid they also drove even more of a wedge between the Phenom and his peers than was already there because of the big bonus and the resulting publicity, which had given cause for *Baseball America* to rank Rick Wilkins as the third-best prospect overall in the Cubs system after only a half season of baseball.

Those broad linebacker shoulders were carrying a ton of that most cumbersome of burdens: touted *potential*. And, even though his clutch three-run homer in the '87 New York–Penn League Championship game had meant treasured championship rings to the fellow Geneva alumni who now made up the nucleus of the '88 Peoria Chiefs, he would mostly have to prove or belie that potential without the cheer or even goodwill of his teammates. And, in truth, that's just about the way he liked it. In fact, Rick Wilkins thought he thrived on it.

CHAPTER

2

Although it was still colder than a starlet's silicone tit, Wisconsin had suddenly become a wonderful place to be in mid-April if you were a Chiefie with the red-ass and back-to-back wins in Wausau.

"Are we having fun?"

Jim Tracy's big feet squeaked as he waltzed an imaginary partner across the makeshift dance floor to maybe the tenth repetition of "For All the Girls I've Loved Before." In between snatches of crooning along with the Julio Iglesias–Willie Nelson duet, whose number he insisted be punched in every time someone put more quarters in the jukebox, he would yuk it up with that grin and repeat the rhetorical question which had suddenly become a communal refrain that otherwise quiet sabbath evening when the Gazebo Lounge of the Wausau Holiday Inn was the province soley of a group of Peoria Chiefs and Tess from Tomahawk.

"Are we having fun?" he'd almost bellow—but of course with his voice it was more a bravura cackle—again and again to one or another in particular but always to the group and cosmos in general.

Always the response would be something along the generic order of "I don't know. It feels like fun." Then that person would turn to another on the barstool next or maybe across the room and pass it on: "Hey. Are we having fun?"

Invariably Trace would follow that with what in the world of baseball is proof positive of just how much fun everyone is having: the insult, usually of the fighting kind in most other spheres.

"You're a bag of dirt . . . no offense." Then the high-sign shrug of the shoulder across the nose. More crooning, more feet squeaking, and if the refrain had been left idle for but a moment he would three-quarter-time by and start it again. "I think we're having fun here, guys . . . *aren't we?*"

"What a question," the Z Man finally said, instantly giving birth to

58

another stock phrase that would endure the season. Unwittingly he'd also cut right to the murky heart of a somewhat quirky issue.

What a question indeed. Because, as incredible as it seemed even at the time, considering what the mood had been less than thirty hours before, we were not only having fun that Sunday night, we were dumbfoundedly reveling in just the fact that we could, much in the fashion of the lost patrol having stumbled onto an oasis. And therein lies the rub.

This was, after all, baseball—of which Earl Weaver once assured Thomas Boswell, "This ain't a football game. We do this every day." And they do it for a lot of days. Consequently, the tradition and wisdom of the game holds that the euphoria of an oasis must always be disciplined by the certain knowledge that it will not last nor that it will never return. It is therefore considered unseemly and un-baseball to wallow overlong in either the trough or the mire.

Not only was this baseball, it was professional baseball. While almost all of those who possess the talent to play this game of dreams for pay had played it—and would have continued to do so—for free at a level far past the point when most must give up bats, balls, and glove for shovel, computer, or order pad, and are therefore the subject of both envy and ridicule by those who were not so gifted or free of spirit, it is nonetheless the source by which they now pay the rent, the light bill, the orthodontist, and the grocer. It is a living, for however long it may last, and at whatever scale. From a million dollars a year with five thousand square feet of rock-and-adobe mansion in Scottsdale to $3,200 and a one-bedroom efficiency for four that most self-respecting hippies from the '60s would've turned up their noses at. For two and a half summers of the working poor, or twenty-two years of fortune and fame. They are, all of them, professional baseball players. It is their job. Rah-rah is for amateurs, football players, and salesmen.

Baseball is also intrinsically America—still the birthplace, cradle, and bully pulpit, if no longer the actual home of the Puritan work ethic. Where work in theory is serious business; it is not fun. If you are having too much fun doing your job, then it is either too easy and frivolous to be dignified as such, or else you're being paid too much to do it.

Both conclusions are anathema to the professional athlete, most especially baseball players. After all, theirs is a game which everyone has played at one competitive level or another. And, because of the democratic nature of the game at all its well-defined and segregated skill levels, everyone has probably done so with just enough success to further foster baseball's greatest illusion and much of its allure—"Christ . . . I coulda hit that pitch." Or "Two mil a year and he's too lazy to use both hands?" Is it then any wonder that professional baseball players have never quite been sure how they should deal publicly—and even privately—with either success or failure.

This is doubly true for the minor league ballplayer. Not only is he very insecure within his endemically insecure profession; but, after having achieved part of his impossible dream, while still chasing the rest of it, the minor leaguer must have that very dream trivialized not only by the fact that every swingin' Sam thinks that he probably could've done just as well but also by the fact that there is a son, grandson, nephew, brother, or *husband* who should be given the opportunity to take his job away from him—and does he know anybody that can maybe take a look at Johnny?

It is only coincidentally a fact, but as good as any other case in point, to note that even the raven-tressed Tess from Tomahawk had both a ball-playing brother and husband she talked to Trace and Kranny about during those four high-flying days in Wausau when the Peoria Chiefs were dealing with that paradox of paradoxes, instant minor league prosperity and its dangerous handmaiden, irrational optimism, in a fashion which would, through it all, become somewhat of a hallmark of the 1988 ballclub: an odd but appealing mixture of bemused cynicism and understated bravado which enabled them to look either a gift horse or a Trojan horse straight in the mouth and pull its tail.

"Maybe it's been so long I wouldn't know fun from baby shit . . ." the Kran-dog had said at one point that night while watching the Trace Monster clown for the benefit of the contingent of Chiefies scattered in little groups throughout the large and otherwise mostly empty lounge not really knowing what else to do but smile a lot, needle one another unmercifully but strangely enough only a little raucously, and bask for as long as it lasted in the redemptive good cheer of their manager.

". . . but whatever it is, it's something those other fuckers *aren't* having. And that's what it's all about. I think. Isn't it?"

What a question.

When Rick Kranitz took pause to observe and then so eloquently define the oddly indefinable by the splendid method of determining what it was not, a trio of us were again engaged in being badly overmatched in witty repartee with the irrepressible Tess.

Shortly after Kranny turned back around to rejoin the sport at hand—the getting-quite-competitive verbal jousting to see which if any of us would be the first to impress the bubbly, dark-eyed, bodacious beauty with the caustic wit—Jim Tracy waltzed on over and, after bumming his one cigarette for the week, lit it with Tess's lighter, which he then, leaning over the bar, promptly tossed for a perfect swish into a garbage can about ten feet away.

"Hey! What's with you, Slick?"

"They call 'em disposable, don't they?" the Shooter explained to all and went back to his dancing.

"That's a manager?"

"Why not?"

"I thought baseball managers were supposed to be all gruff and serious. He's a clown . . . from the ozone layer!"

"Yeah, well, eighteen runs in about the same number of hours would even put a song in the heart of Dick Williams . . . who ain't got one. Whatcha think it's gonna do for the Shooter?"

"So you guys got ten more today, huh?"

"Kranny . . . ya hear the way she said that? That's us she's talking about. Is that head music or what? Ozone layer, hell. We done stepped into the Twilight Zone!"

"I told you I was going to change you guys' luck," Tess said as if that was the end of that and turned away to fill a drink.

Rick Kranitz leaned back on the barstool, glanced about the Gazebo Lounge, sighed, and smiled. "Look at those guys. What a difference a day makes, huh?" Then, after a pause, "Fuck it, I don't care what anybody says . . . winning *does* make all the difference in the world."

"You ready to go get a win?"

That's exactly the way Phil Hannon had said it. Not with swagger. Not with hope. Just fact. It had been about ten minutes of four in the afternoon on Saturday, the Chiefs' first day in Wausau. The square-jawed youth with the always twinkling eyes had said it in greeting as he'd stepped out of his room to join the procession making for the bus that could be heard idling in the parking lot.

Forget a 1-and-7 record. Forget that his base-running error had probably cost a ballgame only hours before. Forget the gloom that had lain as if a shroud upon the family throughout the past night and day. Forget and forgive that it was with more than a little skepticism that at least one of us had greeted Jim Tracy's pronouncement over lunch that "this ballclub is about to explode on somebody . . . and God help the team they do it on."

With Phil's incongruous-under-the-circumstances words, spoken in a singsong alto-tenor Missouri combination of Southern drawl and Midwestern twang, said with a conviction rendered absolute by their very casualness and by who said them, I for one was now suddenly prepared to bet if not my own mortgage, then certainly the mother-in-law's that the Wausau Timbers, Midwest League affiliate of the Seattle Mariners, were in for a group of trouble. Our Gentleman Jim center fielder had just announced that the Chiefies had turned from prey to predator.

While the first winning streak of the 1988 Peoria Chiefs season had surely been prefaced by Rick Wilkins and foretold by Phil Hannon, it was Lenny Bell who quickly rendered the matter somewhat evidentiary.

With two down in the first, and Eddie Williams dancing off second after a single and a stolen base in his first appearance in the lineup since

Opening Day, "Ding Dong" crushed an inside fastball and sent it straight—and damn quick—over the left-field wall.

The Wausau Timbers, apparently not yet aware of their place in the predestined order of things, impudently pricked with fate by then proceeding to hammer starter Brett Robinson all over and out of the yard. The shyly beaming brand-new poppa (a little beauty named Ashley, born Opening Day) left the contest with one out in the sixth and the good guys down 5-3. Trace had gone out to get him after he'd served up his third gopher ball, a two-run blast by the nine-hole hitter, no less. Luckily the other two homers had been solos.

What happened thereafter was as predictable as it was also unpredictable. Predictable in that the bullpen-by-committee came on to throw one-hit shutout ball over the remainder. Totally unpredictable (based on record, not predestination, of course) was that after being held hitless since the first, the Peoria Chiefs bats sizzled in the sixth inning and then finally exploded in the seventh and eighth for six runs on ten hits. The decisive blow was dealt by Bob Strickland; a two-out, three-run bomb over the right-field wall in the seventh.

Answering power with power, the punchless Peoria Chiefs actually won a slugfest. Having suffered the deflation of a thunderbolt lead vanishing in a hail of haymakers, they'd been able for the first time to come off the canvas swinging lights-out punches of their own.

Most everybody got into the act, too. A season-high total of twelve hits had been spread among eight of the nine starters. Only Jossy Rosario had come up with an oh-fer day.

In fact, other than a starting pitcher getting pasted, the Chiefs had played virtually flawless baseball. Aside from a passed ball, they'd played errorless in the field. At the plate they had hit, they had hit for power, sacrificed, hit behind runners, and hit with men in scoring position, and they'd done it all in the clutch.

The bullpen surely did its job. Mark "Ollie" North, the Alabama squire, one of Earl Winn's boys, who because of the presence of Gabby Rodriguez was forced to play the limited role of second-fiddle left-handed reliever on this ballclub, had nonetheless played it to perfection. Getting the only two outs he'd been asked to get, clean-living, stout-hearted Ollie had also gotten the win by virtue of the fact that his two-thirds inning of work in the bottom of the sixth had preceded the explosion in the seventh. Greg "Silent Kal" Kallevig, caring not a whit that in his fourth season of pro ball he was not only back for his third tour with the Peoria Chiefs but for the moment was relegated to right-handed middle relief, had loped his studious, silent-to-an-exasperating-fault, six-foot-four Minnesota-farmboy and A-student body out to the hill and given up only one hit and walked none through the seventh and eighth. Of course, the Z Man was brought in to close the deal in the ninth, collecting his first save of the season in his always flamboyant way. Two strikeouts, a walk, a balk, a mini-tantrum, but no hits or runs. Good night, Timbers.

*   *   *

It was shortly after the one-thirty start of Sunday's day game when perhaps the Timbers did indeed realize the futility of bucking fate. Playing uninspired, can't-catch-it, can't-throw-it, can't-hit-it, bad baseball, they fell behind early en route to an embarrassing licking. Then they quit. Literally. Down 10-2 after seven, apparently coming to the conclusion that whatever developmental value there was to any further endurance of their humiliation was negated by the numbing cold and a stiffening northwest wind, the Wausau Timbers surrendered unconditionally, choosing not to take the field in the eighth. By agreement the remainder was "colded out" and the game was announced as official, and then everybody hightailed it in search of warmth. Two in a row for the Chiefies!

However, while the Chiefs had again collected hits in double digits, it must be noted that we hadn't actually offensively overpowered anyone that frigid afternoon. Of the then season-high total ten runs scored, only three had been earned. It had not been pretty baseball. It held little for the connoisseur to appreciate. However, since all this ugly was happening to somebody else for a change, the third win in ten tries for the Chiefs had an aesthetic value which was nigh on priceless to those who so recently had been sure that bad things were only supposed to happen to *them*.

"Can you believe it . . . they quit!"

"Why not . . . we own 'em and they know it."

"Yeah, you're right . . . everybody gets to own somebody. Even us."

Billy Mel had certainly "owned" them at least. Which was the one aspect of game ten that baseball purists could savor. Particularly if their interest lies in watching the development of raw, but promising young pitching talent.

While he often didn't have a clue where his breaking ball or his 88-90-mile-an-hour fastball was going, his loosey-goosey right arm was particularly "live" that day, which meant that wherever the ball was going, it was getting there with movement. Consequently that left the Timbers likewise clueless; eight strikeouts, four walks, one hit batsman, no runs, and only one twisting, windblown pop-up that dropped in for a single, through the first five and two-thirds innings. Then, after two quick strikeouts in the sixth, with the score a comfortable 10-zip, another "duck fart" found the right-field chalk line for an excuse-me double. When Mel walked the following batter, Jim Tracy, wanting the young and particularly sensitive hurler to leave the game tasting only success and not failure, went out, congratulated him, gave him a one-liner to make him smile, and then brought in Gabby Rodriguez.

While the Cuban-born, Las Vegas–raised left-hander with the flowing two-tone mane, earring, and that flashy, but loose and easy, on-the-Strip manner which wears so well on his powerful, sculpted six-foot-four, 190-pound frame is in every way the antithesis of the impressionable, gangling long drink of water from the land of Thomas Wolfe and Catfish Hunter, in terms of pitching development there are more similarities than differences. The most glaring of which he promptly displayed by throwing his first pitch to the backstop, moving the runners to second and third, and then walking the batter on three more not even close. Thereupon another similarity showed itself. Obviously struggling with his release point, visibly frustrated, and his concentration fragmented, after getting behind yet another hitter, he zeroed in on the strike zone and not a target within the strike zone and served up a hit-me-please-before-he-calls-it-a-ball, down-the-hopper BP fastball which fortunately was only lined into centerfield for a two-RBI single instead of out of the yard altogether.

While Billy Mel would later fret about the two earned runs now attributed to him, they seemed to settle Gabby down and he finished strong with two strikeouts in the seventh. Good afternoon, Timbers. Hello, "Are we having fun?"

What a question.

Richie Zisk is fond of observing, "There's gotta be something wrong with us. Out at the ballpark, where we can't have any, we talk about women and whiskey. Then when we go into the barrooms, where there's plenty of both, we talk about baseball. Figure that out."

We've tried, Richie. It's just that every time we get a good start at it we end up talking about baseball. Or women. Depending on where we are, of course.

In fact, not long after Kranny had determined that winning was to losing what feast was to famine, we, with the benefit of Tess there to lend perspective, had begun to muse upon just that phenomenon when Bill Melvin came up to the bar alongside us to fetch himself a beer. Naturally, the Kran-dog immediately left hanging in midthought and midsentence whatever profound insight on the matter he was about to offer now that the opportunity for a much more important discussion had presented itself. Turning to the young pitcher, Rick Kranitz asked, "What did you learn today, Mel?"

"I wanted to talk to you about that, Kranny."

"Good."

Then the pitching coach and his pupil gathered up their drinks and went and sat at a table where for the next hour and a half they quietly dissected every hitter and situation from the game just played; those two earned runs; a career; a life; and a dream.

Maybe next time, Richie. Perhaps when we're not having so much "fun." But then you or Trace might be there and some kid struggling with the bat will show up and we'll start having too much fun again to worry about the fact that our priorities are seemingly bass-ackwards.

The incidental truths of *Bull Durham* high jinks and ribald frivolity notwithstanding, and even as blessed enough gospel that most of them happily are, perhaps that strangely ambiguous Sunday night in the Gazebo Lounge serves as a more prosaic snapshot of what is the real essence and "fun" of life in the minor leagues:

That omnipresent, osmotic process by which the collective wisdom of the game is passed by the chosen who went before to the newly chosen who are attempting to follow.

Scouting departments might bird-dog, cross-check, and sign them. General managers and farm directors might set their monetary value and if, where, and for whom they will play. But it is an organization's minor league staff of managers, coaches, and instructors who are responsible for teaching bonus-baby amateurs how to play, think, and live as professional baseball players.

In the major leagues, American Legion, and NCAA they play the game. In the minor leagues they teach the game. Even as they live it, breathe it, do it, and talk it on-call twenty-four hours a day, seven days a week, from March till September.

Richie Zisk wasn't particularly talking about the piss-and-vinegar young minor league ballplayer in the "we" of his denoted irony. He was talking about the teachers. Who, not unlike good teachers anywhere, are the dedicated, overworked, and underpaid foundation of their profession.

"That's not our call. The scouting department makes the decision as to whether or not they think a kid has the physical tools and mental aptitude to maybe play in the big leagues . . ."

It's spring training and Bill Harford, the man who now hires and fires the passers of the Chicago Cubs torch, is sitting in the small stand of bleachers along the third-base line of diamond #2 of the Fitch Park minor league complex as Richie Zisk and Jim Tracy run the "bastard play" drill.

". . . but once we get him, we have to teach him. That's what we're all about. That's what we're required to do."

He watches the endless repetition being made fun by Richie and Trace turning the fake-bunt-and-chop-swing drill into a game with bubble gum being the trophies for the winning group.

"We've got a young staff, too. And the other encouraging thing about our staff is that probably eighty-five percent of them were at one time Cubs. They were part of our system. And that's the key. They know our program, they know how we run it. They know what we expect. They know the hours we put in.

"When you're looking for somebody that can teach, it's a good idea to look within the organization. Because you've dealt with them as a player, you know the kind of work ethic they have. The kind of personality they have. Whether or not they're going to be able to get along with their players. Communicate. Motivate. You know, it's a tough business for them, too. There are even less openings in the big leagues for managers and coaches than there are for players. And it's tough year after year to come back and back and just be a worker. But they're paying their dues all over again. They have to get that experience. You talk to a Tracy or Loviglio [Jay Loviglio, Winston-Salem manager and former big leaguer], guys that have been managing only a couple of years, they'll be the first to tell you that it was a lot different from what they expected. They made mistakes. They learned things. And year after year they get better and better. At handling situations. At handling people."

Again the increasing competitiveness and spirit of the drill captures his attention—ballplayers whooping and hollering for the fun of it amid the tedium and sweltering heat of spring training?

"Whoohoo, baby! I see you." Mick Kelleher, his signature ballglove rolled up and stuffed behind him in the waistband of his uniform, has wandered over from diamond #4—the infield only, half-diamond—to get in on the fun.

"Match point . . . one run in. One out, man on third. Will he?" Richie calls out the situation. And the not-so-mock drama.

The mechanical "hummer" swallows a baseball and then, its wheels spinning, shoots it toward the plate.

"Uh-huh . . . double Johnson!" crowed Trace, the man feeding the hummer, as a ball goes chopping over first base fair and then skips across the right-field foul area and into the left-field corner of diamond #1.

"Whoohoo . . . oh, my!" says the Killer.

"Give me some room here, fellows. Everybody's going to get a piece," says the Bat Doctor as half of the Cubbies on diamond #2 crowd around him for their gum.

"Lucky hit" is the refrain from the other half who have just lost.

". . . at the same time, we don't want to infringe upon their realm," Bill was now saying. "They're running the ballclub. That's their job. That's what we hired them to do. And they have to be given the opportunity to do it. I want to give them the chance to use their own ideas without thinking that Big Brother is looking over their shoulders. We hired them to do a job. We think they can do the job. And they're going to do it."

". . . boy, grind is not the word for it. There has to be a tougher word. But you do this because you love it. Certainly not for the money, at any rate. So you just deal with all the rest that comes along with it."

Tony Franklin, almost thirty-eight years old that spring, had already been coaching and managing in the minor leagues since 1979. This would be his sixth year with the Cubs organization. Although for the 1988 season he would be the roving outfield and base-running instructor, the five years previous had been spent managing at the low A and Rookie League levels. His four years at Geneva and one at Wytheville gave him more time in grade as a manager than any other member of the Cubs minor league staff, including the seven managers who would be skippering ballclubs that season, all of whom were also younger than Tony. Having come to the Cubs from the Baltimore Orioles organization early in the Dallas Green years of rebuilding, he was now a senior member of the staff Dallas and Gordon Goldsberry had built.

On the first day of minor league spring training exhibition games, he was leaning against the chain-link fence behind home plate of diamond #3 watching players he'd managed as rookies vie now for spots higher up the ladder. As he did so he talked about managing at a level where not a small part of the job is being a "daddy."

". . . you'd better be. Otherwise those kids will be going south on you, you know? If you've been a student of the game, if you've had good teachers yourself, the baseball part of managing shouldn't be a problem. You're teaching the basics. You assume they know nothing. It's the things that happen off the field, with the youngsters sometimes, that'll have you walking the motel room at three in the morning talking to yourself. Every manager, I don't care what level he's at, wants to win. But of course you can't do it at the expense of developing. And so much of that development is up here"—tapping his head. "There's a lot of growing up to do. A lot of maturing. And that's going to cost you ballgames and some sleep. But it's the first time a lot of them have to pay rent. Rather than going out and having a good time, they have to put a little money away to pay a light bill, or a gas bill, or keep a refrigerator stocked with some milk—hopefully it's milk and nothing else, you know? There are a lot of distractions . . . lot of distractions, a kid can always find a good time out there in baseball. So, it can get a little tough managing at that level. It gets frustrating. At the lower levels I think we should all have a degree in social work."

Tony "the Professor" Franklin laughed and then paused for a moment to watch Bill Melvin pitching against the San Francisco Class A club that would become the Clinton Giants of the Midwest League in two and a half weeks. He'd had Billy Mel at Wytheville in 1986 when the then nineteen-year-old had gone oh for the season in his first year of pro ball (0-8, 7.17; with 42 BB in 58 IP). The kind of year when a kid a whole lot less sensitive and impressionable than Bill might've gone south at any moment. But he hadn't. Instead he came back to win ten games the next year pitching at levels higher than the one he'd failed—and learned—at so humiliatingly the year before.

"He struggled, but he never quit, the knucklehead. And he wanted to learn. He was a mess, but a joy to manage. He's the kind of kid you pull for. He'll only stop trying to learn when you get tired of talking. Of course, sometimes you have to say it all over again. They forget quickly at that age."

Mel finished up a strong two innings. Then Mike Aspray took his dog-

and-pony show of the strike zone to the hill and soon had overeager Giants-maybe-to-be wailing at air.

". . . these kids come to the game with a dream," Tony was saying now. "Hopefully a good percentage of them can fulfill those dreams. But we all know that's not going to happen. Yet they're here because they feel they have a chance to do it. The scouts who signed them think they can do it. So it's up to us to help them in any way we can. Not only on the field but off the field as well. It's all part of the job."

". . . as far as Triple A players, there's a different way of handling them. That's the big part of managing at higher levels—going out today and pressing the right button with your players."

Pete Mackanin wouldn't turn thirty-seven until the 1988 minor league season was into its last month, and he looked even younger than that. His youthful appearance is all the more striking considering his baseball résumé, which with the coming season, his first as the manager of the Cubs' Class AAA Iowa club, would then span a period of exactly two decades in pro ball.

"With the younger ones, A ball, even Double A, it's more important that they understand the fundamentals. You're much more of a teacher at that level. You also see an inferior brand of baseball. So you have to have patience."

The journeyman infielder's sixteen-year playing career had begun the summer of Woodstock when he was signed out of high school by the Washington Senators and had ended with Ronald Reagan beginning his second term. He had played nine of those sixteen years in the big leagues for four different teams, two in each league. Immediately upon ending his playing career at Triple A Iowa for the Cubs, he'd been asked to join the organization's minor league staff. His first assignment had been Peoria. As a rookie manager in 1985 he had piloted the Chiefs to a divisional title and into the championship series in their first year as an affiliate of the Chicago Cubs. In 1986, although finishing second in the division, albeit with an even better record, he'd again taken the Chiefs into the championship series. So successful had he been, he was promoted the following year all the way up to the position of Coordinator of Minor League Instruction, responsible for supervising the field personnel for the entirety of the Cubs farm system. Now, for 1988, he would be skippering the flagship of the minor league fleet. He was the rising star of the organization. It was almost a foregone conclusion among many who should know that Pete Mackanin would be managing in the big leagues soon—perhaps before he turned forty.

While he was aware of all the talk about his ascendant mobility, he was more than content with his current job, and after he and his pitching coach, Big Jim Wright, had finished putting the Iowa club through a brisk situations workout on diamond #1, he was ruminating upon what he had already learned were the differences between managing at the Triple A level as opposed to Class A.

". . . but going through these drills with my guys? They've all heard it for a number of years. They know what to expect. They know what we're trying to accomplish. Oh, maybe there's a guy who has gone through his career not doing something the best way, then it's up to me to convince him that it isn't. But this? Man, you saw that workout . . . this is *easy*. On the field it's a walk in the park with the older guys."

He laughs and starts to push the shopping cart holding the Iowa club's equipment toward the nonimposing white-brick, one-story combination fieldhouse, clubhouse, and office complex which sits at the hub of Fitch Park.

"As long as they're doing it properly, that is. There's a tendency, of course, for some of the older guys to slack off a little bit and give it that ol' 'We know what we're doing,' you know, 'We've heard this all before' . . . but unfortunately they don't always do it the right way. They don't know it all. But then that's easily corrected. If they've gotten this far in their career, as a teacher you're only making minor adjustments."

If the teaching and molding part of the job has decreased, however, another aspect of managing has greatly increased.

"The hardest part at this level is motivating. Because almost nobody wants to be here. You've got young prospects hungry to get to the big leagues and they're so close they can smell it. You've got some—sometimes more than you like—but some veterans, guys who've been around, who may be on their way out, a former major league player who's trying to hang on. Or a Triple A career guy who is frustrated, has good years in Triple A but never gets the chance. And you've got guys in the middle who could go one way or the other. They can blossom into a major league prospect, or they can start that slide back down the ladder. So when you've got a combination like that, everybody's frustrated. Those trying to get there and those trying to get back. And that's hard to deal with. But then that's my job."

The 1988 Peoria Chiefs broke spring training with an average age of 22.3 years. Other illuminating demographic details of the twenty-three-man squad which began and ended (barely) the month of April with Peoria include:

The youngest player was still eighteen (reserve outfielder Horace Tucker). The four next youngest were twenty.

The oldest were twenty-four; there were five of them. And no less than three of these would be twenty-five before the World Series would officially end the 1988 baseball season.

There were no rookies. Thirteen of the twenty-three were in their second season of pro ball (the least-experienced had appeared in nineteen professional games prior to the '88 season—both Boswell and Tucker).

Six were beginning their third year, four their fourth. (It is a somewhat revealing comment on the prospective relative lengths of minor league careers by position to note that of the four fourth-year players, three were pitchers, Green, Kallevig, and Zarranz; and the fourth, Strickland, had been signed as a pitcher.)

None of the twenty-three had yet played above the Class A level. Five, however, had spent at least some time at the "high A" level with Winston-Salem.

No fewer than seventeen Chiefs had played either college or junior college baseball. Only two of the non-Latin players had signed out of high school (Tucker and Eddie Williams).

The highest-drafted player had gone in the third round (Williams). The next-highest, Bill Melvin, had gone in the eighth. Six Chiefs had been drafted between the tenth and twentieth rounds, six between the twentieth and thirtieth. Including the four Latin players, who were not subject to the draft, nine of the twenty-three had been signed as nondrafted free agents.

The highest-profile player, according to the national baseball media, was Rick Wilkins, the only true bonus baby on the club. (Although Eddie hadn't done badly for himself, his signing bonus was somewhat less than a third of what Rick had gotten even though he'd gone twenty rounds higher in the same draft.) Three others had been highlighted as players to watch in *Baseball America*'s annual preseason evaluation of the twenty-six major league farm systems: Massicotte, Caballero, and Rosario.

We can at least statistically deduce that the methods used to manage such a ballclub must fall, with even more complexity, somewhere in between those required for the starry-eyed and/or hayseed rookies of which Tony Franklin spoke and those sometimes bitter, often jaded, and always frustrated older ballplayers which Pete Mackanin described.

As might be understood by professors of second-year law school students and teachers of eighth-grade English classes, educating, counseling, and motivating such a not atypical "middle to high" full-season Class A ballclub is pretty much of a flying-by-the-seat-of-the-britches proposition. While all of the nothing-new-under-the-sun methods might be tried, they are not so true—and, perhaps more so than at any other level, they have to be almost daily modified and individualized not only player by player, but also by groups according to the relatively wide range of ages, maturity within that particularly tumultuous range of eighteen to twenty-five, experience, and development. On and off the field. With this understood, let us note that almost nothing Jim Tracy and Rick Kranitz will do—in and out of uniform—during the 1988 season will be done without calculating its result.

Which is why, for all of his crooning, waltzing buffoonery, Jim Tracy actually drank very little that Sunday night in the Gazebo Lounge. As soon as various means toward several ends had been successfully employed for the evening, he went up to his room sober as a judge to do several more hours of the monstrous daily load of paperwork a minor league manager must churn out on top of his full-time daddy, coach, captain-at-sea, judge-and-jury, and social worker responsibilities.

Means and ends? His Clyde Cadiddlehopper performance was both a reward and a blessing bestowed. Jim Tracy is very much aware that his personality is one that inspires devotion and familiarity as opposed to the usually accepted norm in the coaching business of an arm's-length respect always bordering closely upon hatred and fear. He is also aware that he is indeed funny; that his players, not unlike the rest of us, genuinely enjoy his antics. Therefore, with his ballclub, he will bestow or withhold this favor accordingly. For effect. Since he is loved, his players feel a very real sense of personal guilt when this by-nature buoyantly garrulous spirit is rendered by their play into a bereaved morosity. Not unlike children anywhere, they would do almost anything to see a beloved father smile and whistle at the end of a hard day at work.

They'd done good. Hence the reward and blessing. Of course, he had also contained any untoward overconfidence by his reminder of who they were, the long task still at hand, and the venerable institution of which they were representative: "Are we having fun?"

He had also not neglected to remind them of exactly what they were, and that the institution was much larger than any of them: "They call 'em disposable, don't they?"

In further testimony to the actual shrewdness of their outwardly clowning mentor, after Monday's game was called on account of even colder weather well before the Chiefs even went out to the ballpark, when Jim Tracy the ex-ballplayer instinctively knew that, with a night off *and* a winning streak, there would now be a much larger and more raucous gathering of party-hungry Chicfs down in the Gazebo Lounge that night, he stayed away entirely. These were not babies. While they still needed a daddy, the role was more effective if used only in small doses. They also needed space, and if they were going to have a real party, as much as the Shooter in him ached to be there, he had paperwork to do.

If it can turn a Marc's Big Boy $5.95 all-you-can-eat salad bar and "Jimmy Buffet" into an epicure's delight, perhaps winning *does* make all the difference in the world. The discovery of this phenomenon is of no small consequence after maybe the seventh or eighth hour-and-a-half-long breakfast, lunch, and dinner "meeting of the board" at the eatery with the most bang for the least bucks just up the street from the Wausau Holiday Inn.

While the Chiefs might be winning—and make no mistake about it, as calculated as its manifestation might be in the presence of players, the Shooter is an infinitely happier man when he's winning—there were still some disturbing realities underneath the sheen which Trace knew weren't going to just go away because everyone was suddenly less inclined to see them. In truth, it turns out that Jim Tracy is the sort of professional baseball man who frets over a winning streak as much as he savors it.

This for-management-only fretting, of course, can only be done in the company of the "adults." Therefore, when on the road, Tracy and Kranitz basically had but two options for places to do so: a selected restaurant table or the motel room. Since there was the benefit of food and waitresses at the former and only our own company, cable TV, and paperwork at the latter, the observation about winning's effect on the palate was not only significant but sorely put to the test.

In fact, from the first afternoon in Wausau, even before the offensive explosion he'd predicted had taken place, Jim Tracy was already worrying about the effect that very explosion might have on his ballclub.

"I don't like it, guys . . . this orchard we're going to play at is a bandbox. Balls get up and flop out of there. With our pitching and these pull-crazy, all-swing-or-no-swing dumdums, this ballpark was ordered for us by Saint Peter."

"Goddam, Trace . . . that's just what we need. What's not to like?" Kranny said as he surveyed the yard-and-a-half-high double-chocolate-fudge chocolate cake Angie had just set down in front of him.

"Yeah . . . but then we've gotta go to Rockford where they've got this humongous orchard. Uh-uh, from little to big? Mess up a young hitter every time . . . right, Angie? Better bring me one of those things too. Why didn't you tell me I was gonna want it when I saw it. It just sounded terrible. I know, you wanted an excuse to come back and break my heart again. . . . 'Angie . . .'" And the Shooter started croaking the Mick Jagger tune of that name as the tall, willowy, very patient waitress who would over the course of the Chiefs' stay in Wausau be unanimously appointed as our designated waitress blushed, giggled, and then headed back toward the kitchen.

"Fuck Rockford . . . we need some wins here" was the logic of the Kran-dog, spoken just before he dived into that cake as big as a breadbox.

"My Mule's got a point there . . . don't he?"

"Could be, Trace . . . and I don't think you'd get any argument from Pete Vonachen, either. Damn, that does look good . . . Angie!"

"Yeah, you're right. We'll do it for the boss. But still. . . ?"

Conversely then to what might have been expected by the uninitiated, that addictive heap of chocolate goo was ingested as often as not through those four days in Wausau with as much attention being paid to what was wrong, what could go wrong, or what was right but could end up being wrong, as there was to what was undeniably "Are we having fun? Fuckin' A" right.

After the win on Saturday, the slugfest win? While the offensive barrage had thrilled him, one of Jim Tracy's most repeated refrains during his continual, habitual replaying of one game until the next one takes its place was: "I went one batter too far with Robbie . . . I knew it at the time, too. I'd made up my mind to make the move . . . and then talked myself out of it. My bad . . . my bad."

Rick Kranitz was able to listen to that for just so long before the Kran-dog in him was compelled to say, "Give it a break, big guy. That's what they're here for . . . to learn how to work out of situations like that."

Lenny Bell's rifled homer in the first inning that had jump-started the now resurgent Chiefs? Jim Tracy mostly chose to mark the danger that could be lurking there. "Jesus, Mary, and Joseph . . . he hit it like he was mad at it, huh? And that's gonna be the problem, guys. You watch, he's gonna be looking to turn and hammer everything for the rest of the series . . . except now all they're gonna throw him is junk away."

"Be fools not to," agreed Kranny, who has about as much fondness for all hitters as he does all umpires. "But then if their staff could put it where they wanted it every time they'd be pitching in the Kingdome. Not here." After a pause, and a gleefully wicked smile, the Kran-dog added, "'Course, I know where I'd put it. In his fucking ear. That ball got out *too* fast."

"Yeah . . . just like I hit 'em off you in the Coast League, huh, Mule?"

"Trace . . . when are you ever going to remember it right? You only faced me once, and I struck you out on a three-two slider at your knees."

"Did not."

"Did so."

"Did not."

"Fuck it, remember what you want."

"That's better. Can't forget who's the mule here and who's the buggy-master."

Jim Tracy didn't forget to spend a goodly amount of Sunday morning's batting practice trying to explain to a not at all convinced Lenny Bell, "Look, you're already set up halfway into the next county . . . you've already hung out a sign for every pitcher saying, 'Come in here, please.' So now that they've seen what you can do with it when they do, that sign reads 'Do not disturb.' So whatcha gonna do?"

The big, broad-shouldered third baseman considered the question for a moment, then remembered the correct answer he's been taught but is yet to learn: "Go to right field with it."

"Ding Dong gets the prize. But how are you going to do that if you can't cover the plate away?"

"You think I should move up on it?"

"What I think ain't important. While I know what I would do, you're the one that's gotta be comfortable and believe. So, whatcha gonna do?"

"Get closer, I guess. How about here?" Lenny moved a good six to eight inches closer to the plate.

"Yeah . . . let's just try that. Okay? See how it feels."

From that stance, Bell lined the next two pitches from Kranny into right field, one-hopping the wall with both.

"Feels good, huh?"

"I guess so . . . I mean, yeah."

"All right then, maybe we've learned something."

However, on each ensuing pitch he set up a little bit farther away, until soon he was right back where he'd been before, a mile away, but smiling away as he still continued to blast line drive after line drive.

"Fuck it," the Shooter mumbled. "You can't teach 'em nothing till they're flat on their ass and bleeding. And I'm trying to do it when he's on a roll? I gotta have more rocks in my head than he does."

Batting practice of itself was another source of worry for Jim Tracy. Not the quality of it. But the absence of it. It seems that in Wausau, Wisconsin, high school baseball takes precedence over the minor league version of the game. While this misalignment of priorities is perhaps forgivable when one considers that spring is a very iffy and maybe three-weeks-tops affair in those parts, it is nonetheless vexing to the minor league manager who brings a team hitting .197 to town only to find out it can't hit or take infield because Johnny and his aluminum bat have the diamond. In fact, the Sunday morning Trace tried to teach Lenny Bell something he wasn't ready to learn would be the only pregame BP the Chiefs would take in Wausau.

"I don't know, big guy . . . looks like these kids do better when you're not teaching them anything."

"Angie, you gonna let him talk to me like that? Mule . . . if it proves anything, it's that slop you throw messes 'em up for real pitchers."

"Good . . . then you can start taking both turns of BP. Won't offend me. My arm's still tired from that time I struck you out in the PCL."

"In your dreams, Kranny. In your dreams. But if we ever get to hit again, I'll be so damn grateful I will throw every round!"

While Rick Kranitz is by nature more inclined to accept good fortune where it lies and not beat it to death with theories upon its legitimacy or suffer angst over its inevitable departure, there were some problems with the albeit winning Chiefs that were still so glaring he not only had to agree with Trace about them but even bring them up himself.

"Trace . . . it's really starting to get inside of Mass's head. Maybe we ought to move Cabbie up in the rotation."

"Have him open the series in Rockford?"

"Yeah. It'll maybe pump him up. Also give me an extra day to work with him. Plus if it doesn't work, at least he'll be pitching in a bigger ballpark."

Since Jeff Massicotte, the number-two man, and Eduardo Caballero, the number-three man, had pitched the doubleheader in Appleton, the change could be made at this point without too greatly effecting the regulated routine and rhythm of the five-man starting rotation.

"It could be done now . . . Jesus, can you see him getting lit up in this yard? At forty bucks a dozen . . . balls be flying outta here enough to bankrupt this nickel-and-dime operation. And we'd be left with a real basket case on our hands."

"So, you want to do it?"

"Have to get Colbie's permission first. And he might wanna run it by Gordon or Billy."

"I'll explain it . . . it's justified."

"Hey, I'd never doubt my Mule . . . we'll ask."

"Yeah? You haven't sat Jossy down yet," and there was another problem which continued unabated even as the Chiefs won.

The sweet-faced, self-effacing Dominican second baseman was still hearing footsteps on the pivot, and was all but an automatic out at the plate. Jossy had come to Wausau 2 for 30 on the season and there was as yet no evidence of the infielder who'd been named to the Appalachian League All-Star team in '87 while spraying line drives around to the tune of a solid .301 batting average and twenty-seven RBI in sixty-six games at Wytheville.

"They want him to play. And based on last year, it's hard not to agree . . . I mean, it *is* the same guy. But it sure is getting uglier and uglier to watch."

"Trace . . . he's going to get hurt."

Jim Tracy dropped his head and stared at his big knuckles for a moment. Then he looked up and said very quietly, "You know . . . I hate to even think this, much less say it. But I'm starting to wonder if maybe he ain't got . . . well, a little yellow in him. Jesus Lord, you don't ever wanna stick a kid with that kinda label . . . but dammit, he might be more than just timid. There are times he looks flat-out afraid out there. And I'm not just talking about around the bag. But the way he's bailing out at the plate, and the look in his eyes I can see sometimes when he does, makes me wonder."

"I don't know, Trace . . . it's kind of hard to believe he could've gotten this far and be afraid of a baseball. And if he is, he sure found a way to deal with it last year. But then I'm seeing the same thing you are. What are we going to do about it?"

"The Killer can't get here until sometime in May. But Tony's gonna join us before we leave here. Maybe he can do some good."

"He'd better. And I hate to sound like a broken record."

"Sure you do . . . but that's why I keep you around, Mule."

"Just keep me around long enough for Castillo . . . him I'd pay to work with. Almost." With that Kranny brought up a subject that had suddenly become a part of every one of those Big Boy's or motel-room board meetings; and a shining example of something which is very right, also being wrong—for somebody.

Frank Castillo had just turned nineteen when the sharp but unexplainable pain he felt while running on the sun-kilned, brick-hard surface of Fitch Park had finally been confirmed as a stress fracture of the lower right leg, exactly one week before the Peoria Chiefs opened the season without one of the brightest lights in all of the Chicago Cubs much-vaunted minor league system as the ace of their staff.

The year before, in his first half-season of pro ball, Frank Castillo, the inscrutable, implacable high schooler out of El Paso, Texas, had almost methodically won eleven and lost only one. He had been honored as Appalachian League Player of the Year and named to the Topps Rookie All-Star Team (selected from all the short-season rookie leagues).

Borrowing a metaphor from the record business, Frank Anthony Castillo was a ballplayer on the chart with a bullet. Then came the stress fracture, a prognosis of from six to eight weeks laid-up, his dismay—which he so typically took in stride—and Pete Vonachen's wailing and gnashing of teeth.

Word had now arrived, however, that the El Paso Buzz Saw might be well ahead of schedule on his mending. That possibly the injury hadn't been as serious as first thought. At any rate, he had started running, and if all went well with that, then perhaps his debut as a Peoria Chief was imminent. Very good news, right? Not necessarily.

"Eleven pitchers? Like we need another hole in the head." Jim Tracy was chawing on a chicken-fried steak and the notion that in minor league baseball it is possible to have too much of a good thing. "Our staff is too good as it is . . . everybody we got is useful. We carry eleven, that means somebody's gonna sit. Now we got an unhappy ballplayer—"

"And that shit's contagious," was Kranny's amen.

"You're damned right it is. And we need that like we need two holes in the head."

"So? Somebody goes down a notch." The stupid one of us thought it was simple enough.

"No," Kranny said with a solemnity he only adopts when he's really troubled, or about to pull one of his capers on the unexpecting. Now he was troubled. "With all the teams set and the situation pretty well stocked back at extended spring training . . . more than likely somebody would have to be released."

"And that's the problem. We ain't got a pitcher deserving of a release. There's not a one of 'em I could recommend to be released. You, Kranny?"

"What a question."

"It'd be y'all's decision?" I asked.

"It would start with us . . . we'd be asked to finger somebody. It's our job. Then, unless Gordon or Billy had strong feelings on the matter one way or the other . . . it would end with us."

"Fuck it. If he comes, we'll just go with eleven. Don't want to. But there's nobody I wanna send home, either."

Of course, there still remained the two problems which had from the start been the most consistent bogeymen of the Peoria Chiefs: team strikeouts and Rick Wilkins's lack of run production. These two malodorous apparitions continued to monopolize most of Jim Tracy's concerns about his ballclub; they had also become all but synonymous in his dissertations.

Fact: while the Chiefs had hit for double figures in the first two wins at Wausau, so had they also struck out in like numbers. Twenty-two hits had been accompanied by twenty-one K's.

Fact: while Rick Wilkins had only two of those no-contact outs, he had also driven in only one of the eighteen runs, giving him three RBI on the season. Of the starters, only Warren Arrington, the nine-hole hitter, had less with two. (Of course, it's not like anyone else was feasting on ducks-on-the-pond soup either. As a team the Chiefs had driven in only thirty-two runs.)

Fact: eighty-nine strikeouts with only thirty-two RBI in ten ballgames factored into something the Shooter couldn't fathom except for knowing that it smelled like something one had best hold his nose in the presence of.

Fact: while Rick Wilkins's lead in team strikeouts at thirteen was indeed being pushed hard now by none other than Lenny Bell with twelve, Wilkie's two strikeouts in Wausau had come with men on base, and both had come at one of those conspicuous moments in a baseball game when perhaps the contest itself is in doubt.

Fact: any way you sliced it, an analysis of the numbers continued to red-flag a team with serious run-production flaws built into its structure, of which strikeouts were still the too obvious symptom; and, because Rick Wilkins was "the Man" in the three-hole spot, sent here to produce runs, but wasn't, and was still leading the team in strikeouts, he was the most visible manifestation of that which was still rotten in Denmark.

Result: his hangdog, weight-of-the-world mopiness continued even as his teammates won; and as he was now also taking his frustrations with the bat back out onto the field with him.

"Trace . . . he's gonna cost us a game. He nonchalanted that passed ball. And that was just one he got caught on. He's been doing that half-assed 'ole' shit. My guys are starting to bitch. They're afraid to throw some of their best stuff with men on third."

"I know . . . and now he's throwing like a popgun, too. I guess if he can't hit, he's decided he'll really make us feel sorry for him and not be able to catch it or throw it either."

Several of us were huddled in the corner of the visiting dugout trying to think warm as we watched two high school teams go through that really dumb ritual of lining up to shake hands after one or the other had just won or lost one of the sloppiest baseball games any of us had seen played in a while.

"You know," said Brett "Robbie" Robinson, "that's about the caliber of baseball my high school played." The remark was greeted by an awkward silence, and uncertain looks all around.

Finally the Z Man said, "What's the matter, guys . . . at least *he's* honest enough to admit it."

A moment of thoughtful silence. Then, "Hey . . . my high school team was dynamite. We kicked ass!"

Zarranz picked up his ballglove from the dugout steps and said out of the side of his mouth, "You knew it'd be him to say something, didn't you?" Then from the top step, "Hey, Wilkie . . . guess that ballclub was so good you didn't have to call for too many breaking balls down, huh?"

As Rick Wilkins took a beat or two figuring out he'd just been insulted, Jim Tracy came around the corner of the dugout cackling and rubbing his big hands together.

"Let's go, men . . . we can get at them fuckers now."

"About damn time. Let's put this one in the bag and get the hell out of Dodge . . . gotta be warmer in Rockford."

"Not at four-thirty in the morning it won't be."

"No shit."

Getaway day is always a bitch. Not only is it going to be a long day, but there is the matter of motel check-out times coming three or four hours before you're ready to leave. Minor league owners aren't particularly fond of paying a full day's rate on a dozen-plus rooms just for ballplayers to sit around in until time to get on the bus and head to the field. And motel operators aren't in the business of gratis boarding. They do, however, like the business that a good relationship with a minor league circuit can provide. Therefore an accommodation is arrived at whereby the motel will "hold over" four rooms for late cleaning (in time for the non-reservation drive-up business). Consequently, getaway day always begins hectically with everybody having to pack up, check out, "pay your goddam incidentals, all right?" and then move everything into those four rooms for several hours of close-quarters hanging out.

In Wausau the situation was made somewhat more complicated by the fact that the Peoria Chiefs could not dress or shower at Athletic Park. While there had been some effort to jazz up the quaint old ballyard in accordance with the newest trends in the marketing of minor league baseball (a picnic area down the left-field line, for instance), nothing as yet had been done to upgrade the visiting team's clubhouse. Not only was it cramped and inadequate (however clean and freshly painted), there was no heat or even hot water.

In this case, Pete Vonachen would be lighter in the wallet by the price of four rooms for an extra night so his ballclub could go back and change and shower after the game; it also, of course, meant that it would be just that much longer a day, night, and morning.

Aside from the dressing facilities, however, Athletic Park isn't a bad ballyard at all. Small, yes. But the lighting is new. The playing field is good if not excellent. And they have perhaps the best "Brats" anywhere (as in sandwich delicacy, not ill-mannered rug rats). Plus that chipped-rock-and-mortar wall and facade—and those giant living Christmas trees—give it an ambience unique in the Midwest League. And although the franchise had just been bought by a group of doctors from Fort Wayne, Indiana, and was going through the sticky transition from popular local ownership to absentee ownership, it was, by the prevailing standards of Single A, as professionally run an operation as could be expected for a club that on a good year could expect to draw but sixty thousand fans.

Of one thing we may be certain: Jack Roeder, the general manager, was astute enough as both a baseball man and a businessman to not try and make up the lost game with a doubleheader on a night so cold only eighty-five people showed up anyway. Exhibiting an understanding of the game and those who have to play it, he would also let Pete Vonachen have those extra concessions at a doubleheader in Peoria in July. Wonderful fellow, he—we would only have to play one.

Even though the score was still 0-0 at the time, the third win in a row for the Peoria Chiefs became a *fait accompli* when John Green built a fire out in the bullpen. It had taken a little ingenuity and perseverance, but what had had its humble beginnings as a broken bat, a scrap of paper, and a Bic lighter by the start of the second inning was one grade-A, hand-warming, backside-toasting bonfire.

It must also be noted that by the time the Grinches-that-be ruled that the fire had to go at the close of that half-inning, the good guys had already sent seven men to the plate, loaded the bases, and scored two runs on only two singles when the Timbers, apparently taking their cue from the high schoolers, booted two routine ground balls, both of which should've been cinch double plays. Only Bell's lead-off single, the first of his three hits that night, had been a blow struck with much authority.

It was not the Wausau folks who demanded the fire be put out. They seemed to enjoy the spirit of the event as much as anyone. After all, these are the same people who get a squealing, elbow-in-the-ribs, knee-slapping hee-haw out of a roly-poly guy named Spike running around the bases with a broom between innings doing a spastic bump and grind at each one as he sweeps and shimmies to a honky-tonk hootchie-kootchie reserved just for his routine. It was pretty-boy umpire Mike Pietro, he of the thousand balks, and no love for the Peoria Chiefs in general and Rick Kranitz in particular, who was working the bases that night. Twice he took it upon himself to halt the match and march out to the bullpen in the left-field foul corner and do his indignant fire marshal impersonation. Even after the Wausau grounds crew, along with the management, staff, press box contingent, and what few fans were in attendance had booed his first trip out there, and then applauded when shortly thereafter the fire—with a little help, of course—defiantly flamed back to its full glory, he still was zealotry-bound to prove who indeed was running this baseball game.

While the Chiefs' bats and the bad baseball played by the Wausau Timbers might've so far negated any not so subconscious desire on the part of him and his partner Vince Rainforth to officiate over what to them would have been the equivalent of the righteous of this world triumphing over the sinners, this he did not have to take.

(His thoughts on which of the two camps the 1988 Peoria Chiefs belonged to can perhaps be best expressed in his own words, spoken to Jim Tracy before the first game of the series on Saturday: "I want you to keep a collar on Kranny . . . you hear?")

And since nothing happens in a ballyard after a game has started that an umpire doesn't say happens, his Smokey the Bear stance was in the end as successful as it was silly.

But the Chiefs had two runs and with Aspray hitting spots within spots with different speeds it appeared that the dauntless duo of Mike & Vince would have scant opportunity for further effect upon either the flow or the outcome of the ballgame.

This seemed to be even more of a given when Mike continued to conduct a five-hit, shutout symposium on the art of first-pitch strikes, lead-off outs, and empty-bases, meaningless two-out singles through seven with a now 3-0 lead courtesy of Lenny Bell's third hit on the evening, a wall-banging double to left, which so unnerved the Timbers starter that he then immediately thereafter threw two wild pitches in the general direction of Bob Strickland, depositing Lenny first at third and then into the dugout with the third unearned run he'd allowed on the night.

However, since relief pitchers are also in the minor leagues to develop and here was a classic case for exercising the muscle of your setup-and-then-lights-out strategy of bullpen management which has become so entrenched now in professional baseball, Jim Tracy trotted John Green, the arsonist or Prometheus depending on either the minority or majority viewpoint, out to the mound to start the eighth.

Now, while any competent umpire this side of blindness can call balls and strikes on Mike Aspray from a La-Z-Boy recliner with but little opportunity for the use of any judgment that if wrong didn't threaten the wrath of the big umpire in the sky, not to mention baseball purists on either side, John Green's knuckle curve is a different matter altogether. Here there was ample opportunity for sublime larceny with impunity.

While the veteran right-hander's control is such that he can also pretty much put a baseball where he wants, his out-pitch depended for its success upon the fact that where he wanted it to go was only a mirage of the actual strike zone. Therefore, on this night, if the Wausau Timbers didn't oblige and go to hacking, it was a lock that Greenie the fire-giver wouldn't be getting any called third strikes.

However, to the visibly seething annoyance of Mike Pietro, his partner in righteousness behind the plate Vince Rainforth was powerless to strike a blow for the establishment when the Timbers proceeded to whale away for three quick outs on a soft 1-3 comebacker, a nubbed slow-roller 4-3, and a swinging K on a full-count breaker in the dirt which Wilkins deigned to smother—barely, and none too vigorously.

The Chiefs didn't score in their last turn with the bats, so it was still a 3-0 ballgame when John Green faced the Timbers center fielder Jim Pritikin to lead off the bottom of the ninth—three outs away from waving the broom out of town instead of riding it?

And the tall, slender left-handed hitter was all too willing to do his part, it seemed. After quickly hacking himself onto the wrong side of a 1-2 count, almost as an afterthought he waved weakly but not even in the vicinity of a knuckle-yakker that neither he nor Wilkins appeared to give a damn had eluded them both. Unfortunately, the thought that he should run to first base occurred to Mr. Pritikin well before Mr. Wilkins decided that maybe he'd best go retrieve that live hand grenade now resting quite placidly behind home plate and about a yard out from the backstop. Still, since it's a lot closer from the plate to there than it is from the plate to first, even though he had a head start, it shouldn't have been a race Jim Pritikin could win. And he wouldn't have—if he hadn't been the only one running! Weighted by the burden of a 0-for-4 day—and with it the certain knowledge that he would leave Wausau with the same batting average with which he'd arrived, .200—Rick Wilkins sulked his way back to the baseball not even in time to make a throw.

What's this? A strikeout, but no out, and now the tying run in the on-deck circle. Greenie stared darts at his "what the fuck?"-shrugging catcher, looked up into the night, sighed, and then got DH Ruben Gonzalez to line out easily enough to left field. Ray Williams, however, the Timbers' right fielder, possibly more attuned to the sensitivities of the game within the game, worked Greenie to a 3-2 count and then laid off a bender at the knees and on the black away which Vince Rainforth almost fell all over himself calling ball four.

The fat's in the fire—but then there ain't no fire, just that gleam in Mike Pietro's eye. Then, as soon as Rick Sweet, the Timbers' manager, announced he was sending a left-hand-hitting pinch hitter to the plate, and Jim Tracy popped out of the dugout signaling for Gabby Rodriguez, there were curses and venom in the mouth of John Green.

"Aw, fuck . . . Trace?"

"Gotta do it, Greenie."

"Yeah . . . I know. But still . . . fuck!"

With Gabby in the game, the plot of course thickened. Vince Rainforth knew the troubles the big left-hander sometimes had finding the plate— he shouldn't even have to work at it to give this next guy a free pass. But Gabby is nothing if not a born rebel. He quickly jumped out ahead of Mike McDonald 1-2, threading BBs. This called for some serious application of the umpire's fine art of squeezing or expanding a strike zone to fit a given situation without risking the validation of total skullduggery.

Vince was up to the task. He missed three straight close ones, and the bases are loaded with only one out.

Time for the Z man. Time for a K.

Z delivered. Some pinch hitter with the name of Lorenso Sisney wasn't about to catch up with one of Z's fastballs up and in; particularly not after Z had made him look like his name sounds on the pitch before by throwing him a 1-1 change-up that drifted in belly-high and at least a day late down the middle of the plate.

Alas, neither could Wilkie when, with two outs now, Z threw the same combination of pitches to third baseman Tony Woods, only to see the high hard one skip off the top of Rick's mitt. Another passed ball. But we got folks running all over the place this time! Not the least of which were the two guys racing toward home plate—the runner from third, and Z.

For all of his flamboyance, Fernando is an excellent athlete, and he gets there well ahead of Pritikin. Then he waits. It seems that the only guy who isn't running, isn't running toward the one thing that Z needs; by the time Wilkins lollygags his way toward it and throws a dispassionate lollipop to Z, all the eyes-blazing pitcher can do is catch it, slap his glove against his thigh, spit, and say:

"Goddam, Wilkie . . . just goddam! You hear me?"

"Hey, what's with you?" The big catcher shrugs. Then he puts on his mask, squats down, and as if nothing at all has happened calls out, "Let's go here. Two down . . ."

Z stomps back up on the mound and is so livid he promptly balks Williams in from third. Well, at least Mike Pietro saw a balk. Whatever he saw, it was sure to his fancy, because it was with uncommon and undisguised glee that he announced the fact to the heavens and beyond.

Katy bar the door. Without a hit, a 3-0 ballgame is now a nail-biting 3-2 squeaker with the tying run 90 feet away.

Figuring that his chances were better if he just let the batter hit the ball, as opposed to all of the apparently bad things that could happen if he tried to get him out, Z grooved a fastball that Woods skied into center field, where Phil Hannon, who'd prophesied the whole thing anyway, gathered it in like manna from heaven and headed for the bus.

Whew!

Despite the efforts of the avenging Archangels in blue, and the non-efforts of our own "the Man" to the contrary, destiny just couldn't be denied and the Peoria Chiefs were now 4 and 7.

". . . it's bad enough he ain't driving in any runs for us. But does the sumbitch have to give 'em to the bad guys?"

"We won, Trace."

"Damn right we did! And you know something? Mike Aspray is a pitcher . . . and there ain't no higher compliment than that."

Goodbye, Timbers. Thanks for having us.

*   *   *

As minor league bus rides go, two hundred miles is but a hop. In further perspective, in an age where getting from any here to any there is increasingly regarded as an almost instantaneous proposition, the distance between Wausau, Wisconsin, and Rockford, Illinois, is little more than a thought and then a hello. For the Chiefs, however, it might as well have been the distance between two worlds, two eras even. Because, after eight days spent transported back a generation into the anachronistic time bubble of the old "bushes," we were back in the Big Time!

Big city. Bright lights. Brand-new franchise in a brand-spanking-new baseball stadium. Blaring rock-and-roll over state-of-the-art sound equipment. Media blitz in a media town which takes its cue but not back-chorus role from the really big city just down the interstate, whose suburbs start but an exit or two away, Chicago. The "show time" excitement. The *Price Is Right, Let's Make a Deal,* and *Gong Show* hype and hoopla of the "new" minors. Attendance that is counted in four digits instead of two. And a three-game-winning streak to boot?

We done died and instead of to heaven they sent us to a place almost like home! A place in fact that was trying for all its worth to ape the success of home. They also sent us a new Jeff Massicotte. What more could we ask for? Four in a row. In fact, we expected no less.

"Print it. It's done," said the twenty-one-year-old right-hander from Meriden, Connecticut, who would shortly be taking the mound to open the first of a four-game series with the Rockford Expos. "I've got it . . . I can just feel it, you know?" And this was coming from the same young man who before each of his last two outings had been so uptight that, totally against his otherwise quick-witted, slyly gregarious nature, he had not allowed himself to even look at much less talk to anyone!

Now, minutes before he again had to go out to that dirt circle and wrestle with his very personal demons, he was laughing. "We come two hundred miles south . . . and it's colder still! What'd Pete do, order this shit to follow us around so nobody can get a head start on him in the attendance race? Fuck it. Let's just get this shit on and over. Should be able to find some fun in this town. You think?"

While we would indeed, in the immediate interim, Jeff "Massacre" Massicotte went out and had about as much fun as any pitcher should be allowed—lest the guys with the bats in their hands become superfluous—and put a whole different twist to his nickname. Massacre, as in thirteen strikeouts, no runs, no walks, and only three hits over seven innings' work. Realizing for the first time that as a starter he didn't have to rear back and throw each pitch as if the fate of the Western World hung in the balance, he relaxed, and that sweeping, dipping, three-quarter-overhand-delivered two-speed "slurve" which had marked him as a prospect with a big league ticket was suddenly back—in spades.

Of course, such performances by a pitcher do not win baseball games.

The very best they can do is effect a tie regardless of how well they pitch. Think about it.

Fortunately Jeff didn't have to. After his seven innings of fun, Jim Tracy said, "Atta baby," and turned a 5-0 lead over to steady Mark North so he could get in on the fun too.

As heartening to the Shooter as was this seemingly miraculous turn-around to a problem which had plagued him not a little, so was the who and the how of the occurrence of those five runs. As in most ballgames, it'd been one big inning. In this case the third. With bases loaded and one out in a 0-0 ballgame, facing a 3-2 count and staring right into the jaws of the probability of an inning-ending double play, Rick Wilkins clutched up and doubled his RBI production for the season by banging a bases-clearing double off the wall in right center! Then, after Lenny Bell couldn't get out on the corner with enough wood still left and fouled out to first, Elvin Paulino, the left-hand-hitting, grinning, nodding coño-head who Trace had been preaching "Go the other way, or I break your fucking neck" to in pidgin Spanish since the day they first laid eyes on each other the spring before, took a pretty good fastball down and on the corner away and deposited it closer to the Rock River than the back of the left-field wall for a two-run wrong-way homer. Hello, Rockford. Good night, Expos.

"Damn, Mule . . . what'd you do with Mass? You in the voodoo business these days?"

"Nope . . . just kept telling him how good he was. What did you say to Wilkie?"

"It wasn't that," the Shooter chortled. Then he slapped the table, leaned back, crossed those big arms across his chest, sighed, smiled a smile so real and so big it was bigger than he was as it enveloped us all, and said, "Don'tcha love ever' one of 'em. I mean, Jesus, Mary, and Joseph . . . these kids have turned it around, huh?"

"It's sweet, Trace."

"Sweet? I'm telling you, it's happening. I believe we've got our ballclub back. We've turned a corner here, gentlemen."

"Gotta believe what I see."

"Five and seven, Kranny? You realize if we just take two out of the next three from these fuckers, we go home seven and eight after what could've been the worst scheduled road trip in the history of organized baseball?"

"Think Pete will give us a parade?"

"He just might do it, too," the Shooter cackled. Then he leaned forward and said, almost conspiratorily, "You know, this really *is* fun!"

Yepper.

In truth—and you'll just have to take the word of that man over there waiting for a bus on the matter—it just doesn't get much better than this.

CHAPTER 3

SOMEWHERE BETWEEN A Hardee's in Rockford and a Shake 'n' Bake in Peoria, while rolling and nodding south on US 61, finally heading toward home and hell to pay for somebody, at something before dawn on the Sunday morning of April 24, a brief but evidently not isolated thought had been thunk.

"Back in the real world they've got a word for this, you know."

"Yeah."

Try "schizoid." Flights of a too manic, supernal fantasy butt-edited jarringly with disproportionate crashes of a too depressive ultrareality of the shitcan school of self-flagellation all within a metaphysical structure of the certainty that none of it really matters anyway!

But then that's crazy. Or so they say. And this was only baseball. Minor league baseball at that. Where the platitude "It matters not whether you win or lose, but how you played the game" isn't just some schoolmarmish beatitude no one ever believed anyway, but is in theory and fact the rule which governs its very structure and reason for being.

Riiight!

But it is true, nonetheless. It is also true, however, that the message of the method must necessarily depend upon which corner of the street you're working that day. Certainly any corner you're working with Pete Vonachen will beat to a different rhythm put to an old public-domain melody. Or any other of his fellow breed of entrepreneurial minor league owners. Wins and losses can also suddenly become *very* important when a farm system's budget and/or department heads are up for corporate review.

Any minor league manager worth his too small salary likewise is not without some vested interest in the league standings posted in the sports pages of the newspaper he reads every morning. And even if his job isn't as traditionally perilous as that of his major league brethren, now that he

is no longer putting playing numbers in the permanent records of baseball—the most-documented sport in this solar system—only a manager
with the brain-wave activity of a hickory stump isn't at least aware that
those numbers changing daily in the W and L columns are *his*. Forever-
more. The final totals to be duly noted in the obituary columns of the
Sporting News.

And the ballplayers? Suffice it to say they'd best not affect any posture
exposing that fundamental truism unless they're hitting a solid .300 with
power and ribbies, or an ERA in the twos and lower. And even those
kinds of numbers can forever be tainted within the society by an insidious
label—"He's got an attitude"—which can only be mitigated to a tolera-
ble level of clubhouse slander by continuing to post those superlative
numbers consistently up to and throughout a major league career. Yet it
can be taken to the mountain that no minor leaguer ever got to the bigs
on the strength of his farm club's won-loss record. And every would-be
knows it. Even as that within him that made him a ballplayer to begin
with allows him to psychologically embrace the abstract concept of no-
fault/pass-fail/win-lose about as indifferently as he would repeated pokes
in the face with a sharp stick.

Minor league baseball then can be likened to living and working within
the Big Fib. An insular society where the truth is by nature understood to
be unworkable so the Big Fib must, for the general good if not the very
existence of the whole, be instituted, believed, and evangelized as gospel
by the very folks who best understand the truth.

And of course that is crazy only if you stop dancing as fast as you can
long enough to think about it.

But it isn't crazy even then when it's all so reasonably articulated by
one of the system's newer, brighter, up-and-charging keepers of the Big
Fib. One who though young for his position of power is learning quickly
how to juggle and minstrel a corner with the best of them. And as the
wheels and blacktop hummed thoughts together into a semiconscious
stream, the words of Bill Harford, as spoken on a blazing hot, dry, clear-
blue afternoon at Fitch Park in Mesa, Arizona, just some few weeks before play back into the mind's ear.

"That's what I'm saying . . . winning is a by-product of what you teach.
If it's sound . . . and you have talented ballplayers . . . you will win ballgames. At every level. And since the real goal is to win at the major
league level, they might as well start learning to win at the minor league
level. . . .

"But at the same time we don't want to forget what we're all about.
Our job is to get as many guys to Jim Frey as we can. The Red Sox are
always under .500 in their system but look how many they get to the big
leagues. Winning a championship at Peoria or Winston-Salem with a
bunch of players who you know can play at that level—older players,
good minor league players, but who in our opinion aren't big league pros-

pects—at the expense of young players who you believe are, then you're not doing anybody any good. . . .

"But believe me, we want to win. It makes everything run smoother. And if it keeps Pete Vonachen happy and from burning up the phone lines, that's not bad either."

He hadn't ended the matter there. "We also want to start to create something where they know *we're the Cubs*. That they know when the Cubs come to town we're coming first-class, the kids are going to be well behaved, well dressed . . . and you're gonna have a tough day. We're gonna do the fundamentals right. We're gonna play the game hard. And we're there to win."

All of which brings us to the inescapable conclusion that no matter from which corner your particular soap-box was grounded, the first sixteen days of the Chiefs' season had come up a cropper. And as the fall was damn fast, so was it far.

". . . I was on the top step from pitch one." Jim Tracy was happily yukking through maybe the sixth rehash of Massicotte's gem in about a dozen hours. The Shooter's ritual replay was even more ebullient and animated now that for the third morning his "adult" audience was larger by one with the addition of Tony Franklin.

"I'm telling you, Tony . . . I mean, you gotta understand, you didn't see it. All you saw was the numbers in the reports. But the kid had been a disaster in his first two starts. About like giving a firebug the keys to a bomb factory! But then, whoom! Whoom! With that hard slider? Just breaking off those yakkers and mowing 'em down . . . 'Jesus, Mary, and Joseph, what have we got here?' I'm saying. But I'm saying it sitting on the bench now! He got me off those steps in a hurry."

"He looked unhittable to me. But then a lot of them looked that way when I played," laughed Tony, the ex-infielder whose glove had gotten him to Triple A, but whose bat had assured that a nine-year professional playing career spent mostly with the Cincinnati Reds organization would end when he was twenty-eight back where it had started, in the Class A Florida State League.

The impeccably dressed roving instructor with the diction and manner of a college professor then took a sip of coffee and observed, "So what's the deal here? I thought I was coming to visit a terminally ill patient. I almost stopped to pick up flowers and sympathy cards. But since I've been here all I have seen is what could pass for the old Big Red Machine. It is fun, guys . . . but you don't need me."

"They got well in a hurry, Tony," said Rick Kranitz. "I guess it was only one of those eight-day viruses . . . but believe me, this isn't the same team as just a few days ago."

"Yeah," Trace said. "Just relax and have a good time getting into Harford's pocket . . . and wait'll you see those knee-bucklers from Eduardo. Christ, wait'll those Rockheads get a look!"

For three watershed innings that Thursday night of April 21, looking at Eduardo Caballero's knee-buckling yakker—and then either flinching embarrassingly, or swinging at where it was supposed to be but wasn't anymore—was just about all the Rockford Expos could do.

In fact when Mr. Elbows-knees-ass-and-head-jerks went out to take the hill for the bottom of the fourth that godawful cold, wet, miserably dreary night at Marinelli Field, so dominant had the stringbean right-hander been that only three would-be-Expos had even been able to put the ball in play, much less hit it safely.

He'd also had a 2-0 lead to go with his fledgling no-no when he'd started his pre-pitch ritual of the sleeve tug, the dirt scoop, the crotch pull, and the two-handed skull crush of his ballcap down onto his head before toeing the rubber and looking in for a sign from Herbie Andrade for the second pitch of that fateful inning.

Even now in retrospect who can say that everything that thereupon suddenly went wrong for the 1988 Peoria Chiefs—and stayed that way for a very long time—wouldn't have happened anyway even if Edgar Caceras, the Rockford second baseman, hadn't fisted a little bleeder into short right field for a leadoff single? This is particularly true considering that almost everything that did go wrong was as reaffirming to fact and form as it was betraying faith and hope. We just know that it did.

The next bad thing to happen, however, like the leadoff chink itself, was not in the least predictable. After a nubbed slow-roller resulted in a fine running scoop and flip by Jossy Rosario to Eduardo for a racing bang-bang 4-1 putout, with Caceras advancing to second, Scott Mann, the Expos' twenty-six-year-old DH, who'd just that day been sent down from Double A to bolster an offense off to an even slower start than the Chiefs, spanked a hard, one-hop single into short, straightaway center field, which Phil Hannon (regarded by no less than Jimmy Piersall as the best defensive center fielder in the Cubs' entire organization) let get by him for his first error of the season, and the score was now 2-1.

From that distance, as hard as the ball had been hit, and with Phil's accurate if not outstanding arm, there had been every likelihood that Mr. Caceras would've been dead meat. Instead, the score was 2-1, still only one out, and Mann now at second.

Any professional scouting report on Eduardo Caballero will include some question regarding his apparent loss of concentration and com-posure whenever anything inexplicable, untoward, or just not to his fancy starts happening around and about him. This already diagnosed tendency had been duly discussed and then further documented into the system by Tracy and Kranitz in their game reports.

So it was certainly no surprise when the Panamanian Devil—that rarity, a strikeout pitcher with excellent control—then stomped, contorted, and muttered his way through a long-drawn-out process of walking the next two batters to fill the bases.

And it was absolutely no surprise, but just a cold, fist-in-the-gut shame, when the next batter rolled a tailor-made double-play ball and Jossy Rosario took Marty Rivero's flip for the force only to then be knocked halfway into left field on the pivot as his intended relay to first instead wound up in the Chiefs' bullpen and two runs scored.

Thus did the seemingly bottomless slide of the original edition of the '88 Chiefs begin.

Because even though the Expos would score only once more that night after Jim Tracy went to his bullpen, the Chiefs were also suddenly back to shopping for clutch hits at the bargain-basement counter. Their seven hits on the night had produced only two gift runs in the third. Back-to-back walks and back-to-back balks had been followed by Eddie Williams's seeing-eye single to right. And even in that high-water-mark half-inning just before the fall, there had been ominous signs of what was to be. Instead of the big inning it could've been, it was lamely truncated when Fast Eddie, all on his own and to the hopping, yapping chagrin of Jim Tracy, tried to steal third with still only one down and was out by a day and a half. Naturally, Phil Hannon promptly singled with now nobody to drive in and was then thrown out attempting to steal second on the very next pitch.

In the fourth, seventh, and ninth we had ended innings with either the winning or tying runs on base. The two in the seventh had been a second-and-third situation with only one out. In the ninth it had been second-and-third with nobody out. But *nada*.

The seven hits had been matched by seven strikeouts. Four of which were evenly divided between our three- and four-hole hitters, Wilkins and Bell. A night off from behind the plate for Rick so he could maybe think about his attitude back there hadn't appeared to take the pressure off him with the bat either. As the DH he had gone hitless in four at bats. And Bell, after experiencing only his second 0-for-4 game of the season the night prior, had gone 1-4. Now his 6-for-12 binge in Wausau had been countered by a 1-8 fast so far in Rockford, with his strikeouts mounting along with his obvious inability to cover any part of the plate from the outer third on.

On top of a relapse of offensive anemia, we'd also committed three errors, one passed ball, two wild pitches, and walked seven.

If this was the corner we'd turned, then it looked a hell of a lot like where we'd just been only worse.

Much worse. As if all that mess wasn't bad enough, it also appeared that we'd been snatched around that corner by a gang of thieves. And we ain't talking about on the field.

Most of the bloom was off the Rockford lily for the Peoria Chiefs well before the start of that second game. It had vanished in a frozen moment with an indignant, anguished, bellicose howl from Jim Tracy only minutes after we'd swaggered off the bus and into the modern, spacious visitors' clubhouse at Marinelli Field.

"We been thieved!"

While it is true that besides a scoreboard the other as yet major unfinished aspect of the brand-new stadium was heat anywhere, it wasn't just the cold that rendered Trace's words written in a staccato ack-ack of vapor puffs—he was smoking. The bastards had stolen his major league jersey!

"Hey, Skip . . . some of my stuff's missing?"

It was Rick Wilkins. His fine, new, official Chicago Cubs warm-up jacket he'd gotten in big league camp was gone. As was his game cap and jersey.

"Sons . . . of . . . goddam . . . bitches," slowly, venomously spit the Shooter before he threw his uniform pants against the wall. "And you know it had to be an inside job."

Because of the lack of heat, almost none of the Chiefs had wanted to shower in the clubhouse the night before. But since it was a well-equipped, otherwise most commodious facility, with only two quite secure entrances or exits, there was no reason not to mostly dress there and also to leave whatever one didn't want to be constantly toting back and forth from the Howard Johnson's. The doors had been locked by our trainer, Steve Melendez, when we'd left and the keys were said to be accessible only to the chief groundskeeper and select members of general manager Tom Shannon's staff. In fact, whenever Stevie and Lee Kline came over with the laundry, or the team itself arrived, there would be a wait while someone went and rounded up a key to let us in.

But not only did the thieves, whoever they still may be, have an in, they also turned out to be selectively elitist in their larceny, possibly with an informed eye at the collectors' market. Only the Phenom and the Shooter had been victims.

"That's low. My major league jersey?" Jim Tracy had the pain in his voice and the look on his face that sometimes come when the basic good in man is again reminded of the incomprehensibly petty but undeniably evident baseness that is also always there. "I was gonna give that to my oldest boy when he got big enough to appreciate it. Now some sumbitch is gonna be wearing it in a beer league softball game!"

"Trace . . . I don't think you have to be worrying about that," said Kranny with a face you wouldn't want to see on a judge if you were a defendant. "The low-life scumbag has probably already sold it as Sandberg's."

"Jesus . . . I didn't think about that." Then that look again. "The cocksuckers . . . I was wearing that 23 in Wrigley Field when Ryno was still at Double A with the Phillies. Hell, when he goes into the Hall of Fame and they retire that number, I'm gonna be a great trivia question—who was the last Cub to wear that number before him. And now I ain't got it."

"Yeah, but Wilkie . . . how come him?" wondered Melendez.

"I guess they read the baseball media . . . figure his stuff is like investing in the futures market," said one of us.

"Well, they aren't reading the box scores. Dumb mothers, serves 'em right if he tops out at A Ball!"—only from the Kran-dog.

So after enduring both the thievery and that ballgame, even the native Rock heads will perhaps understand, if not restrain their umbrage at, Jim Tracy's two-word, repeated assessment of his wife's hometown.

"Fuck Rockford."

To be sure it was always followed by no shortage of amens.

That blasphemy, however, was perhaps a bit too general for Rick Kranitz. Ever the pragmatist, he knew our fate lay in the charts—the game charts. So he cursed them.

Pissed at his pitching staff, a ballclub, a town, and life in general at the moment, he chose to take his wrath out on two clipboards. As soon as he climbed on the bus he flipped on his overhead light and started spewing a steady stream of verbal abuse at the pitching chart and the game chart that the two next-scheduled pitchers in the rotation must sit behind home plate in their civvies and keep with any variance from absolute accuracy coming at the peril of their souls and their wallet. No names were used. He profaned no ballplayer. And neither did he look at any. Only at the charts. As if it was their fault. Yet every pitcher listened. And every pitcher cringed. One or two of them might've even learned something in between the obscenities.

Almost nothing is ever all bad for all time in baseball. Even that horrific, foreboding day (which had, truth to tell, begun with the worst snow flurries of the trip to date). And of course, at the time we certainly had no way of knowing that, in the overall scheme of things, that second game in Rockford wasn't anything more than just another ballgame. Consequently, within an hour and a half of its conclusion, that's about all it became.

Albeit a particularly bad one. For the first time, within the volumes of words and phrases used to replay that game, there were precious few which could be termed positive, and even then it was a stretch—and from a negative.

"Trace . . . Herbie calls a better game than Wilkie," the Kran-dog had observed.

"I noticed. Shame he's not a prospect." Then, after chewing on that irony for a while, Jim Tracy said, "You know, we learned something else tonight."

"What's that?"

"Jossy might be timid . . . but he ain't no creampuff. Jeez'em'tally . . . that dude almost broke him in two, and he's up grinning and whistling before Stevie's even up the steps to run check him out. Whatever he's afraid of it ain't pain."

"If he was, perhaps it would be better. Then he'd find a way to get to the bag quicker. That's where the problem lies," said Tony Franklin. "For some reason he's getting there late. And it's not because he's not fast enough . . . it's mechanical or situational."

"Can you fix it? Mick can't get here for a while."

"I can try. But it's hard to fix a lot during just a few minutes of fungoes at batting practice."

"If we get that! Goddam weather. Goddam road trip. How the hell you supposed to teach this game if you can't get on a ball diamond?"

"That's why they pay us the big money, Trace," laughed Tony Franklin without mirth.

"Riiight. I swear, you know what's gonna be the best thing about finally getting home? We'll be able to work out."

Rick Kranitz thought about that for only a heartbeat, then, "Trace . . . I'm sorry, but the best thing about going home is knowing we don't have to come back!"

True. But certainly not definitive.

"Not to beg a point, Kranny . . . but *that's* the best thing about going home," Mario had said.

" 'Beg' don't do the sentiments justice," I agreed.

Rick Kranitz followed our gaze across the parking lot until his eyes too came to rest for a moment upon the easy task of looking at Dawn and Holly.

"Okay . . . so I lied," he had answered simply enough before returning to his perusal of the hot-off-the-press, twenty-page special souvenir tabloid the *Peoria Journal Star* puts out annually on the Chiefs.

That little scene, while it surely represented the only undeniably good thing about any part of our second day in Rockford, was also a not unheeded reminder that the absolutely best thing about going home was the very home we were going to—which of course meant it could also be the very worst—Peoria.

With Meinen Field only two more wake-ups and a late-night bus ride away, our natural longing for journey's end, already as wistful as it was problematic, was particularly piqued by the fact that now, on the last leg and inward bound, some very welcome seagulls, heralding home and anchorage, had come up to meet us; and they'd brought some of the fruits of the harbor with them.

When Jeff Reeser and Phil Theobald had decided to drive up to Rockford to pre-welcome us home from our fifteen-day trip into an arctic purgatory (indeed scheduled with the complicity of Pete Vonachen because he wanted someone else to have to try and draw fans out to ballgames in weather best suited for penguins), their gesture of support for the wanderers was also partly impulsed by the fact that we'd been winning. "Greeser" and "T-Ball" like not to absent themselves when there are good times to be had.

Phil, the grizzled man of letters, Civil War history, Jack Daniel's, and chain-smoked cigarettes, the primo sportswriter at the *Journal Star,* and Jeff, the Chiefs' young and dandy Director of Promotions, had also wanted us to see the special tabloid fanfaring an expectant season with a compendium of almost everything one needed to know about the 1988 Chiefs, which that morning had been distributed to some few hundred thousand folks in the environs of Peoria and north-central Illinois.

"I've never seen anything like this in the minor leagues."

Kranny had first said that some two weeks before when television cameras and a throng of fans had been the first thing the Chiefs had seen when they'd stepped off the plane from spring training to begin a three-day whirl of media and public idolatry in Peoria before having to hic off into the hinterlands for the longest road trip in the recent memory of anyone in the Midwest League. He'd said it again, with more amazement still, when all three local network affiliates, numerous radio stations, and almost a thousand fans had come out in 40-degree weather just to watch the first workout of their 1988 Chiefs at Meinen Field the night we'd arrived. And again when well over a thousand had paid good money to come out for the Meet the Chiefs Night extravaganza in the Grand Ballroom of the Continental Regency the following night. And then Opening Day?—which had begun at dawn with the first of the many continuous and overlapping live remotes that would be broadcast from various parts of Meinen Field that day right up through the marching bands, fireworks, and skydivers which presaged just the commencement of the Gonzo Opening Night festivities—What a question.

So when he'd said it again as he leafed through north-central Illinois's largest daily newspaper's yearly homage to a Single A baseball team, there was no longer any amazement in the statement, just acceptance of fact. And the acceptance of what that fact could mean for a 5-and-8 ballclub with still two more games to play before landing back in the middle of all that rabid, expectant glitz which is the phenomenon of Cubs minor league baseball Pete Vonachen's way in Peoria.

"This is big league all the way . . . I'm telling you," Kranny had added as he closed up the special tab.

"So is that," Mario and I said in almost the same breath.

Rick Kranitz studied the stunning blonde and ever so cute brunette talking with John Green and Lenny Bell as we waited for Trace to come on so we could get back to the motel.

"Ehhh . . . Triple A at least," Kranny had finally said in appreciation of the two young ladies, who represented yet another aspect of baseball at Meinen Field unique to the Midwest League, if not all of minor league baseball—the Peoria Chiefs Spirit Girls.

Phil and Jeff had not just brought a newspaper section with which to hail and hearty a winning streak, they had also brought Dawn and Holly, two of the stars of that troupe of lovelies. Pete Vonachen had long since figured correctly that a pretty face in an attractive little costume will sell more programs and better assuage the grumbles of a standing-room-only crowd than old fogies in VFW hats. So of course with all that incentive from home, we lost.

"Well, one thing's certain," Kranny had said as he looked again at the full-color close-up of a beaming, yukking Jim Tracy on the cover of the "Play Ball" tabloid. "There's no slipping into town quiet-like . . . in a couple of days we're going to be either some very public heroes, or some very embarrassed bums."

"Yeah . . . but not lonely ones," said Mario as our attention was again drawn back to Dawn and Holly. "I mean, we could be going home to someplace like Burlington."

"Peoria definitely has its advantages, Kranny."

The pitching coach of the Peoria Chiefs had smiled then and said, "Just remember, guys, we aren't the ballplayers."

If perhaps some kind of cosmic grace period exists, some suspended moment before destiny becomes history, when the hounds of fate can still be called back, then surely such a moment came and went when, only shortly before the National Anthem, the heavens themselves opened up in indignant judgment and poured a gully-washer on any such nonsense and Friday night's game was called before the Rockford grounds crew could even get the right side of their brand-new tarp wet.

"So whatcha think of this yard, Wilkie?" Rick Wilkins had been standing apart, hefting the ubiquitous bat as he glanced about Marinelli Stadium.

"Not bad, actually . . . pretty nice yard. 'Course, after South Bend? But then the only thing better than that could be Wrigley Field . . . and that's the only place I wanna be."

That's when the deluge came. While it came down in thunder-clapping bucketfuls, it did not come down long. But then since this was still early in the shakedown cruise for the new Rockford Expos franchise, the grounds crew was still trying to figure out how the damned tarp worked, let alone start rolling it out, when, within five minutes of the first splat, as we watched with quick dread a baseball diamond turning into a rice paddy, we heard the quick-draw decision of general manager Tom Shannon come booming over the most obnoxiously loud sound system in the entirety of the Midwest League. The words we feared the most.

". . . doubleheader tomorrow! First game will begin at six-thirty!"

Thus was destiny not denied her poetic injustice. The Chiefs would have to play a night doubleheader on getaway-home day.

"Fuck Rockford!"

That sentiment in its less general and more whimsical connotation was, at least in spirit if not in surety of any success, responsible for the fact that the partying we did that night had a different tone. We also, for the first time, did not do our partying en masse. All of Rockford became the milieu as groups of the family went off in several directions looking for whatever adventures an unexpected night off in a real city might hold.

Being in Rockford, some of course had the company of visitors from home. Trace had a group in from the suburbs of Chicago. Mario had a lady friend up from Peoria. However, most of us were chasing tips about the local night life generously offered by friendly natives—"The least they could do, the goddam Rockheads." A very disjointed, raucous night unfolded.

One group of us was shanghaied by this goofy guy named Guido—he wrecks automobiles for a hobby—when he assured us he knew exactly how to get to some jumping sports bar with a name like Cubbies West that was supposed to be roasting a pig that night. John Green had heard about it. We were supposed to meet Greenie and company there. Kranny just happened to mention that fact to Guido, who was sitting on the barstool next to us at the Howard Johnson's lounge and peppering us with every baseball opinion he ever had.

While we did eventually and at different times connect with various other roving bands of the family, too many of us perhaps got a much more thorough tour of the Rockford social scene than its charms merited. Guido didn't want us to miss anything.

We didn't. At least not the joints. But perhaps we should have. If memory serves. Which in this case is all too sketchy. I'll just take Kranny's word on the issue.

"Fuck Rockford."

"Not tonight."

"Fuck Guido."

It was as anticlimactic as it was redundant. Would that it had been as swift as it was ugly. But no. On the coldest night of them all, when we who were still mostly packed for the sun of Arizona had by this time resorted to bringing blankets from the motel to ward off frostbite when and as best we could, the Peoria Chiefs chose to play their sloppiest baseball to date, assuring that sometime about dawn we would be slinking home to Peoria a 5-and-10 ballclub.

So cold and redundantly ugly was it that Tony Franklin had quit the dugout almost from the first, and shortly thereafter, while huddled under one of those blankets in the unenclosed press box, gave his assessment of the situation.

"'The Boys Who Would Be Cubs'? Not likely. Try 'The Boys Who Won't Be Cubs.' Absolutely Under No Circumstances Will Ever Be Cubs."

Mario had liked Tony's wit so much he had shared it with the listeners at home. He had to say something about that mess going on down on the diamond of Marinelli Field that Saturday night of April 23. And a little humor is always helpful in whiling away the many insufferable moments encountered by a broadcaster trying to keep his audience tuned in during a 6-2 and 5-1 double-dip spanking.

Unfortunately, from the vantage point of the moment, it appeared that Tony's line—which would also endure the season—was perhaps all too accurate. It was that bad. All of the redundancies came home to roost that night. We even invented one.

On a night when the Peoria Chiefs should've been madder than hell but not play like it, instead, "Goddam, we played horseshit!"

Trace punched every croaking syllable as he undressed layer by thermal layer and punctuated his sentences with yet another fling of garment at the wall.

"We can't goddam hit it!" Six singles and one double over two games in fourteen innings.

"We can't goddam catch it!" Seven errors, and ten now in just three games.

"We can't goddam throw strikes!" While we only walked a total of seven for both games, it was always at the wrong time.

"And we can't goddam think!" We'd also balked three times, John Green on consecutive pitches to score a run in the first game; Z balked a run in in the second.

And then there had been that play in the bottom of the third. It was the capper, pun fully intended:

"I didn't know that ball hit off his head. Did it . . . did it really?"

"Jesus Christ, Trace . . . when a fly ball suddenly bounces thirty feet in the air, you don't reckon it hit off his glove, do ya?"

"Aw, Horace . . . God love him. He ain't got a clue, does he? But tell me where there's a sweeter kid anywhere. Jesus, Mary, and Joseph, though . . . that ball hit him in the head?"

Horace Tucker, who'd been added as an afterthought to the Peoria roster only hours before the plane had left Arizona, had gotten to start his first game of the season that night, playing right field in the second match.

While Tucker's one at bat before being lifted for a pinch hitter had prompted Tony Franklin's comment (first to us and then the micro tape recorder James Colborn had decreed become a working tool of every Cubs roving instructor)—

"He's overmatched in this league . . . I mean, look at him. He's only eighteen. He's scared to death. He's got the tools . . . but he's just not ready yet. Maybe he should have gone to junior college."

—it was a lazy fly ball to straightaway right field off the bat of Archie Cianfrocco that somehow wound up hitting Horace square in the head, instead of the glove he was holding only inches away for just that eventuality, that perhaps best epitomized the developmental quandary to date.

"Can't anybody here play this game?" After almost an hour Trace was down to the final layer of long johns and jock, and not caring that he was quoting Casey Stengel, had wound down to where he was just sitting on the metal folding chair in that freezing visiting manager's office shaking his big head from side to side. "What kind of team is that, huh?"

Then, in a hoarse, cracking whisper: "I just don't know what I can say to 'em anymore . . . you know what I mean? I just don't fucking know."

For one thing it had been a much colder team than the home boys. Which was the reason the Peoria Chiefs were beyond war-paint mad well before taking the field that night.

Our already bad blood toward anything Rockford was poisoned yet further when I chanced to stumble on that weasel sumbitch Tom Shannon filling propane heaters for the home team's clubhouse and dugouts. It seems that they'd been doing it throughout the series. This fact had been brought back up by Kranny as Trace was now almost dressed.

"Trace, I'm telling you. It's this town. We aren't this bad."

"Yeah? Goddam thieves and dipshits for sure! And you know? Just a couple hits here or there, and we could be going home a .500 ballclub. I mean . . . and the conditions we been under during this whole trip? Rain, snow, too cold for a well digger? It could be worse now."

"Yeah." Kranny actually smiled just a little. "Just think, we could be going home like the Orioles . . . zero and fifteen!"

"Yeah . . . you're right. Fuck Rockford and the horse they stole to ride in on . . . we're going to Peoria!"

No one said a word from the ballfield back to the motel. If you blinked your eyes you did it quietly. Then, as Lee pulled into the parking lot, Jim Tracy turned around in his seat and asked what time it was.

"Eleven-twenty."

The bus pulled to a stop, and he stood up and turned around. His voice was low and forced. His sentences clipped. The personification of restraint mightily tested.

"Gentlemen. Go in. Shower. Change your clothes. Bus leaves at one o'clock. Eat here. 'Cause we ain't stopping."

A long pause. There was a rustle here and there as if perhaps that was going to be all. Then.

"I strongly suggest that youse guys get some sleep on this bus!" The voice was louder now, an edge was showing. "You've got a two-o'clock game tomorrow. When we get to Peoria I'll let you know what time to be at the ballpark."

Another pause, longer still. But there was no rustling anywhere. And the explosion came soon enough.

"We played horseshit baseball tonight! We are horseshit! And if what I think is true? That youse guys were out chasing pussy last night and that's the reason? Which is the only thing I can figure out! Well, I'd just better not think that! You understand? Because if that's the case? There *will* be some changes here, gentlemen. . . !"

Jim Tracy's big neck twitched as he harangued on. It seems that the Shooter had indeed thought of something to say to his ballclub.

THE 1988 PEORIA Chiefs would play twelve of their next sixteen games in the "friendly," pristine confines of Meinen Field.

While that might be merely a statement of scheduled fact, it also serves succinctly to present a good news–bad news joke that, while we went through it, was about as funny as being invited to spend an evening with Michelle Pfeiffer only to have her end up slapping you around all night.

"It's like investigating a train wreck. You know? Except you know all the victims," Richie Zisk had said toward the end of those sixteen days which saw the Chicago Cubs organization react to "Pete's Problem" first by trying to fix what was broke, and then finally starting the process of replacing it when it still wouldn't work.

"If we'd known you were coming we'da baked a cake!" Rick Kranitz had cracked at one point early on during the fix-it-quick days. When there were enough cooks for this puzzlingly sour soup that on any given day at Meinen Field one could've called a staff meeting of the Cubs Minor League Department and had a quorum.

All things considered, then, perhaps the gods of baseball, and even Pete Vonachen, will forgive the fact that, at that time and given our druthers, we'd just as soon have been anywhere but home.

And not Wrigley Field, either. Which was precisely where we were also scheduled to be on the seventeenth day "After Rockford." Where the 1988 Peoria Chiefs would have to suffer the ignominy of a day in their honor. Now that *is* crazy! I don't care who's doing the saying.

We would also learn during those sixteen days that all of it mattered a great deal to a lot of people. Almost from the beginning. But then at least we did have that almost . . .

If "After Rockford" we were not going to be allowed to slip into town quietly, at least we had the good fortune to be able to do it quickly.

With more than a little anxiety about how our Homecoming act might play in Peoria, there was comfort in the knowledge that we were coming home only for a four-game series with the Beloit Brewers before then having to strike out for our first venture into Iowa. But there was another blessed quickness about our return. That moment of almost . . .

With our "second Opening Day" game being a two-o'clock start, there had been time only to crash, bag and baggage unpacked, for about three or four hours wherever it was you'd crashed for those three days before and then get out to the ballpark.

And since the Sunday-afternoon game was indeed being promoted and administered with much of the trappings of an Opening Day—with Pete off selling Chiefs at some sabbath luncheon, and John Butler and staff already busily engaged in pregame helter-skelter—we'd been able to pop out onto the diamond of Meinen Field after almost no contact with, and mercifully little feedback from, the Home Front. Twice blessed then, that allowed our first impressions to be those only of joy!

If it ain't heaven, at a little after eleven o'clock on Sunday morning, April 24, to the Peoria Chiefs, Meinen Field damn sure had whatever was in second place beat all to Rockford and back.

A beautiful, bright, cloudless blue sky with an actual *sun* shining big and round as the grin on Jim Tracy's face. The temperature was in the mid-50s, but it might as well have been Hawaii for how it felt to us.

Surely *this* was a new day. And what is not possible or well and good on such a day? So there was a bounce in every step, and a song of "things are sure to change now" in every heart as the Peoria Chiefs, laughing and prancing, stretched, ran, and played short-and-long toss before taking batting practice in the impeccably groomed ballpark that welcomed their return all dressed up and sparkling like a beautiful girl awaiting a prom date. And not at all unlike just such a date, there was that same exhilarating sense of thrill and promise.

That very thrill and promise was only enhanced by the personage of the first emissary from the land of the Big Cubbie Bear to arrive at the scene. You see, Jimmy Piersall was also waiting for us. And of this you may be certain: whatever the adventure, it can only be heightened by the presence of the only baseball legend and great of the game who is fond of reminding friend or foe—and there is no middle ground—that "I'm crazy and I've got the papers to prove it." Of course, we two-dozen-plus wandering sons of the Cubbie Bear, who'd not had the benefit of his unique company since we'd had to say goodbye to him back in Mesa, were decidedly of the former category.

Therefore, after his quick-tongued, loose-cannon, graveled yet squeaky-voiced salutations and greetings of outrageously baudy, ethnic needles and jabs had been rat-a-tat-tatted around aplenty so that every Chief had felt the welcoming reaffirmation of an individualized sting, and we were now spiritedly spread about the billiard-table-smooth-and-just-as-green diamond of Meinen Field for batting practice, even the most pessimistic one among us soon couldn't help but surrender to the prevailing sentiment of the storm survived, fair winds ahead when he leaned upon the batting cage and heard that unforgettable voice muse:

"Tough road trip." Then, "I know owners like that sort of thing this time of year. Get those bad-weather games out of the way. But that was fucking ridiculous!"

He paused as his eyes darted around in observation. Then the pronouncement, as if from on high: "But you're gonna be all right. Good pitching."

A moment later those constantly darting, piercing eyes had suddenly stopped, widened, and then sparkled as Jimmy Piersall remembered something. "That's what I wanted to do! And there's that cocksucker now . . . I didn't know where he got off to. Got something I been wanting to show that soul brother . . . whatever the fuck they call themselves these days . . . I guess that's not it, though. But lemme get him now, before . . ."

Then, as so often happens with Jimmy Piersall, whose body—and tongue—are always jumping to catch up with his mind, a sentence and thought was left hanging and he was running off toward center field with a bat in his hand. Once out there, he commenced teaching Phil Hannon a completely different batting stance.

"It's easier to get a lawyer into heaven than it is to get people out to watch minor league baseball on a weekend afternoon," Pete Vonachen has said on more than one occasion. His marketing experience had led him to conclude that while a major league game is an experience, therefore a justifiable exception, "Mama's not giving up her barbecues or letting Dad off from cutting the grass for no minor league game!"

It is no coincidence, then, that only five such scheduled games appeared on the Chiefs' 1988 home calendar, and that all of them were early in the season when the weather was most likely to be problematic. Pete was not at all displeased then—and in fact seemed a little surprised and even vaguely perplexed—when 2,477 paying rear ends were in and about their seats for the first of them when George Spelius, president of the Midwest League, as part of the pregame festivities, gave a speech and presented Pete the award for Peoria's again leading the league in Opening Day attendance.

In support of Pete's theory, and not any apparent contradiction by numbers, it must be noted that minor league baseball in Peoria, Illinois, *is* an experience.

It is Heartland pizzazz. It is Mid-America state fair family thrill, excitement, and something for everyone. It is Show Time in Peoria—whose very name, through legend and fact, has long stood as the standard of a tough house to play.

It is—as it was that gorgeous Sunday afternoon—a chance to whoop! oooh! holler! and ahhh! as you watch would-be major league "Stars of Tomorrow" only minutes before they must again "Play ball" with nothing less at daily stake than their careers and dreams, all line up behind second base and one at a time try to throw a baseball through about an 18-inch circular hole in the Q on the doubie-deck signboard in left center field on the very off chance that it might go through and win airfare for two to anywhere in the world in the "WQ105 Ball Toss."

It is a chance to hear "The Star-Spangled Banner" performed as a haunting, soulful, compelling saxophone solo by one of the best barbers *and* musicians in Peoria, Dave Parkinson. And then it's a chance to sit down with your beer, butterflied pork chops, pizzas, nachos, cheers, leers, jeers, and tears as "Hard Luck Mike" Aspray took a 5-2 licking he didn't deserve from the Beloit Brewers on an afternoon when the Chiefs outhit an opponent 12 to 8 but could score only two runs for the eighth time in sixteen games, and the fourth in a row. The sun, blue skies, and pizzazz notwithstanding, the Peoria Chiefs were now on their second four-game losing streak of the young season. And counting.

Mike Aspray holds umpires up to some rather high standards. At the very least he expects them to have the same command of the strike zone he does. On that balmy Sunday-at-the-park, plate umpire Mike Huber's reflexive response to this affront upon his apprenticed profession was to come up with a standard all his own: a strike zone about the size of a cigar box that also happened to be situated right over the middle of the plate and at a height somewhere between the belt buckle and the belly button.

When young Mr. Aspray had contended with this rigid censorship of his art well enough to take a 2-1 lead into the fifth, young Mr. Huber then countered by shrinking the damn thing to the size of a pocket pack of panatelas. And while that soon ended any further doubt about the outcome, it in no way ended the debate.

Pete Vonachen will wear out three or four pairs of shoes during a baseball season. That afternoon it appeared he might accelerate the attrition as he relentlessly paced the terraced levels of wide-opened Meinen Field working the crowd, name by glad-hand name recalled, with all the skill and instincts of the successful restaurateur he once was. That was when the Chiefs were batting.

With the progression of the obvious war of wills transpiring between one of his pitchers and one of those so vulnerable foils in blue, Pete Vonachen was not going to miss an opportunity to both put on a show for his fans and also vent some of his very real frustrations.

So, to his normal frenetic ramblings, whenever we were in the field, his act now included traipsing the full length of the bright blue rail separating the box seats from the bleachers, stomping and snorting his way down one foul line and then the other, just blasting away.

"You wimp. . . ! You gutless son of . . . something! The blind! That's it! You gutless son of the blind! What? What a wimp! What you wearing under there . . . a slip? Oh . . . you can't see, but you can hear! Well, hear this. . . !"

The crowd loved it. Huber squeezed even tighter. Pete was up to that. The Chiefs weren't. But it was a hell of a show. Which of course was the idea. Our Homecoming might've been a miswritten melodrama with the good guys losing, but it brought the house down.

It also must be noted that if Pete wasn't in true fact panicking yet, he nonetheless thought it was already past time for it. There had been another visitor from Wrigley Field that afternoon. Scott Nelson, Assistant Director of Scouting, who'd been there for the real season opener, had hied his droll but scattered buckshot wit and cherubic face down to lend his moral support for our "reopener." And in between all the ranting and boosterism, Pete had repeatedly also found the time to sit down behind Scotty and pump him for information on how certain players were doing at either Charleston or Winston-Salem. Every time he'd come back it would be with a couple more names on his shopping list.

"What's Sullivan doing? Big boy . . . hits 'em hard, I hear. And Stevie Hill . . . is he playing every day, or sitting? He needs to play, you know . . . and the folks love him here . . ."

With a disarming charm and an endearing candor that in the end only lets you learn what he thinks you should or need to know, Scott Nelson had adroitly fielded all of Pete's probes and innuendos without once breaking official party ranks. And while doing so, he had managed to not only momentarily placate a not unimportant man in the Chicago Cubs scheme of things, but he had also made him laugh. Which, on that day, and ever increasingly in the days and weeks to come, was no easy task.

"You don't very often lose a baseball game to umpires. But this was one. They fucking stole it from us!" Jimmy Piersall said.

"He squeezed him big-time. No doubt about that," agreed Tony Franklin.

Then Jim Tracy looked up at Rick Kranitz leaning against the jam of the door which separates their offices and said, "One of us should've gotten tossed tonight, Mule. You know that, huh?"

"Goddam, Trace . . . it's not like we weren't trying. But Jesus! With Pete carrying on like that, who had time to pay us any mind?"

"God love him . . . I told you he was something. Didn't I?"

Meinen Field in those days was beginning to feel and sound a whole lot like spring training.

The next to arrive was Bill "Gabby" Hayes, the Cubs' roving catching instructor. He'd made it in early the very next morning, just in time for "early work." Selected-personnel morning workouts are mandatory at the lower levels of the Cubs' farm system when at home, and weather permitting. A list of those expected to be there is posted on the bulletin board each evening. The last thing a Cub minor leaguer does before leaving the clubhouse is look at that list. Not to do so could cost him some money.

However, with this being the first opportunity for the Peoria Chiefs to hold such workouts, and with all the concerted attention our shame was occasioning, there would be no problem with truancy during these days of intensive reinstruction.

While Jim Tracy was effusive in his joy at being able to work with the middle of his batting order at the batting cage, the most immediate and pressing reclamation projects involved Jossy Rosario and Rick Wilkins.

Before we would get out of town, Tony Franklin would send thousands of ground balls scooting out toward the middle infield where Jossy, with the accompaniment of Marty, Boz, and Sergio trading off at shortstop, would turn double play after double play.

"Ducks can't catch! That's why they don't have gloves!"

Trying to halt that creeping, off-balance duck walk so many infielders erroneously pick up somewhere along the way, Tony had said that so many times it no longer needed to be translated.

And one of the first things big ol', good ol' boy-walrus Bill Hayes had done was to set up "the hummer" in the bullpen so that it would spit ball after ball into the dirt as Rick Wilkins crouched, lunged, and grunted again and again.

"I want you to block every fucking pitch! I don't care whether it's warm-up. New pitcher coming in. Men on base. Practice. Whatever. You understand me? You catch every fucking ball from now on! Make it a habit. Every fucking ball, go get it!"

Yepper, it was enough to make you nostalgic for the cup of vegetable soup and crackers of lunchtime at Fitch Park!

However, on the first day of all this, that second day "After Rockford," we were also aware that our sense of misery-loves-company delight and bemusement at all of the empathetic support hastening to be at our side during this spring of our perplexing discontent could change quickly.

Gordon Goldsberry was due in that evening for game two of the Beloit series. While we understood that there might not be a better baseball man to have around than he during any moment of crisis, we also understood that he was the Boss.

No offense, Pete.

It was baseball's social hour. The gates to Meinen Field would be opening soon. The Spirit Girls were dusting off the chairs in the box-seat sections. Others of Director of Stadium Operations Mike Nelson's regimented personnel were scurrying about on last-minute pregame duties. From the speakers above the uncovered grandstand came some much-amplified, very good rock and roll.

"Turn now! Have to start those hips . . . start to turn back . . . now! Go get it! That's the way to pull that belly button," Jimmy Piersall had said. Then, apparently satisfied with Warren Arrington's last swing, he'd allowed himself a glance around at a ballyard which at the moment was stepping in its bustle to the sounds of Elton John's "Levon."

"Fucking music! Put that shit in the toilet! These ballplayers don't need to be entertained!"

(Of the many things prevalent in our society for which Mr. Piersall has no use, one of them is rock music of any kind.)

Just as Jimmy had made that observation, and had turned back to watch what Gator was going to do with the next offering from Jim Tracy, Pete Vonachen, all dressed up from a speaking engagement and sporting a fine cream-colored sport coat, joined us at the cage.

Without a hi, bye, or at your leave, Jimmy Piersall greeted the owner of the Peoria Chiefs with: "That's why you're five and eleven, Pete. It's that goddam music!"

"Unh-unh," corrected Peter of Peoria. "We're only oh and two with that music."

Piersall's attention darts again. "Goddam! Don't hit Jossy any more balls!" he hollers at Greg Kallevig, who had just been following the normal routine of nonstarting pitchers standing off to either side of the batting cage and hitting fungoes to the infielders during batting practice.

"Christ! He won't be able to play tonight. Son of a bitch! Had him out here all day. Over four hundred ground balls! Goddam!"

Then, in the next breath, "Nice jacket, Pete. Is that the one you wore when you were up there crying to Jim Frey?"

"Aw . . . Jimmy, would I do something like that?"

"What? Goddam! You whined so much Frey said, 'Get your ass down there. Bullshit the man!' So I'm just here to bullshit you, Pete. 'Goddam, go baby-sit Pete!' he told me."

"Well, if he wanted to send somebody to bullshit me, they sure sent the right man. But seriously, Jimmy. I was just up there to see Harry. That's all. Then I get this message that Jim wants to see me. So I went on up."

"And what'd you tell him?"

"I said the obvious—'Hey, we just need a couple of sticks.'"

"And what'd he tell you?"

"He just said, 'Yeah, I know. You're off to a tough start. I'll see what I can do.' And that was the end of it. I swear, Jimmy."

"Right!"

"Hey . . . if I did say any more than that, from the way you guys are popping in here like rocket scientists to a fizzled launch, then maybe somebody's starting to listen for a change."

"Yeah. You belch. Harry hears it. And we jump. Nice jacket, though."

Sure enough, it was at that moment that Gordon Goldsberry suddenly appeared at the cage. With his first words after hello, we quickly realized that the boss, at least for now, wasn't there to add to our misery.

"Well, Pete, I hope you found out you can't send your team to the north pole and expect them to win too."

Gordon Goldsberry is a soft-spoken, innately gentle man. His voice and manner are almost always the embodiment of reasonableness in thought and modulation.

That demeanor did not change as he had to smile and nod through the virulent return of the old "Massacre" Jeff, the Chiefs coming up on the short end of an 8-5 batters' turkey shoot, and the relentless lobbying of Pete Vonachen.

Of course, as far as the game was concerned, there was actually very little reason for change. A baseball man such as Gordon Goldsberry knew that there is precious little one should conclude about any one ballgame. This is most particularly true about any game where both starting pitchers are well gone by the third inning; a game where there are a total of twenty hits, seventeen walks, twenty-three left on base, and five errors!

With a very shaky 3-1 lead in the top of the third, Jeff had promptly walked the first two men he faced. The fifth and sixth men he'd already walked on the still very early evening. They would also be his last. Only moments thereafter, a catcher by the name of Tom Torricelli hit a laid-in groover about to the back of their team bus parked behind the batting cages behind the left-center-field wall for a three-run homer that would in the end decide the issue as it decided Mass's stay upon the mound before that ball even came down.

Gordon Goldsberry's face flickered only slightly. Then he turned to Donna Vonachen, Pete's saint of a wife, and asked after the grandbaby.

Gordon Goldsberry does not wear that gentility only in public. Even in the privacy of Jim Tracy's office his counsel, spoken quietly, thoughtfully, was a sermon on patience and faith in the system and the game that was so much bigger than all of this.

". . . we have to have patience, gentlemen. It's a tough thing for these kids . . . the road trip. And each of us, we have to remember times when we were hitting a buck-seventy. Or less. It happened. And we have to remember back when we all went through something like this. . . .

"They went up there and played in that cold. . . . We can't give up on kids in three weeks. That's not what we thought of them when we sent others home and them here. Look at Grace. He's right now hitting .180

at Iowa. Is anyone down on him? Absolutely not. He'll still be in Wrigley
. . . maybe any day now. No. We can't get down on them now . . . we
owe them more than that."

Jim Tracy, of course, had nothing but agreement with all of it. And
then some.

"Gordie, I'ma tell ya what I know. This is a *good* ballclub. It was a
good ballclub when we left Mesa. And nobody can convince me that
they're not going to turn it all around. Hell . . . maybe tomorrow!"

There were times that season when one would've sworn Jim Tracy was
clairvoyant. On balance, perhaps just a few more times than one also
would've taken an oath that he was jinxed. On the occasion of the last
two days of the four-game home stand against the Beloit Brewers, he
proved to be the former. As the weather turned nasty, so did the Chiefs.

There is surely only coincidence and nothing more in the fact that Pete
Vonachen had a speech to give and wasn't there until afterward that very
cold night when only 165 true-blue-frozen Peorians were at the vigil when
the 1988 Peoria Chiefs won for the first time at home, Tuesday, April 26.

There was, however, absolutely nothing coincidental, ulterior, or un-
characteristic about Jim Tracy's mood after Eduardo Caballero, taking
full advantage of a whipping crosswind, bent yakker after yakker past
numb-fingered Brewers for seven innings, striking out ten, as his teammates, seemingly energized by the ugly elements, played perhaps their
best baseball to date while staking the skinny Panamanian to a 5-1 lead
before he took his frozen fingers to the bench and let the Z Man finish
the job with perfection in the eighth and ninth.

"Now *that's* my ballclub!" was Jim Tracy's greeting to everyone who
poked his head into his office.

"I'm telling ya . . . that's the ballclub I had in spring training! Those
boys just got a little lost wandering around Wisconsin, Pete . . . but
they're back!" And then he would turn to any one of us who had been
there and ask, "Am I right? That's the ballclub we knew we had, huh?
God love 'em . . . I'd take ever'one of 'em to war with me."

That night they might've looked even better than spring training. Behind great pitching, they had played errorless defense. At the plate,
"Jeez'em'tally . . . even our outs were rockets! Huh?" And the nine hits
that hadn't found a glove were timely. "That's the way we did it all spring
. . . get a man on base, move him along, then drive him in. Am I right?
Gracious . . . this game is fun when you play it right."

Amens all around.

If there is one constant that lies beneath the grace and, to the casual
observer, the seemingly effortless simplicity of baseball when played at its
very finest by even the greats of the game, it is that it takes a goodly
amount of work to get it right so that you can have fun.

But then since this is baseball, where the only real constancy is time-lessness and that everything—given enough of it—will all come out in the wash anyway, there are as many opinions about what is right, what it takes to get it right, and what's it all about anyway, as there are ways to have fun when it is right.

It is not surprising then that in those days when we were critically ill, yet fully conscious, while all those eminent baseball surgeons were laboring over us, we could now hear at least a second or third opinion on most everything.

Shortly after "Massacre's Return" and the fifth loss in a row, Jim Tracy and Rick Kranitz had found themselves alone for a moment.

". . . don't ask me right now where else these kids could play, but I *know* they can play in this league . . . and we've gotta get it out of 'em. And sooner a whole lot better than later!" Jim Tracy said.

Then he leaned forward, big elbows on big bony knees, and added in that little-boy wonder at horrors: "Kranny, I'm afraid things could get real ugly around here if we don't start winning soon."

It was during that brief conversation when, even though fully aware that the already bad weather was forecast to get worse, the two men whose ballclub was being so thoroughly probed, studied, and prodded by others made the decision to go to full-squad full workouts in the morning sessions.

Not unlike most overachievers in any discipline, the Shooter *had* to believe hard work was the way to make right whatever it was that had gone so terribly wrong. At that point anything else would've been tantamount to admitting that what was wrong had never been right and perhaps couldn't be fixed at all. This Jim Tracy could not do at any cost. Not then. Not yet. It was bad enough that he could not sleep for trying to figure out how to put the pieces of the puzzle back together. But to also suspect that they do not fit? Unthinkable. Which was why Jim Tracy really *wasn't* sleeping.

". . . it's too much. You don't want to leave your game on the practice field! Spring training's okay . . . but even there they're getting crazy with it, to tell you the truth. And these fuckers are having to play every day!"

Jimmy Piersall is hitting fungoes to his "Soul Patrol" outfielders—Eddie, Gator, Phil, and Horace—as he gives his thoughts on the work-cures-all ethic.

". . . sure you wanna stay sharp. But I never saw any guy get to the big leagues because of what he did in a practice! They only count those fucking numbers in the games, you know! Those black bastards have to go out every night! Trying to do something so maybe they can get the hell out of here and get some real white pussy! And we dumb shits are running his game out of him that morning! Who's fucking stupid? Us? Or them?"

Of course the never repressible Mr. Piersall had said all that in between every "That'sa baby!" as he progressively hit fly balls a little farther away and a little closer to the wall, giving the Soul Patrol a longer and more difficult run and chance with each one. And this was after he'd already spent a good part of the morning in a determined continuation of the crash-course process of making Phil Hannon believe in his brand-new batting stance.

"You know, sometimes we forget that big leaguers are gonna get there whether we fuck 'em up or not."

Jimmy Piersall is nothing if not generous with his thoughts if he thinks you really give a damn. Somewhat later that morning he was still continuing to share them as he worked and watched.

"And the other dumb fucks aren't gonna get there no matter what we do. You've got to be very good to play this game. And we can't teach good! Maybe better. But if the good ain't there? Go home and get a shoe-shine stand! But then if we told them all the truth, and they did all go back to the ghetto or hicksville, we'd have to all get honest jobs ourselves!"

Mr. Piersall also had his own thoughts on perhaps why this team was struggling in particular, and why in his opinion there was less developmental bang for the buck in general in the much-condensed and streamlined "new" minor leagues as opposed to the vast bushes of the late 1940s.

"These kids know they're going to play every day. The prospects . . . the starters. So there's no one pushing them. When I played? There were so many fucking ballplayers! Hungry! Snapping at your heels! Hell, it was a goddam job! And you were afraid to even come into the fucking dugout for too long. Some dago take your job away! But these kids? You think Wilkins is worried about having to sit his big ass on the bench?"

However, having said that, Jimmy went on to say that Rick Wilkins was going to play in the big leagues. And that there were several other players on this club besides some of the pitchers that he believed were bona fide major league prospects. For instance, he was adamant in his conviction that Jossy Rosario was going to be a big league infielder.

But then Gordon Goldsberry also believed that. Just as he too was convinced that, no matter the current wholesale struggling, the '88 Chiefs had more than perhaps the industry mean of three or four real prospects.

And he also was out there teaching in the cold and wet. He spent most of his time at the batting cage. He might be the boss, but the ex–big league first baseman who once played for Rogers Hornsby also happens to be an intuitive yet flexible and, of course, patient instructor. He also enjoys it.

With everybody else slinging defense at Jossy, Mr. Goldsberry instead chose to perhaps let the bewildered young man regain his confidence by taking some of his frustrations out hitting the damn ball instead of fielding it ad nauseam. In short time, with Trace on the mound chunking and yukking encouragement, Jossy was smiling for real for the first time in days as he hammered line drives all over the yard.

On a particularly well-hit liner into right center, Gordon had chuckled and said, "That'll feed your family."

"I did it for eight years . . . just like that!" agreed Jim Tracy. "Tell him, Stevie." And when it was translated, Jossy grinned and nodded and then hit the next one harder.

"Chico . . . cut that out! Jesus, Mary, and Joseph, will you just cut that out!"

"Watch your lips," said John Green as he stood to the side of the cage swinging a bat. He was next in to hit. John Green the pitcher? Correct. Which was why Gordon Goldsberry was soon having even more fun.

For several days now Trace had been letting Greenie hit with the extra men at BP. He had been musing more and more on the fact that the ex-University of Arizona third baseman might just be called on to win a ballgame with a bat instead of only trying to save one with his right arm. With Gordon and everyone else there, it was a good time to run that possibility up the system flagpole. It also could've been construed, of course, as a statement of just exactly how much patience and faith Jim Tracy really did have that the guys who the system had sent here to drive in runs were really going to do it. However, for whatever negligible developmental value there was to it, Gordon Goldsberry, the man who ran that system, had as good a time as everyone else as he watched the young man he'd seen grow up hit the ball pretty damn good.

And then always there was Tony Franklin's authoritative, now almost perpetually scolding voice.

"Don't let me see you get your hands below the waist," Tony Franklin admonished and then hit another fungo toward the center of the diamond.

". . . like a boxer! Then your first move is here, right? No crunched-up first step forward . . . because that's all you can do from that position. At the very least you will have to come *up* . . . before your first move to the ball, see? See how easy this game can be if you'll just let it?"

Then "the Professor" paused in thoughtful deliberation of his metaphor as he flicked idly with his fungo. Suddenly there was a mischievous grin on his face.

"What it is . . . is rhythm!"

At that moment Bob Strickland happened to be passing by on his way to the water fountain at the end of the dugout.

"Strick? Put down your glove and come here. Now don't be embarrassed . . . show me your Ali shuffle."

It took some prodding, but eventually big Bob was bouncing around as best he could in an awkward caricature of the famous Ali footwork.

"See? That's the problem with this ballclub . . . no rhythm! Better stop before you hurt yourself, big man . . . damn, we're just going to have to paint you black," laughed the black instructor.

Then, "Hey, Trace! I've found your problem . . . no rhythm. Maybe these honkies need to be on a dance floor instead of here!"

"No fucking way we should play in this shit!" Gomer Hodge, the Beloit manager, said to the Brewers' hitting instructor Lamar Johnson just loud enough for us all to hear after they'd passed the batting cage with only uncharacteristically terse words of greeting on their way to the third-base dugout.

"Fuck 'em," said Jimmy Piersall.

And then someone asked Pete Vonachen why we were indeed going to play a baseball game under conditions such that nowhere else in the Midwest League would it even have been considered.

"Because we're not pussies! Some of these other owners? They could give a shit . . . they're not baseball people. If the schedule calls for it to be played, and it's even possible, we're gonna play it!"

Then Peter of Peoria looked at all the baseball men standing around the batting cage and added, "God didn't intend for baseball to be played in seven innings."

If that be so, then He proved His point that very evening. Because after seven innings of the last game in the Beloit series the score was still a frigid 0-0. Ollie North, getting a spot start because of the doubleheader in Rockford, had pitched brilliantly through six innings of wind and freezing rain, allowing only four popsicle singles. But he would only have the gratitude of his manager and an ERA that now read 1.20 to show for it. Because it was during Greg Kallevig's two perfect innings that, in the eighth, with Gator at second, Lenny Bell, who'd continued his slumping ways "After Rockford" with a 1-for-9 slate in the first three games at home, "waited for the fucking wind to die down" and then singled hard through the left side for his second hit on the night, driving in the ice-breaking run. Which soon became two. And that was enough for Z's third save with another perfect close, Silent Kal's first win, and the occasion of the 1988 Peoria Chiefs exiting the Southern Division cellar for the first time since the eighth inning of Opening Day!

Hotdiggitydamn! Iowa here we come.

But first we had some dancing to do.

While Tony Franklin might have been jesting when he made his observation about what this team really needed to do, Jim Tracy wasn't at all when he told Mike Nelson and Jeff Reeser:

"You gotta get these boys out . . . after what they been through the last few days? Jeeze'em'tally . . . they gotta be like caged animals! I'm telling ya . . . take 'em out, will ya? Let these kids have a little fun . . .

even if ya gotta show some of the fuckers how to do it! And I don't care what . . . long's they're here when the bus rolls at eight."

Whatever stereotype you might have previously encountered concerning P-Town—forget it. It's a jewel of a city where a good life can be lived, and a good time had.

That night and morning we definitely had the latter. And not too many had to be shown how. It was also interesting to note how much rhythm some folks suddenly develop when they're dancing with something besides a ball and glove.

We'd just crossed the Mississippi into Iowa and Lee Kline had pulled the bus over for a pit stop on our way to Cedar Rapids. It was with ringing grogginess and parade-ground mouths that some of us stood there blinking at a beautiful, real spring morning and heard the Shooter cackle, "We can't play in this! We need to order us up some sleet and cold and shit. You know those 'mudders'? Well, we're colders!"

Then he turned back to the east, across the rise and bluff and river, toward Peoria, and eventually said, "Golly damn . . . I mean, it's tough when you split a series at home and feel like you're glad to get out alive! Isn't it?"

"Damned glad," Kranny corrected.

Then Jim Tracy yukked and turned around and said, "Wait'll youse guys see this yard we're coming to. We're talking baseball here, gentlemen! She's a beauty, fellows. Privilege to play in her, I'ma tell ya. So let's just go up there and get us a couple before we go calling on them Waterloos! Jeez'em'tally, gentlemen . . . we just hold our own on this little trip, and then we got eight straight ones to make up some ground at home."

"We'd better. I wouldn't want to go back if we don't," said Kranny, giving flip voice to the unspeakable dread we all carried within us as he yawned and stretched and headed back to the bus where almost all the ballplayers had chosen continued sleep as a remedy to the sweet poisons of the night rather than a stretch of the legs, fresh air, and a place to piss where the door handle didn't bang you in the ass.

Even though that ringing grogginess was gone at least for the ballplayers, it still perhaps could be all too easy to blame again just those same sweet poisons for the fact that only a few hours later the Peoria Chiefs would be able to manage only two hits, no runs, but twelve strikeouts, and take a 5-zip waxing from the Cedar Rapids Reds to get us off and stumbling into a four-day Iowa "train wreck" which would ensure that the unspeakable soon became an uproar.

But whiskey, women, and song had damn little to do with it. To think so would be a grave disservice to a young man by the name of Mike Moscrey, another pitcher who would be in the big leagues inside a year. With a nasty, dive-bombing slider, a good-moving fastball, and uncanny control, the twenty-year-old Mr. Moscrey "privileged" and bewildered us with a perfect game through seven. It was such a performance that when this gem was broken up cheaply on a chopped slow roller by Bell down the third-base line, with the score already 5-0, even Brett Robinson, our starter and loser, who by that time was sitting in the stands helping with the charts, felt cheated out of witnessing perhaps the game's greatest rarity. All of us were then twice relieved when Mike Boswell—the kid who "shouldn't even be in this league!" except for the fact that Jim Tracy didn't agree and had more than once already saved him from the ax— slammed a legitimate pinch-hit triple in the ninth.

Twice relieved? Well, it could only get better. They sure as hell couldn't have anybody *else* that good. Could they?

"Is Jossy overmatched?" Jim Tracy almost whispers it.

It's another Mark's Big Boy. In a lovely little city with a rushing, babbling river running right through the middle of downtown. Another late-night eat and wake. For whatever the gloom, we are back on the road, on our own, and there is that closeness and unity of real purpose of mission that for this ballclub, because of the phenomenon that is home, can only be felt on the road.

". . . I mean, really? Is he going to hit?" The Shooter is only idly doodling with his food.

"You mean is he going to live long enough to hit?" says the Kran-dog. After a couple of games of discernible improvement on his footwork around the bag, our second baseman was back to peeking at the runner on every pivot, and getting clipped, and worse.

"I mean, is he ever going to do any of it? Christ . . . I keep hearing what everybody says about him, you know." And here Jim Tracy's voice drops even lower as he reflexively glances around him as if the air itself might be wire-tapped. Then he asks the question which is of course the quintessence of what all of this is really only about anyway.

"But I've gotta wonder, is he even good enough to play here . . . much less any higher? I mean . . . does this kid even belong in pro baseball?"

That question is answered by no one. Only a very long silence as now almost everybody can only pick at his food. And it is not just our fondness for a sweet, bewildered kid who only works hard and smiles no matter what. That question speaks too directly to the inevitability of the changes in our family we know have to be coming.

Finally Trace croaks, "Sergio's starting at second tomorrow." Then he goes back to silently pushing little piles of peas together with his fork before looking up again and saying with a stiffened jaw, "And I don't feel bad about Horace not getting any playing time, either. He'd just embarrass himself."

Then Bill "Gabby" Hayes, God love him, breaks the doom as, after eating heartily, he pushes his plate away and says, "Trace, you remember that guy in Midland who used to blow himself up?"

"You mean Captain Dynamite?" And soon the Shooter is yukking and grinning as he and his old teammate regales us till our sides hurt about some "fool who used to get his jollies off traveling around ballparks getting into a box with a bunch of dynamite and blowing himself to kingdom come," and that night in Midland, Texas, when he almost actually did.

"I swear . . . I wanted to hit him. I thought I was going to!"

"Trace . . . I was gonna kill him!"

"Goddam . . . I know, Mule! Why'd you think I told him just to get the fuck out of the ballpark? So I wouldn't hit him . . . and you wouldn't go to jail for murder. Fuck him."

"The fucking idiot!"

We would play only one good game on that road trip. It was a shame we lost it. It's a shame anyone lost such an incredibly suspenseful game. It was, however, a far greater shame that on that night of April 29, upon the occasion of our second game in beautiful old Veterans Stadium, Jim Tracy and Rick Kranitz would have cause to be angrier with a ballplayer than at any other time that season. The ballplayer was Fernando Zarranz. For the next several days, however, by his manager and coach he would be referred to or addressed only as that "fucking idiot!"

Because not only did the Z in him cost the Peoria Chiefs to lose perhaps too much of a heartbreaker to the powerful Cedar Rapids Reds 2 to 1, it also cost him two hundred dollars and a three-day suspension.

"The fucking idiot, if he shows his ass one more time he's *gone!*"

It is also a shame that Fernando had taken his string of seven relief appearances on the season without yet allowing a run with him when Tracy sent him out to hold the pass long enough for us to be able to throw the top of our batting order at them in the top of the fourteenth.

It seems the Reds did have someone else at least as good as Mr. Moscrey. In fact, he would beat Moscrey to the big leagues by some months. His name is Scott Scudder and all he did was strike out fifteen in eight innings before giving a 1-1 ballgame over to a staff that seemed to get better every time they trotted somebody else out at you. But the Chiefs' pitchers had responded in kind, and after Mel had mowed, flinging hard and all over, through seven, striking out eight, and Kal had thrown groundout after groundout for five more scoreless innings, Fernando was summoned in to a real nutcracker of a ballgame.

Z walked the first man he faced. Then, when the next man bunted the first pitch at the same time base umpire Jim Hacker called "Balk," and only a second or two after that trickling bunt popped in and out of Elvin Paulino's glove, Fernando jerked his head around in what-the-fuck amazement a couple of times and then, screaming like an obscene banshee, he charged Mr. Hacker and commenced to thumping him in the chest with his glove!

Jim Tracy literally threw Z off the field. He also had to go deeper into his already overworked bullpen. So overworked that Trace had no one else warmed up and had decided it was Z's game to win or lose. So now with men on first and second and Steve Davis, a dangerous left-hand hitter, up, Trace had to hurriedly get Gabby Rodriguez ready.

"I swear I didn't know it was like an injury . . . I thought he'd only get eight pitches, and I'm pleading with Malone for mercy, you know, and he says, 'Jimmy, he gets all the time he needs.' Goddam . . . if Gabby had only gotten eight pitches and would've gone out there and hurt himself or something . . . I *would've* wrung Z's fucking neck! How the fuck can a veteran like him let his team down that bad . . . tell me! He knew what I had left out there . . . fucking idiot!"

Gabby didn't hurt himself, and Steve Davis for a change didn't hurt us. Gabby struck him out while he was trying to bunt the runners up. Trace then looked at big old Jim Bishop, the Reds' third baseman and clean-up hitter, a right-handed batter, walking to the plate, and with the game on the line knew he had to play the percentages tired bullpen or not, so in comes Greenie. And Mr. Greenjeans had him 1-2 when the big, surly guy, who'd been lipping off since we'd arrived, sent the next pitch off to kick up chalk down the left-field line and we lost.

Bad enough you have to play thirteen innings of that kind of gut-check baseball and it's one o'clock in the morning before you even get on the bus to drive to Waterloo, where you've got a day game in twelve hours after having just suffered the futility of thirty-two strikeouts in two ball-games, but to lose it too? That way?

"The fucking idiot!"

"Hey, he's a prospect in my book," Tracy says of Bill Melvin's performance that night. Then he says, "And what a difference a year makes . . . I've got Eddie and Polly down as prospects now."

He means it, literally, book and all. It's another motel room. It's more paperwork. But now it's not just their daily reports that Jim Tracy, Rick Kranitz, and Bill Hayes are kibbitzing over as they stretch, yawn, and scribble, it's time for the "Monthly Prospect Report."

"Hey, Kranny?" Bill Hayes looks up from the batch of forms he's hunched over at the table by the window and glances to the television screen, where Alan Alda and Ann-Margret are getting involved.

"What?" asks Kranny from the combination desk and dresser where he's working on his batch.

"Do you have Mass as a prospect? I mean, is he a prospect?"

Kranny looks up, and he too watches a moment or two of the movie before saying, "Yeah. He's gotta be. I mean . . . not by the way he threw the other night." Then, "But, yeah . . . you gotta put him down as a prospect."

"Yeah . . . I know I've got to, too. But I can only give him a three on his curveball . . . ?"

The Cubs use a grading scale of ten, with a five being "major league average." In the case of a position player, each of the five "tools" will be so graded. With pitchers, each pitch in their repertoire will get a number.

"Yeah? I only gave him a two," laughs the pitching coach.

"But . . . I'm gonna have to go with threes all across the board!" explained the catching instructor.

"You've gotta go with what you saw," says Kranny.

"Shut that door," says Jim Tracy from the bed where he's stretched out with his batch of forms. "Jesus, Mary, and Joseph . . . with Melendez's room next door, guys be popping in here to say 'Hi, Skip' and then look down to see their name on a prospect report that says, 'Tops—Double A'! I don't need any wholesale resignations. Not yet."

"If we could just score three runs a night we could win some ballgames!" Jim Tracy had said that on the way to Waterloo as he bemoaned the fates of a ballclub that had scored three or fewer runs in fifteen of the twenty-one ballgames played.

"If you want three runs a game out of this bunch, you'd better activate yourself," Kranny had told him.

"Don't think I'm not thinking about it, either!"

"I didn't think you were taking all that BP just because you couldn't hit the fucking idiot."

"Just three fucking runs would do it, I'm telling ya."

Not in Waterloo. It might've even taken more than the Shooter's bat to overcome the sixteen runs the Indians piled on the Chiefs' three during our two days of fun and humiliation in yet another truly lovely Iowa river burg. The two days immediately preceding Richie Zisk's "train wreck" metaphor. However, since it was inevitable, it somehow did not seem so calamitous that first afternoon when Mike Aspray finally had a bad game and got hit hard and we lost 6-1.

So much so that we were soon more than solaced by the fact that we had an evening free in a college town. And that right across from the Holiday Inn—which wasn't actually in Waterloo but in Cedar Falls—was a nightclub called Spinner McGee's, which shortly after sundown was descended upon by the family of the Peoria Chiefs with an abandon that provided for the passing of a decidedly raucous good time, John Green dropping a cigarette and burning the ass end out of my britches as he scrambled to elude the clutches of a husky Amazon bent only on his conquest, and a group of drunks then descending on a still very much awake Jim Tracy doing paperwork at something like three in the A.M., who then happily kept him company until the dawn of a new day bearing a new game.

While that man over there waiting for a bus might think he sees a pattern developing here, any such conclusion is suspect because of the fact that Jeff Massicotte, who partied but little, then proceeded the next afternoon to jackknife us into total train-wreck shock with a performance that would have Kranny seeking to institute negative digits into the Cubs arithmetic.

In fact he was already dressed and had joined the suspended Zarranz and me up in the stands by the top of the third inning, with the good guys already down 7-1, after his fifth start of the season had lasted exactly one inning, during which time he'd given up six hits, walked two, committed four balks, and allowed five runs. However, by the rigid quirks of base-ball scoring, because of the balks and one error, none of the runs was earned. Jeff's already bloated team-high ERA of 6.91 would not be af-fected.

Possibly for that reason, and any myriad others the human brain might employ in its efforts at rationalizing that which is too painful to accept in its obviated form, Jeff was more confused and belligerent than he was despondant.

"So what's the deal, man . . . did you balk?" the Z Man had asked.

"I was talking to Marty, he said I balked . . . so, I don't know, but I guess I probably did."

"It's their thing this year, bro . . . the Commish wants it, so they're going fucking crazy with it, you know. We just gotta adjust, that's all."

"The way they're interpreting the rules, I guess I did balk in their eyes. But, jeez . . . that's how I've always pitched. Suddenly they want to change a rule, and I've gotta change what I've been doing all my life? It's not like I'm trying to deceive the runner. I do it every time!"

"It's a bitch, man . . . lemme tell ya."

"I mean, we're here in the minor leagues to try and work on things to improve ourselves . . . why can't they work with us? Why can't they help us and we'll help them? We're all trying to get to the same place?"

"It ain't fair, bro . . . but it's real."

"Shit . . . we're trying to work on something, and they take us com-pletely out of our rhythm. That's what happened to me. They took me completely out of my rhythm!"

"Hey, man . . . don't take it so tough. You're probably out of the rotation, and you're gonna be back in the bullpen."

"What do you mean? I didn't pitch a bad inning! I had good stuff. I had a good inning. There wasn't a ball hit hard off me. What'd they hit? Maybe only—"

"Mass . . . you gave up six hits, and they were fucking ropes, man."

At that moment Lenny Bell poked his head out from around the corner of the dugout and said, "Z . . . isn't that that girl?"

"What girl?"

"The girl from last night. Down there behind the plate. See, over there?"

"I'll go check it out."

Fernando got up and strolled the small, covered grandstand of Municipal Stadium about as subtly as he does most everything else and was soon back.

"No, man . . . you oughta see that broad. She's got an ass about two feet wide! That's not her . . . that's that girl's been walking up and down here all the time. I'm telling you, that's not her."

"Oh," says Lenny, hanging over the top of the dugout while now Mark North is getting hit hard after also being called for consecutive balks that had caused Kranny to explode out onto the field and, in the rhubarb that followed, found out, with no small insult to his dignity, that only Trace is allowed to go out to chew on umpires without it being considered an official trip to the mound.

Lenny was still looking around the stands in search of faces from the night before who'd made nighttime promises to at least come and see us off, when Mass, who'd been sitting there smarting from Z's bluntly stated dose of reality, now had the opportunity to counter, "So what's your story? What the hell happened to you out there the other night? Huh?"

While Fernando Zarranz might thrive on fooling everyone else, he almost never tries to fool himself. Afterward, at least.

"I just didn't have my stuff, man. I don't know . . . it was like I was out of it, disoriented, you know? I'd been up and down in the bullpen all night. I just didn't feel right. I should've told Trace, but you always think you can do it . . . and then I'm throwing balloons up there! It just didn't feel right. I guess that's why I did it. I just blew up. It was wrong, man. You know what I'm saying? I'm sorry and I gotta pay. But I didn't have my stuff, man. And it was weird . . . like I was someplace else. I didn't have my stuff, bro!"

And what was Lenny Bell doing in the dugout anyway while his teammates were enduring what turned out to be a 10-2 shellacking?

For the first time that year, Ding Dong, after getting suited up, and almost as an afterthought on his way out to loosen up before BP, had stopped to glance at the lineup that had just been posted by Stevie Melendez on the wall of the visitors' clubhouse and saw his name listed down on the bottom under the "extra men" heading. He hadn't done a double take. He had just stared at it for a moment. Then he'd said, "Okay."

He also went out, jumped in there with the extra-men group during that batting practice, and started slamming baseballs all over and out of quaint little Municipal Park.

Jim Tracy had watched his now badly slumping third baseman do this for a while, then he'd said, "I believe he got the message. I left him a wake-up call . . . and he's answering it."

Rick Kranitz was metaphysically opposed in the extreme to the literal translation of the always ambiguous balk rule that the Commissioner had suddenly ordered be enforced for the 1988 season. He was decidedly on the pitcher's side of the controversy that would rage throughout organized baseball for most of the summer.

Therefore, Jeff Massicotte thought he would get a sympathetic response when he used much the same words explaining his performance to his pitching coach that he'd used up in the stands with Z. Wrong.

"Goddammit . . . you'd think you would fucking learn! Give them what they want. Once? Okay. Twice? Three times? Four! They're not going to change. They've proved their fucking point. So how much intelligence does it take to figure out 'come to a stop'? Make a mental note, 'I will come to a stop'! Come hell or high water . . .' "

And when he'd also told Kranny and Trace that he felt he had in fact pitched well except for the balks? Very wrong. At least to say so. Especially at that time.

"Who's he fucking kidding?" barked the Kran-dog.

"No one but himself," said the Shooter, sitting on his stool and in no hurry to do anything, much less get dressed and get on that bus and head back to Peoria with a ballclub now nine games under .500 (7-16).

"And that's a very dangerous thing to do in this game. The one person you'd better not kid . . . not be realistic with is yourself. You can have your dreams, your ambitions . . . but you've gotta know when you're fucking up. When you're horseshit. What it boils down to is personal standards. They've gotta be pretty fucking high if you think you wanna play in the big leagues! Maybe he's just told us his are only 'good enough.' "

Kranny wasn't inclined to be that philosophical at the moment. "Mass is out of there! He won't get back in . . . it might be time for him to go back to Charleston! Castillo? That spot's open *now*, Trace. . . !"

For once Jim Tracy didn't get off the bus first. Instead he sat there in the first seat, aisle right, and stared stonily out the window as he waited for all the ballplayers to get off and file in deadly silence into another all-American budget-priced eatery. Then, only after Stevie Melendez had gone out to assure him that all of them were seated, and that he had indeed been able to secure a table for the "adults" that was completely away from any Chief, did he get off the bus and come inside.

Even then the silence continued. It was Appleton revisited. Only worse. Much worse. We knew what was ahead of us. Peoria. Where we would have to play eight games against the same two clubs that had just swept us. The two teams with the best records in the whole fourteen-team Midwest League against the team with the worst. Where we knew that neither Pete nor the Cubs were going to take it anymore. Where we knew "changes are coming, gentlemen." Where, while waiting for those changes, we knew we would also be the first Chiefs team to have to prove or disprove a much-debated point: would Peoria support a loser?

That we knew all this, and were each in his own way thinking only of these things to the exclusion of war, peace, romance, or sustenance, was perhaps best evidenced by the first words spoken.

"You know, I've been staring at this menu for five minutes and I couldn't tell you a thing on it . . . I haven't read a word," Rick Kranitz had said.

Trace just laid his down, put his elbows on the table, and buried his head in his hands. Then he looked up and said, "Stevie, I know these boys only hit .230 last year . . . but some of them hit the ball *hard*—didn't they?"

The trainer who had been with most of the Chiefs at Geneva in '87 could only shrug and offer, "Sometimes. I guess," and go back to studying his menu. All of this wasn't going to stop Stevie from eating.

After a few more sighs, and long, slow shakes of his head, Jim Tracy announced, "Don't you people be surprised when I put John Green in there to hit."

"We're waiting on it, Trace," said Mario.

"You want to get a message to those guys?" Kranny asked as he nodded toward the ballplayers huddled far on the other side of the partition, eating in the communal solitude of prisoners. "Call early-work BP for tomorrow morning, and just put Greenie's name on the board . . . they'll get the message!"

A little later, only picking at a salad, the Shooter said, almost defiantly, "I've got to believe this team isn't horseshit . . . I've gotta believe! If I give up on them, they'll give up on themselves. And goddammit . . . there's some kids on this team that can play! This is not a bad ballclub!"

And for the first time it sounded like Jim Tracy was trying to convince himself rather than somebody else.

After a while, Kranny said, "Trace . . . there's only one thing really wrong with this ballclub. And now they're finally sending the right guy."

"Yeah, you're right. Harford said the Bat Doctor will be here tomorrow. Maybe he can do something."

He did what he could. And the fact that we were able to win even three of those eight games at home meant that what Richie Zisk did was not inconsiderable. Considering what it was beginning to be evident he had to work with. And under the circumstances.

On the night of the last game of the Beloit series in Peoria, the night we had moved out of last place and then got to stay there for all of a day and a half, the Peoria Chiefs' team batting average had risen to .223, the highest it had been since Opening Day. And that was, of course, *the* problem.

For all of the debated wisdoms which swear that pitching is anywhere from 60 to 160 percent of the game, and that those "nonathletes" are the ones you can never have enough of, it is 100 percent of a certainty that you're not going to win very many games unless you also have at least some folks who can hit the damn thing.

While the Peoria Chiefs' pitching staff would, over the course of the 1988 season, mostly only give the Chicago Cubs' player development people cause for continued belief in the promise of its varying grades of preevaluated potential, there was before, and would continue to be, more than a little doubt that perhaps the scouting department had overevaluated the dubious promise of some nonpotential thumpers.

"Why are we only drafting skinny little kids who can run and maybe hit singles? We play eighty-one games in Wrigley Field, for chrissakes!" Jim Frey had said any number of times, to any number of people, that spring training of 1988.

While that might've been somewhat of a rhetorical simplification, and while not *every* Peoria Chief was skinny and little, we were perhaps far too close to the mold of the banjo-hitting, run, and peck-for-a-base-at-a-time team that the new general manager of the Chicago Cubs had made it very clear he didn't think held any future for "impact" upon the "kind of team I think it takes to win in Wrigley Field."

The Minor League Department, still administered and staffed by men of the recently deposed regime, and headed by a man who held the dual title of Director of Minor Leagues *and* Scouting, Gordon Goldsberry, was of course very much aware of their new boss's public and behind-closed-doors critique of what, after spring training, he *actually* thought was in the much-vaunted Cubs minor league system. Therefore they had gone into the 1988 season with no small vested interest in the offensive productivity of those "skinny little kids" they as an organization had drafted and were now developing. Most particularly was this the case with the lower levels of the system. Where the fruits of the most recent drafts would now have to prove the validity of the methodology of their selective planting. And in the Chicago Cubs system, no minor league team is as visible—or as close—to Wrigley Field as Peoria.

But so far, "We couldn't hit water if we fell out of one of them *big* boats!"

The question, of course, was, would we ever? And it seemed a lot of people were asking it. Seldom has such a fuss been made over hitting a ball with a stick as would be made in the days—and weeks—to come.

It was the fourth night—actually morning—of that eight-game home stand. Mike Aspray, only a few hours before, had given up only two runs but had seen his record go to 1-5 when the Cedar Rapids Reds had burst our two-day soaring balloon with a familiar 4-2 handcuffing. A group of Peoria Chiefs had been lubricating their frustrations back at the apartments they'd finally been able to move into the night we'd returned from Iowa. However, the presence of only two Spirit Girls made for a lopsided mix. Therefore, with a bottle or two of schnapps in hand, and the potential for improving that mix if they could find this place someone had told them about in the neighboring community of Pekin, they'd piled into John Green's "rent-a-wreck" and ventured forth.

They never found Pekin. They were still looking for it when they were stopped by a patrolman in the town of Canton, well south and west of Peoria. This officer of the law looked at John Green's driver's license, then into the car, where Spirit Girls and ballplayers were none too successfully trying to quickly hide all spirits even as theirs were all too obvious, handed Greenie back his license and said, "Look, you guys just be careful, all right?"

"Yes, sir!" said a much-relieved John Green, who only a beat later had cause to start laughing his ass off when the copper had added, "And Jesus . . . get them people to send you some sticks!"

Then, giving up on finding Pekin, and with directions now back to Peoria, they were later standing in the parking lot of one of that city's after-hours downtown watering holes when a couple of vocal local yokels started mouthing off and using the ineptitude of the Chiefs as their focal point. Soon John Green had cause to laugh even harder.

"Hell, I didn't even get to throw a lick!"

He didn't have to. Elvin Paulino laid out the mouthiest one with a single left hook that put him facedown and as still on the pavement as if he been shot in the back of the head with a .45. John then turned and saw Mike Aspray pounding the living daylights out of another.

"Goddam . . . mild-mannered Mike? And I'm telling you, he would've killed that dude if we'd have let him. I think every time he hit that fucker it was for every hit we never get when he needs it!"

While we would indeed have a good laugh over the events of that evening then and in the future, they also perhaps serve to illustrate a period of time when a lot of doubts from within were coming out, and a lot of doubts from without were coming in. And no one, perhaps even the powers that be themselves, understood that better than veteran Mr. Greenjeans himself.

On our very first night back in town, as young Chiefies, at midnight, were sleepily milling about the parking lot outside the Meinen Field clubhouse trying to gather bag, baggage, and transportation to move into apartments they had not even seen yet, John Green, who'd of course been this way before, had leaned back against the car that was already there waiting for him and Z, and Gabby knowing that their place had already been prepared for them by certain young ladies, and was speaking right to the heart of the issue:

". . . frankly, what we've got are some guys here overmatched. Most of 'em. Fact about six out of eight. Or seven out of nine, depending on how you look at it and when. It's okay when you've got three, four, maybe five that are overmatched. Because the other ones will carry them until they can catch up, get a chance to ease up to the level of this league.

But we don't have that. We've got at least seven that are overmatched at this point."

"Yeah, man . . . and the other two are struggling."

An observation: when big leaguers take batting practice, maybe four out of every five swings result in a hard-hit ball; with the minor leaguers, maybe only one or two.

And then there is that *sound*.

It is midmorning of another blazing blue day in Mesa, Arizona. The time of the day when half of the big club comes down from Hohokam to take their batting practice at the minor league complex.

"I'm telling you the secret is in the sound. It's all magic," I had suddenly announced to Richie Zisk as we leaned on the batting cage of diamond #1.

"Think so?" he had said.

With three batting practices going on around us on three different fields, I had said, "Listen."

So we did. And as we did, we had also strolled between the three full diamonds. And being the serious man he is, Richie had pondered it. And every time we heard that very special *thwack!* the Bat Doctor would look to see who had made it and smile. Even when our backs were turned, and sometimes dozens of yards away, we confirmed that you could tell a major league hitter, even a marginal one, from all but only a very few of the 150 or so minor leaguers also present.

"So that solves it," I had said. "It's all in the sound. And if it's magic, you can't teach it. Instead, what you do is go around listening for that sound. Then, when you hear it, sign 'em up and make room for 'em in the big leagues."

"It's that simple, huh?"

"Gotta be, Richie."

"If that's so then I'm out of a job."

"Oh. Forgot about that."

"Also, that sound has to come from somewhere. And the only magic I really believe in is a two-oh count with runners in scoring position. Therefore my job is to take that sound and turn it into—"

Thwack!

"—that one over there. Maybe it is inborn. I don't know. But if it is, then teaching them what I've already learned about what works and what doesn't work can't do any harm."

"Developing natural but raw ability that's *already* there?"

"Maybe. But then you didn't hear the sound some of those over there made when they were over here, now did you?"

"Oh. . . ?"

"Uh-huh."

*   *   *

Pete Vonachen isn't one to stroll and listen. And he isn't big on patience. And the only magic he knows is all black or all white and is only as good or lasts as long as the last victory or the last defeat.

While this manic-depressive herk-'n'-jerk would run the gamut during that home stand, it was decidedly at that point which looks and sounds a whole lot like panic early that first morning of our return from Iowa.

"We've been pooped on!"

Pete had called for a meeting of his staff at eight o'clock that morning. While John Butler, Mike Nelson, and Jeff Reeser sat in the big paneled office waiting to find out what would in fact be the marching orders, they first had to sit through a pacing bombast that would sometimes go from his office, into the business office, into the foyer, and back.

"Shit right on us, is what they did. So, I've called 'em for the last time! *They* can go oh for the rest of the season—I don't give a shit! I ain't talking to anybody again!"

He stops, spins around, and bangs the ticket counter a good lick. Then. "All I know is my contract is up next year! And there are twenty-five other teams that would love to come here!"

Another swipe at the counter and he's back at the door to his office. "Parity! That's all! I understood when they said they were going with the Charleston team—but they promised me parity! They promised they wouldn't stack Winston-Salem!"

Then he tells his daughter Mikie, who's filling in until a new office manager can be hired, "Fax me the stats from Winston-Salem!"

He paces and rants on until he gets the stats.

"Goddam! Those son of a bitches are hitting the shit out of the ball!"

Then he sits down at his desk, suddenly calm as can be, and says, "The gate's gonna be bad," and proceeds to announce he wants immediate cutbacks on stadium personnel, advertising, all expenditures, "cut everywhere!"

Such was the wind in Peter of Peoria's sails that first day.

"This is panic city around here, huh?" Mike Nelson said afterward.

In truth and nothing but, it was a bleak and tense home we came to. There was that feeling of slow death everywhere. And the only sense of optimism was akin to that reserved for a loved one possibly on death's bed but still fighting for life—there's always hope. "Isn't there?"

Jim Tracy was very much aware that Pete had (and despite his vow of only hours before would continue to do so, that very day in fact) been burning up the phone lines to Wrigley Field. Because, usually right afterward, Bill Harford would then call Trace.

The Shooter was torn. A fiercely loyal *and* fiercely competitive man, he wanted to give Pete Vonachen a winning baseball team almost as much as he wanted one himself. But he is also a baseball man.

". . . those kids have been here. At this level. They've done what they can do here. It's time for them to be at Winston-Salem. They earned it. . . .

"And I wish he'd just leave the shit alone . . . get out of it and let me deal with my job and my bosses like it's supposed to be. 'Cause he doesn't understand what he's saying. Or just saying it because he understands and wants it anyway. But there ain't a hell of a lot of help out there Billy and Gordon can send. I mean, goddam . . . they're juggling numbers up there like crazy trying to get us some ballplayers! But don't he know that to really help us they'd have to rape two ballclubs? Both Winston-Salem and Charleston. And I can tell ya, they ain't gonna do that."

One of the first real moments of that bedside, against-all-odds-but-hope optimism, which would soon burst into full-blown euphoria, was that same Monday morning, when perhaps the single most welcome face from spring training walked up to the batting cage and sang out:

"The Bat Doctor is here, gentlemen. There will be an exorcism at home plate in five minutes!"

Then he smiled and added as an aside, "Gotta try something. Maybe a little 'magic'? Get rid of the demon on their back that's been eating up all that *sound*?"

After the short frivolity which ensued, Richie then settled in just to watch and observe for a while.

"Have to diagnose before you try to cure."

But when Jossy was hitting, he had seen something he hadn't understood and wanted to at least probe its perimeters. And while he mostly just encouraged and boostered in pigdin Baseball Spanish whatever Jossy did, he also had quietly let Kranny know to keep moving the ball in and then away.

Because of the one-game benching of Bell and Eddie Williams's on-and-off-again hamstring problem, and most particularly now with Zisk there and James Colborn and Bill Harford due in soon, Jim Tracy had only been able to sit "the prospect" Jossy down for that one game in Cedar Rapids.

Now he watched Zisk working with Jossy for a few minutes and then stepped well back of the cage and said, "Fear factor. You know how after they come inside on him, he's finished? He just wants out of there and then waves at the pitch away?"

"Can that be corrected?"

The Shooter got as solemn as a deacon and even quieter when he answered, "No. And God that's why I hope it's not that." Then a moment later, just as quietly, but in a far different tone, he added, " 'Course, I'd also like to get Boz into the lineup. He's come off the bench and hit the shit out of the ball! He deserves it. A lot of people don't believe in that kid. But I do. A lot like I was, and if Jack Hiatt would've given up on me back in 1978 . . ."

The Bat Doctor's orchestration of a brief ceremony of crossed bats, a spit, and a couple of mumbo-jumbos seemed that first night to have left the voodoo at the plate for the wrong team. Eduardo Caballero, otherwise pitching well, made at least three mistakes that left the ballpark as home runs for the Reds and the Chiefs could barely hit it out of the infield.

So it was after a 6-1 licking and now the second five-game losing streak in a week and a half that Jim Tracy sat in his chair and now not even able to shake his head just stared at the floor and in a voice breaking and cracking with the weight of the words he was finally saying, spoke the unspeakable:

"You know who I'm hurting for the most . . . these kids. They're overmatched . . . and they're just going to keep going out there every night and get their brains kicked in."

Richie Zisk chose to concentrate his initial efforts on the middle of the batting order. So that Tuesday morning, he put all ice-breaking hocuspocus aside and went to work with Wilkins, Bell, and Paulino.

The Bat Doctor saw no mechanical defects in Rick Wilkins's swing that would account for the .210 batting average. It was still that quick, short, compact swing with almost textbook form. What he wanted to do was to get him to use it! To stop watching pitches he could hit, and then swinging at ones he couldn't because he was always behind in the count. So with Rick he only hung on the cage and talked the philosophy of hitting.

"You don't go to the plate saying, 'If he throws me a good pitch, I'm going to hit it.' No, just the opposite. 'I'm going to hit it unless it's a bad pitch.' You're going to hit that little son of a bitch every time—until you know *you* don't want to!"

That theme of "aggressive hitting" would be a point he would preach throughout his stay. To every hitter.

But with Elvin Paulino, while the major league bat speed everybody saw in the fun-loving Dominican's swing was also still there from spring training, Richie saw a bad habit that had creeped back in. He was overstriding.

"Stop . . . now, set up again." As Elvin assumed his stance, Richie Zisk put a ballglove about six inches in front of his right foot. "All right? *Poquito?* Little bit. Pick it up and lay it down." Then he pointed at the glove and said, "If you step on it, you're in some deep shit!"

Polly did the first time, and popped up weakly, cursing. *"Me coño!"* Then he kept his foot behind that glove and started lining shot after shot into both gaps.

"Hold that feeling . . . freeze that memory! Draw yourself a line if you have to! *Sí?"*

Lenny Bell was next. And his problem everybody knew. Except him.

". . . I had you up *here* in spring training, and what'd you do? Only the hottest hitter in camp. But now look at you. Drop the bat . . . just hold it out over the plate and just drop it, let it fall."

When Lenny did so, from the end of the bat to the outside of the plate there were still about three or four uncovered inches.

"Can I draw you any better picture than that? Move on up here." Lenny did, and, of course, banged balls around just like he always does during BP. Unfortunately his average after "Play ball" had now dipped to .247. So while Lenny whaled away, the Bat Doctor reinforced the lesson with a steady stream of batting logic:

"You like the inside pitch . . . you're an inside hitter? So make sure *every* pitch to you is relatively inside. How do you do that? Just like Nettles . . . crowd the fucking plate! Eventually they're going to have to come in there . . . because you've also got the outside covered, and you're forcing them to come to *you,* give you your pitch sooner or later, right?"

Then he turned around and said for all to hear, "And when you get your pitch, hit it hard! Don't look at it, don't foul it off, but hit it hard somewhere. That's the difference between a major league hitter and a minor leaguer, they don't miss a pitcher's mistake!"

It was while Lenny was banging away that Trace and I commented on the irony that everything the Shooter had been saying for weeks was now being repeated almost verbatim by Richie and these guys were taking to it like it was suddenly gospel. There was no coincidence to the fact that what Richie was saying dovetailed with Jim Tracy's methods—he and Richie Zisk almost share the same brain when it comes to the art of hitting.

Richie had thought about our comment. "Damn, you know that just might be part of the problem here!"

The Bat Doctor waited for Lenny to belt a couple more and then he said, "See? Now isn't that what Trace has been telling you all along? If you would've listened then, you wouldn't be out here on my fix-it list. No, you'd still be hitting that .350 and be back in bed with that little squeeze."

Then Richie Zisk called everyone to come in around the plate and pointed at Jim Tracy. "Gentlemen, the Shooter didn't get his nickname because he was handy with a gun or a beaver shoot. He got it because he could flat-out knock the shit out of the ball . . . and what he says about hitting? You take it to the bank."

It was just about then that Pete Vonachen came literally skipping out onto the field with a smile no one had seen on him in too long, danced a jig, and announced:

"We're getting Glenn Sullivan! And then maybe Stevie Hill right after. Damn! I knew this organization wasn't going to let me down . . . let us wither and die on the vine! Hurry this shit up, I'm taking everybody to lunch!"

Jim Tracy had been aware that one combination of player moves being discussed as ways of bolstering the Chiefs had in fact been that of sending Glenn Sullivan, a big, potential power-hitting first baseman, down to us from Winston-Salem, a young man that both Tracy and Pete had lobbied hard to get assigned to Peoria back during spring training. And he also was privy to the fact that it had been determined to give Jossy a little longer, and then if he still didn't come around, that he would be going to Charleston, and that Stevie Hill, Jim Tracy's second baseman at Peoria in '87, who wasn't getting a lot of playing time at Winston-Salem, would then be sent to us. And that in any case, Horace Tucker was history.

What Jim Tracy didn't know was that the deal was done.

"Christ . . . that ain't official," Trace whispered. Then he thought a minute. "Hell, yeah it is . . . and I bet the moment I walk into that office after BP, the phone's gonna ring and it's gonna be Dollar Bill."

He didn't have to wait that long. Only minutes later Big Nellie came running up and said that Bill Harford was on the phone and wanted to talk to him *now*.

As he started to walk to the clubhouse, Jim Tracy said, "I know one thing . . . Jay Loviglio must be steaming down there in Winston-Salem!"

"That's not quite the aggression I meant . . . but goddam you gotta love it, right?" Richie Zisk had said as we watched the fight.

Absotively and posilutely!

You see, that heady pop of glorious remission was in fact made manifest not by a pop at all, but rather by as fine a forearm-shiver as you'll see on any football field, delivered by one John Green, which rearranged the topography of Jim Bishop's face.

Although, truth to tell, the evidence was already there by that time. The aggression Richie had asked to see had started in the first inning with a Rick Wilkins double off the Reds' Mr. Moscrey to drive in the first of the seven runs he gave up in only two and two-thirds innings, which proved yet again that "payback's a bitch." And most of the damage done to that very fine pitcher who had humiliated us only five days before was done by the three Chiefs Richie and Trace had spent the morning working with.

And in further truth to tell, Eddie Williams really shouldn't have tried to bunt on them with a 7-zip lead. But then considering the famine they had gleefully watched us bloat through, one would've thought they would understand that it was not gluttony. They didn't. So in the tradition of the game, they plunked him the next time up. But then baseball tradition also demands tit for tat.

John Green sat out in the bullpen and said, "If Trace puts me in, I know which one I'm going to hit."

"What a question."

So, when starter Brett Robinson, who'd allowed only three hits, started having control problems in the sixth, with no one wanting to even think about blowing a 7-1 lead, and the call had gone out for Greenie, everybody who knew anything looked at his scoresheet and waited.

Which was why in the eighth inning, with big, hot-dog-mouth Jim Bishop at the plate, after Greenie had made him look foolish on a knuckle curve low and away for strike one, and then busted him back high and tight on the next pitch for ball one, Jim Tracy turned to Bill Melvin sitting on the bench next to him in the dugout and said, "Better put your pencil down."

Then when Greenie came back inside again, and the giant third baseman almost jumped out of his spikes in an effort to knock the ball into the cemetery across Nebraska Avenue, but ended just screwing himself into the ground when he came up empty, Jim Tracy had added, "Better put your clipboard down."

But actually then came a moment when it all almost didn't happen. "Goddam . . . I had him set up for the strikeout. And I'm thinking, 'Shit, that's more revenge than hitting him.' So, I'm thinking he's going to be looking for the breaker, and already had my mind made up to come back inside. But then . . ."

Then Bishop spit. Not in his hands for better grip. Not into the dirt for determination. But no, he looked out at Greenie, leaned forward just a little, and spit toward the mound.

"Jesus, Mary, and Joseph . . . put everything down, boys! We're gonna rumble."

It was a good one, too. Not your usual grab-somebody-and-roll-around-trying-to-make-it-look-good-but-for-God's-sakes-don't-get-hurt kind of stomping, snorting baseball brawl. No, from the first lick, this was a street fight—with casualties.

Mr. Bishop's biggest mistake wasn't charging the mound, it was that moment of hesitation brought on by disbelief when he saw John Green drop his glove and start coming to meet him! That moment of hesitation cost him a badly broken nose as Greenie's forearm put an immediate end to his further participation in the battle royal. Which was now widespread. And which of course we won. Decisively. Four of theirs went to the emergency room. We went to celebrate.

"Goddam . . . somebody clipped *me*!" Jim Tracy laughed as he rubbed his jaw, then just beamed. "But how about my Jossy, huh? Jossy the 'Aggressor'! When the umpire started throwing people out and he said, 'Rosario,' I go, 'What?' And he goes, 'He was the aggressor.' Goddam! Jossy? Kranny tells me he was 'Kid Rosario' out there."

It was true. Little Jossy had literally dived into the melee throwing not at all amateurish, and deadly accurate, left and right combinations on anything he saw wearing red. That was not only something to laugh and marvel over, however. It was also something that perhaps was revealing about a mystery and a concern that had reached the highest levels of the system. Which is why, that very night, Jim Tracy had called Bill Harford to tell him they had found something else Jossy wasn't afraid of.

Surely now *this* would be a real corner turned? To a man, we believed it. That next day everything and everyone at Meinen Field had a special glow and buzz.

And leading the cheerleading now was Pete Vonachen. He wasn't even upset when we learned about midafternoon that the Sullivan deal was off for now. There had been some injuries at Winston-Salem the day before, and neither Sullivan nor Hill could be spared at the moment.

Of course one of the reasons Pete Vonachen took that news so well was that it was coupled with the fact that they were instead sending us Pookie Bernstine, a twenty-eight-year-old outfielder who had hit .288 just the year before at Triple A!

"Now . . . see? They really do care about us! I mean, that's sending in the cavalry. Christ, he was on the forty-man roster just last year!" Pete said.

There was one small, yet also quite poignant complication with the for now aborted Sullivan deal. Horace Tucker.

Sure that it was a done deal, Pete, wanting Chiefs fans to understand that everything possible that could be done to give them a winner was being done, had instructed Jeff Reeser to release the details of the move to the press. Including the fact that Horace was being sent back to Mesa for "extended spring training." Phil Theobald had already put it in his "Chiefs Chatter" column, which is distributed at every home game.

But Horace had not been told. Not wanting him to hear it from some fan that evening, Jim Tracy then had to hurry up and call Horace in and give him the talk every manager dreads.

"God love him . . . he understood. I thought I was going to be the one to cry . . . but he knew he was overmatched here, and that down there at least he'll get some at bats . . ."

Jim Tracy was saying that when the phone rang. It was Bill Harford. The move was off. Tucker didn't have to go. Unless Trace wanted him to. Bill would leave the decision entirely up to him.

"Goddam, Billy . . . I just finished giving him the goodbye-and-go-get-'em speech!"

He thought hard, but quickly, and then made up his mind.

"I wouldn't be doing him any good if I kept him. I can't use him, Bill. We know he wasn't ready to come here in the first place. No, let him go on down . . . I'll just go with the three extra men I've got."

And early that next morning we all said goodbye to the first member of the family to leave us.

*　　*　　*

Trace had overheard and understood just enough of a conversation in Spanish for him to cackle, "Jossy . . . you worried I fine you fifty dollars? No. You protect your teammates, I give you fifty dollars!"

Jossy just smiled, basking in his newfound stature. He was Kid Rosario. The hero of "the Fight!"

Bob Strickland is in the cage.

"Hold up a minute," said Richie Zisk. "Now . . . show me your slap shot."

"What?" asked a quite confused Strick.

"You played hockey, right?"

"Yeah . . . but how'd you know that?"

"Never mind. Just take your bat like it's a hockey stick and show me your slap shot."

Feeling quite foolish, and not understanding at all why he was being asked to do so, Bob went ahead and did it.

"Hold it!" Richie had said. "Now look at your hips and your hands. Did they open in sync?"

You could see a light bulb go off in the eyes of Bob Strickland.

"That's your key . . . freeze it and remember it," Richie had said.

The balloon soared higher the next night when Bill Melvin, Greg Kallevig, and Fernando Zarranz held the Reds to two runs on five hits, and Bob "Slap Shot" Strickland rapped a two-run homer that just nicked the right-field foul pole. While it caused quite a fuss, and got Marc Bombard, the manager of the Reds, tossed from the match, it counted all the same, the first dinger by a Chief at home, and we went partying off into that very good night with a 4-2 win, absolutely convinced that the all-but-left-for-dead were not only alive but were world beaters.

And Peter of Peoria's spirits expanded further. As did his generosity.

While hitting was the major emphasis at that time, the balk situation also came in for its share of long hours of "early work."

James Colborn, the Cubs' Coordinator of Minor League Instruction, had particularly liked one of Kranny's pre-warm-up lectures on the subject:

"Stop and let 'em take a picture of you! Say, 'Hey, is that good enough for you?' Pose for a fucking picture. They'll have to see that. If they don't, fuck 'em, and I'll go to war for you. But you gotta give me that stop."

He had not, however, been at all fond of Mike Aspray's pitch selection the following night. The night the balloon burst and those two dudes were left lying on the pavement outside Thumper's.

"What's with all the change-ups?" the former twenty-game winner in the big leagues had turned and asked Richie Zisk.

"Hey, don't look at me. Harford says he wants ten percent change-ups thrown every game."

James Colborn, certainly the only pitcher in the history of major league baseball to have both a no-hitter to his credit and a master's degree in sociology from the University of Edinburgh, Scotland, almost never raises his voice. He did then.

"But that's our job! There has to be some thought behind it! Sure the percentage is right . . . but who is he to tell us how and when to throw it? Where did he ever pitch? That's bullcrap! We're supposed to be teaching situations to these kids . . . not just some random nonsense that fills up a pitching chart to fit his bookkeeping!"

"Don't shout at me—I'm the wrong guy. Talk to him!"

"I will!"

That ballgame wasn't over ten minutes before Pete Vonachen was slamming his briefcase around his office and yelling, "We're over-matched."

This tirade had been occasioned not only by the loss—which is usually enough anyway—but also by the fact that José Cardenal, the hitting instructor for the Cincinnati Reds, had pointed out that at least five of the Cedar Rapids players had been sent back from Double A just to help bolster a team that was strong on pitching, but had appeared in spring training to be in need of offensive support to be competitive in the Midwest League. Mr. Cardenal had meant no harm. In fact he was actually trying to assuage the sting of defeat for an old friend. It had far the opposite effect.

Despite Rick Kranitz's vow to the contrary, Jeff Massicotte would get one more start. James Colborn wasn't ready to give up on his experiment yet.

That yet lasted all of one and a third innings when the Waterloo Indians came in next and gave Mass a nightmare case of *déjà vu:* six runs, four hits, three walks, and one balk, and "He's out of the rotation!"

Quite officially now, as Bill Harford also sat there in squirming, embarrassed bewilderment while whatever wisp left of all that wonderful of only a day and a half ago was now blown away 13-4.

"Come on, Donna . . . I can't take this bullshit anymore!" Pete Vonachen had said in the third inning and gone home and left Harford, Colborn, and Zisk sitting there without even a word of goodbye.

"Was that a subtle hint?" Bill Harford had said as he watched the Chiefs' owner make a show out of storming out of his ballpark while Cubs brass were so visibly present.

"Not so subtle, was it?" answered the Bat Doctor.

"Childish," said James Colborn.

*   *   *

"I'm starting to get hurt in my pride, and I'm starting to get hurt in my pocketbook . . . so you can bet your ass something is about to change around here! They're fucking with the two things I value the most."

Even though we had managed to squeak out a 7-6 win the next night, the very manner in which we had won it now had Pete Vonachen as livid as if we'd lost.

"Goddam . . . send me a player to help and then not play him! What's wrong with sending in a ringer—isn't winning a part of development, too?"

Pookie Bernstine had just won the ballgame with a two-out clutch hit in the bottom of the twelfth inning in his first start as a Peoria Chief. Wonderful. Except that Pete had been told that very same night that Pookie was there as a player/coach—with the emphasis on *coach*. That he was not there to keep some prospect on the bench. But rather to be used sparingly, while he learned the ropes of his second baseball career as the newest member of the Cubs' minor league staff of instructors and coaches.

"I'll be goddamned. Let him go learn to coach at Instructional League. He's here . . . and I want him playing!"

And we wanted the hell out of there. Anywhere but there.

"I told you things could get real ugly, didn't I, Mule?"

"Ugly I can take . . . but this is like sitting on a goddam ticking time bomb or something. You see Billy? I almost feel sorry for him . . . the way he's tiptoeing around."

Bill Harford wasn't the only one. Just about everyone else appeared to walk and speak around Meinen Field now like they were at either a funeral or an execution.

Except Z. Who now had his own radio call-in show.

And the Waterloo Indians. Who knew exactly what a whipping boy is for—to pound on. Which they did. For two more days.

Then, with Pete and staff and family and Boosters Club and even a television crew caravaning with us, we were off to Wrigley Field for a "goddamfuckinghorseshit!" day in our miserable honor.

And then Madison, Wisconsin.

"I never ever thought I'd be glad to be going back to that state. You know how they say everything is relative? That is living and dying proof of it," the Kran-dog had said.

CHAPTER 5

"YOU LIKE THAT swing, Billy?" Jim Frey asked Billy Williams.

"Looks like he could have that power we're looking for," answered the Hall of Fame slugger and Cub immortal who, after surrendering his position of Hitting Instructor over to Richie Zisk the season before, was now serving as Special Player Consultant.

"Yeah . . . but it's a short swing, too. Like that swing a lot," Frey said and then hit the remote control to back up the videotaped scouting report on a college third baseman projected by most in baseball to be a sure first-round pick in the draft coming up in exactly three weeks.

"What do you think about this kid?" Mr. Frey then asked Gordon Goldsberry. "How do we have him?"

The Director of Minor Leagues and Scouting, who'd been perusing a current Peoria Chiefs stat sheet, looked up at the TV screen and said, "High. But not as a third baseman. Good strong arm. Good body. I'd make a catcher out of him."

"Yeah . . . look," Jim Frey said as now the young man on the tape is taking ground balls. "See how his knees come in every time?"

Then, as the tape rolled on to other amateur prospects that the Cubs and the other twenty-five major league teams would soon be deciding whether and at what price to invite into the fraternity of professional baseball, Gordon's thoughts returned to a group already in—and who were now so close at hand.

"What are we going to do with this kid?" he asked Jim Tracy as his fingers stopped at Jeff Massicotte's numbers of 1-5, and ERA of 7.52. "Does he just not like being a starter? Is he happier as a reliever?"

"It looks that way," Jim Tracy said, and then added, "We don't know whether it's just that he's happier relieving . . . but it also has something to do with fear of failure. Whenever he's successful, it then brings out a fear of failure. Colbie got into his head a little bit this last time in. You know that thing about his dad. . . ?"

"Yes," Gordon nodded. Then, far more paternally than just administratively, he furrowed his brow in thought as, with the videotape flickering just over his shoulder, he went back to staring at that stat sheet. Then, "Is the kid a loner?"

"No. Not at all, in fact. Pretty much the opposite," Rick Kranitz told him.

"What about that Castillo kid?" Jim Frey looked up from the TV screen and said, "I like him."

"Going slower now than we'd thought," Gordon answered. "Probably still a month."

That's when Billy Williams grinned and said, "Hell of a rumble you guys had down there, huh, Shooter? That's all we've been hearing about."

"Yeah, Trace!" Jim Frey said forgetting all about the video now as "the Fight" became a blow-by-blow subject of much jocularity and interest, with Jim Tracy beaming and yukking and miming and everybody trying their damnedest to make our visit to Wrigley Field as unpainful as they could by letting us hark back to a moment of conquest rather than dwell on the weeks of vanquishment.

And of course it was Gordon Goldsberry, brandishing the stats sheet, who perceived and then celebrated the most tangible result of "the Fight."

"I know one thing, gentlemen . . . looks like that fight was the best thing for Jossy. It lit a fire under his tail, huh?"

"'Kid Rosario' . . . I'm tellin' ya, Gordie, I believe it did the trick. That Chico is playing some ball!" Jim Tracy yukked just as Bill Harford came by and told us it was time to go downstairs to the Stadium Club for our luncheon.

In truth, everybody treated us far better than we deserved. Which made it all the more embarrassing. But even that could be gotten used to, and was, and almost put aside entirely with everybody so going out of their way to make "Peoria Chiefs Day" at Wrigley Field the reward it had been planned to be anyway, regardless. With all those important folks doing their best, the Peoria Chiefs would have been ingrates of the worst kind if they had not soon started making the best of a bad situation.

Their first-ever visit into the clubhouse they all dreamed of dressing in some day had netted them loot by the armful, given to them by their big league brethren and Yosh Kawano, the ageless equipment manager. Ballgloves. Spikes. Bats. Batting gloves. Warm-up slickers. Half-sleeves. Etc., and everything major league. Zarranz had a boxful. Bill Melvin a shopping bag. Herbie had two bags. Then, clutching all this largess, they had been treated to a gourmet buffet in the plush and exclusive Stadium Club. They had then gone out and sat behind home plate to watch Orel Hershiser pitch against the big club while their manager and owner went up to the press box to be on national TV with Harry Caray. All this for a badly struggling Single A ballclub.

There was, however, another reason the Peoria Chiefs were determined to pass this day as painlessly as they could get away with. This was their first scheduled off day of the season. And if this, the first of only three such days scheduled into a 140-game season in four and a half months, had to be given over to public festivities at a *ballpark,* they, being young men and ballplayers, were not going to let it too radically interfere with the activities normally associated with a day when no ballgame would have to be played.

Which had started as early as seven o'clock that morning when John Green and Fernando Zarranz had seen that the bus had not rolled out of the parking lot at Meinen Field without several cases of contraband beer.

Then there was all that Budweiser out at Wrigley. At a game that went fourteen innings! This very length also occasioned an inevitable dispersal of some of the family.

Which was why, when the game had finally ended with the big club losing, and after Jim Tracy, looking around at the state of some of his Chiefs, and knowing that we had to get into Madison at some kind of decent hour, had thought better of our scheduled visit to some of the famous Cubbie watering holes just outside Wrigley's ivied walls and called for the bus to roll *now,* it couldn't for some time—not until a grinning but nigh on sightless John Green finally came hustling up in his stupor to tell us that Z was "lost, man . . . he's wasted, Trace! Gotta go look for him."

In proof that Greenie was perhaps only fuzzy of eye but not of imagery, while Trace was deciding the wisdom of letting the last person to have seen Z go looking for him in that condition, Fernando appeared and, just muttering Z-isms, staggered his strut to the back of the bus and crashed.

Sometime after midnight, after we'd checked into the Regal 8 Motel across from a big, splashy-looking nightclub called Sergio's, we were mostly all nursing hangovers of various degrees and gathered in foggy groups throughout a Denny's restaurant, trying to get down whatever we could that would make the ache of too much liquid fun, for too many hours, in all that sun, and with all that hoopla, go away.

Jim Tracy was tired and dispirited, but also so much more obviously relaxed now that we were back on the road. He had drunk very little, as usual. Now, as he looked about the restaurant at his ballplayers, and then out across the street at that nightclub, and the city beyond it, the city where the year before, with a winning ballclub, the ulcer that now made him pay dearly for every drink he did take when he felt like he wanted— or needed—one anyway, had hemorrhaged and sent him to the hospital, he was speaking his thoughts on partying ballplayers in general, and John and Z in particular.

"I don't care . . . they're men. And with their ERAs?" (Green, 2.45; Zarranz, 0.68!) "Now maybe if it was up in the fours or something, I might say something. But they can do as they please as long as they pitch like that." Then his voice had trailed off and there was a tightening of his jaw, even as there was a tiny smile, as he was now slowly shaking his head.

We followed his gaze up to the counter, where Jeff Massicotte sat forlornly hunched over his elbows. Looking like death warmed over and then refried after an afternoon spent soaking up the sun and revelry of the notorious "bleacher bum" section of Wrigley Field in an attempt to forget, drown, and bleach his troubles, Jeff had only minutes before been able to rouse himself enough to come on over to the restaurant and because of his pasty, sick-as-a-very-old-dog pallor and shuffle had been immediately greeted by a chorus of "Grandpa!" from his teammates.

So, maybe sick of spirit and sick of stomach, and still buffeted by the wake of the failed "experiment," at least Jeff Massicotte had now been able to regain the nickname he'd had long before he'd been stuck with "Massacre"—in both its connotations. There was comfort in that.

"He really does look like Grandpa from *The Munsters,* doesn't he?" Jim Tracy said as we walked out of a Denny's emptied now of all Chiefs save for Jeff sitting there slumped over and only staring at his eggs.

"Yeah . . . and maybe he won't pitch like it now either," Kranny added as we walked on across the wide avenue toward sleep.

No one went into Sergio's. Not that night.

One of us, however, could not drift off into a much-welcomed numbness after such a day on that seventeenth day "After Rockford" without the rerunning of two pictures across the memory's projector in those last few moments before sleep is there and thoughts are . . .

. . . of twenty-eight-year-old "Pookie" Nehames Bernstine standing apart for a moment right after we'd stepped out into the sunshine of Wrigley Field that morning. Standing apart from the oohs and the ahhs and the jokes and the barbs and the preening and cavorting. Standing apart, his face a hard, distant mask, save for the now glistening eyes seeing both the near and so distant, as he looked around at the ballpark that up until only a month before he had always believed he would play in, but now knew he never would.

. . . of twenty-year-old Rick "the Phenom" Wilkins also standing apart in those moments, and later. And he too took no part in the country-cousin-come-to-see-the-big-house gawking. But his face had been anything but a mask, and his eyes had sparkled for a whole different reason, as with the assuredness of the man-to-the-manor-born he had surveyed all that he believed was sure to be his.

CHAPTER

6

WHATEVER WINNING IS, it's obviously not losing, yet seldom is that otherwise cosmically nebulous distinction between being a "winner" and a "loser" more precisely delineated than in the world of baseball. In fact it is so precise, it uses a number to separate one from the other, .500. This number is so important to both the business and mystique of the game that the digits upward and downward of that number, representing to the nth degree how much one team is one or the other on any given day, are published every given day in the sports pages. Right after the number of wins and losses and *before* the Games Back column.

While this seemingly preferential placement of this number in the major league standings is understood to be but a logical formality, since it's really the Games Back column that holds the daily tale of the tape upon which so much of the national psyche ebbs and flows from April till October, it is very little understood, yet even more logical, and certainly no formality at all that, in the minor leagues, where this number is also published every day, when viewed from the perspective of the player development personnel for the twenty-six big league teams, it is listed exactly in its correct priority. "Playing .500 ball" is *not* just a figure of baseball speech to a major league farm director, his general manager, and the corporate bean counters to whom they both answer. Minor league owners be coddled or be damned.

We make reminder here of the Big Fib syndrome for both the purpose of perspective and as another sneaky way of presenting a good news–bad news oversimplification of perhaps the most pivotal period of the 1988 season for the Peoria Chiefs.

When we'd escaped Peoria and the debris field of the "train wreck" for Madison, Wisconsin, by way of our day at Wrigley on May 10, the Chiefs were eleven games under .500 (10 and 21). Thirty-eight days later, when Rusty Crockett, the last player picked by the Chicago Cubs in that June

138

draft, played his first professional baseball game in Burlington, Iowa, on June 17, the last day of the first half of the split season, sparked his first rally, drove in his first run to make a 4-2 game of it, and then Pookie Bernstine, playing in his 755th professional baseball game, all in the minors, tripled to make a 5-4 victory of it, the Peoria Chiefs were still eleven games under .500 (29 and 40).

In other words, for thirty-eight days, while Pete Vonachen alternately screamed, pouted, gloated, ranted, and then finally even worse, and while the Chicago Cubs went about methodically stirring the organizational pot to find the right mix of "saviors" to send to our rescue, we treaded water. Exactly. Nineteen wins, nineteen losses. We played ".500 baseball."

The bad news was that we were still eleven games under over all. The good news was that when Rusty Crockett started his second professional game the next day, everybody would *technically* be back to 0-0.

While the Chicago Cubs minor league officials might've been able to take some cautious optimism from the fact that they'd apparently stopped the bleeding, we were still far below the organizational "critical" point; and the arbitrary artificiality of the split-season format the Midwest League went to beginning with that season, for the purpose of sustaining fan support with two pennant races, had but mostly only cosmetic developmental value to them, and was factored not at all into their organizational bookkeeping.

Of course it suddenly had a great deal of value to Peter of Peoria. And he hadn't been cautious, or optimistic, about anything long enough during those thirty-eight days to notice whether the bleeding had stopped or not.

To what extent he had factored our treading-water heroics into *his* bookkeeping is best exemplified by the fact that when Rusty Crockett would spark his first winning rally at home, Pete Vonachen would have to watch it from the roof of the toolshed behind the clubhouse. Because three days before that last game of the first half, Pete had either "lost it completely," or only enough to ensure that *his* fans still had reason to come out to the ballyard, and had gone out onto the field and, among a great many other things, had thrown a forearm shiver at an umpire!

Now, while Pete's blow had had none of the pop, nor quite the same intention, as John Green's, it had occasioned a hell of a lot more ruckus, of course. He would be a thousand dollars poorer (and fifty thousand richer because of the publicity) when George Spelius, the president of the Midwest League, researched through the annals of the National Association and the Commissioner's Office and could find only two applicable precedents in the history of organized baseball, split the difference between banishment and a circumstancial slap on the wrist, fined him, and suspended him for twenty days.

Whether he actually lost control or had calculated the effect—and even those of us who should know cannot agree to what degree *both* elements were there, just that they *were* both there—is unknown. But to whatever degree it was the former must in all accuracy be mitigated by the fact that for this manic-depressive, perfectionist workaholic, the 1988 Peoria Chiefs' way of treading water was all just a bit much.

In fact, the Chiefs' way of treading water during those thirty-eight days could be likened to floating on a beach raft with a scotch in one hand and a honey in the other while periodically something dark and nasty from the deep comes up and jerks you down for what always seemed like too long past the last gurgle, only to then instantaneously spit you back up into the sun, the booze, and the babe and you're wondering if it happened at all until you look and see the newest teeth marks.

So if Pete went a little crazy, we rather enjoyed it. At the very least it proved that we *weren't*—because even though we might've wanted to throw a hissy-fit the way he did, we didn't. And at a time when, with all the mind-fuck of either heaven or deep water that such clearly defined streaks of won or lost ballgames by the Chiefs prompt in Peoria and its environs, we were having some rather serious doubts about the reality of it all ourselves. Because, as prophesied by that sage and oversized Puck, Jim Tracy, in Sergio's in Madison, Wisconsin, it was at a time when there was "gonna be blood on the floor!"

And there was blood on the water every time that monster came up and bit us.

By the time the first real "savior" came in a small and unheralded package, we were already well on to being a different team, a different family.

But before we examine what changes those thirty-eight days of spasmodic, yet numerically perfect mediocrity had wrought upon the family, perhaps it is best if we again let Richie Zisk first express what was certainly the most didactic epitaph of that period of time—and indeed, truth to tell now and let the whole cat out of the bag, perhaps upon the entirety of the mystery that is the subject of this inquiry.

He had said it up in Kenosha, Wisconsin, during the high-cotton days of the 7-of-9 string and explosion of forty-seven runs that had instantaneously combusted from the vacuum of the 2-and-6 slow suffocation of twelve runs. It had been that night when he was "getting deep into Dollar Bill's pocket" by picking up via his expense account the tab for a special and most appreciated gesture of a peer-pure, "atta baby" celebratory night of feast and spirits. And it had been only a couple of hours after Bill Melvin had won his second start in a row, four days after he'd first so publicly found and then lost "The Lady in Pink," to even his pitching record, if not yet his love life, to 3-3 and drop his ERA to 2.97 by throwing a no-hitter against the Northern Division defending champions and again powerhouse Kenosha Twins. A "no-fucking-hitter!" that, unfortunately in stupid fact, will forever be recorded as a one-hitter because one adolescent scorekeeper stood his myopic but principled ground against some hard behind-the-scenes lobbying by an impressive array of baseball brain trust (including from the Twins) and called a comedy of errors by Sergio Espinal and Eddie Williams a hit, and would not budge.

Over a platter of walleyed pike and the cackling, yukking din of a relaxed and ebullient Shooter on a roll among comrades and away from the pressures of Pete and Peoria, the Bat Doctor had paused to think about it all and then had said:

"As you're finding out, there's a hell of a lot more to it than just bats and balls and playing the game, huh? I mean, there's so much going on the average fan doesn't understand that it's mind-boggling."

Then he'd listened to Kranny, Bill Hayes, and Trace try to outdo each other in coming up with their best baseball stories having to do with defecation—a most popular pastime among those who at one time or another had to play the National Pastime in places where that bodily function is not always so adequately provided for—and then had returned to his thoughts about it all and had mused:

"Actually kind of mind-boggling to us too, isn't it? If we could just find some way to measure, to reach down inside, and find out what separates a guy with tremendous talent . . . that makes it . . . from the guy with tremendous talent that doesn't . . . Christ, we'd all make a lot of money. You know, if we had something that could screen everybody before they even put a uniform on . . . to see if they have that one intangible they need, but only time and the game will prove they have . . . the ability to *adjust*."

But then as he also pointed out only a little later, as Jim Tracy was then occupied with asking the waitress if *she* could figure out how in the devil a pop fly that had popped in and out of two fielders' gloves could be ruled a base hit:

". . . 'course, it's pretty fucking hard to adjust to much of anything when that monster keeps coming up and biting you in the ass."

How does a ballclub whose team batting average had dipped as low as .194 fully a month and a half into the season, and had never risen above the .217 that it was on the last day of the first half of the split season, play .500 baseball for thirty-eight days while going against the teeth of the best that the Midwest League had to offer? Pitching.

In the spirit of giving top billing only to those who earned it, any examination of who we were and how we got that way on that hotter-than-hot night of June 17 in Burlington, Iowa, must begin with "them fucking nonathletes—and God love every one of 'em . . . except Z, he's getting enough of that from half the dollies in three states. But the fucker's getting the job done, huh?"

He would again that night. In fact the Z Man had gotten his second win of the season, to go with his nine saves and an ERA of 1.36, when he'd made his twenty-third appearance on the season in the bottom of the ninth and blew the Atlanta Braves farmhands away 1-2-3 after Pookie had capped the comeback with his triple to put the good guys ahead.

Nothing new about that, right? Aside from the occasional, inevitable relapses of being "that fucking idiot," Fernando Zarranz, on the diamond, had been mostly doing what the Chicago Cubs had decided they had wanted him to do when, during the last week of spring training, he'd been reassigned—partly upon his own urging, we should note—from the Winston-Salem roster to Peoria's so that he might prove himself in a new role that just might finally get him out of A ball and perhaps beyond—the role of "closer."

However, who Z relieved, and the circumstances, do tell us something.

When "Five-and-two-thirds" Eduardo Caballero didn't even make it to his new nickname after again dominating hitters through four innings of one-hit shutout ball only to have it all blow up on him in a hail of rockets in the fifth and sixth, and Jim Tracy went out to the mound to get the ball and wait with catcher Herbie Andrade for a reliever to face the predominantly right-handed-hitting Burlington Braves, it wasn't John Green or Greg Kallevig they waited on, but lefty Gabby Rodriguez.

That scene leads us back to a time when we looked like sure bets to break the all-time record for batting futility in the Midwest League (.211); and Fernando had Z'd his way back onto Jim Tracy's "I'd better not see him tonight . . . or there really will be some blood on the fucking floor!" list.

John Green was so mad he hadn't even stopped to take a shower. He beat even Herbie out of the clubhouse, and he didn't stop to flirt with the local college girls as Herbie always did and would in only moments. He burst out of the visitors' end of the cinder-block clubhouse at Warner Field in Madison, Wisconsin, took the graveled parking lot outside the mobile home that serves as the administrative offices of the Madison Muskies in those long, head-down strides of his when he's like that, and stormed onto the bus empty of everyone but Mario and me, who at that moment wanted no part of *that* visitors' clubhouse.

"What happened?" he demanded of the universe at large, but of us close-hand as soon as he'd stomped up the steps and seen us sitting there in the same dismayed shock, but far less anger, than he. "You guys were behind the plate—did he just not move fast enough?"

We had nothing more to offer to what he himself had seen. The same thing that all the other ballplayers save one from both teams had seen. The same thing the 204 people who'd come out to chant "Muskie Bait" for eleven excruciating innings on a truly beautiful Wisconsin spring night had seen—the thing that had sent them home "Muskie Clapping" happy indeed when Rick Wilkins, after striking out twice en route to another oh-fer evening, had dropped a swinging third strike on Ozzie Canseco (yes, José's twin brother), chased it only halfheartedly and then only as an afterthought as big, fast Ozzie first started for the dugout in disgust but then beat it for first base safely enough to soon be the winning run as the Oakland As' farm club beat John Green and the helpless Peoria Chiefs 3-2 on our second night back in Wisconsin and our first game after our "off day" at Wrigley Field.

"Goddammit . . . threw him my best pitch, and it was nasty! He swung out of his ass, man . . . out two! But no, there's that big sumbitch on base. Jesus! You know?"

Greenie then stomped on to the back of the bus, where he pounded his fist into a headrest.

"Goddammit! I'm tired of losing like this. I'm just sick of this shit!"

He wasn't the only one. After another deadly-silent ride back to another motel, Jim Tracy was still so beyond words that he couldn't stand up and give his usual instructions and schedule for the night and the next day. Instead he'd just leaned across the aisle and whispered "Four-forty-five bus" to Stevie Melendez. And while the Peoria Chiefs' trainer was relaying—and expanding on—those terse marching orders for the next twenty-four hours in first English and then Spanish, the Shooter exited in a posture of complete dismissal and went straight to his room.

John Green wasn't far behind him. He really *was* sick and tired of "losing like this." So, for well over an hour, he sat in Jim Tracy's room as they quickly came to an agreement on just how sick "everybody" was of losing like that; and then did not disagree completely on what should be done about one of the most obvious reasons that we were losing in "such horseshit ways."

But Jim Tracy wasn't quite ready to take it totally upon himself and bench one of the "hottest fucking prospects—my ass—in the goddam organization!"

Instead, right after Greenie came out and started quietly spreading the word among the family ("Don't be surprised what happens"), Jim Tracy had called the big catcher into his room and read him a "warning riot act."

The Shooter was pissed. Not only had Wilkins's passed ball in the eleventh surely lost the game, the two consecutive passed balls he'd committed in the fifth tied it at 2-2, where it would stay for a while with Hard Luck Mike pitching eight innings of five-hit ball before giving way to Greenie in the ninth on another night when Aspray would have to try and balance the frustration of a 1-and-5 record with the fact that his ERA was now 2.25. So Jim Tracy knew if he couldn't shock the Phenom out of his problems with some finally tough talk, his pitchers were about to do it for him, and not with talk.

"We can't be losing games with passed balls! Bad enough those guys scrap out there on that hill and you sumbitches can't score 'em any runs

. . . but you giving 'em away because you're pouting! You carrying that sick bat of yours with you out there onto the field just ain't gonna get the job done! *You* ain't gettin' the job done. And I heard all these great things about you? People I got a lotta respect for told me you could do it all. A leader, they said. Great defensive catcher. Could hit. Great arm . . . *but!* What I'm seeing? Well, it sure ain't what I've been hearing. Fact is, you ain't shown *me* nothing, pal! And you'd better get this shit together . . . 'cause lemme tell ya something, you may not believe it, but there's a place over there on that bench for your ass too!"

So Rick wouldn't be on the bench the next night when Greg Kallevig would get his first start since his sparkling but so-quiet 3-0 record and otherworldly ERA of 0.84 in eleven appearances out of the bullpen had gotten him moved into Jeff Massicotte's place in the rotation. But Jim Tracy had sent Wilkie at least part of his message. He moved him and his .193 average down from his prized third spot in the order to the fifth.

Rick got the message. But to prove how much he didn't like it— worse still, that he didn't understand it—he'd responded to this public insult to what he truly believed was his God-given dignity and destiny by being even more sullen and sulky than was his norm and pouted his way through another oh-fer night, while Greg Kallevig threw a complete game thing of groundout beauty in his first start in almost a year, only to lose 1-0.

There had been a lot of oh-fers that night, but Rick had twice stranded scarce runners in even scarcer scoring positions, once striking out almost desultorily upon the occasion of getting the hit-and-run sign from Jim Tracy on a 3-2 count! Another message received. Another message misunderstood and therefore responded to in kind—a defiant, why's-everybody-always-picking-on-me kind.

No passed balls, however. But then he really didn't have much opportunity. What's to catch when Greg Kallevig throws a complete game in eighty-four pitches, with only one walk and one strikeout? Think about "them groundouts, will ya?"

Unfortunately, Jim Tracy was also thinking about *all* the ways the Chiefies had for making outs at a time when their facility for doing so was almost uncanny. Because that was the night, with Greg Kallevig's stoic, heroic performance breaking the Shooter's big heart, and the hitters shattering his faith in all that's beneath heaven, when Jim Tracy, the baseball purist, in his desperation, trashed perhaps one of the most sacred "rules" of the game, and by so doing surely displayed the most sterling example of the almost total futility of those first eight dreadful, water-torture days immediately following our visit to Wrigley.

In the eighth inning, with two outs and a 1-0 count on Lenny Bell, his four-hole hitter, Jim Tracy had Phil Hannon try to steal third in the hope against hope that the catcher "would maybe throw the fucker into left field or something! Anything! Just steal a goddam run!" But he didn't.

Phil was out by yesterday. And not long after that Jim Tracy gave one of the strangest bus speeches he would give all year.

Conversationally, and with a practiced casualness, he'd told Lee to turn the light on, stood up, and, in a voice much more like the favorite uncle and not the Dutch one, begun with a question:

"You think youse guys could do me a favor?"

He'd actually waited for a chorus of mostly silent nods and grunts in the perplexed affirmative.

"I want youse guys to go out . . . all of ya, together . . . drink a few beers. Even if it's just soda pop for some of youse. But I want ya to get together, relax, enjoy yourselves . . . *but,* talk some baseball. I want you to take Pookie with you . . . and I want you to ask him some questions. Find out what it takes to be a professional hitter. I can't fault the effort most of youse gives me for two and a half hours out there. If I'd had this much effort last year I'd won the fucking league! And youse guys know what kind of talent I had last year, right?"

He paused again for nods and grunts and now a few words as they realized there didn't look to be a hammer coming behind this soft-glove treatment.

There wasn't. "So go relax . . . together . . . and then don't lose that feeling of togetherness. Because when we break out of this thing that's got ahold of us . . . and we *are* . . . somebody's gonna pay dearly for this frustration we're going through. So go have a good time . . . but I want you talking baseball. Will youse do that for me? Will ya? One-o'clock room call. Four-forty-five bus. Good night, gentlemen."

The Chiefies were only too willing to oblige. And jumping Sergio's was even more jumping that night, as there was a lot of "togetherness" going on. And there had been *some* baseball talked. But as Pookie said at one point before he too just started relaxing and having a good time, "Some of these guys just don't know enough to ask questions about . . . and some of the others think they know too much to learn anything from a guy they just saw get released in spring training, you know?" Then he dismissed the bitterness he still was wrestling with over the so recent end to his once so promising career and turned his attention to the particular bit of "fun" going on at that moment in Sergio's.

Sergio Espinal, thinking it only proper since they'd appropriated his name for their establishment, managed to sweet talk a pretty young thing into rigging the drawing for a $450 leather jacket so that his buddy Lenny Bell would win it. She was willing in her complicity, just wrong in her understanding of her instructions. Marty Rivero got the coat.

And Greenie and Fernando got the girls. Of course, there was nothing unusual about that. And it wouldn't have been an issue at all if one of the young ladies hadn't locked her keys in her car. But because she did, at a little before four in the morning, everybody in the wing of the motel where the Chiefs' rooms were was awakened by Z banging on the door to his and Greenie's room as he tried to explain the urgency of his problem while John was having none at all with his. Then we were treated to the ensuing Keystone Cops routine and commotion that went back and forth in the corridor for the next several minutes as John Green and Fernando Zarranz, both well past their four sheets to the wind, and two young ladies, one amorously interrupted and wanting to get back to it, the other frantic, went about trying to keep everything as quiet as possible—even of course as it got hilariously louder—as they tried various attempts to solve the several problems at hand. Eventually all was solved, after a fashion, and everybody went back to sleep.

As something of the further measure of Jim Tracy's attitude toward ballplayers "just being ballplayers" as long as "they're getting the job done," and as another profound statement on the utter futility of those days when the Chiefs were averaging 1.33 runs a game, the Shooter's sudden announcement over the last of the remains from another long breakfast that midmorning was both revealing and not surprising.

"I'm going to DH Greenie. Not maybe . . . going to!" Then, with a wink and a smile, "'Course, think I'd better wait until tomorrow."

He said that about ten o'clock. A little less than two hours later he got a phone call from Bill Harford. A few minutes after that, he called John Green's room, woke him up, and told him he wanted to see him.

"Aw shit, man! I knew I was in trouble . . . I knew Trace heard all that shit. I knew he knew I was boning this chick at four in the morning . . . and here it comes. Right? Fine city and big-time lecture."

Jim Tracy saw that look on Greenie's face when he walked into the room, so he played along.

"You guys think I'm deaf! That was you out in the hall at four in the morning, wasn't it?"

"Jesus . . . it was the fucking keys, Trace. I was in my room before . . . but yeah, it was me. But, Skip, I ain't got the fifty bucks . . ."

That's when the Shooter had smiled and said, "Guess you'll just have to owe it to me. . . . Greenie, you're going to Pittsfield!"

Within minutes of that stunning news, and the news that he had to leave *now,* pandemonium broke out in John Green's room as every member of the Chiefs poured in to share in his found-money fortune while he, in a state of hungover, delirious joy, accepted all the backslapping and whoops and hollers while also trying to quickly pack his one small bag, and decide with his roommate Fernando what they were going to do about such things as all his stuff being back in Peoria, the lease on the apartment, the rent-a-wreck, utility deposits, mail, all the things that one has to think about when one has to move across-country, except you aren't home when you have to do it; they even discussed who would get possession of his blond Spirit Girl.

But mostly the talk was about going to "Double Fucking A!"

". . . last year it looked like light-years away! You know? I always thought if I could pitch Double A, I might pitch in the big leagues! So. . . ? If I go up there and do well? You never know, you know . . . you just never know!

"I always wanted to pitch at least Double A. That was my goal I set this off-season . . . to get to Double A. And then evaluate everything from there, you know? To go on or not."

"You're going *up* is where you're going!" pointed out Jeff Massicotte, who was indeed happy for John Green, but also not unmindful of the fact that he would now be *the* right-hand setup man out of the bullpen. "Whohoo, what a question! And you're gonna get plenty innings now, Mass. Give 'em hell . . . you can do it, you hear?"

"But what's the deal?" Rick Wilkins then had to ask along with his congratulations. "Injuries up there, huh?"

And there had been. That's why the break for Greenie, and the rush. Greenie knew this, so he looked up and smiled and said, "I don't care . . . just give me the ball."

Then he was gone. Within two hours of the first phone call—there would be a flurry, it's not easy to arrange on a moment's notice how one is to fly from Madison, Wisconsin, to New Britain, Connecticut, but that's just one of Stevie Melendez's many jobs—and with twenty-five dollars scraped together, and his last bummed pack of cigarettes, and that one bag, Mr. Greenjeans had gotten on one of those small commuter prop-jets and flown away from the family.

While there is a quite tangible, engulfing joy—however bittersweet—which betakes a low minor league baseball team when a very popular and much respected ballplayer gets whisked by the Baseball Gods into that rarefied air of the land of the multiple A's where the next phone call can get you to the promised land, and while Jim Tracy took perhaps more delight than anyone in seeing "Greenie get his shot," the very circumstances of that joy we were suddenly awash in occasioned the Shooter to also have to belay some of it long enough to perform a task much less pleasant. He had to explain to Greg Kallevig why the news wasn't for him.

John Green and Greg Kallevig had come into the organization at the same time, on the same team. They had both started their professional careers at Wytheville in 1985. They were both twenty-four, in their fourth year of pro ball, and seeing their third stint at Peoria. On the day that Green was called up, these two men, whose careers had been so closely parallel, had these comparative stats: Green—0-1, 2.18, no saves, 13 appearances, 20 innings pitched, 21 hits, 5 earned runs, 6 BB, all out of the bullpen; Kallevig—3-1, 0.90, no saves, one game started, one complete game, 40 innings pitched, 27 hits, 4 runs allowed earned or unearned, 6 BB.

Greenie's numbers were fine indeed, right? But Silent Kal's! Now you understand Jim Tracy's dilemma that day when he had to tell Greg Kallevig *something*. When in doubt, Jim Tracy is always more comfortable with the truth.

"No doubt about it, on numbers alone, and on the reports we send in, it should've been you. But this is your option year. It's more important for you—and the organization—that you get innings pitched. And that you put up some big numbers. For Greenie? It's now or never. They needed a quick Band-Aid up there, that's all. So this is his one shot. If he doesn't do it, then it's the slide down the ladder. You didn't want this shot, Greg. Too risky. You do it here!"

Now, after all that dawn's comedy, midday jubilation, and truth-telling, we of course had a ballgame to play. And on such a day we were damned and determined that we would not have to suffer the ignominy of our *third* five-game losing streak in exactly twenty-one days.

Jim Tracy still wasn't quite ready to bench Rick Wilkins. He just batted him fifth again. Rick pouted more, had another oh-fer night, and again stranded two runners in scoring position. But it looked like it wasn't going to matter. With Eduardo actually getting into the seventh with his dominating act before faltering, and Jeff Massicotte coming on for his second strong relief appearance, and "Kid Rosario"—still streaking in the flush of his "Agressor" rebirth—getting two hits and scoring twice, and big Bob Strickland a clutch triple, our feast of seven hits had us a 4-1 lead in the bottom of the ninth when Fernando Zarranz took *his* hangover to the mound.

And suddenly those runners Wilkins didn't drive in meant a lot as we lost 5-4 and then it was shock. And for the first time real tears. Professional baseball players sat in a professional dugout and cried after Rick Wilkins lost another swinging third strike on a big breaker delivered down and away from Gabby Rodriguez for what would have been the third out as the winning run skipped across the plate while the big catcher, who along with Fernando Zarranz was the only other ballplayer without tears in his eyes that night, gave late and flagging chase.

While the Shooter had a moment there when the glistening in his shell-shocked eyes was also the stuff of tears, it was only a moment and then there was only the fire. That night when he'd again only been up to leaning across the aisle to whisper the orders of the day to Stevie in a rock-hard rasp, the message was just a little longer than the time before.

"*We're* gonna go drink some cocktails tonight . . . and if I see one of the son of a bitches in a bar, I'm gonna pinch their fucking heads off!" Then he'd gotten up, taken a disgusted sweep-look back at the dark and silent bus, and added just before stomping off, "Tell 'em! Exactly the way I said it." And Stevie did. In both English and Spanish.

Jim Tracy had not raged over Rick Wilkins's performance that night when the "adults" did have Sergio's to themselves. It was just the same old bad news. Bad news that was quickly dismissed with a decision he'd been delaying having to make. "Well, he sits. Jeez'em'tally, though . . . will those phone lines be buzzing from Jacksonville, huh? Mama and Papa Wilkins will turn that van around and be in Peoria by the time we get back! He's probably on the phone with 'em right now . . . and how does somebody tell them that they're part of the problem to begin with?"

"I don't know, but somebody better," Kranny had replied before chugging down a beer, slamming it back on the table, and then, by muttering the one-letter curse word for the night, "Z," returning the conversation to the subject that was their rage that late evening when Jim Tracy, with two-fisted company, *did* pour some alcohol on that ulcer and torment of his.

The man who only twenty-four hours before had told his ballclub to "go out, relax, enjoy yourself" was now fuming. "For twelve goddam appearances he goes out there popping ninety with his fastball . . . and tonight? He can't throw eighty? Can't throw fucking strikes? Worst fucking performance I've seen by a fucking pitcher in my whole fucking life! Because he's out all hours of the fucking night chasing goddam pussy! Drunk! And then he lies to me! 'Wasn't me, Skip'! Everyfuckingbody heard it. John Green was man enough to admit it! And this son of a bitch lies to me! Oh, goddam . . . I'm tellin' ya, Kranny, I see him—or anybody else—out tonight, there will be blood on the floor."

That graphic refrain of wrath at everything and everyone that might be even remotely perceived as being responsible for all of the inexplicable torment which Jim Tracy was now all but convinced was a curse would not be abated by the fact that we won the next night with Rick Wilkins on the bench for "the first time in my life, man! You understand? And it stinks!"

There is little to bolster the spirits about a ballgame won 2-1 in the eleventh on a balk. Not unless you're Jeff Massicotte, who got the win by pitching four strong innings in relief of Brett Robinson, for his third good outing since being sent back to the bullpen. Nor did it lessen much the following night when, on our first night back at home for a four-game home stand with the Clinton Giants, Jeff "Grandpa" Massicotte got his second win out of the bullpen. Even though there was not a little satisfaction for Trace and Kranny in how we won that particular game.

Bill Melvin, without his best fastball, had still been able to pitch nine complete innings of seven-hit baseball against a ballclub that was leading the league with a .263 team batting average, had the second-best record in both divisions, and was only one game back of the Southern Division leaders, the Cedar Rapids Reds. It was unfortunate that the score was 2-2 after one earned, and one unearned run was the only result of that first really "pitcherly" performance by Billy Mel. But then the Kran-dog's once again favorite reclamation project, Jeff Massicotte, had pitched a flawless bottom of the tenth after we'd taken a 3-2 lead in the top of the frame. And how did that happen? And why was Jim Tracy shaking his head in a very personal sense of teacherly satisfaction? Rick Wilkins, who had surprised almost all of us by coming out that next afternoon at Meinen Field a much-chastened, humbler young man, the pouting and sullenness gone with the night and his thoughts even before he saw his name penciled in in the clean-up spot, put his 0-for-21 slump behind him, drove in the first run of the game with a double in the first, and then, with two outs in the tenth and Eddie Williams at third, hit the first pitch he saw hard through the right side and the Chiefs won.

Twenty-six days after Silent Kal's first start, while we were again on the road, but at a much happier time, another phone call came from Bill Harford and we had to hurry up and get him to an airplane for another joyous, sudden, though not unexpected goodbye.

Greg Kallevig had taken Jim Tracy's truth to heart in his characteristically silent, studious, stoic, yet so gentle and selfless way and then had proceeded to post by at least thrice the best numbers of his four-year journeyman career.

Drafted out of South Dakota State as the Cubs eleventh pick in the '85 June draft, he had been used almost exclusively as a starter in his first two professional seasons—Wytheville in '85, Peoria in '86—with decidedly mixed results. He'd always exhibited excellent control, but without overpowering stuff, his hits-to-innings-pitched ratio had always been high, accounting for the 6-7, 3.81, 5-9, 4.53 records he'd posted respectively. In '87 he'd been moved to the bullpen and had started the year at Winston-Salem. After twenty-seven appearances, and a 5.17 ERA, he'd been shipped back to Peoria. There, under the encouragement of Jim Tracy, and the tutelage of then Peoria pitching coach, Joe Housey, he'd begun to find some success throwing a "heavy" sinking slider and, while again his hits-to-innings-pitched ratio was too high, had improved his numbers to 3-1, 3.28 in ten games, four as a starter. That improvement, however, had not impressed enough people within the Cubs organization to keep Greg Kallevig's name off the "bubble list" during spring training 1988.

The Chicago Cubs have an almost Athenian democracy about player releases during the spring. At least three times during those three and a half weeks of minor league spring training, the entire Minor League Department will gather in front of a big white Magic Marker board with a list of names under consideration to be released. That is the bubble list. One at a time each of those names is brought up for open discussion, then a vote. Every person has one equal vote, from Gordon Goldsberry and Bill Harford through every manager, coach, and instructor in the system. And if only one person votes no—or as it's more often phrased, "I'll take him. He can play for me"—then that name is moved to the other side of the board to be voted on again at the time of the next "cut day," when again just one vote will get that player's name moved to the right side of that board. Greg Kallevig survived every one of those bubble sessions. Jim Tracy had seen to that.

Which was why the Shooter took no small measure of satisfaction in the fact that Greg, in his next five starts, pitching for *that* ballclub, would win three, lose one, get one no-decision, and throw another complete game, while bringing his season record to 6-2 with a league-leading ERA of 1.25.

He'd gotten his sixth win on June 6, in Cedar Rapids, over the division- and league-leading Reds. In the true tradition of a "stopper," it had been a big win. After almost a solid month of commuters, we were off for three nights and four days into our favorite slice of the Midwest League circuit, Cedar Rapids, and Waterloo, Iowa—just in time, too.

We'd just been through a 2-and-7 monster-jerking, which had ended the day before with us being swept in a two-game series with Springfield. The series was decided in the first game when, with the Chiefs down 2-1 in the ninth, with one out and Pookie, who can still flat-ass run, at third, and the count 3-0 on Rick Wilkins, Springfield manager Mark DeJohn brought in a lefty with nothing but a big old roundhouse American Legion curveball, and Rick, who only needed to just put the ball in play and Pookie would score, didn't even take his bat off his shoulder as three of the most perfect rainbows arced across the middle of the plate. Moments later, after Lenny Bell had at least gone down like a warrior with his blade hacking, Jim Tracy had stood in the third base coaching box like a Rodin sculpture for a full minute and then had spun on his heels and walked away, and the silent treatment was there to stay for a while.

While Jim Tracy, staying as true to his vow as he could, tried his damnedest not to display any public approval to his ballplayers, his resolve was sorely tested when suddenly and mysteriously, the very next day, we started playing a little Dr. Longball. Greg Kallevig, without his best slider, went seven and then turned a 4-3 lead over to Massicotte. "Grandpa" held them for an inning and a third, Z slammed the hammer, and we beat the powerful Reds in their own beautiful Veterans Memorial Stadium, truly the perfectly preserved Queen Dowager of Midwest League ballparks.

And when Eduardo Caballero went a full nine innings the next night, throwing a four-hit shutout—the first time in sixty games the 40-and-20 Reds had been shut out that season—with Rick Wilkins *and* little "Gator" Arrington getting into the longball act, and we waved a 4-zip score and a broom on our way to Waterloo, Jim Tracy had to admit, "Goddam . . . if you can't get a little excited over that, then you're dead!"

And damned if we didn't go on to beat the second-place Indians the next night, take three out of four on that trip into "groupie paradise"— all those colleges in Iowa? And not a hell of a lot to do in the heat and worst drought since the dust bowl years?—and end the first half of the split season with an 8-and-4 run that had started the night Greg Kallevig had won his sixth game.

What was amazing about that string—and what would also cause the fuss that had already been bubbling at a high boil to soon erupt into an explosion that would be heard throughout the world of organized baseball—was that after that game we had to do it without Silent "Superman" Kal, who "really does look like Clark Kent, don't he?"

Not thirty-six hours after Greg had gotten us off and running on another of our schizoid percs after another plunging jerk, on the morning of June 8, there was another flurry of phone calls, all precipitated by the first one from Bill Harford.

Situation, Chicago Cubs Minor League Department: Shawn Boskie and John Berringer, two right-handed pitchers, were out of the Winston-Salem rotation because of injuries at the same time.

Solution: Joe Kraemer, left-handed pitcher, who was struggling a bit at Triple A Iowa, would be sent down to Double A Pittsfield. John Green— who hadn't been given much of a shot at all by Double A manager "He can't play for me and get me another one yesterday!" Jim Essian, but enough for him to look at Greenie's 5.51 ERA in sixteen innings over six appearances and stoop to his trademark bellowing—would go down to Winston-Salem. Bill Kazmierczak, right-handed pitcher, who had been making a mockery of Carolina League hitters, would be sent up to Pittsfield. Greg Kallevig would be sent up from Peoria to Winston-Salem. And to be sent to Peoria. . . ?

"Nuh-uh, tell him I don't want anybody else. I'll just go with the nine I got," Jim Tracy had said with a tense bark and a disgusted wave of his hand at Kranny, who was on the phone the third time Bill Harford called that morning.

"Hell, I've been going with nine anyway!" the Shooter had added as he spit his dip into the cup on the dresser like he wanted to knock the Styrofoam bottom out of it and then muttered John Gardner's name. In the twenty-four days since the Cubs had sent Mr. Gardner up from Charleston to replace John Green, he had pitched exactly three innings. He had, in fact, just the night before, in a somewhat stormy session, requested to be sent to Geneva if Tracy wasn't going to pitch him. Jim Tracy had said he'd be more than happy to pass that word up the system. That word was passed along, but also put on hold the very next day when the system was too busy making moves which meant that at least numerically, if not in participatory fact, John Gardner would remain a Peoria Chief for a while longer.

Situation, Peoria Chiefs Professional Baseball Club, Inc.: a struggling 24-and-36 ballclub that, in the words of its owner, was "the laughingstock of Peoria! And that means I am! And that means somebody's gonna pay!" was losing its number-one pitcher, the league ERA leader, the only

Chief who was a cinch to be named to the All-Star Game coming up next month. And this ballplayer was going to Winston-Salem, not Pittsfield. Of course, Winston-Salem is not "up" to Peter of Peoria! That it all surely could only be a conspiracy of betrayal and a total injustice to the "crown jewel of the organization—that's what they tell me and then stick a knife in my back!" was even more infuriatingly proved to Pete Vonachen by the fact that Winston-Salem was only two games back in a race for the first half title in the Carolina League. "Oh! It's okay to win for 'development's sake' for an absentee owner with a fucking new toy— but not for me! With all I've done for the no-good bastards!"

Solution: none but rage and more phone calls to Harry Caray.

As soon as Jim Tracy had hung up the phone after Bill Harford's first call that morning of June 8, he'd shaken his big head hard a couple of times, pushed his glasses back up on his nose, put in a load of dip, and said, "Jesus, Mary, and Joseph . . . can you hear Pete screaming when he hears this, huh? Good thing he's in Florida. Give me time to buy some ear plugs. I mean, how am I gonna explain *this* to him? Goddam . . . he just doesn't understand!"

And he still wouldn't about ten minutes later, when Jim Tracy, sans ear plug, had to try and explain it to "the Boss" even before he'd had the chance to explain it to Greg Kallevig, because of course there are telephones in Florida too.

Trace was not a little torn himself, however. And was himself not thrilled, or even in total agreement with the system's solution to the problem in Winston-Salem. He had in fact fretted throughout Kal's run about the eventuality of the Cubs moving him up. But he is a baseball man and an organization man, so he gave a straight, methodical, however terse party-line delineation of the situation and then held the phone away from his ear and let Pete rant for a while before saying, "Boss . . . we gotta get Kal on an airplane. You take Donna on a boat ride and we'll see you in a couple of days," and then hung up the phone.

This was a Wednesday morning. They needed Kallevig to start Friday night for Winston-Salem. Therefore, along with the bustle of arranging to get a ballplayer out of Waterloo, Iowa, to Roanoke, Virginia, where he would meet up with the Spirits, there was also the matter of getting his normal second-day-after-a-start throwing on the side in. So while Stevie Melendez went into his frenetic but efficient act, Kal and Kranny had to hustle out to Municipal Stadium early to get the "side work" done.

That's why when the rest of the Peoria Chiefs had arrived at the visitors' clubhouse that afternoon, Silent Kal was already back in his civvies, bag in hand, hoping to get away before what was sure to be an embarrassingly emotional scene of farewell. But Kranny had held him back with a few more words of encouragement partly because he knew that team goodbyes are a ritual that must take place.

Because it was the quiet, gentle giant who reads Vonnegut but doesn't swear, smoke, drink, or have any eyes but those for his fiancée, Rene, a student nurse back in Peoria, the goodbye for Greg Kallevig did not have the raucous pandemonium of John Green's promotion. But in many ways it was more touching and more sincere. It was over quickly. A handshake all around. The big guy nodding, and smiling, and shuffling his feet as he aw-shucksed his way over to the door.

It was Phil Hannon who then phrased the essence of that goodbye, and what, given Greg's history with Peoria—this was actually his *fourth* base-ball season in Peoria; he'd played for the Peoria Pacers of the Central Illinois Collegiate League the summer before he'd signed with the Cubs—was uppermost in everyone's mind, not the least of which Greg's:

"Hey, Kal . . . no offense, but don't come back! We don't want to see that ugly face until spring training."

That was picked up by all, and it was to a chorus of "Don't come back, no offense" that Silent Kal waved one last time and walked out of the clubhouse.

Greg had made this trip before. It was not like John Green jumping to "Dubs." While he was happy for "another shot at a step up the ladder," he had his reservations.

"I just hope they use me. I'm in a rhythm. Everything is working for me right now. All my pitches. I hate to break that. And with Rene about to graduate. To pick up and leave everything right now? But it's baseball. They want me there. I go. I just hope they give me a chance to stick."

With that, and a copy of *Slaughterhouse Five* under his arm, Greg Kal-levig boarded another small prop-jet to begin the first leg of a zig-zag-zig flight schedule that would eventually land him back in "high" Single A.

So we're back to that scene at the mound in Burlington, Iowa, the last game of the first half of the split season, where Jim Tracy and Herbie Andrade are waiting on Gabby Rodriguez to come face Rich Casarotti, the Braves' second baseman, with two men on and one out and us al-ready down 2-1 in the bottom of the sixth. But why isn't it Jeff Massicotte they're waiting on?

Since that morning back in Jim Frey's office when Gordon Goldsberry had looked at Jeff's stats and wondered, "What are we going to do with this kid? Does he just not like being a starter?" "Grandpa" had gone a long way toward proving the point he'd tried to make all along.

On that day his record had been 1-5, with an ERA of 7.52. Eighteen appearances out of the bullpen later, pitching mop-up, middle, and long relief, his record was 6-6 and he'd whittled that mountainous ERA down to 4.08. In those thirty-eight days, he had worked his way from a finger-in-the-dike, batter-or-two blowout Band-Aid role to being the workhorse of the bullpen.

In the five days prior to the last game of the first half of the split season, Jeff had made three appearances, pitched eight shutout innings of gut-check baseball, and won three ballgames. *He* wasn't coming out because Jim Tracy didn't want to perhaps "Jesus, Mary, and Joseph, blow the kid's arm *out* . . . not after my Mule's done worked miracles and the kid's got a career again!"

While Jeff "I tried to tell 'em, but they wouldn't listen!" Massicotte felt he had proved his point on "their fucking experiment," the Chicago Cubs, and particularly Jim Colborn, saw it from a different perspective. In fact, to Jim Colborn, the experiment had succeeded exactly as planned.

"He had to go through that. But now he's exactly where we'd wanted him to be. He got a lot of work early . . . and we'd pretty much projected that for him. The breakdown. But he had to fall apart before we could fix him. Sure, it hurt him inside. But it helped him as a pitcher because we were able to get him to work on some mechanical problems that, though he'd been successful in rookie ball, we believed would prevent him from playing higher baseball."

Whatever. At least everybody agreed on one thing: Jeff Massicotte was right where he belonged and doing fine. "For now," Jim Colborn had added, understanding full well that just "mechanics" had not been all of Jeff's problems.

Sitting among the scouts who outnumbered the fans in the small section of box seats behind home plate in all but dilapidated Community Field in godforsakenly forlorn Burlington, Iowa, watching that seemingly routine scene unfold out at the mound in the bottom of the sixth inning that evening of June 17, were three young men who knew it to be anything but routine. In fact, Bill Melvin and Brett Robinson had put down their clipboards and pencils, and Mike Aspray his hot dog, and had themselves remarked upon the significance of what it had meant.

Mike Aspray had finished his between-starts pitching on the side, and with the heat and the unimaginable grind of *everyday* life in the minor leagues—where a "travel day" is just another two-hour bus ride and then a game and then a two-hour bus ride home (that's a commuter, and also only $5.50 meal money), or a four-to-six-hour bus ride and a game and then a motel just in time to get up, talk about it, and then do it again— had showered early and had come up to catch whatever breeze there was and help Brett and Bill with the pitching and game charts, and eat, and look at girls, and talk baseball. (When we weren't sneaking glances at and marvel-talking about the "Lady in Pink," who was no girl, but indeed all lady, and was sitting just around the corner of the fenced backstop, on the first-base side, and who by this time was *the* talk of our small world.)

Mike Aspray's song of thirty-eight days, while a tune of unjust woe, needed few words, and was sung in the abbreviated language of shrugs and old clichés with which one acknowledges an as yet unaccepted but nonetheless unquestionable fact. "Hard Luck Mike" was the title of that discordant melody.

Aspray, a nondrafted free agent, had been signed for less than a song out of California State University–Dominguez Hills. And even though this unheralded "roster filler" had already surprised everybody but Gene Handley, the scout who had signed him, by going 6-0, 2.45, pitching almost exclusively from the bullpen at Geneva in '87, his first half-summer of pro ball, as a starter now, pitching in a league loaded with number-one draft choices and hitters with as much as five and six years of professional experience, for a "pitcher without the hammer," his 3.34 ERA had the Cubs minor league officials now believing that perhaps they might've stolen a song that just might pitch its way into some higher baseball, possibly all the way.

Unfortunately, one of the more esoteric numbers we shrugged and clichéd off that day, the one most eating at the resolve of this patient, handsome, dark-haired, soft-voiced, fun-loving Californian, was thirteen—that's how many times in his fourteen starts the Peoria Chiefs had scored three or fewer runs.

"I wouldn't believe it either . . . except it's happening to me," Mike had said, looking over Brett Robinson's shoulder at a not at all esoteric number that was eating at his pride, fuck his resolve.

"It's crazy," Brett had agreed, with his finger pointing at that ugly 3-9 won-loss record of Mike's. While we talked and waited for play to resume, we also glanced at an updated stats sheet. Though quasi-verboten to Peoria Chiefs by Jim Tracy, stat sheets are nevertheless so ubiquitous as program inserts or handouts at minor league ballparks that the numbers that are already burned into their soul *without* their having to see them in print are always available not only to them, but also to the good folks who pay to come out to cheer or jeer while speculating upon which of them might *really* be a "Star of Tomorrow" as advertised on so many of those programs.

"But I'll trade all the runs they seem to score for me . . . for your earnie right now," Brett added as his finger then moved across from that 3-9 alongside Mike's name out to the number that he, unlike most young minor league pitchers, already understood was the only one that really mattered, and then down to that corresponding number of his own. "And smile right through those two-o'clock feedings."

Brett "Robbie" Robinson was smiling and even chuckled as he spoke those words in that tone of rueful irony of the truth he is so disarmingly fond of using with self-deprecating candor.

But he wasn't smiling on the inside, where a fine young man and talented pitcher was fighting all the same odds and having to make all the same "adjustments" as his teammates in his quest for that impossible dream—plus one very tiny one that was also so large that it gave perspective to almost anything held up next to it.

*   *   *

Thirty-eight days before, on that first morning in Madison after we'd had our day at Wrigley, when Brett Robinson's line had then read 1-3, 7.20, it wasn't just Jeff Massicotte's place in the starting rotation that Jim Tracy and Rick Kranitz thought that they perhaps should be concerned with filling.

"They're hitting him like a redheaded stepchild," Jim Tracy had said of one of the four married Chiefs, the long, tall, but not lanky, or shy, just quiet and modest almost to a fault, nondrafted free agent signed *after* he'd already received his B.S. degree from Illinois Wesleyan University.

"Just one more bad outing, Mule. Right?"

"It's looking that way . . . but, Trace, he's running himself ragged. Every day's a commute for him. And he sure isn't getting any sleep. Hell, he's gotta be happier than any of us to get away from home!"

True. But how could a twenty-four-year-old first-time father, while surely feeling relief from some of his labors, be happily unconcerned about leaving his month-old baby daughter behind with a touch of the colic? Not Robbie anyway. Even though it did mean that for three days he would not have to make the seventy-five-mile drive between Decatur and Peoria before every workout and after every game.

On the seven hundred to nine hundred dollars a month—for *only* four and a half months a year, by the way—that most second- or third-year Single A ballplayers make, the matter of housing is made manageable only by the practice of from two to four (and more) players sharing the expenses of an apartment. With a wife and infant child, that sort of arrangement was not one of Brett's options. With the baby only being born Opening Day, the immediate two-week road trip, and the finances involved, Robbie & Family had chosen the option so many young marrieds do—staying with the folks until you work it all out. Brett had not yet been able to do that.

"I know it's tough on him, Kranny . . . we've all been there. He's just gotta choose whether he's gonna be a ballplayer right now or a daddy," had replied the Shooter, who'd not seen his wife and three sons (the youngest of which was only months older than Brett's daughter) since he'd left for spring training and they with a moving van had left for Florida.

"Tough decision . . . but then that's what mamas and grandmas are all about," had added Jim Tracy, whose wife, Deborah, was at that very time going about the rigors of setting up a new home for them after the decision had been made to sell their home outside of Chicago so that they could be close to her family now that Trace had recommitted his life to baseball and would be God only knew where six months out of each year while he attempted to reclimb that ladder to the big leagues as a manager and she tried to raise three boys on less than half of what Trace had earned in the business world the two years he'd been out of baseball.

"If it was easy, everybody could do it, Mule. Fair or not, one more bad outing. . . ?"

"What's gotta be . . . has gotta be," the Kran-dog had said.

"Been beating me around pretty good," Brett Robinson had said later that night as he sat by himself at the counter at Denny's after calling home and finding out that it was indeed only colic. "But I'll have some rest before my next start . . . I've just got to recover. I know what Trace is thinking. My job is on the line."

Three nights later he went to the hill and pitched seven strong innings of three-hit baseball, Massicotte went four more, and we avoided a four-game sweep at the hands of the Madison Muskies and won the first game since we could remember.

While it's a numerical fact and oddity that we did indeed score more runs whenever Robbie pitched over those next five weeks, he'd also fought a stalwart holding action against that "one more bad outing" threat he always knew during that time was only two bad outings in a row away. In a seesaw battle of advances and fallbacks, aided eventually by the fact that he'd been able to find a mobile home rental they could afford that was still a drive away but not a commute, he'd gained more ground than he'd lost.

But on June 17, as we watched the big left-hander with the flowing mane and the high leg kick pop Herbie's mitt with his last few warm-up tosses before trying to bail Caballero out of the five-and-a-third jam he'd once again contorted himself into, Brett Robinson knew that his 4-5 record and 4.12 ERA still kept him all too close to that "one more bad outing."

Yet the baby was fine, in those thirty-eight days his won-loss record had been better than the team's, and the missus was up and about and feeling fine enough now to sometimes bring the baby out to the ballpark when we were at home and sit with the other wives . . .

. . . but mostly girlfriends. The "real" ones from "back home" that had long since started arriving at different intervals for four- or five-day stays here and there throughout this midseason period when we would make only three short overnight road trips in two and a half months. And the local "part-timers" who would shamelessly, publicly, and heart-breakingly gullibly "get lost" for those days when either the real girlfriends or the ballplayer's parents were in town, only to blithely reappear instantly upon the departures and be just that quickly accepted back into the by now expanded and coed nuclear "family" of the Peoria Chiefs; a communal, insular, yet quirkily permeable society which operated under the injunction that since the truth could only hurt somebody, and since usually it's the person who doesn't deserve it, and that most of all it could hurt *me*, I'll cover for you, you cover for me. Besides, what does it all matter anyway since it's only for now, and this isn't the real world anyhow. So anything and everyone is accepted for what they think they are at that moment, and that's just fine.

And that was even for "groupies." Who by this time were very much a significant part of the family and its intrinsically schizoid life; but then the thin, albeit vehemently defended, line between a groupie and a part-timer is perhaps only that of the latitude between maybe having only one or two ballplayer loves-of-my-life-for-a-summer-when-I-was-young-and-different-and-belonged! for a season instead of three or four (or more—and in some sadder cases, most!).

But the "Lady in Pink" was neither of those. That was the problem. However, it was viewed as anything but a problem at the time to Bill Melvin, and the immediate family of the Peoria Chiefs, including the adult contingent—even Trace and Kranny at first. "Nuke" could hardly believe his incredible good fortune. And the rest of us were just flat-out jealous that the thirty-five-year-old, breathtakingly sensual and *Vogue*-beautiful, wealthy divorcée sitting there apart from the wives, groupies, girlfriends (real or part-time) in both space and style that evening in Burlington was exchanging discreet glances of goo-goo eyes with the gangling, so unworldly twenty-one-year-old, instead of please God why not one of us?

Which was why Billy "Nuke" Mel was certainly more upbeat in our commiserating reminiscences that stiflingly hot night even though his now 4-6 record and 3.60 ERA had rather suddenly begun to raise the first whispers of a puzzling developmental question concerning a thought-to-be bona fide "prospect."

When Bill Melvin had pitched and lost the last game against Waterloo at home the night before we'd left for Wrigley Field, his record had been 1-3, 4.13. In his next start, he'd gone nine and pitched well, and Massicotte had gotten his first win out of the bullpen when we'd won the last game of the Madison series in extra innings.

In the next, at Quad Cities, on May 20, Billy Mel had again thrown wild and hard but effectively for seven innings and had gotten his second win on the season when we'd won our second game in a row after that lowest of the low; which, of course, this being the 1988 Peoria Chiefs, had immediately preceded the halcyon 7-and-2 days of the "exploding bats . . . Jesus, Mary and Joseph!" The night when Jim Tracy was so suddenly ebullient again that he'd carried on a running gag and conversation with the Quad Cities home fans about waving runners around third to the tune of seventeen runs in two nights—"Exploding bats, what can I say? But my arm's getting tired . . . you folks wave the next one in, will ya? That's my drinking arm!"

Which was why the very next night, May 21, after we'd just beaten *Springfield* 2-1 at home in front of 5,100 screaming Peorians on, believe it or not, "*Bull Durham* Night," a promotional night for the movie, we, all but en masse, and led by none other than the Shooter himself, were partying hearty at Spirits in the Père Marquette Hotel, when suddenly this heartstopping beauty in a clinging pink designer mini-sheath, that *everyone* had either eyed or taken his shot at from the moment we'd arrived but to no avail, had *Bill Melvin* out on the dance floor as we then marveled and oohed as she and he did all but *Last Tango* for the next thirty minutes or so before she then just vanished, as if into thin air, off into the night, leaving us all, but mostly of course the by now dizzy moonstruck country boy, wondering if it hadn't all been some scene out of some cosmic movie only we had seen.

Mel was devastated. And intrigued. And since Jennifer, his hometown sweetheart, who had just been up for a visit, had tearfully admitted to him in her last phone call that she had actually kissed this other fellow "she had some feelings for," Bill Melvin had then set about in bewronged earnest to play private eye and find her whom he and we knew then only as "the Lady in Pink."

He was able to find out a great deal about her, but not her, as it turned out that this prominent Peoria socialite, recently divorced from a much older prominent and quite successful Peoria businessman, had flown off to Las Vegas for vacation the very morning she'd so bedazzled Mel—and us.

So Billy Mel took his heartache up to Kenosha, Wisconsin, and earned Midwest League Pitcher of the Week by throwing that "no-hitter" that wasn't, for his third consecutive good outing, his second win in a row, and a slate that now read 3-3, 2.97.

And then five days later, on a commuter to Clinton—

On a night when we discovered the true realities of both the shocking racism still rampant in Mid-America, and exactly some of the heartbreak that awaits those who may think that catching and marrying a ballplayer is a ticket to the Promised Land. The night when Terrie Bernstine and Charlene Hannon, the lovely, quite proper wives of Pookie and Phil, the working mothers of their children, who on weekends and holidays would drive great distances to be with their husbands as often as finances and circumstances allowed, were not allowed to sit in the mostly empty section of box seats at Riverview Stadium, the section behind home plate with the protective screen that would shield the three toddlers they had with them from foul balls, but also be close enough for them to see Daddy play, because—"we don't have to sit with their kind." You see, they were stig-matized into a category that the president of the Clinton Baseball Club, Inc., Bill Gardner, perhaps most offensively yet accurately delineated when he tried to explain the policy: "I don't know what everybody else in this league does, but we've got a problem with baseball wives . . . how do we tell them from the other whores and tramps . . . if we let 'em sit wherever they want, then soon we've got nothing but that kind of thing going on down there with the paying customers. And we got a complaint on those two." And that complaint's root cause had been aimed at the other cross that baseball wives such as Terrie Bernstine and Charlene Hannon have to carry with them as their husbands chase a penury dream in places like Clinton, Iowa; they are white, and their husbands are not.

—Billy Mel, a true young gentleman of an old but new Southland, took the hill and pitched hard, wild, and *vengeful* for eight innings and we took our justice with a 6-3 paddling of the second-place Clinton Giants, and Mel won his third game in a row.

Then, the day before Mel's next start, the Lady in Pink called *him*. She had returned to learn from her friends about this young ballplayer who'd been sleuthing all over town after her. The one she did indeed remember dancing with the night before she'd left to "just get away for a while" from the hassles of a divorce, even one as reasonably amicable as hers appeared to be. She thought the whole thing sweet, and strange, and flattering, as she too was intrigued by the "only in a movie" romance of it all, and putting aside the "utter impossibilities of our ages" for the moment, she agreed to meet and have a laugh over his "detective act."

So they did, a casual, fun picnic-brunch "date" the following midmorning. That evening, Saturday, June 4, Mel had gone down to Springfield and mowed hard, wild, and *glowing* for eight 5-hit innings only to lose 2-1 when Rick Wilkins had watched those three straight 3-0 curveballs swish by totally unmolested with Pookie pawing the dirt *less* than ninety feet away.

But while Mel, as is his wont, took that particular loss as hard, if not harder than anyone, he was able to put it aside as only a memory perhaps a little faster than the rest of us.

Because that picnic date had night-blossomed into something full, romantic, passionate and thrilling within twenty-four hours. Bill Melvin, the impressionable, sensitive, ever so polite country boy from North Carolina, was soon being pampered, dressed, fed, and yes, "truly loved . . . I know I've never felt this way before about any man," by the sort of female almost all of us only know and fantasize about from the movies as he was now sporting around town in either a red Jaguar or a black Corvette, wearing expensive new clothes, and now had a roomie of one in a "mansion, y'all! It's something like you see in one of those magazines!" That is, of course, when they weren't spending romantic wee-hour nights and intimate, blissful dawns up in Chicago staying in hotels and frequenting restaurants and nightclubs the likes of which Billy Mel had definitely only seen in the movies.

Suddenly, Bill Melvin was living the big league life as a pitcher on a Single A ballclub. And naturally, with all of the "family" having gone together to see Ron Shelton's fine baseball film, *Bull Durham,* and with the all too obvious life-imitating-art happening for real right in front of our more than bemused eyes, Billy Mel had gained a new nickname that would spread throughout baseball and still be with him long after the season had ended.

However, even as a promotional poster for the movie depicting "Nuke Laloosh" in a jockstrap and garter belt had been altered to feature Bill Melvin's face instead of Tim Robbins's, and affixed to his locker by his teammates, it appeared that perhaps the parallels to the fiction might be a case of art imitating life in a less humorous way.

In his very next start, June 9, up in Waterloo, when we were going for a clean sweep of our four-day, three-night forage into Iowa, on a night when "Nuke" knew what was waiting for him at the end of that game and the five-hour bus ride home, he went out and got absolutely shelled for nine rockets—including three doubles and a homer—and we lost 6-2. So? Every pitcher has a bad outing. What had red-flagged that performance in a puzzling way to Rick Kranitz was that a young, healthy pitcher, who normally throws 88 to 90 miles an hour, was all of a sudden getting the ball up there at best 83 to 84.

But only puzzling. And while it had registered as something to watch for—being discussed by Trace and Kranny and then duly noted in their daily reports—it was soon all but forgotten amid the suddenly on-again euphoria of the first week of that final 8-and-4 stretch before the end of the first half of the split season.

Nuke's next start? On Tuesday, June 14, Bill Melvin's again only 83-to-84-mile-an-hour "heater" was the fuel for nine more rockets in only a five-inning stint that included a double, triple, and home run, plus a balk and a hit batsman, and he was gone from the zoo going on around him for his earliest exit on the season, down 4-zip.

And it was that night—even amid the overshadowing torrent of words spoken that had little or nothing to do with why everyone was there to begin with—that the words "Leaving his fastball in the sheets?" were first spoken by Rick Kranitz and Jim Tracy.

It was also that night that the Lady in Pink was given another cryptic moniker. In fact it was John Butler, the general manager of the Peoria Chiefs, a young man who not only was the one responsible for getting all the little things done that ensure that "Pete's Phenomena" in Peoria actually works but had also played this game at a competitive college level before then going into its administration, who had sat later that night in his office with Trace and Kranny over a bottle of medicinal bourbon he'd pulled from his closet—there for just such nights—and been the first to make the "Black Widow" analogy.

"You know . . . she lures her lover in, beds him, drains the strength out of him . . . and then eats him!"

We had all laughed. Trace and Kranny as hard as the rest of us. And then, back in their office, they'd further discussed this puzzling trend in the development of a young "prospect" and again noted it in their daily reports. But now the mystery had a suspect. And from that night on, as far as management was concerned, the Lady in Pink was referred to as the Black Widow.

But Bill Melvin was in love. And, to his further befuddling, stupefying, bumping-into-walls mixture of amazement and joy, which afflicts men of all ages at such times, was added the astounding-to-him fact that so was

Angela. (Yes, we finally give name to a wonderful lady; and for the only time in this work, we will not give the true name.)

Three days after that calamitous and eventful last start of his, Nuke, while he spoke with some concern about his now three *losses* in a row, his mood of wonderful mitigated that very concern.

He was "just having a little problem reaching out and getting on top of the ball." A mechanical problem that he was "working on with Kranny," but would have "straightened out soon." Particularly would this be the case, he wanted us to understand, since "I've never felt better. I feel great. Rested. Honest, never felt better in my life! I swear, guys. Eating better and sleeping better than ever."

But in any case, whatever the problem might be, it *certainly* couldn't have anything to do with that gorgeous lady sitting over there trying not to look at him too often lest it embarrass him and call any more attention to herself than her totally unplanned, and never dreamed-of, yet so public entry into the "family" of the 1988 Peoria Chiefs had already occasioned.

"Aw, look at her, y'all . . . isn't she something? And golly jeez, can ya believe it . . . she *likes* me! I swear, y'all . . . nothing like this has ever happened to me in my life!"

Surely not. And since such times as that generally happen if they happen at all but once in a lifetime, in all probability it'll never happen again—those times that, when they are happening, always seem like too much, and when they are over, never enough.

With Nuke and Robbie having returned to their pencils and clipboards, and Hard Luck Mike and I looking out toward the bullpen now that Gabby has walked Mr. Casarotti to load the bases with still only one out in the bottom of the sixth, that night of June 17 in Burlington, we can take note that "Ollie" North, the baby-faced, but not baby-sized, and definitely man-spirited left-hander, is up and throwing to Rick Wilkins.

Mark North had been given the first shot at filling Greg Kallevig's spot in the rotation. Just six days before, on June 11, at home against the same Burlington Braves, Jim Tracy had given Ollie the ball and then the would-be-Braves had commenced to almost immediately make him sorry that he had. Brian Hunter, the Burlington first baseman, in his first at bat, sent out toward Nebraska Avenue the first of two home runs he belted off of the willing, but on that one night not able, Mr. North in the five innings before the Trace Monster took that ball away.

"I gave him his shot . . . and he shit all over himself," Jim Tracy had said. Which is why Ollie's now back to his role of second-fiddle left-handed setup man. "It's a bitch of a game. And it ain't equal. Sometimes you only get a shot . . . and you gotta produce *then*. Or it's another man's turn."

We did not lose that game Ollie North started, however. Here was a "mop-up situation if ever I saw one . . . so, he's been crying to show what he can do or send him where he can play? Hell, here's the ball,"

Jim Tracy had also said that night after he'd sent John Gardner out for the sixth inning. And all he'd done was throw *mad* BBs, hard, hardheaded, and just wild enough to pitch four innings of shutout, one-hit baseball, striking out five and walking no one, as the Chiefs again played longball and won a slugfest 7-5. John had his first career win at the full-season Single A level.

"I'd forfeit before I'd pitch him!" the Trace monster had said in a pique only four days before in a Mark's Big Boy in Cedar Rapids, Iowa, after just having left that stormy session when John Gardner had basically said, "Play me, or send me the fuck out of here!" among other things.

"Goddam . . . now that's what I like to see!" the Shooter had said after those four mop-up innings. "Kid come in there and want to show me something? He sent me a message . . . and I got it. You think he won't get the ball again five days from now? He earned it. Jeez'em' fuckin'tally . . . you think that don't get my dick hard? See a kid say it and then do it? God love him, that's why I love this game!"

That five days later had been the day before that Friday evening in Burlington where Gabby has now given up a sacrifice fly off the bat of the second hitter he faced, Braves catcher Brian Deak (whose two-run homer in the fifth had started Eduardo's once again inevitable collapse), and another earned run has been added to Eduardo Caballero's already team-high total, and we're now down 3-1 in the sixth inning of the last game of the first half.

And six innings was exactly how many innings John Gardner would get as a Peoria Chiefs starter. In those six innings the day before, young Mr. Gardner had again pitched mad, hard, hardheaded, but this time a lot wilder and turned a 4-2 deficit over to Jeff Massicotte after allowing four runs on six hits and four walks—three consecutively—but seven strikeouts.

"Goddam hardheaded *thrower* . . . that's all he is. He either blows them away. Walks them. Or they hit the peepee out of it!"

Which is the reason he too isn't warming up down in the bullpen now that Scott Bohlke, the Braves centerfielder, has just looped a double to right which Pookie plays well enough that only one run was added to Eduardo's tally and we're now down 4-1. And was only partly the reason he would not get the starting nod five days hence again.

That reason wasn't throwing in the bullpen either. In fact, he was yet to throw a pitch as a Peoria Chief. But then that's only because Carl Hamilton, a Triple A pitcher, who'd been on the major league roster just this past spring training—and was in fact at that very moment technically still on the forty-man roster—had arrived from "extended spring training" with Rusty Crockett only the afternoon before, after having spent the first two and half months of the season rehabbing the mysteriously ailing left arm that had just so recently had him tagged as the preeminent rising young pitching star in the Cubbie Bear firmament.

And of course there is Gabby Rodriguez himself who's just gotten shortstop Jerald Frost to ground out to Rusty Crockett to end the inning with no further damage done to the Chiefs or Eduardo's ERA. Then, after a two-out single by Herbie Andrade is all we can muster in the top of the seventh, the Braves quickly load the bases with only one out in the bottom. Gabby then gets Brian Champion, the Braves' big DH, to roll weakly into a 6-4-3 doubleplay to once again pitch out of a jam that would affect his ERA. And then, after Rusty drives in his first professional run, on his first professional hit with two out in the eighth, Gabby also once again turns a ball game he's held within reach to Fernando Zarranz.

Which pretty much sums up the story of Gabby and explains how and why the big, flamboyant left-hander, for his team-high twenty-six appearances on the season, had a record of 0-1, no saves, but a sparkling, team-leading ERA of only 1.30, even better than Fernando—his sole soulmate, running mate, roommate, and mischief mate since the departure of Mr. Greenjeans—who got all the saves, hence all the glory.

What of the "Panamanian Devil"? He of the "knee-buckling yakker," the human can opener of elbows, and knees, and skinny bones all coming at you in herks and jerks, with always that all-or-nothing look in his eyes in a face always at war between expressions of bewilderment, a sly grinning cunningness, and fear.

And, as we had finally found out over those thirty-eight days, *fear* was the operative word. And not the kind of fear and reticence of such things as an inside fastball that had finally gotten Jossy shipped down to Charleston, either.

As Eduardo sat like a broken scarecrow in the corner of the dugout, with his head in his hands, his record was 2-8, 4.07. Second only to Aspray in losses, and just barely third behind Brett and Mass for team-worst ERA. He also had ninety-four strikeouts for his eighty-four innings pitched, far and away the team high, and on a pace to shatter the Peoria Chiefs record for strikeouts in a season. His ninety-four strikeouts also were fourth-best in the league at the halfway mark.

His major developmental problem, as previously discussed, was that for all of his "dominating stuff," he would almost always have that "one big inning" about the fifth or sixth, and almost always it would be precipitated by something seemingly out of his control happening around him that would then cause him to lose his concentration and his anyway always precarious composure.

Then had come that night in Cedar Rapids ten days before, the night before the Cubbie Bear had swooped in and taken Silent Kal away from us, the night when Eduardo had shut out the powerhouse Reds with a complete-game, four-hit gem for only his second win on the season to go with the already eight losses. Then, just five days later, on June 12, at home in front of 5,227 very screaming Peorians, against the first-time-visiting South Bend White Sox, he'd again gone the route only to get a no-decision.

But to Rick Kranitz, that performance had been even more gratifying than the shutout over the Reds—because Eduardo had also struggled. Between the shutout in Cedar Rapids and that gutty no-decision in a winning cause five days later, Kranny, with the help of Stevie Melendez as translator—although, in truth, Eduardo actually understood and spoke more English than he wanted people to know he did—had finally been able to dig out of the young man what at least the mental problem was.

He was scared to death. He went to sleep every night and woke up every morning afraid that because of his won-loss record he was about to be released and sent home. Home to him was an impoverished region of Panama. Home was a place where the last time he'd been able to get a call through, he'd heard the sound of machine-gun fire in the background. Home was where on that very same phone call he'd learned that a boyhood friend of his had recently been found by the side of the road with no head or legs, only a torso left by Noriega's goon squads, but listed officially in the local paper as a suicide. Home was a place that he wanted desperately to get his family away from by "making big league . . . then all come. Buy house . . . big farm. No more . . ." and here he'd mimed a spraying machine gun.

"Can you believe that?" Rick Kranitz had said after a session where he had explained to Eduardo that the Chicago Cubs do *not* release major league arms, with a major league breaking ball—an arm that was leading the entire Cubs minor league system in strikeouts at the time—at the age of 21, no matter what their won-loss record was. "He actually thought every time he lost, or even got hit hard, we were going to immediately ship his ass home . . . the next day!"

Then Kranny had shaken his head in amazement. "Actually, that's the problem with most of these kids, even the ones who *should* know better. They just don't understand how the system works and what we're here for. But . . . while the other guys are out there trying to pitch and win with the fear of going home and having to tell their friends and neighbors why they weren't good enough before going on about their lives as their incentive, this poor kid was going out there pitching like he had a *gun* to his head. A real one!"

For all of Kranny's patient reasoning, however, from the way Eduardo was sitting in the corner of that visitors' dugout in Burlington, Iowa, on that evening of June 17, it appeared that the Panamanian Devil was seeing that gun again, rather than the Chiefs coming back to win that last game of the first half of the split season.

Bill Harford and the wintertime master pin board in his office at Wrigley Field. Starting with the Cubs on the left, he plots all of the teams in the franchise.

Spring training morning run: 150-plus anonymous Cubbies at Fitch Park

Mike "the Killer" Kelleher at Fitch Park's diamond #1 as minor league spring training exhibition games are underway; Big Jim Wright *(left)* and Peter Mackanin seated

"What phone? Tell Peter I'm watching baseball and catching some rays." Scott Nelson, Assistant Director of Scouting.

A yukking Jim Tracy on the cover of the *Journal Star*'s special *Play Ball!* tabloid

Rick Kranitz wearing his Kran-dog face

Photo by Robert Hunt

Who needs the Dallas Cowboys' Cowgirls? We've got the Spirit Girls!

Courtesy *Peoria Journal Star;* photo by Linda Henson

First "Meet the Chiefs" workout at Meinen Field; Mike Aspray, Opening Day pitcher, in foreground

A soft-spoken, innately gentle man, Gordon Goldsberry

The family Bernstine: Terrie, Pookie, and Kiki

"I wancha to give all the credit to my guys, the staff. . . . Me? Just tell 'em I'm gunpowder mean." *(Left to right)* Pete Vonachen, Mike Nelson, Jeff Reeser, John Butler.

Courtesy of the Chicago Cubs

Photo by Robert Hunt

Leo Durocher once said that this man, Jim Colborn, was "too smart to play this game!"

The never repressible Jimmy Piersall with one or a dozen things on his mind and on the move

personal collection

Gotcha, Richie . . . the Bat Doctor, Richard W. Zisk, Fitch Park Diamond #2, spring training, 1988

The "Professor," Tony Franklin

"Hit It Lee" Kline and the Iron Lung

Opening Day hype—the book writer "interviewing" Cub immortal and Hall of Famer Billy Williams

Courtesy *Peoria Journal Star;* photo by Linda Henson

Photo by Robert Hunt

The Phenom, Rick Wilkins

Marty Rivero demonstrating
how to come across the bag
and not get creamed

The "Soul Patrol" outfield: *(left to right)*
Warren Arrington, Phil Hannon, Eddie
Williams

The Z-Man, Fernando
Zarranz, always has time for a
youngster and an autograph.

Photo by Al Harkrader

Brett "One More Bad Outing" Robinson going about having a pretty damn good one

Courtesy *Peoria Journal Star;* photo by Al Harkrader

"Kid Rosario" has the ball, but Andres Santana gets the bag and a steal early on in the 18-inning, 1–0 loss to the Clinton Giants at Meinen Field.

Burlington Brave Rick Berg is out—and so was Gerald Frost on the back end of this Rusty "Davey" "Rocket" Crockett routine airborne 4-6-3 doubleplay.

Peter of Peoria working the house after his grand entrance and release from the paddy wagon

Photo by Robert Hunt

Surely the only "pig" Zarranz
ever kissed, as he's one of the
seven booby prizers in the
Kiss the Pig contest

Photo by Robert Hunt

Which one is the clown? *(Left to right)* Gabby, Z, Boz, Cap, Grandpa, and
Pookie, with Max Patkin, the Clown Prince of Baseball, in the middle.

Mass, Z, and Gabby are all smiles with the Famous Chicken in the Meinen Field clubhouse.

Wilkie's "quick bat" has just been fooled and jammed during the 8–7 win of the opener of the Remember Appleton series.

Silent "Superman" Kal with the "best midgets in baseball"—*(left to right)*
Steve Hill, Russell Dee Crockett, and Warren "Gator" Arrington

Kal in the process of getting Appleton Fox Darryl Robinson to ground out
in a 5–1 win; Herbie is catching.

Courtesy *Peoria Journal Star*; photo by Al Harkrader

"Doubleheader tomorrow"—two Spirit Girls watch the opener of the "Pay back's a bitch" series with Rockford being washed away.

Photo by Al Harkrader

The El Paso Buzz Saw coming at you—Frank Anthony Castillo

Author's personal collection

"Sold"—Pete Vonochen *(left)* and the new owner, Clar Krusinski; *(seated, left to right)* Michelle Vonachen Shaddid, Donna Vonachen, Josette Krusinski, Bragita Krusinski

Courtesy *Peoria Journal Star;* photo by Linda Henson

The big man with the big hands, bigger heart, and a proud lipful of dip—the Shooter, James Edwin Tracy

CHAPTER 7

THE PEORIA CHIEFS of the first half of the 1988 Midwest League season did of course hit the ball hard *some* of the time. And while a ballclub among the league leaders in team ERA, but by far and away dead last in team batting average, that plays exactly .500 ball for thirty-eight days under some damn crazy circumstances must tip its grateful cap to the heroes of such a stand of perfect mediocrity, it is still and always will be an absolute that we would not have won a single one of those thirty-eight games if those "real athletes" had *not* hit that little round son of a bitching thing every now and again. As obviously was the case that night of June 17, when those guys that swing the sticks prevented Eduardo's record from being an even more *"merde!"* and murderously terrifying 2 and *9*.

In fact we actually had the lead first that hot night in Burlington. Mike Boswell, leading off the top of the fifth inning, had hit his first professional home run—a truly prodigious blow that just missed the Marlboro Man sign that seems to be at every minor league ballpark, horse and rider rising high above the outfield fences, and kept on going until it disappeared into the barrenness of that old Mississippi River town gone to incestuous, never-ended-the-Depression, ugly and withering seed—and we were up 1-zip.

And the Shooter, over there in the third-base coaching box, had jumped about as high—and then rooster-strutted his jig of joy—as had the Boz the instant he knew that ball was history. And why not? Twice more since spring training Jim Tracy had been able to save a kid he "just can't give up on" from the "blood on the floor" ax that fell all too soon after he'd first prophesized it that night up in Madison, Wisconsin, three days after we'd left Wrigley.

So bully for the Boz. And we all felt that way, too. Because no one worked harder, deserved it more, or was better liked by his teammates

183

than Mike Boswell. However, his first-ever pro dinger did occasion Billy "Nuke" Mel to look up from his clipboard and be the first to wonder out loud the question that had popped into at least three of our heads maybe only a second after we'd watched Boz almost stomp home plate through the gravel-pit surface of Community Field at the end of his home-run trot that was more a galloping polka:

"I wonder how Strick's doing?"

That's right, Mike Boswell was DH'ing that evening of June 17, partly because four days after that night in Madison, as the suffocating run drought continued, on May 17, Jim Tracy had *not* been able to save the first sacrificial lamb offered up toward its end. Naturally it would coincide with the first of the two "private" tantrums Pete Vonachen would throw before the final so public one.

Things had actually gotten so bad that Jim Tracy went and bought some rope. First thing Monday morning, May 16, our second day back in Peoria after those eventful, crazy, maddening, and so futile four days up in Madison when the dandelions were out in the full bloom of a glorious Wisconsin spring but our bats were not, and even though we'd won the night before to make it two in a row, Jim Tracy, after suffering through a week in which the Chiefs had scored a grand total of nine runs, on his way to "early work," had stopped at a hardware store and bought a length of white, medium-grade rope.

The Shooter wasn't going to hang himself. But *something* had to be done. And as much as Jim Tracy might sometimes have wanted to, that rope was not for the purpose of hanging Pete Vonachen, either—or as perhaps would have been more appropriate, gagging his mouth and tying his hands well away from a telephone. Nope. The Shooter wanted to shackle his ballplayers. Literally. The hitting instructor in Jim Tracy had decided that the common thread running through the batting woes of the Chiefs was that old bugaboo overstriding.

So that morning before the second game of a four-game home stand against the Clinton Giants, being the astute teacher that he is, Jim Tracy picked out the team leader, Marty Rivero, had him take his regular stance, then took one of the three pieces of rope he'd cut from that length he bought at the hardware store and, just like shackles, tied an end around each ankle, with just enough slack that Marty could hobble, but anything more and he'd fall flat on his face.

"Now . . . hit!"

There was much joking, immediate chain-gang references, of course. But after at first a couple of awkward, stumbling lunges, and the answering chorus of hoots, damned if the .179-hitting shortstop hadn't started tattooing the baseball to all reaches of Meinen Field. Marty was thrilled.

So was Trace, because not only was Marty thrilled, he was a believer. And while he had also put the rope on Jossy, Strick, Gator, and Elvin that morning—with varying degrees of success—it was Marty that he most wanted to believe in the "rope trick" (as it would soon be called throughout the Cubs minor league system). If Marty believed, he would sell it to the rest.

Which was why the Shooter was even more thrilled when, that afternoon, for regular batting practice, with everyone there, Marty had *asked* for Trace to "tie me up again." No matter that there were by then already some fans and even scouts sitting in the stands waiting for the evening's game. And again the Cap had blasted the ball with regularity—all the while extolling the virtues of the rope trick. He'd even convinced his roomie to give it a try.

"I feel like a criminal," Rick Wilkins had said after he'd been chided into letting Jim Tracy shackle his ankles.

"Yeah . . . well, you think the way you're hitting ain't a crime?" was the Trace Monster's reply.

"That's brutal, Skip."

"Shut up and swing . . . and don't fall on your fat ass."

Rick did, and even though he hit some shots with it, he fought the whole idea and, for his last round of swings, had taken his off and then hit three little "duck farts."

Bob Strickland had not complained at all, however. He just let Trace tie on his shackles, adjusted his stride as best he could, and went on about his business as uncomplaining as always.

Pete Vonachen watched all this, and his jokes about a "chain gang" were of a darker humor. Which was improved not at all when right after that first rope-trick batting practice, the Chiefs went out and got only two hits off a young gentleman by the name of Tom Hostetler, who at the time was leading *the world* with some numbers that staggered the imagination but not Jim Tracy's conviction that it all had to be a dreadful master plot somewhere; the anemic Chiefs were supposed to "adjust" and hit at the same time against "them numbers!": 7-0, 0.50, fifty-four innings pitched, and *seventy-five* strikeouts.

We got waxed 7-1 on one of those nights when Mike Aspray's control was perhaps a bit too good and he got roughed for eleven hits; and on a night that, for the first time in the four-year history of the Cubs affiliation with Peoria, the Chiefs were booed, taunted, and jeered by consensus in their own "friendly confines."

But by the next afternoon's batting practice, Jim Tracy, undeterred from his diagnosis, was back with ropes for everyone. And while there was still some resistance to the method, there was no stopping "Tracy's madness." It was no longer optional. During this second rope-trick batting practice, as the manacled Chiefs were being laughed at and teased by the Clinton Giants, and jeered and hooted at by the early-arriving fans for "Kodak Picture Night," Pete Vonachen stood on the landing of the press box at Meinen Field, watching the tied-up Chiefs and the surly—and smaller-than-expected—crowd trickle in.

"I never thought I'd ever see this . . . after all we've done for them," he said as he gestured toward the fans coming through the turnstiles below. "But then can you blame them?" he added even as he was holding a league stat sheet which showed that Peoria was comfortably ahead in the league attendance race as usual, and in fact was right on pace to equal if not break the attendance record they'd just set the season prior. "Going to Rocky's—hell, even to the library—is more fun than coming out to watch this!" he then said, gesturing down at his "hog-tied Chiefs."

"I just feel so powerless. It's something I can't control. If something's wrong, I can fix it. I can either fire what's wrong. Or hire somebody who's right. Or maybe it's a problem I can fix by throwing money at it. But this? All I can do is watch and burn . . . and talk! But they're not listening. I call, I soothe, I ask nice . . . nothing! Well . . . there's one person they have to listen to!" Then he slammed his fist down on the railing and demanded, "What time is it?"

Without waiting for an answer he then went down the steps two at a time, saying, "If I hurry, I might have time to catch Harry before he goes on the air!"

Down on the field, Jim Tracy stepped out from the batting cage where he'd just finished taking some pretty serious batting practice himself. The Shooter was taking more and more BP in those days, and it wasn't the getting-out-the-frustrations kind. He wasn't at all sure the rope trick was going to work and he really *was* sick of losing one-run games; he had in fact already brought up the idea of activating himself with Cubs officials, but their answer for now was that that was why Pookie had been sent there, to be the player-coach, and they weren't going to panic just because Pete Vonachen was.

"Who's he going to call this time?" Jim Tracy asked as he watched Pete hustle down the left-field line toward the offices, but then quickly added, "Don't tell me . . . I don't want to know. I'll find out soon enough."

Then Jim Tracy, being Jim Tracy, put all that aside and put his mind back on the job he was sent there to do.

"You see Serge's face when he saw he was DH'ing tonight?" he asked.

"Did you see Dana's face when she found out 'Baby' was in the starting lineup?"

"Who's a bigger pain than her, huh? Nobody. But then I guess every ballplayer oughta have a wife that good-looking and that dedicated to making sure *she* gets to the big leagues. It can only help . . . if he could just put a sock in her mouth, huh?"

A spit of dip. Then, "But he's earned it. These 'prospects' have had a chance. And I've gotta get that boy to Double A . . . time's running out for ol' Serge. Gotta give him his shot. He's never had a shot at playing every day in three years of pro ball. And the only thing that's gonna keep him in this game is versatility. So I'm gonna play him all over. Maybe at second, or short and even over at third . . . and DH some . . . gotta have him in there, though. Nobody else is getting the job done. Maybe he will."

Perhaps so. And Sergio did get two hits as the DH that first night of his run at being a Peoria Chief regular. But then that was the night that for eighteen innings, and four and a half hours, it appeared that out of nineteen professional hitters from both teams, *nobody* could get the job done!

Which was why, after Kal had thrown ten shutout innings, Grandpa four more, and then Z another three, and four of the Giants' pitchers had done the same, stranding sixteen Chiefs base runners—in scoring position in the fourteenth, fifteenth, sixteenth, and seventeenth innings, no less!— that when Z went back to the hill in the top of the eighteenth and quickly got the first out, the score was still 0-0. Which was why the very few people still left from the 1,100 that had showed up to watch the affair were beginning to discuss who to send out for some ham and eggs.

We needn't have bothered. Elanus Westbrooks, one of the stars for the University of Texas in the College World Series less than eleven months before, lined a single to left, Tony Michalak, the Giants' third baseman, hit a sharp but possibly catchable ball under Polly's glove into right, and then a catcher by the name of Ham—I swear it's true—lofted a sacrifice fly to center field and the score was 1-0. We went down 1-2-3 in the bottom of the eighteenth. You could've cut the despair with a knife.

"How could so many scouts have been wrong?" Phil Theobald had said as we watched that despair troop in that zombied daze toward the clubhouse and then just stood there in the all but empty park alone for some minutes longer, both of us not quite ready to face either the Trace Monster or Peter of Peoria, who had shortly before huffed by around the other side of us making like one pissed-off banshee in the direction of the clubhouse behind the left-field fences of Meinen Field. Then, finally, knowing that the unavoidable is best faced head-on, we started making that same trek all the zombies and the Monster and the Boss had made.

While we were doing so, and steeling ourselves for whatever predictably unpredictable but surely volatile scenes experience gave us every reason to expect were awaiting us, we were surprised by what seemed like such a minor one, under the circumstances, come running out to meet us. While the scenes to follow were ugly and sad and bitter indeed, this minor one was in some ways, for the purposes of this inquiry, every bit as revealing.

It was Z who came charging back out of the clubhouse, half naked, madder than hell, and jumped in Phil's face at about the point where we'd reached the bullpen mounds.

"Theobald! How could you have called that a hit?"

Taken aback for a minute, his mind surely not focusing at that moment on that one ground ball that had just barely eluded Paulino's glove, Phil, the sportswriter but also official scorekeeper for all Chiefs home games, then shook his head in disbelief when he realized what Fernando meant, and jumped right back.

"Because I saw it as a hit . . . and that's the way it's gonna stay. Or do you wanna leave it up to Trace? Wanna ask him?"

Not on Z's life. So he just stomped around a bit: "Goddam horseshit fucking call and you know it! Jesus Christ! *You* could've caught that fucking ball!" Such as that for another minute, then he stomped back to the clubhouse.

"We've just lost one to nothing in eighteen innings and all he's worried about is his ERA? What does that tell us?" Phil Theobald had asked as we'd then continued on our way in Fernando's wake.

"Just the truth," I said.

Pete Vonachen is a good man. Many times a brilliant man. This incorrigibly competitive curmudgeon, he is not loved and admired by scores of ballplayers, employees, and friends and neighbors far beyond Peoria, without just cause.

He just can't stand to lose—at anything. Most particularly not his ballclub. And most particularly not that summer of 1988. He was also very tired and very frustrated; and though he was trying to hide it, his health was slipping. Like any driven, self-made entrepreneur, with all the vices prone to such men who squeeze life for every drop it has, he had for some forty years been burning more than one candle at both ends and sometimes in the middle.

This is noted only as fact, and not as an excuse for any culpability he surely shares in the chain of events which, while they did not begin that night, certainly started coming to what would in the end be a most unseemly head when Pete Vonachen had slung his leather note satchel across the small lobby and just missed hitting one of us as he was conducting a top-of-the-lungs tirade for the benefit of everyone within the walls of the Chiefs' office and clubhouse complex in general but, in particular immediate proximity, John Butler, Mike Nelson, Jeff Reeser, and other assorted staff members, which included two of his children, plus his wife "Saint Donna," who could only listen for a minute or two before she'd heard enough and told him she'd get home on her own, thank you.

". . . no good motherfuckers! I'll never sign another PDC"—Player Development Contract—"with those lowdown cocksuckers ever again. Motherfuckers can't hit! Never will hit! Goddam sons of bitches. Fucking Pookie Bernstine! If he's a Triple A hitter, I'm a Chinaman! Not a one of the cocksuckers can hit! Goddam fucking Cubs! Let me die here! Send me nothing but puss hitters . . . !"

Then, suddenly, he had stopped and looked at every one of us to make sure that we weren't just cowering, but were actually listening to what he was saying—and most especially what he now made a very deliberate and even louder point of saying so that anyone within sound of his voice could make no mistake about its meaning.

"And they sent me a *puss manager*! He wants to 'God love 'em' all to death! I know one fucking thing . . . if Pete Mackanin was managing this ballclub, he'd have their asses so reamed out they'd be shitting on inner tubes for a month! And he'd be running their tongues in the dirt every day, all day, until the motherfuckers either quit or started winning! But not Mr. Nice Guy back there! I've got nothing but puss hitters . . . and a *puss manager*!"

The walls of the Meinen Field offices are by no means soundproof.

While Jim Tracy had heard and his Trace Monster heart had been both broken and enraged at what he'd heard, he was not allowed the luxury of expressing either emotion at the time because his big Shooter's heart was instead having to reach out to Bob Strickland, who at that very moment was sitting in Trace's office not taking at all well why he, at twenty-four years of age, was being sent back to Charleston and the lowly South Atlantic League.

While Jim Tracy had again been privy to, and had had his input upon, the discussions within the Cubs' Minor League Department regarding just this player move, he had not known that it had been in fact a concluded discussion until after coming in from those eighteen innings of total futility and hearing it as a message on the Wang system of telecommunications used by the Cubs.

"And don't think that was any fun either," Jim Tracy had said after Bob had finally given up his protestations at the seeming unfairness of it all, and had left with big shoulders drooping and still moist eyes to tell Jackie that they had another long move to make.

"He took it hard . . . didn't he?" the Shooter had said, staring at the floor of his office after hearing Bob slam the outer door to Kranny's office. "But I didn't lie to him."

No he hadn't. He had let Bob contest the "unfair" and "why me?" facts of the matter: that though he was only hitting .236, on this ballclub that just happened to be second only to Lenny Bell's team-high .239; that, though he who had been sent here to drive in runs had but only eleven RBI, on this ballclub that put him only one back of the team leader, Phil Hannon no less, who had twelve RBI to go with his .187 batting average; and that those eleven RBI in seventy-two at bats were exactly how many "the Phenom" had in his 131 at bats, and one more than Lenny Bell had in his 139 at bats! All of this—which he of course knew and understood by rote—Jim Tracy had let be pointed out among a flow of hard, bitter words of hurt and anger, then he'd held up his big hand to slow the big man down and gestured toward the front offices and said:

"Strick . . . you know what's going on here. They're sending me a Double A player back here? A guy who had success here last year? And you know LaPenta can only play first base and DH. I'm gonna have to play him. And I've got Elvie? So all you're gonna do here is be a bullpen catcher for the rest of the year? Nuh-uh. That's not doing you any good. Go down to Charleston. They need help, and you need at bats. You're having trouble getting behind the ball. You need to swing . . . and I ain't gonna be able to get ya any. Strick, I'ma level with ya, I could've kept ya . . . but for what? So you stay here all year and be a bullpen catcher? Is that what you want?"

Of course there was an extra bit of truth that Jim Tracy did not think needed to be told to Bob Strickland, but would express shortly after that door had slammed.

"As tough as that was to do . . . at least it wasn't the Boz. I ain't givin' up on that kid. Saved his ass again. Plus it makes more sense. Boz is more versatile . . . and he's younger."

But soon the Shooter was out of words to say. There were too many other ones ringing in his thoughts until well toward dawn as he just sat there in his underwear staring at the floor.

We'd all wondered if she would show up. For some of us, the favorite distaff member of the nuclear "family" of the Peoria Chiefs. The so pretty, sedate, but bubbly one, the one who never complained or had an unkind word for any person. The one for whom Richie Zisk and I most enjoyed trying to win a dinner for two at one of the sponsoring restaurants by giving her the answer to the daily trivia question contest more often than we did the other wives and girlfriends—even as we tried to appear even-handed about it; but all the ladies of the family knew.

But Jackie Kubaz was there in her usual place in the "family" section of the box seats behind home plate in Meinen Field that following evening, Wednesday, May 18. And while there was pain in her eyes there was only a smile on her face. And as always only positive things to say about a very negative situation.

"Not come? We're going to beat these guys tonight. Plus, for the first time in his career, they've actually given us a little time to move." (Bob had been told he didn't have to be in Charleston until Friday evening.) "So I've had a whole day to do everything. I can't believe it. Got everything packed. Took care of the utilities. Even got our deposit back from the landlady! I feel so proud of myself. This is the easiest move we've had to make. So I came out here to relax, say goodbye, cheer us on, and look forward to a leisurely drive down to West Virginia."

It was exactly then, only a minute or two before we were about to stand up for the National Anthem, sad to be saying goodbye to Jackie, the light of our home-plate vigil group, but also relieved and buoyed by her undaunted spirit, that Big Bob suddenly appeared in civvies, when only some twenty minutes before he'd been suited up for his last game as a Peoria Chief in case Trace might need him to pinch-hit.

We'd all turned in surprise when we saw the big man standing over us with this most unusual, big smile. And we were even more surprised at that smile, but no longer his presence, when all he could do was stand there with that smile plastered on his face and abruptly announce, "We have to leave now . . . they need me to play tomorrow night."

Jackie had taken that news without a flicker on her sunshine face. But that look on Bob's face had more than puzzled her. Her first words after hearing the news which meant that they would *now* have to jump up and make an all-night drive and dash instead of the so well-ordered departure she'd spent the day preparing for were: "But, honey . . . why are you smiling?"

Bob shuffled his feet, struggling with the embarrassment and shame which is always there when a ballplayer has to publicly deal with such situations, and said, "What else can I do? I'm sure not happy about any of it. But they tell me I've got to go. So I've got to go . . . now!"

And with that, and thus with only just a handful of quick goodbyes and very best wishes over the last notes of the Star Spangled Banner, Bob and Jackie left the "family." Then the rest of us sat through another scoreless nine innings of Peoria Chiefs baseball as we lost 3-0 to the Clinton Giants to drop to the then season low of fifteen games under .500 with our third loss in a row in a four-games series where we scored but three runs and were shut out completely over the last thirty-one innings.

I really didn't want to hear any more. But Pete Vonachen did. And he did so with glee. Like a little boy in his eavesdropping glee, he'd even grabbed me by the elbow as I was getting the hell out of there and had then sent whispered, giggling instructions for the rest of his staff to gather just underneath the high little windows that ventilate the Peoria Chiefs locker room so that we could all better hear and bear witness to the fruits of his Machiavellian methods.

They were not pretty. But Pete Vonachen loved it. He would giggle, jiggle, and punch the otherwise still night air with a stubby fist in gestures of "Go get 'em" conspiratorial gloat as Jim Tracy roared at his ballclub that night in a voice that croaked itself into a choking, screeching hoarseness which would've been almost comical except for the naked pain exposed.

". . . come June there's gonna be a lot of fucking Peoria Chiefies playing at Wytheville and Geneva! How can I keep going to bat for you with Billy Harford when you're hitting a buck seventy-five? Tell me that! Huh? I can't! And I won't!

". . . and you know what? Come next year, you're gonna be reading the *Sporting News* about *other* people . . . and you're wondering 'What happened?' while you're out there trying to get a fucking job!

"I see you out there friendly with those other guys, joking around with 'em . . . then come seven o'clock they shove it up your ass! They love you in this fucking league! Everybody in this fucking league loves to play you, you cocksucking sons of bitches! Yeah! They talk friendly to you! They like you! Because you're an easy fucking win for 'em! You're twelve and twenty-seven! Twenty-seven times they've shoved it up your fucking ass!

"You're out there running the streets all fucking night long! And they're shoving it up your ass? Come pretty fucking soon . . . you're gonna have all the time to party you want! 'Cause you ain't gonna be in baseball! You're gonna be on the outside looking in! And that's where I wantcha all right now . . . outta here and outta my fucking sight!"

And then they filed out of that door, one at a time, heads down, not daring to look one way or the other, walked past a beaming Pete Vonachen, got in their cars with the women who waited in the parking lot for them every night, and drove away.

Later that night, long after Pete Vonachen had gotten into his Buick a chuckling, heel-clicking man, Jim Tracy was staring into the Amaretto Sour he'd been nursing for at least a solid, brooding hour of speechlessness as Rick Kranitz and Mickey Kelleher had tried to talk about anything but baseball. But then baseball being baseball, and baseball men being baseball men, every conversation eventually leads back to baseball. So, when the Killer had finished telling a story about when he'd once worked on a fishing boat off of Alaska—and just exactly how much that experience had always made him damn grateful for baseball—the Shooter had finally broken his long silence and, in a voice reserved for the confessional, had said:

"I lost it tonight, guys. It might've been the right thing to do . . . and everything I said was true . . . but I didn't do it for that reason. Tonight I let Pete Vonachen manage *my* team."

Pete Vonachen took his staff to lunch that next afternoon. His spirits were higher than they'd been for some time. He was relaxed, gregarious, generous, funny—he was Pete Vonachen. He had won. Something.

"Watch now," he'd said, jiggling those jowls with a big satisfied chuckle. "Plus I've got Harry stirred up. From now on it's let-Harry-Caray-do-the-talking time. On the air! He'll put the pressure on 'em. So, I'm done talking . . . let's eat!"

About three hours later, Mario Impemba was standing in the visitors' clubhouse of John O'Donnell Stadium in Davenport, Iowa, when a very bitter Jerry LaPenta answered a simple "How you doing, Jerry?" from the young broadcaster, who hadn't seen him since the end of the '87 season, with:

"Not too good, 'Impromptu.' If these fuckers could hit I'd still be up there!" The once-again-Chiefie had said it loud enough for everyone else in the clubhouse to hear. Then he'd gone and thrown his stuff at a locker and stomped on out to the field to be alone for a while before suiting up.

"Okay . . . and I don't suppose him hitting .205 at Pittsfield had a thing to do with it, right? Another happy face around here. Just what we need," Mario said as we watched Jerry LaPenta disappear into the cata-comb-like tunnel of the old stadium.

Then, without Jerry LaPenta in the lineup—and a very much happier and relaxed old Shooter suddenly back among us, even before the first hit off "them exploding bats," because Jim Frey had taken time out from his big league woes to call a Single A manager and bolster his spirits with tales of how they'd "all been through times like this" and not to worry because "we know what kind of a job you're doing and under what hand-icaps you're doing it!"—the Peoria Chiefs buried the Quad Cities Angels 9-1, with Brett Robinson being the benefactor of *thirteen hits* and one less run than we'd been able to manage in a whole week of games!

Then the next night, right back in that grand old tomb of a once grand old ballpark, we scored eight more and won again. This time with Jerry in the lineup as the DH—but pulling an oh-fer in his first game back as a Chiefie.

"Goddam," Jerry LaPenta had said. "If these son of a bitches would've done this a few days ago, Pete wouldn't have had to cry-baby me back down here!"

"It's the rope trick," Jim Tracy had said.

And it might've been, because throughout that 7-and-2 stretch of won-derful, the Peoria Chiefs proudly wore their shackles at every batting practice, and scored forty-seven runs.

Those shackles, while no longer mandatory, were still being worn dur-ing batting practice by most of the Peoria Chiefs hitters that evening of June 17, in Burlington, Iowa. In fact, if one had been at that game and had been particularly observant, one might've taken note of the rope ends hanging out of the uniform pockets of some of the Chiefs who came out of the dugout to meet Mike Boswell in "low-fiving" celebration of his first professional home run.

Not the starters, obviously. Their by now individualized, braided, and even colorfully decorated shackles had been tucked away in their equip-ment bags. But most of that game's "extra men" had them. Jerry La-Penta and Sergio Espinal had them hanging out of their pockets.

But wait a minute. When the Boz had hit that dinger and occasioned Billy "Nuke" Mel to wonder out loud about the fortunes of Bob Strick-land, that had sent our thoughts back to the events of exactly a month before: to not only the night when Strick had gotten the bitter news, and Pete had uttered some more than bitter words, but also to a time when a Double A hitter was being sent down to plug up a sinking-fast lineup, and a Single A utility player was about to be given a shot at being a regular in that lineup.

So why were Jerry LaPenta and Sergio Espinal "extra men" that last day of the first half of the split season? And why wasn't it one of them who had been in that spot to hit the home run instead of Boz?

Quirk of fate? Surely. But then everything in baseball is a quirk of fate; just as certainly as everything in baseball is also the product of a timeless, methodical continuum which is governed in the whole and in the end by anything but those individual quirks which give the game its color but not its character and design.

Jerry "I'm a Bitter Bob" LaPenta is a left-handed batter with a power hitter's build and a power hitter's stroke. Mike Stanton, the Braves' starting pitcher that evening of June 17, is a left-hander. Therefore, Jerry's not DH'ing could easily enough be explained by the logic of both baseball percentages and tradition. Except that when Jerry had hit .280 with some power at Peoria in '87 and won himself a promotion to Double A, he had done it as an everyday player, hitting lefties often better than he had right-handers. He had not been projected as, nor had he played as, a platoon hitter. And he had not been sent back to Peoria to become one. But he *had* been sent back struggling.

He still was now a month later. So his .192 batting average at Peoria had more than a little to do with why he wasn't the DH that day. Even though that was the *highest* it had been in the thirty days since he'd arrived. And was in fact the product of a recent surge that had raised his average some fifty points, and which had also begun to only somewhat improve his "attitude."

After sitting out that game in Davenport the first day he'd arrived, Jerry had been inserted into the lineup the next evening and went on to start eleven of the next thirteen games, mostly as the DH but occasionally at first base.

But with only five hits during that time, and a .143 batting average, and after striking out three times and grounding into a double play on the night of June 1, Draft Day, Jerry LaPenta, even louder this time, would be heard to say:

"Hey, what do I need this shit for? I've got a degree . . . I'm not like these other clowns. I can go home and get a good job as a stockbroker making thirty grand a year and get married. I'm no slave to this horseshit organization like these other poor fuckers. I don't need this shit!"

Not surprisingly, he was benched that following day, when Jim Tracy had been heard to say:

"I'm about to shitcan him *and* his fucking attitude!"

Not entirely, however. Not on this team. Six times in the next twelve games, Jim Tracy would put "Bitter Bob" back into the lineup in hopes that Dr. Longball might suddenly have returned his magic to Jerry's swing. And twice it had. It was his three-run homer up in Cedar Rapids that had given Greg Kallevig his sixth win two days before he'd been called up, and had catapulted us out of the jaws of the monster for that 8-and-4 run. And then June 11, against the Braves at home, it had been his two homers that had prevented Mark North from being the loser in his one and only shot at the rotation,, and had won John Gardner his first game above Rookie Ball. But, still, he was hitting .192; and although those three home runs tied him for the team high with four other Chiefs who'd been there from the first, as far as Jim Tracy was concerned, the verdict was still out on both his effectiveness and his "attitude," and both would have to improve further yet before he would again be an automatic pencil-in in the starting lineup.

And Sergio? Jim Tracy had been true to his word. Sergio Espinal had been given his "shot." After DH'ing that long ugly, pivotal, lowest-of-the-low night of May 17—the night that also it had been decided that "Kid Rosario" was definitely just puzzling Jossy again and might not be such a puzzle at all but a mistake in developmental philosophy—"Baby" had started twenty-seven out of the next thirty games, all at second base.

He'd made a hell of a run at it. Going into that night of May 17, Sergio Espinal had only forty-five at bats in the then thirty-seven games played on the season, and had an average of .200. Despite those two hits he'd gotten that first night during the eighteen-inning marathon, the New York City "flash" by way of the Oklahoma State Cowboys got off to an initially slow start. But then he'd gotten hot, and by the end of the exploding bats days of 7 and 2 joy, he'd gotten his average up to .241 by May 28, second on the team only to Lenny Bell, who only four days before had had to take *his* hot streak and his .275 batting average to the bench with a controversial bum ankle.

But once it got around that Sergio Espinal couldn't hit a slider if his wife Dana's life had depended on it—and from the way she would scream and holler and jump up and down in total abandon, wearing those so revealing short skirts and loose-fitting bodices, every time he got a hit, or, wearing those same provocative clothes, would throw herself over whoever was near in wailing anguish every time he didn't, and with the way that he would look first to her immediately after whatever he had just done, it appeared to everybody, Cubs minor league officials included, that perhaps it did—his batting average started nosing down to the point where it was that day of June 17, .215, only fifteen points higher than it had been exactly thirty days before when he'd been given his chance to play himself into the lineup to stay, or play himself out.

Which was why the third of the three games that Sergio would be on the bench for during those thirty days had been only the day before, June 16, the day *before* Rusty Crockett had been available to start his first professional game at second base.

Which was why Dana Espinal was sitting right behind us that evening digging her fingers into various arms and moaning into various shoulders every time Rusty did anything and alternately asking "He doesn't really look that good, does he?" and "Dear Lord . . . what do you think this means for Baby? Are *we* in trouble?"

On the night of the draft, Pete Vonachen hadn't bothered with shouting through walls. After slamming a cold drink across the press box and drenching one very pissed-off Phil Theobald, he'd marched right into Jim Tracy's office. Among all of the other words we've already heard him use in his diatribes against the then 1988 Peoria Chiefs—and he used all of them—he had ended this tantrum to Trace's face with the summation that:

"They're all a bunch of fucking *donkeys* . . . not a one of 'em's worthy to wear a Chiefs uniform. And if Rick Wilkins is a prospect then I'm a fucking Chinaman! And Lenny Bell is nothing but a gold-bricking crybaby who don't know that a little fucking pain is part of this fucking game . . . and he ain't gonna have no fucking career he's so fucking worried about jeopardizing by playing in a little pain if he don't get his ass out there and do the fucking job! Or get his fucking ass to Charleston where he fucking belongs! I'm sick to death of it all! And you'd better do something about this shit! Or I will!"

Then he'd slammed the door to Trace's office so hard on the way out that all of the Shooter's pictures and mementos from his family had fallen off the pegboard, and stormed out of the clubhouse shooting unabashed dagger eyes at the beaten and now stunned Chiefs standing there who'd at least thought that the sanctum of their own clubhouse had provided them some small protection from an outside world that seemed to be closing ever so ominously tighter about them.

After a day and a half of brooding over Pete Vonachen's "over the fucking line!" tongue-lashing in full view of his ballplayers, Jim Tracy had locked the door to the visitors' clubhouse in Clinton and given those very same ballplayers a tongue-lashing of his own. Again it wasn't pretty. Almost all the same words were used as the last time Pete had provoked such a response. There was only one thing different. Since it was before a ballgame, he couldn't tell them to get out of his sight. But he could tell them that he wasn't going to "even talk to you fuckers again until this shit ends!" and begin the silent treatment.

With Bell saying now that he was *very* ready to play—and also privately admitting, "Hell no, I wasn't gonna rush it back. They might wanna win ballgames, but a ballplayer's career is his body, you know? That's all we've got! But then all this shit? You'd think we were already in the big leagues. I think I'd better get my ass back in there. They take this shit serious around here, don't they?"—and with Jim Tracy wanting to make sure a "third base 'prospect' for the Chicago Cubs, and they're *scarce* ya understand" was indeed "fully, verifiably sound," Boz had started again at third and Trace had "eased" Lenny back into the lineup as the DH. He went 0 for 4 in his first start back since the injury, but with two RBI.

Lenny had shown himself to be "100 percent," and after all "he is the prospect," so he moved back into his third-base spot to stay as that batting average had then steadily slipped to the .250 it was that night of June 17 when he was still the starting third baseman even though he only had "eighteen fucking RBIs! Halfway through the goddam season! Now, I ask you . . . how's that even possible?"

But "'prospect' or fucking not," Jim Tracy had not forgotten Mike Boswell. While there were people "I've gotta play," in the sixteen games that followed daily along in the aftermath of the second-lowest of the low, "fucking draft day," June 1, Jim Tracy had found a way to slip "my man Boz" into the starting lineup seven times: at second, at third, and as DH.

Unfortunately, the six hits he'd gotten in those seven games, while they always seemed to come at an opportune moment, still meant that he was hitting "a goddam buck seventy-eight" halfway through the season, no matter how you sliced it up. But the Boz wasn't done yet. Because, one more time, on that perhaps just plain old craziest of the thirty-eight days, June 14, when Pete went nuts and Jossy was *smiling* because he was going to Charleston, Jim Tracy had "saved the Boz again!" And it had been a "prospect going down . . . not a 'suspect.'"

How exactly did we win that last game of the first half of the 1988 Midwest League split season?

In the top of the eighth, with the score 4-1, Phil Hannon worked a walk. Pookie Bernstine, starting in right field, then lined a hard single to left for his second hit of the night, putting runners at first and second with no outs. Lenny Bell then sent a broken-bat pop-up to shortstop for an infield-fly-rule out; and Jerry LaPenta, pinch-hitting for Marty Rivero, skied weakly to shallow left field for out number two.

Same old tune then, right? Get 'em on (sometimes) but don't get 'em in (most of the time). Not this time. Well, at least halfways.

And "half" was the prefix before several of the descriptive phrases used to note the youngster who was then walking up to the plate—as in "half-pint" and, more pointedly, "Jeez'em'tally . . . we're in a hole *I* can't see out of, and they send me half a ballplayer?"

Rusty Crockett, fresh out of the University of Texas and ten days of "mini-camp" in Mesa, in his fourth professional at bat, did what Lenny Bell, his ex-Longhorn teammate, had been able to do but eighteen times in 228 at bats on the season, when—after digging his back right foot into the dirt and gravel in that determined, quietly cocky way of his, and pointing his bat right at that sweet spot he was daring for as he stared out at the pitcher before bringing that bat back one last time to wait to see if that dare would be taken, left elbow up high and shoulder turned slightly in and down—he drove a first-pitch fastball hard into centerfield, scoring Phil Hannon from second to make it 4-2 and leaving Pookie now at second. Where he would stay, when Mike Boswell, his heroics for the day having already surpassed their quota, struck out on a damn good 3-2 curveball. But we're "half" way back.

Z then wrapped two punchouts around an excuse-me single to right and a caught-stealing in the bottom of the eighth, and it was last-licks time for the good guys. The last chance to prove that in those thirty-eight days since the "train wreck" we would not be losers; but had indeed "played .500 ball" during a period when there had been more than just one "inside" bet made as to just how far under that magical number we *would* fall.

Elvin Paulino led off the inning with a hard-earned base on balls. As did Herbie, in only his forty-ninth at bat on the half-season, ensuring that his .156 batting average would not change.

Up steps Warren "Gator" Arrington, who aside from one of the two position players who would not appear in that game of June 17, was perhaps the Peoria Chiefs batter most responsible for whatever contribution those guys that swing the sticks had made toward our being in a position to be 19-and-19 over those thirty-eight "no dog would have" days.

As late as that ugly night of June 1, our "Who's shorter than him? No body! 'Not any longer.' Ah, you're both midgets!" everyday left fielder had been hitting .189. He had spent the then fifty-three games played batting in either the eighth or ninth spot in the order, whaling away with a long, whip-handled bat and even longer stroke, still believing he could hit the home runs he'd grown accustomed to hitting with the aluminum bat during his All-American days when he'd helped lead Troy State University to two consecutive NCAA Championships.

However, on June 6, up in Cedar Rapids, Jim Tracy, after several days of attempts at persuasion by suggestion, had taken that bat away from him, handed him a big, heavy, stubby one instead, told him if he tried to hit one more home run he "was gonna chase his skinny ass all the way back to Montgomery" with just that very "club," and moved him into the lead-off spot with orders to just "chop that fucker and haul ass!"

Ten days, ten games, twenty-one hits, and twelve runs scored later, Gator had raised his average some forty points to .229; which, on that evening of June 17, as he stood just out of the batter's box looking at Trace for the signs with two on and no outs, was good enough on this ballclub to be second behind Ding Dong's team-high but slipping fast .250.

Hot hitter or not, however, the situation called for a bunt. Trace gave the sign, Gator, who was still trying to "adjust" to the ingrained, lifetime notion that he was no longer a "fence buster . . . I really was. Ya shoulda seen 'em. Tape-measure shots, and if I'm lying I'm dying. Ask Earl," and had never been much of a bunter, gave it his best, but fouled off two attempts and was quickly down in the count 0-2. Fortunately, it was soon enough 1-2 when a reliever by the name of Jaime Cuesta threw one in the dirt that got by Mr. Deak, and the runners moved up anyway.

Gator didn't really have to look to Trace for a sign now, but he did. The Shooter said, "Don't look at me. There they are. Let's go, midget number one." So Gator smiled, spit, and then hit a "heavy" piss-cutter that got inside the third baseman before he could even dive, and we've got a tie ballgame!

Phil Hannon then tried to move Gator to third, but he got a bit too much of the ball too early and grounded out to short. One out and the go-ahead run was still at second base. Not for long. Because Pookie Nehames "Send me a Triple A player and then not use him!" "If he's a Triple A hitter, I'm a Chinaman!" Bernstine immediately slammed a triple off the signboards in the left-field corner, for his third hit on the night, and 5-4 Chiefs.

Which was still by no means a certain win with the other guys, who led the league in both batting average and home runs, now guaranteed last licks. So collecting an insurance run wouldn't hurt. And with Pookie at third with less than two outs, there were of course any number of ways we could have done so.

"I don't need to get a hit here," Jim Tracy might've said a hundred times since the first day of spring training as he would discuss this exact situation in drills or BP with his ballclub. "All I gotta do is get him in . . . I don't even have to hit it hard. A duck fart. A fucking old four-three rollout. But guess what? I got me an RBI. And I'll take one of those every day over a base hit. 'Cause that's where the money is, gentlemen . . . that's how you feed your family. Get the Cadillac. And make your manager happy. Fuck a batting average and the sportswriter who first came up with it."

So what did Lenny Bell do? He looked at the now drawn-in infield, then out toward the outfield fences, thought about how two RBI would perhaps better help *his* cause than only one, then stepped in and tried to jerk the first pitch he saw back toward the Mississippi River, but instead lined right into the shortstop's glove for the second out.

The infield moved back to normal depth as Sergio, who'd taken over at short in the eighth after LaPenta had pinch-hit for Marty, stepped to the plate. And with Dana Espinal about to squeeze my arm into hot boudin, and another reliever by the name of Mr. Chad Smith falling behind in the count to "Baby . . . Oh, the pressure's on Baby, isn't it? Come on, Baby, you can do it! Please . . . he *can* do it, can't he?" some of us turned our eyes to the on-deck circle and silently asked the baseball gods to please let "Baby" get a walk.

Billy "Nuke" Mel's thoughts again were not as silent. Looking at Rusty

Crockett taking his practice swings, Nuke had said quietly—but not quietly enough so that Mrs. Espinal didn't try to burn holes in the back of his head with those blazing black, half–Cherokee Indian eyes of hers— "There's just something about him, huh? I don't know, but I think his coming might just make the difference around here, y'all."

Then he'd thought about what he'd just said, looked at me, as we'd then both grinned and shrugged and, with just those silent grins and shrugs, had reflected back three days prior, to the day we had found out that Rusty was only *coming,* and what a "golly damn difference. . . !" just *that* day had been.

During the last weeks of May and the first couple of weeks of June, much of the talk and buzz among baseball people is about the draft, that annual ritual when not only is the game and business perpetuated and replenished, but so are the American Dream and the Big Fib. That infinitely thorough, minutely orchestrated to the last index card of the last part-time "stringer" in the last corner of Podunk, USA, monstrously complex and expensive names-out-of-a-hat pull, when some 1,200 to 1,400 young dreamers will be offered the answer to their dreams if only they can be among the four or six out of a hundred of all the thousands from *all* the other drafts before and yet to come who will ever play a single day in the big leagues. That's the generally accepted percentage of ballplayers who sign a professional contract and then go on to make at least one appearance in a major league baseball game—4 to 6 percent!

While this annual event grips all of organized baseball during those few weeks, aside from the offices of the twenty-six major league scouting and player development departments, and those thousand-plus homes where that phone will ring and a decision will then have to be made, perhaps nowhere else in baseball was the draft having any more of a gripping effect than in Peoria, Illinois, where on the day of the draft, Pete Vonachen was seeing his most cherished dream come crashing about him in a 20-and-33 ball of shameful fire.

But as much as he pissed and moaned through April and May, he had not actually given up hope yet that his *demanded* wish could still come true. After all, in June of '85, his first year being affiliated with the Cubs, the draft had sent him Rafael Palmiero, the Cubs number-one pick that year, and all he did, fresh out of Mississippi State, was hit .297 with fifty-one RBI in only seventy-three games as he helped lead the Chiefs to the play-offs through the second half of that season.

In 1986 the draft had given him a double dose of timed-capsule relief. Mark Grace, a twenty-fifth-round pick in '85, had not signed, but—much like Rick Wilkins—had held out, played more amateur ball while he watched his stock rise higher until he finally signed for close to first-round money just in time to report to Peoria for the start of the '86 season. And all this fresh-off-the-aluminum-bat slugger did in his first season of pro ball was hit .342, the only rookie to ever lead the Midwest League in batting. Then, with that June's draft he was sent Peoria's own hometown hero, Joe Girardi, and all this fifth-round pick and fresh *graduate* off the campus of Northwestern University did was hit .309 in sixty-eight games through the second half and throw out every runner in sight. The two of them—with considerable assistance from Dwight "Smitty" Smith, of course, who hit .310—led Peoria again to the play-offs and one game away from a championship.

In '87, the draft had sent him big Mike Harkey, the hard-throwing right-hander, California State–Fullerton College World Series star, and Cubs number-one pick, who, while he didn't consistently display the bang the Cubs knew was in that long right arm down the second half, just flat-out scared enough hitters to be more than a little effective on the field, and a box-office boost off the field which helped to set the Midwest League attendance record, as that ballclub, powered by the fuel of '86's second-round pick Jerome "Juice" Walton's .335 batting average and 102 runs scored, and under Jim Tracy's steerage, had fought for a play-off spot down until the last day of the season.

Surely then, lightning—and Gordon Goldsberry's scouting department—could strike again.

So the word "savior" had started cropping up into the conversations one could hear in the box seats and the bleachers, at Boosters Club meetings, in the bank lobbies, and of course in the administrative offices of the Peoria Chiefs. Then had come actual draft day itself, and the Cubs had taken Ty Griffin, a "goddam *second baseman* who's going to the goddam Olympics anyfuckingway!" And we already know what commotion ensued that very evening. But then Pete had remembered that "saviors" don't always come in first-round packages.

Therefore, as the new signees had gathered down in Mesa for ten days of indoctrination and conditioning, and so that their varying skill levels could be scouted one against the other before then being disbursed throughout the system to teams and levels that those skills had been adjudged to merit "without getting a kid in over his head too soon," that word "savior" was again cropping up particularly and most frequently from that big paneled office with almost as many autographed and framed pictures of Baseball Legends hanging on the walls as Margo Adams has in her scrapbooks.

We were awaiting those assignments with no less interest than Pete Vonachen. This is a watchful time for the family also. After all, those some thirty new signees, plus the guys who'd been left at "extended spring training" nursing injuries or honing up on certain deficiencies in their game, have gotta go somewhere. And unless it's to one of the two rookie teams, anyplace else they go means somebody's gotta leave.

That only obvious fact can have any number of imagined and imminent dire circumstances for a Single A ballclub that kept bouncing between twelve and fifteen games under .500 and whose collective batting average had never gotten above .216. While for the most part the starters acted as if they could give a shit—"What they gonna do, bench me and put some rook out there? That's what they added Charleston for. My job's safe"— it was also mostly in the spirit of whistling past a graveyard. The utility and role players? They just grinned and bore it, refusing almost to discuss it; and why not? Dana Espinal was doing enough fretting and fussing and equivocating over the impending eventualities to go around for all!

Jim Tracy and Rick Kranitz? Their thoughts on the whole affair perhaps best exemplify what was mostly the marked ambivalence of that "waiting for the savior" time, those two weeks from draft day until crazy day.

"I wish Pete would say something about a fucking 'savior' to *me*! I'd tell him what they did to the *real* Savior, and then maybe show him!" the Shooter had said while he sat at his desk filling out daily reports, as Kranny did the same at his desk just around the opened door between their two offices and dressing rooms.

"Nuh-uh . . . I've got what I need. These kids are gonna come around. *This* is my offense! I don't need any ballyhooed ballplayer . . . green and still wet . . . coming in here. . . . Shit, they think a kid can come right off the fucking playgrounds and turn this shit around? This ain't American Legion here! Kranny. . . ?"

"I'm listening."

"You think a kid can come right out of say even a major college program, hell, even a high draft pick, and immediately make an impact on a ball team in this league?"

"I don't know," answered the pitching coach who'd been drafted out of Oklahoma State by the Brewers in the third round of the 1979 June draft and immediately sent to *Burlington,* Iowa. "But I'll tell you this. There were three of us like that sent to this league the year I was here . . . and you know what? All three teams were horseshit when we came . . . and they were horseshit when we left!"

The Shooter got a laugh out of that, then said; "See? Fuck the draft . . . we're just gonna play the cards we got."

Of course in the very next breath he'd leaned back in his chair and rubbed his big jaw, spit a dip at the dead can of Seven-Up, and said, "Course . . . if they've got a right-handed hitter with some punch, one of them boomers with the sound you like, I'd like to get him up here."

"Hey, what about a pitcher, Trace?" piped up the Kran-dog. "I wouldn't mind me a left-handed starter . . . and the way Robbie's throwing, that spot's still a question with me."

"Yeah! And maybe they've got. . . ?"

It was with all this "savior" contention and ambivalence going on now almost hourly that we played and won or lost every day for the next two weeks waiting for the Word from Mesa.

It came shortly after nine o'clock Tuesday morning, June 14. We were getting the Cubs' *forty-fifth* pick, Rusty Crockett, a five-foot-seven, part-time college center fielder that the Cubs wanted to turn into a middle infielder; and Carl Hamilton, a Triple A pitcher still on rehab who would be on a strict pitch limit at first but at least would numerically bring our pitching staff back up to the norm of ten. And, of course, Jossy Rosario would go to Charleston.

That was it. So Jim Tracy, after dawdling over that fizzle of a piece of news for as long as he could, went on around to the front offices to relay it so that the necessary arrangements could be seen to, was surprised by the nonchalant way that Pete took the news, then went back to his office to busy himself with the affairs that phone call had occasioned for him.

First thing was to tell Jossy. But there was no answer at the apartment where our four Latin players roomed together. That was not unusual. Herbie liked to sleep on mornings when he didn't have to come to early work. Therefore he often just unplugged the telephone. Or if everyone else was still there and sleeping he'd cover it up under pillows and laundry and such.

So while Stevie Melendez was dispatched to get him, Trace saw to his most important affairs: mulling over what it all meant and why. He clicked his tongue, shook his head, sighed, and said, "High expectations, huh? Ol' Jossy . . . but he's only twenty. Right now he just doesn't have the bat speed. We all saw it. But then the fight? Hell, he's a new man . . . or at least we saw him that way, anyway, so maybe that was what fooled me during that spurt."

While his defensive play still sparkled, by the end of May, Jossy's average had peaked at .188 and fluctuated downward from that. That's when Trace had decided to bench him and see if that would awaken the bat that had hit so well at Wytheville the year before. Then Bell had gone down and Jossy had had to stay in the lineup until his return. But even the day before Bell had returned, Jossy was back on the bench. Through June 1, Jossy had started forty-eight of the then fifty-four games. In the following thirteen games before the Word, he'd started four.

"Hell, we solved that timidness out at the bag," Trace mused. "And that spurt bought him another couple of weeks . . . but it's just plain evident that this was a case of overestimating his success at Wytheville, and then pushing him up a level too far too soon. So now he's gonna be where he should've been, Charleston. There he'll play every day . . . and get his self caught up. Best thing for him, he's young . . . and he's still a 'prospect,' they aren't about to let him go . . . too much talent. Yeah, Jossy's gonna be fine."

Trace paused there for a moment. Then, "You know Billy and them wanted to move him three weeks ago, don'tcha? But I vetoed it then, stopped it. Said let's give it more time."

Another pause as he dropped his head. Then, without looking up, the

Shooter confessed his baseball soul to that floor he's always staring at: "But . . . this time . . . I agreed."

So did Jossy. While most of the news was delivered through translation and pigdin baseball Spanish, the words in English that came out of his mouth matched in enthusiasm the not at all bewildered or forced smile that was shining on his face. Almost proudly he'd said to Trace, and everyone else after he came out of that office, "Me go down. Me play every day. Charleston. Is good!"

That hadn't been the chore that Trace had dreaded it might be. So, after Jossy had left the office to go spread the *good* news, the Shooter's spirits were greatly lifted as he continued to talk about all the much-expected moves that weren't.

"You know, Eddie's name kept coming up," Jim Tracy had said about "Fast Eddie" Williams, our .208-hitting right fielder—one of the only two position players who would not appear in that last game of the first half. "Jesus, Mary, and Joseph . . . it's a sin to have to watch that kid try to switch-hit, ain't it? I mean, when I send him up there and he's gotta bat from the right side, I wanna turn away. It hurts me to watch, and it's embarrassing . . . to him too. But they wanna make him a switch hitter . . . and Richie still thinks he can do it. Yet I ain't gonna tell ya I argued too hard against them moving him when they brought it up. But I deferred to the Bat Doctor on that one."

Then he checked the date on a new can of dip, thumped it hard and fast in his fingers like one would castanets, put in a lower-lipful, shook his head just a little, and said, "'Course, the verdict's still out on some of these kids. I think there's still more moves coming, and not from the draft."

Then he laughed, put on his best Shooter grin, and said, "What about my man Boz, huh? Everybody and their sister thought sure the Boz would be history today, am I right? All of ya . . . hell, Pete was so sure of it, I think just that surprise might've kept his mind off thinking about what we *weren't* getting!"

Then he slapped his desk, yukked again, stood up suddenly, and said, "But I stood right up to all of 'em and said 'No!' 'Nuh-uh,' I said, 'he's become a valuable member of this ballclub. He's come off the bench and helped out!' They got some rookie who can come do that? That's the hardest job in baseball!"

He sat back down and thought and spit for a while and then said, "I *gotta* stand up for guys like Boz. After my first season and a half of pro ball, everybody in the organization wanted to send me home except for one man. So what if some of these kids everyone's pissing and moaning about now turn out to be Jim Tracys . . . or how about this, a Don Mattingly or a Ron Guidry? People wanted to send *them* home, right?"

Then he thought a little more, got that Trace Monster solemn look back on his face, and said, "But Jossy? Well, sometimes you just have to face reality in this game . . . and there was no more saving him. I did my best, you know I did."

He stared back at that floor for a moment, then looked up smiling again and said, "But he ain't going home . . . and you saw it, he was happy! What a sweet kid. God love him . . . but his bat's just not quick enough . . . yet."

That sweet kid was scheduled to fly out early the next morning. But he was out there that afternoon for his last game as a Peoria Chief, happier than at any time since the days just after the Fight, and perhaps actually since we'd left Mesa some two months plus back.

"Me go down! Me play every day! That is good! Yes?" he kept repeating with that "sweet Jossy" smile to well-wishing teammates and fans throughout batting practice that evening.

And it was with that smile that he had to enter that game in the eighth inning when not only had his manager long since been ejected from the contest, but also *three* of his so-soon-to-be-ex-teammates! So Jossy was in there, and will forever be able to say that he appeared in what was surely one of the craziest games in the annals of organized baseball. A game which ensured that when Jossy flew away only a few short hours later, *no one* would have thoughts left over with which to mark and mourn his passage from the family.

Even at the time, and certainly in retrospect, I suppose the climactic event of that night's Circus Maximus was all too predictable. But then again, at the time and also in retrospect, it also seemed to come right out of the *blue*—pun fully intended.

After all, we'd just won three in a row at home, and six out of the previous eight. Pete Vonachen had for several days been almost his old self. In fact, over the last couple of days he'd been engaged in a running gag and practical joke with his manager: Trace had placed some spare-rib bones and assorted leftover trash from a celebratory, let's-make-up eat-in—that Pete had sprung for and had hosted in his office—in Pete's desk drawer; that of course demanded a "gotcha back," and things had accelerated somewhat hilariously and absurdly thereafter, with just that very early morning Pete having one of us dig those now rank but very same ribs out of the dumpster, which he then went and stuffed into Trace's shoes in his locker.

There had also been that "No explosion?" over the news of who was coming up from Mesa. After having worked on other business matters for a while that afternoon, he'd spent most of the next couple of hours anticipating and planning for the next move in the trash war with Trace.

During batting practice he could be seen proudly giving a guided tour to a distinguished-looking gentleman, a man he introduced as Clarence Krusinski, his guest for the evening, "a prominent real estate developer down from Chicago . . . might just wanna do some investing here. Peoria needs some apartment complexes. So everybody be on your best behavior, right, boys?"

So with all that, his seemingly prevailing good spirits, his ballclub winning, and an important guest on hand for the evening's game with the Quad Cities Angels, one would not have guessed that to be the night when Pete Vonachen would be at his very *worst* behavior.

While we would lose that game when Billy "Nuke" Mel's mysteriously disappearing "heater" had been pounded in the fifth inning for four runs on four hits, all rockets, including a homer and triple, it was a low, screaming rocket hit by Sergio Espinal in the third inning off the Angels starter, David Holdridge, when the score was still 0-0, that had started all the ruckus.

As would be proved—and reproved ad nauseam—by all three of the local TV stations on the news broadcasts that night and for days to come, that rocket had not been caught by a diving Kevin Flora, the Angels shortstop, but instead, as everyone in Meinen Field saw, was *trapped,* and it wasn't even close.

However, base umpire Rich Roder wasn't close either, so he panicked and guessed and guessed wrong. He called it an out. Fifteen hundred plus people bellowed at once. Plate umpire Mark Widlowski shrugged and turned away when Trace raced out of the dugout looking for somebody to make right an obvious wrong. Rich Roder then took enough tobacco juice in the face to give him lung cancer and sent the Shooter off to finish managing this ballgame hiding behind the Day's Inn signboard in the left-field corner.

Things deteriorated from there. There was already bad blood with this umpiring crew. It had been Roder and Widlowski who had called all those balks on Mass up in Waterloo six weeks before. But still it should've ended there. However, Mr. Roder and Mr. Widlowski then commenced to committing the umpire's cardinal sin—they lost control of the ballgame.

With all of the verbal abuse being hurled their way from the fans, and knowing that it all stemmed from one of them being out of position and the other not paying attention, they started second-guessing themselves and blowing routine, even more obvious calls, for both teams! Now they had the Angels and their cadre of followers screaming at them too.

So what did they do? They panicked even further and started responding to the fans! Not only did they have rabbit ears, they had petulant, whining mouths. They were so concerned with everything going on outside the white lines they even missed seeing a ball clearly tick foul off of Rick Wilkins's bat and then to his knee, and called it a hit-by-pitch and sent a laughing Rick to first base. Of course by the time that happened to lead off the bottom of the ninth, their befuddled, panicked just-wanting-to-run-and-hide-from-it-all anxiety and myopia were fully understandable. By that time it was all over except for the headlines.

Because, as that game progressively became not a game at all but a piece of absurdist street theatre, Pete Vonachen looked around at only 1,500 fans on a lovely summer night, and at his 27-and-39 ballclub who were "getting the shaft from folks more incompetent than they are," and became the loudest, most verbally abusive voice Messrs. Roder and Widlowski heard.

We need not tell here the kinds of things Pete screamed at the top of his lungs from all parts of Meinen Field that night. We already know the down-and-dirty, go-for-the-throat, vituperative crudity that Pete is fond of using when he's either trying to make a point or simply giving vent to his frustrations—which of course are usually concurrent events.

Suffice it to say he used all of the ones we've previously documented, and invented a few more, and all in front of God, mothers, daughters, husbands, and sons.

Under the weight of that considerable assault upon their dignity, they proceeded to leave Rick Kranitz—who now of course is the manager of record, if not in walkie-talkie fact—fewer and fewer ballplayers to participate in this caricature of a baseball game.

In the bottom of the seventh, after being rung up on a called third strike that almost hit him in the Adam's apple, Lenny Bell was already back in the dugout—although still yapping over the call—when Widlowski stopped everything and ran over to the dugout steps, taunted and jawed with Lenny, and then sent him off to keep his manager company. Then Elvin Paulino, who was the batter at the plate when Widlowski had taken off after Lenny, was ejected only a minute later when he struck out swinging! While Mr. Widlowski couldn't understand the words Polly was saying to *himself* as he muttered his way back to the dugout, under the circumstances, he just assumed they were about the same as he'd been hearing, and promptly tossed him!

That's two starting infielders gone inside of a minute and a half. Therefore when we go out for the eighth inning—the score is 4-2 Angels, but by this point perhaps only Jim Tracy cared about such an ancillary thing as that—we've got one reserve left on the bench, Herbie; and we've got a makeshift infield, with Sergio now at first base for the first time in his life.

We've also got a pitcher coaching first base, Gabby Rodriguez. Not for long, however. While having a pitcher coaching first is not an oddity in the minor leagues, what with the limited staffs and all, it is an oddity for one to be ejected from a ballgame while walking back to the dugout after a quick and relatively uneventful three outs had ended the eighth inning with no change in the score. Gabby still doesn't know what he could've done to get a rather sudden and stunning "And you're outta here too!" Maybe Widlowski "didn't like my fucking hair!"

That's when Pete Vonachen lit down beside me for a moment, said, "Watch this," then turned and gave a hand signal to his son Mark up in the press box. Soon the melody of "Howdy Doody Time" was wafting over Meinen Field.

That's when Mark Widlowski walked over to the dugout and told Kranny, "I'm going to empty this bench one at a time until that stops."

Kranny replied, "Whoa . . . what the fuck can I do about it? I have no control over that. Don't you think you're asking the wrong person here?" Widlowski's reply was to point one finger at the dugout while also looking up to the press box and giving the proverbial finger-across-the-throat "cut" sign. Kranny was standing there laughing, but also feeling helpless. A forfeit never looks good on a daily report. So he looked up to where Pete was now literally clawing at the protective netting along the third-base line only some twenty feet away—the same netting that he'd just thrown a folding metal chair against while screaming, "You wimp son of a bitch! I run this ballpark! Ask me! Tell me!"—and gave a broad, vaudevillian shrug of "What now, boss?"

He didn't have to wait long for an answer. Instantly, sending chairs and the people in them crashing behind and about him as he went, Pete Vonachen scrambled to the little gate in the fence underneath the netting and bolted onto the field snorting and stomping like an enraged old bull.

For those who believe it was all an act, perhaps the first thing Pete did when he reached the retreating-in-a-hurry Widlowski about halfway up the third-base foul line was indeed proof enough. He knelt down, clasped his hands in prayerful supplication, and begged Widlowski to "throw *me* out! Please!"

There are of course any number of rules and regulations and applied judgments that professional umpires are schooled in so that they might be able to handle almost every given situation. But a nationally known, charismatic, influential *owner* out on the field pleading in the posture of some soon-to-be-martyred saint to be thrown out of a ballgame that he is not officially even a participant in? A young Single A umpire?

Perhaps Bill Haller, that twenty-four-year-veteran American League umpire and past Superintendent of Umpires for the Commissioner's Office but now New York Yankees scout for the Midwest League, would've known what to do at the moment. We certainly know what he said he would've done just some few short days later: "I'd have kicked his fat, showboating ass right off the field like he wanted. Make a real show of it. While also telling that crazy motherfucker to meet me for a drink afterwards so we could laugh about it."

Mr. Widlowski apparently did not have the presence of mind or perhaps even the wisdom to conclude the affair in the manner suggested by Bill Haller. Instead he plaintively said, "Please leave the field, Mr. Vonachen. I can't throw you out. You're not in the ballgame." Then he thought he'd just escape the embarrassing scene by sidling back toward home plate and leave the kneeling, wailing, tooth-gnashing, Saint Peter to his audience in the hope that he might eventually just go away. Wrong.

Because now Peter of Peoria was kneeling right on the damn plate and center stage, praying hands held high, wailing and gnashing away all the more: "I'm begging you, throw *me* out. You fucking wimp bastard. Have the guts. . . !''

It was at this point that Rich Roder, who'd started all the mess to begin with—and because he knew that, had been lingering back out by second base, reluctant to come to the aid of his partner—finally came running up. It was just that running that was the problem, and gave cause to those who believe that Pete's act was indeed more real than show.

With Pete on his knees facing Widlowski, he heard and soon saw out of the corner of his eye a figure charging right up next to him—and *over* him. Now, Pete Vonachen had never been much of a baseball player in his youth. But he had been a fair-to-middling and rugged football player. He is also a man who has spent a goodly part of his life in saloons and taverns. Places where often a man's first lick is the only one he's going to get when the trouble starts. It is therefore offered here that, at that point—and at *that* point only—it was pure male instinct and reflex that was responsible for the act which turned this circus into national news.

When Pete came up from his knees to confront this bellicose figure standing almost on top of him, he led with a forearm shiver to clear himself some room. That forearm landed squarely in the chest of Rich Roder.

Pete Vonachen had just hit an umpire in what was clearly visible as a hostile, deliberate act of violence. However defensive that act might have been perceived to be by him, he'd struck an umpire a blow, and it was no "accidental" bumping in the heat of a dirt-kicking, jaw-to-jaw baseball dance and rhubarb.

Since there are at least eighteen young, virile men participating in a competitive athletic contest where usually only two or three other men make all of the hundreds of little decisions which can effect the very outcome of that contest, baseball's most sacrosanct, inviolable proscription is that those men in blue cannot *ever* be punching bags.

While there was a second there when all present—even Pete—were stunned by what we had seen but could barely believe, and there was a hush that fell over the night, it soon went the way of the bats and batting helmets that Pete then started throwing out on the field when even his physical assault upon Mr. Roder had left the two umpires still only plaintively, helplessly pleading, "Mr. Vonachen, *please* leave the field," instead of the "You're out of here!" that would have greatly abbreviated the whole affair and prevented its climactic, most costly and sorry denouement.

They just weren't going to toss him. So, after he'd thrown everything he could find loose in the dugout out onto the field, and stomped and snorted around some more to the once again not silent encouragement of his audience, and, being the showman that he is, knowing that one can milk an act too far and that it's always best to "leave 'em wanting more," he hurled a few more epithets and headed back toward that little gate to exit the field and receive the plaudits of his appreciative fans.

But then Fernando Zarranz had not yet gotten into all the "fun" yet, and of course that just would not do. So just as Pete was about to make his grand exit, the Z Man presented him with an exit gesture.

"Hey, Pete . . . you missed one," Fernando had said and came up and handed him a batting helmet he'd somehow overlooked in his house-cleaning.

"Thanks, Z," Pete said, then sailed that one like a Frisbee and climbed under that little gate and it was over.

Roder and Widlowski appeared to give some thought to ejecting Fernando, but then, just wanting this all to end so that they could get the hell out of there, they thought better of it, and the game, what was left of it, went on for six more quick outs, with the final score 5-2.

Now, for those who will never be sure exactly what was going on in Pete Vonachen's head that night, it must be noted here that as soon as he was off the field, there was a relaxed, peaceful serenity in his eyes and on his face that we had not seen since those winter months long before when all ahead was but the optimism of the Summer Game yet to be played, when everybody is still a winner.

"Jesus . . . that was fun. I've always wanted to do that," he said. And he wasn't even huffing, or heaving with the adrenaline one would have thought should be there only seconds after such a performance.

Pete Vonachen at that moment was at peace. And oddly enough (except to those who know and understand and love him) he would remain relatively at peace for the remainder of the 1988 baseball season.

When Rusty Crockett, in the on-deck circle in the top of the ninth inning of that game in Burlington, Iowa, had occasioned Bill Melvin to send our thoughts back three days to that night of June 14, Sergio Espinal had been at the plate with a 3-1 count, Pookie had been at third, there had been two outs, and the score was 5-4 Chiefs.

Two hard sliders later, Baby was walking back to the dugout to get his glove to go on out to shortstop to try and help protect that 5-4 lead. And he did. The first batter rolled easily enough to him for a 6-3 putout. Z got the last two on a pop-up to right, and a swinging K on a fork ball in the dirt, which was actually a 2-3 putout when Herbie scrambled after it and threw the very speedy Al Martin out at first and it wasn't even close.

Thus did Jim Tracy get his hundredth win as a minor league manager and we ended the first half of the season eleven games under .500, sixteen and a half games back of the champion Cedar Rapids Reds, and two games *ahead* of the last-place Quad Cities Angels. We might have been losers, but we did *not* finish last.

And tomorrow?

Well, tomorrow everybody would be back to 0-0. And Rick Wilkins would also be back behind the plate. You see, Rick had not been benched for his play. As much as Mrs. Wilkins had anxiously implored, "But I don't understand . . . he's always started every game before. Since he was seven! Why's he doing this to my boy?" a 140-game season is a long grind. Professional catchers cannot play every day. Although Rick almost did, of those sixty-nine games of the first half he had started in all but a handful, and he had appeared in every one except that last, and that was only to "give him a blow." And if the game had developed differently, Jim Tracy at one point or another would have gotten Rick's "quick bat" into that one too.

Because it was beginning to look like that quick bat was starting to come along nicely. While a .224 batting average might be little evidence of that, it was a far cry from the .180 he'd been hitting just a month before upon the occasion of the only game in which he *had* been benched because of his play.

Rick Wilkins's story of thirty-eight days? Peaks and valleys. When that bat was singing, so was he and base runners were crying. When it wasn't? Well . . . while every Chief was having to "adjust" to something in his quest for the impossible dream, we must take note that perhaps in some ways Rick's adjustment might have been if not the most compelling then possibly the most difficult.

Everything that Rick Wilkins did or did not do to bring glory or shame to either himself or his teammates must be placed in the perspective that nothing in his charmed and All-Everything life had ever prepared him to be the Phenom scapegoat on a badly struggling ballclub in a glass fish-bowl where everybody on the outside looking in knew how much the keepers paid to get this advertised "something special."

And Rick *had* delivered some "special moments." And those so fickle fans *had* sung his praises—only days or moments before or after they had and would again jeer and taunt him.

Since so often throughout this narrative we have had to make note of mostly his failures, it is only incumbent upon us—and perhaps somewhat revealing?—to balance the scale a bit and mention that two of his now team-leading twenty-seven RBI had come on perhaps the most special *good* day of those thirty-eight days. When on the Sunday afternoon of May 22, during the first-ever live television broadcast of a Peoria Chiefs home game, a telecast that through cable was to be viewed far and wide of Peoria, a telecast that featured as play-by-play man none other than Hall of Fame announcer Jack Brickhouse, against the Springfield Cardinals, Rick Wilkins made sure that another complete-game, four-hit effort by Greg Kallevig was not wasted by hitting his first home run at home to tie the game in the fourth, and then an inning later banging a double off the wall to win it 4-2. Big day. Big game. Much hoopla. And "the Kid" came through.

In fact, only two days before that so damnably hot night of June 17 in Burlington, Iowa, albeit in a losing cause, Rick had had a clutch RBI double at home against the Quad Cities Angels when there had been 5,500 people out at the "ol' ballyard"—the biggest crowd since opening day the night *after* Pete had gone out on the field. A double that for a while put the fans' attention back on the game instead of on every move that Messrs. Roder, Widlowski, and Vonachen might've made "the night after."

And just the day before, right there at Community Field in Burlington, he'd hit an absolute bullet right up the middle so hard that it was almost a dead center fielder and an out instead of the single it ended up being.

Yepper. It looked like "the Phenom" was starting to maybe be just that. And if that was the case, what with the "Coming of Rusty" and all, and if the blond Spirit Girl that Rick had inherited from John Green—the one he ignored and disavowed every time Ma and Pa Wilkins and his two little sisters loaded into that van and drove up to Peoria from Jacksonville, Florida—would "let me get some damn sleep . . . four o'clock in the morning she's banging on my window *demanding* it again," then just maybe the second half of the 1988 Midwest League season would be a whole lot more fun than the first.

After all, tomorrow, when we went down to Springfield, we'd be in first place.

CHAPTER

8

SIX TOMORROWS LATER and we were *exactly* back to yesterday.

And that would have been fine if it had been only that yesterday before Rusty Crockett's first professional baseball game—but no, this of course being the 1988 Peoria Chief Schizoids, we'd done a number on even time itself and had time-warped ourselves back to a yesterday almost two and half months before.

And that number was actually two numbers: 1 and 5. That had been our record upon the conclusion of the first six tomorrows after that glitzy, so expectant "Meet the Chiefs" extravaganza back in the bitter cold of April; and was also our record six tomorrows into the "second chance" of the "new" season in the midst of a record-setting heat wave and the worst drought in the Midwest since the 1930s.

But then that exactly wasn't so exact, actually, despite the numerical preciseness of it; and it wasn't just the fact that there were now some 70 degrees of difference between the thermometer of then and now, either—because the climatic elements of how we went about losing five and winning one to get off to the same tumbling start on the second half of the split season as we had the first were every bit as reversed as the temperature. A "world turned upside down" but still the same?

On the third tomorrow of the "Second Chance" an only perplexed and not mad, and in fact a relaxed and almost back to his jolly-old-self-Shooter had been kneeling behind second base, quietly watching and enjoying the sounds of youth and baseball; then, satisfied that the first morning of the Peoria Chiefs–Jim Tracy Baseball Camp was off to a smooth start, he had turned to one of us who was also kneeling on that lush grass in the already burning morning sun, sighed lazily and said:

"Damn funny game, huh? We score more runs in two nights than we used to score in a week and lose?"

"Hell, Trace . . . you realize we actually batted around on an inning for the first time this season?"

"That *was* the first time, wasn't it? Hmm hmm hhmmm . . ." He shook his head in wonderment. "Who'da thought it . . . our starting pitching is letting us down. You know we've had five bad outings in a row now, huh?"

A shrug was the only reply he got. This resident scribe wasn't about to correct him and remind him that it was seven, not five; and that since Eduardo had gone nine innings on June 7 and had shut out the Reds, who were due in that afternoon, we'd had twelve consecutive games where a starting pitcher had either not gone past the sixth inning, or had gotten a loss or a no decision.

A particularly gleeful chorus of adolescent yelps from over where Kranny and Gabby Rodriguez had a group of young pitchers caught Jim Tracy's attention and his smile for a moment. Then he returned to musing upon this most untimely and puzzling reversal in form for the 1988 Peoria Chiefs.

". . . if it weren't for our bullpen? Jeez'em'tally, I don't even want to think about what we *could've* done in the past couple weeks, huh? So what the hell's happened to our starters?"

Then he paused for a moment to watch the "spring training in miniature, ain't it?" going on about us. But then soon enough he gripped the bat that almost never leaves his hands anymore, took a swipe at the grass with it, and said, "Now we expect that from Robbie . . . rinky-dink curveball. Won't challenge anybody. Tries to nibble that rinky-dinker away from 'em and they just walk on down to first. And then Ollie? Shit must be contagious. I mean, goddam, three sliders and bang! Fulton's back in the dugout—but no, he's gotta go roll that puss spinner up there," and then he took another lick at the grass.

Ah, that Saturday afternoon of June 18 when, along with the heat and the diesel fumes, there had been such a feeling of "fresh, new day" optimism in the air as Lee Kline was idling the bus scheduled to roll for Springfield in two minutes—or when Rick Wilkins's black Firebird, as always, would come screeching up at the last second.

We were 0-0. We'd just won two in a row and eight out of the last twelve. We were starting to hit. We had Rusty. Pete was back to being the generous, gregarious, caring "Boss" which had given just cause for him to be perhaps the only minor league owner in America who, upon his arrival for his annual spring training visit, would be mobbed by upward of a hundred professional baseball players as everything happening on four diamonds would come to a halt so that his arrival could be greeted with whoops, hoots, hugs, and sincere backslapping, glad-hand pummeling. We had survived those too crazy thirty-eight days without losing an inch of ground. We had survived the arrival of the Word with the loss of only one member of the family. Fernando's *real* girlfriend had arrived from Miami for another visit that very day, so we knew he would be behaving like an altar boy and could not lapse back to being "that fucking idiot" for at least a week. And we knew we now had what surely must be the "Classiest Groupie in Single A Baseball"—who of course was no groupie—to help cheer us on, "the Lady in Pink."

So, with all that "on a roll" going for us, how could we not have felt that just about all was well with our world and that we were about to go down to Springfield and not only avenge those two heartbreaking losses of exactly two weekends before, but the two losses that had started all our miseries to begin with lo that lifetime but actually only two and a half months ago?

And when sure enough that Firebird came rolling fast into the parking lot only seconds before Jim Tracy was due to come out of his office to be the last person to climb aboard "the iron lung," and Rick got nonchalantly out and strolled to the bus in his king-of-the-mountain manner, with his pissed-off and embarrassed roommate Marty Rivero giving him the devil every step of the way for making *him* late again too, we knew for sure that nothing in our world had changed overnight except for the league standings.

So, "Look out, Springfield . . . here we come to clip your Redbird ass feathers! Hey! Where's the midget? Goddam, 'Davey,' you're gonna have to stand up in your seat when Stevie counts heads! Ya hear . . ."

However. Alas. And so unfortunately. Brett "one more bad outing" Robinson had his second one in a row and was gone after five and a third innings. In his wake he left a six-run fifth when Ollie had thrown gasoline on the fire when he had "rolled that puss spinner" up to catcher Ed Fulton, who sent it back a lot harder and straighter then it came into right center for a two-RBI single. And then an error and another two-RBI single and we're down 6-zip in our first tomorrow of the second half before I'd even finished my first grilled steak, onions, and green-pepper sandwich for which Lanphier Park is so correctly famous.

But then this wasn't the Chiefs of old. With Mark North settling down and pitching one-hit baseball the rest of the way, we didn't furl our sail and lie dead in the water. Instead we slugged our way back from a 6-0 embarrassment in the camp of our archrival to at least make a 6-4 game of it.

Of course in their eighth, Ray Lankford drove a ball into the right-center gap between Pookie and Phil and outdragged them both—and most Chevrolets; the kid can *run,* as well as hit and throw—all the way around for a rare inside-the-park home run that, even under the circumstances, was a lot more fun to watch than the blast he'd hit over the center-field wall off Mike Aspray in the eighth inning of Opening Day, April 8, the last time the 1988 Peoria Chiefs had been in first place. And we ended up losing 7-4.

But we'd "outhit 'em seven to six . . . goddam rinky-dink curveball! One more fucking bad outing, Mule? And that might've just been it! And that fucking spinner of Ollie's? Oh, goddam, Kranny . . . just goddam . . ."

Jim Tracy was still on one knee, idly gripping, hefting, and sometimes swinging that bat as he continued to survey the groups of young campers being put through their awestruck paces by the first morning's contingent of Chiefies scheduled to miss a little sleep but also pick up a little extra cash.

"So, Robbie, yeah . . . but Mel? The kid's a prospect with one of the best arms in the organization . . . and, jeez'em'tally, he just shit all over himself last night."

Then he paused, dropped his voice, got that Shooter little-boy-in-a-museum-of-dinosaurs look on his face, and asked, "You know about that woman, huh?"

Who didn't, of course. So I said, "Ah, come on, Trace . . . you don't really believe that old wives' tale about 'leaving your fastball in the sheets,' huh?"

"I didn't used to . . . but, damn, something's wrong, ain't it? I mean, here this *kid* is trying to handle this *woman* . . . up all night. And you can see it . . . there's no spring in his legs. I'm tellin' ya . . . look it up in your stats . . . since he's been with that woman, he's gone right into the shitter. And I'll tell ya something else. I already talked to him about it, too. 'Hey, it's your career, or it's the thirty-five-year-old rich pussy. Oh, you can have your rich pussy—just as long's you're in bed by midnight, *sleeping*. Especially on the night before you pitch!' But we'll see if it did any good. Tough for a kid like that to really believe something *that* good could be bad . . . whew, come to think about it, any of us at any age, huh?"

"Yeah," I agreed with much understatement.

"Hmm-hmm! She does look good, don't she?" The Shooter took a much more playful swipe at the grass with that bat.

Angie had been looking so good that Sunday afternoon in Lanphier Park that at one point during the four innings (plus one batter) it had taken Billy "Nuke" Mel to finish blowing a 7-4 Peoria Chief *lead* in another hail of nine rockets off his now at *best* 83-mile-an-hour "heater," he had been more concerned with one of the rockets that had fizzled and had popped up backward and was heading in her direction as she sat there in her sunsuit splendor in the box seats down front and just to the right of home plate.

Forget the men on base, the ones that had already crossed the plate, and the one still standing there about to jump out of his stirrups in the anticipation of another chance to swing at another one of those "fucking cantaloupes," Mel had actually come off the mound to watch that foul ball, male-in-love protective concern and *guilt* written all over his still so boyish face, and had stood there using all the body English he could to will that ball *he'd* just thrown from perchance striking his "Angel."

While it came close, it didn't hit her. But of course Ray Lankford then hit the next pitch hard to right center for the second of his three hits on the afternoon. And then soon came around to score the second of the three runs he would score on the afternoon, any one of which could have been said to be the difference since we ended up losing 8-7.

Such a shame, too—the score, not that the foul ball had only startled the so luscious daylights out of her, instead of conking and perhaps bruising that precious flesh—because not only had we jumped out to an immediate one-run lead when Rusty Crockett had led off his third professional baseball game by again crowding the plate and diving that front shoulder of his in front of the first pitch he saw, taken his ticket to first base without rubbing it, and then utilized his speed and instinctive baseball gamesmanship to come around and score his second professional run, but in the top of the second, after the Cardinals had promptly answered back with four runs in their first look at this new in-love version of Bill Melvin, the "new" Chiefs had thrown a five-spot at them, sent ten men to the plate in the same inning for the first time on the year, and the legend of "Davey" Crockett really started to take off as his second professional base hit was a never-any-doubt two-run homer over the score board in left field—"Jesus, Mary, and Joseph . . . what have we got here? Midget Number Two can *play* this fucking game. Who's got better midgets than us? Nofuckingbody!"

But then that afternoon it appeared that any number of Peoria Chiefs batters could play the game. While Midget Number Two would go on to collect two more safeties for his first 3-for-4 professional game, Midget Number One, Gator Arrington, got himself a couple, one of them being a two-RBI double that that big bat had chopped for a damn bullet off the wall in the left-field corner. Marty "the Cap" got two. The Phenom? He also got a couple to run his hitting streak to six games.

And "how about the Boz, huh?" Mike Boswell, starting at third that afternoon, had *bunted* a double. Scott Raziano, the Cardinals' third baseman and an old buddy of mine from back home, thinking it would roll foul, had let it come—it did, right into the bag, and then kicked off into left field while the Boz was standing on second.

Good gracious, the Peoria Chiefs had gotten eleven hits and scored seven runs and *lost*. While the Trace Monster might've had no love for being 0 and 2 on the new "phony fucking season," the Shooter could in no way be "bitter" about his "offensive juggernaut, ain't we? We hit that ball, and stomp that plate enough times, we'll win us some ballgames soon enough!"

As that Monday-morning sun rose higher, and everything fine with "kiddie baseball," and a group of youngsters at home plate hitting under the tutelage of Mike Boswell and Rick Wilkins, Jim Tracy hoisted those creaking, scarred, knotted-up legs of his with that ever-present bat and headed for the shade of the dugout and a closer look at and listen to what to the Shooter is the finest and most soothing art, music, and poetry this world has to offer—a kid with a stick in his hands; any kid, any age.

When one particular twelve-year-old started hitting shots to all fields off of Boz's lobs, the Shooter—who'd just been mumbling and muttering, in a casual singsong cadence, sentences that all had for him the heart-tugging, mind-perplexing words of "Lenny," "Bell," or "Ding Dong" within them—called out, "Hey, can that kid play third?"

The youngster beamed, and several Chiefs chuckled at the dark, inside humor; but when the kid stepped back in to hit some more "baby ropes" off Boz, Jim Tracy, no longer mumbling or muttering, turned and said, "What am I gonna do about that boy, huh? I mean, God love Lenny Bell any more than me, huh? But how can I keep sending him up there *knowing* he's not gonna get the job done? It's not fair to this ballclub . . . and all he's doing is digging himself deeper in a hole that's soon about to cover him up. And what's that gonna do for him?"

Finally, and apparently, he muttered and mumbled himself into a decision, because he then announced, "Boz is gonna play third! I gotta do it. It's only fair . . . hell, he's hitting the ball hard every time."

With that decided, his thoughts again returned to the larger, more general problem currently on hand.

"Aspray's just gonna have to go out there tonight and give us a good one . . . gotta keep us out of the bullpen. Those poor fuckers' arms are gonna fall off. Then where in the hell would we be? We can't score *that* many runs!"

Not long before Mike Aspray was to go to the mound to match up with the Midwest League's youngest and at the moment perhaps most meteoric "Phenom," the Cedar Rapids Reds' nineteen-year-old Butch Henry—the left-handed high school pitching mate of our own still-recuperating Frank Castillo—who was not only 10-and-0 so far on the 1988 season, but after an unblemished rookie season had yet to lose *any* professional baseball game, the Chiefs had one of their most jocular and impressive batting practices in some time: marked by two particularly special *sounds,* both of which were sweet music to Jim Tracy's ears.

The first of those wonderful sounds occurred when we received the message that Bob Strickland had been called up from Charleston all the way to Double A. He had left us a crushed and bitter not-so-young man going all the way back to the bottom, and now, a month later, he'd jumped two whole levels of the Cubs organization up into that strata of "one phone call away"!

And the other sound was that *sound;* but it was a Beethoven concerto that afternoon because we were hitting "pearls." The Shooter had finally gotten John Butler to unlock his stash and break out four dozen new baseballs for BP. And, folks, that's a *big deal* in the minor leagues. "Gracious sakes alive!" Those shiny, new, *solid* baseballs were absolutely flying out of Meinen Field for about an hour that late, hot afternoon.

Then that early evening, second inning in fact, one that counted also took off and would've flown out of Meinen Field—except that this time Mike Boswell *did* hit the Marlboro Man, and his second home run of the season had careened back onto the field and did not have to be run down and retrieved by the youngsters Mike Nelson commissions to do just that. But it was a blast off a hell of a pitcher, and it was a run. The only one we got.

They would get four. Three of them in the first three innings when Mike Aspray was having a little difficulty finding a consistent "release point" on that "dancing pus" of his. But Mike suddenly found it and then retired the next eighteen batters in a row. Far out-dueling the young Mr. Henry, who, though effective, had found himself hit hard and in some small or large trouble in five of the seven innings he was on the hill.

This performance by Mike had occasioned much talk among the at least half-dozen scouts that, with the free-agent draft over and done with, could now be found sitting in the box seats behind home plate at most every game in every minor league city.

"Jesus Christ . . . this kid wad'n even drafted, and you guys realize he's outpitching Henry?"

"Damn funny game . . . ain't it?"

"Goddam . . . play a better baseball game than these two clubs, huh? Nobody!" the Shooter said afterward, yukking and undressing by the hour as the rest of us were wishing he would hurry up so we could go and properly toast our 0-and-3 record on the second half that "don't mean diddley-twat . . . 'cause we're playing some baseball, gentlemen! I'ma tell youse that . . ."

Besides Aspray going the distance and keeping us out of the bullpen Jim Tracy had several reasons to be pleased with that ball game even though we had lost it. He'd tried an experiment. It had worked. And the legend of "Davey" Crockett had grown further yet.

Looking to get as much punch, defense, *and* development into his lineup as he could, Jim Tracy had put Eddie Williams on the bench— "He ain't hitting, and he's taking that out there with him now, too"— Sergio Espinal at second—"Let's face it, he's a smoother infielder than Davey is just yet, and at least the slider will be breaking in to him"—Elvin Paulino on the bench—"That *coño*-head ain't gonna touch Henry, they'd send me to hell if I made that kid embarrass himself on one of those yakkin' left hooks"—Lenny Bell at first—"That's his true position . . . and, well, with Gordon due here tomorrow, maybe that's the only way

I'm gonna be able to save that boy's career. Show 'em that"—and Rusty Crockett in right field—"Something tells me that midget can play this game anywhere you put him!"

It certainly looked that way. Rusty, who'd been a walk-on middle in-fielder in junior college, a part-time center fielder for Cliff Gustafson at the University of Texas (choosing to turn down the Pittsburgh Pirates and their eight-thousand-dollar offer in favor of the Longhorns and their virtually annual trip to the College World Series, only to then two years later, with no leverage of eligibility left, sign with the Cubs for fifteen hundred) had played right field with that same flair and reckless abandon he does everything else on a ball diamond: running like a "*white* wind, huh?" and crashing into walls and diving and sliding and catching everything that "gets past the grass or stays in the orchard."

And Bell? While he had pulled another oh-fer, he'd positively "played the shit out of first. Scoop any better than him . . . nofuckingbody. That's where that boy belongs. And when he learns to hit a two-strike curveball, that boy's gonna play some real high baseball, and you can print that!"

And "Baby"? Well, when he lined a double off the wall in the right-center gap, Mrs. Espinal had jumped up and down, like a gorgeous jack-in-the-box. After she'd finished that lingerie-and-flesh-revealing performance, she'd gotten all the other wives and girlfriends to turn and shoot dagger eyes at one of us who had somewhat earlier been overheard remarking to Bill Haller, the Yankee scout and veteran umpire, "Crockett can play, Bill . . . I don't care if he is really only five-five. Maybe he won't play any higher than this . . . but he's what this ballclub needed to turn it around."

To further account for Jim Tracy's good cheer, it should be noted that Rick Wilkins had also doubled off the wall—"Went the other way again, too! On a hard slider low and away? Right after he'd just looked like an ass on the very same pitch? That boy's making the adjustments, gentlemen. Lordy . . . he keeps that up, we just might make a race at this fucking phony second season!"—to run his hitting streak to seven.

Yepper, and as crazy as it seems, even though we were 0 for the second half, for the first time on that 1988 season we were beginning to understand now just how wonderful it was to be young and a Chiefie in Peoria. "I told you guys this place was special. Just think what it would be like if we were winning too."

"Harry reamed my ass, is what he did!" Bright and early Tuesday morning, June 21, a quite docile, jovial, and even *repentant* Pete Vonachen was sitting at his desk talking about what his best friend Harry Caray had had to say about his going onto the field and hitting an umpire.

"He just happened to remind me—and in language you won't hear him use on the air, either—that the ballfield and the ballgame ain't the business of a baseball owner! That all I had done was make an ass of myself and a mockery of the game. And he's right . . . owner has no right doing what I did . . . and have been doing . . ."

Whoa! Now I was all but convinced that it was about to start snowing blue-eyed blondes, twelve-year-old scotch, good poetry, watermelon, and maybe even winning baseball. Pete Vonachen agreeing that an owner's *place* only included his office, the press box, and the grandstands?

Plus then going on to say, "I'm sorry, I truly am. And I've apologized publicly and privately to everyone . . . including my boys, my Chiefs . . . and Trace. And I'll tell you something else. So what if the Cubs are in a bind because they went with the seventh team this year? We all knew it might be tough sledding at first. But they've always been good to me in the past. And if they don't have any help to send, so be it. It's not my business. My business is to make sure that we don't let down on our end. We're going for the attendance record. And if maybe the Cubs can't put me a professional-caliber ballclub on the field, we're going to keep right on showing this league how to do things professionally up in the stands."

Of course it has to be noted that Peter of Peoria had gone on to say, "'Course, you know Harry's still giving the Cubs hell on the air about what a bad ballclub they sent his good friend Pete. Hey, and I told him to lay off, too . . . but what can I do? He's Harry, and I'm just little ol' Pete Vonachen . . . doing my thing, staying in my place, emptying the garbage, and writing the checks. Oh, by the way, I still think we're gonna be able to get Stevie Hill sent back down here, and maybe one or two others we've been wanting . . . just don't mention that to anybody, all right?"

Thank God he'd added that last speech. Otherwise I would've been posilutely and absotively convinced that the world had indeed turned completely upside down and would've run out onto that field with a *big* net to scoop up all the spoils that were sure to come tumbling down.

While it was still hotter 'n blue blazes, it was another grand, cheerful morning filled with the sounds of baseball and youth and almost no business.

At one point, as Trace, Kranny, and even *Mrs.* Espinal were lounging in the shade of the dugout, Rick Wilkins—who might far too often be sullen with everyone else, but is wonderful and patient and caring with all children—left his group of campers to come get a drink of water from the cooler perched atop the dugout roof.

We had been perusing a stat sheet, so Jim Tracy said, "Hey, Wilkie . . . numbers are starting to look a little better, huh?"

"Nuh uh. Don't tell me." The big catcher grinned. "You know me, I don't want to know . . . just messes me up."

"Yeah . . . well, they ain't *that* good."

"Maybe not . . . but they will be!"

Rick Wilkins came back with that rejoinder to Jim Tracy as if he'd been swearing on the big Bible Mrs. Wilkins had sent up as one of his presents to be opened at the birthday party that *Mr. and Mrs. Peoria Chiefs*—"Mom" Mary Fisher Smith and "Pop" Warren Smith—had thrown for him. The party which he'd been rude enough to arrive over an hour late for and again leave his roommate Marty Rivero beside himself with embarrassment as he, the only other Chief who'd shown up for the event, had had to finally get Warren Smith to come pick him up and then have to entertain the several couples from the Chiefs Boosters Club who were present all by himself until the guest of honor finally made his appearance, opened up a ton of presents, wolfed down the food, grabbed his blond Spirit Girl, and left us all sitting there wondering why in the hell we had bothered—and also just how much longer "the Cap" was going to put up with it.

"Yep . . . he's still got a lot of growing up to do," the Shooter said after Rick went back to working with his young "mashers! Really, Skip," and the escapade of the birthday party, and the ever increasing volatility of the "Felix-and-Oscar" roomie problem, had been mulled over for the umpteenth time.

". . . but I think it's at least starting to happen. Besides, he's hitting . . . and that's what he's here to do. Not win any personality contests. And you know what . . . I think he's gonna go out tonight, bang a couple off that First National Bank sign, and we're gonna shove it right up their . . . behinds."

"Wouldn't be a bad time to do it," Kranny offered. "What with Gordon coming."

"Mr. Goldsberry's coming?" Mrs. Espinal's ears perked up higher at that news; and nothing stops her tongue, even when she knows she's already pushing the limit by being on the field, much less sitting in the dugout.

"Yes, Dana," the Trace Monster said with a suddenly tight jaw.

"Is Serge going to be in the lineup tonight?" she then had the "balls!" to ask.

"No, Dana," Jim Tracy answered through a jaw tighter still.

"Oh."

"And, Dana . . . just a suggestion . . . this wouldn't be such a good time for one of your little *talks* with management."

"Jim Tracy . . . you know I wouldn't bother Mr. Goldsberry."

"Right . . . just like you didn't Pete Mackanin last year, huh?"

"Oh . . . well. . . ?"

No, it definitely was not a good time for Dana, or any number of other members of the "family," to talk to Gordon Goldsberry. (Although, you've got to hand it to her, she did try.)

Because, just about four hours later, for the one and only time, one of us saw Gordon Goldsberry mad. And shortly after that, all that fool's-gold wonderful we'd been experiencing of late would tarnish more than just a little.

Gordon Goldsberry was under a great deal of pressure. With the change in command from Dallas Green to Jim Frey, Gordon, as is proper in such situations, had written and tendered his letter of resignation. But Mr. Frey had not accepted it, had told him that his talents as a *scouting director* were much admired, and that for now they would stay with the status quo and he would retain the title of Vice President, Minor Leagues and Scouting. Mr. Goldsberry had accepted that at "face value," but not without "some reservations about its sincerity," and had gone on about his job.

However, in the ensuing months of late winter and spring, he had been asked to surrender more and more of the actual day-to-day administration of the Minor League Department to Bill Harford. This had peeved him some, but again, when he was continually told that it was only so that he could spend more time "doing what you do best, evaluating talent," he had bitten his already reserved tongue, put aside some of his pride "for the sake of the organization," and gone on with his business—which was now increasingly *only* that of "evaluating talent." Then as the spring had turned into summer, there had been actual player moves which he had not agreed with or in some cases had not even been told of beforehand. All of this as Jim Frey had also started going public with his blunt thoughts on the "quality of all that young talent we're *supposed* to have in this organization." Talent that of course Gordon Goldsberry and staff had been responsible for scouting, drafting, signing, developing, and evaluating.

And what had the the first two and a half months of the season wrought? Iowa, Pittsfield, and Winston-Salem, the three high teams in the organization were all winning: *but* Charleston's record was now worse than ours; Geneva had gotten off to such a bad start the week before that their General Manager had turned it into a publicity stunt and was *sleeping* in the press box of McDonough Field and wasn't going to come down until the Geneva Cubs won another ballgame (or until beleaguered Bill Hayes went up there and shot him—which of course was the suggestion not just a few of us had been offering to good ol' walrus "Gabby" over the WANG); and the lowest Rookie team, Wytheville, while not losing as embarrassingly ugly as Geneva, Charleston and Peoria, did not appear to have much in the way of the "impact players" that Jim Frey was telling the press he believed the organization needed "to bring a World Series to Wrigley Field . . . that's what it's all about, you know? Not just getting a bunch of kids to the big leagues."

And of course, while a major league ballclub's immediate tomorrow might be at its higher clubs, its future is at the bottom—which fact Mr. Frey also was not hesitating to point out to anyone who asked.

And on top of all this, Harry Caray daily was telling millions of television "Couch Cubbies" world-wide just how bad it *really* was down in the farm land of the Big Cubbie Bear. And of course it was Peoria and the problems of "my good friend, Pete Vonachen" that Harry evangelized the most.

The Cubs cannot censor Mr. Holy Cow; and on this particular axe that Harry was grinding, Jim Frey wouldn't have wanted to if he could. That was not the sentiments, however, of the men who ran the Minor League Department—and that included the increasingly ascendant golden-boy, Bill Harford, who while an ambitious young man and not displeased with his expanding responsibilities and importance, nonetheless revered Gordon Goldsberry and Dallas Green as "the men who took basically an office and errand boy, and taught me the business and art of this game."

So, finally, they had had enough. And most especially Gordon Goldsberry, the man whose name or quotes were used in almost every article written in the baseball press about the on-going "conflict of philosophies" between Jim Frey, and his inherited minor league organization that Baseball America (and various other baseball journals) had just that spring ranked as either the first or second best among the twenty-six Major League clubs, calling it a toss-up between the Cubs and Toronto.

This was the background that I must admit I wasn't even thinking about as I sat sunning myself on the bullpen bench just a little after four that afternoon as the Chiefs were limbering up before the start of batting practice, and heard someone walk up behind me and lean on the chain-link fence separating the ballfield from the left-field bleachers.

Turning and seeing that it was Gordon, I felt an immediate rush of that mixture of pleasure, warmth, and *respect* that most people who know Gordon Goldsberry feel in his presence after an absence of some length. But as we exchanged the obligatory "Good to see you again" and "Is it hot enough for you?" there was a rigidity in his face and manner that was more than just his usual quiet reserve and always courtly bearing. Oops! Perhaps just some more small talk was called for here.

"How's everything in Arizona?"

His eyes were hard and fixed, staring out at the Chiefs on the field. "Went well. Got 'em in, got 'em out."

"Sure like the one you sent us."

"Yeah? Might just be sending you some more if some of these kids don't get off their ass! I'm tired of this horseshit!"

Double oops! Gordon Goldsberry seldom curses, and raises his voice even less. Then, after that short outburst, with a stony face he came on around the fence and went and stood quietly just back from the cage like a statue through the rest of warm-ups and batting practice. It was during that batting practice that Jim Tracy, who now had that solemn Trace Monster look back on his face, whispered, "Gordon's pretty hot at some people. Best keep your eyes and ears open . . . something's about to happen around here, and I ain't real sure it's gonna be pretty."

For starters, it sure wasn't pretty how we lost that night. Carl Hamilton, who'd been in the starting rotation at Triple A Iowa just the summer before, but had not pitched in a real ballgame since arthroscopic surgery to remove bone chips from his left elbow during the winter, was on a seventy-five-pitch limit as he took the hill against the Cedar Rapids Reds, starting in Kal's old spot in the Chiefs' rotation, which of course was still very much up for grabs. It still would be when, expecting to go at least five innings with his allotment of seventy-five pitches, he and his *seventy-nine*-mile-an-hour *fastball*—and this kid used to throw pure 90-plus heat!—were gone after three, having given up six hits, four walks, and fortunately *only* three runs. But then John Gardner soon took care of that discrepancy. Pitching just two-thirds of an inning, the fourth, he gave up three hits, *walked four,* and most unfortunately allowed four runs, as we took an 8-3 whipping from the Reds.

"Something's about to happen around here . . . a lot of it . . . and damn quick, too."

It was all enough to make your head spin, your heart break, your eyes pop, and your belly chuckle for joy all the way down to your toes—and all that within a week from the afternoon Gordon Goldsberry finally got mad and Jim Tracy again gazed into his crystal ball and spittoon.

Yepper. It was a hell of a week that, this being the 1988 Peoria Chief Schizoids, of course, would in fact stretch into twenty-one quite incredible days that would see us actually storm the pinnacle before that monster came up and jerked us down to his darkest, deepest den for one last battle. And, all things considered, even though the much "blood on the floor" would come from some of the deepest cuts of all, perhaps Gordon Goldsberry should get mad more often.

Naturally, this being the Chiefs, those seven days which would become twenty-one would begin and then be propelled by both a big win and a crushing loss. The win would come the very next night after Gordon got mad and the Shooter again played prophet. It was also another "damn good ballgame, huh?"

With the Meinen Field toolshed now officially known as Pete's Perch, equipped with a quickly carpentered platform, beach umbrella, barbecue grill, assorted guests, and a wireless microphone, the owner of the Peoria Chiefs served the first day of his delayed suspension having a ball and entertaining fans, ballplayers from both sides, umpires, and even a now-in-spite-of-himself laughing Gordon Goldsberry, as Eduardo Caballero struggled but contorted that "gun" the hell away from his head for six full innings, Jeff Massicotte went two more, scoreless, pitching with mastery and confidence, Z slammed the hammer, and the Chiefs beat the Reds 3-1 for their first win of the second half.

Ding Dong? Well, he again played the hell out of first base with Gordon there watching. But after a bases-empty, one-out, meaningless soft single in his first at bat, he then popped up weakly with runners at second and third to end what could've been the big inning that would have made

Pete Vonachen's rendition of "Take me out to the ballgame" during the seventh-inning stretch a rollicking celebration of "one in the fucking bag, finally" rather than the rollicking, hilarious, but "Hold 'em, boys!" cheerleading that it was. Then, after he'd struck out in his next at bat only a few minutes before Pete, from his perch and with that wireless mike, had sung that song which almost got him fined and suspended even more and longer for not "following the intent or spirit" of his suspension, Jim Tracy, shaking his big head sadly, and steeling his big breaking heart for what had to be done, called Lenny Bell back and pinch-hit for him in the bottom of the eighth with again two runners on base.

Baby? With Gordon there to watch and make his decisions, Jim Tracy had again started Sergio at second. While he played his as always stellar defense, being in the middle of two crucial double plays, he hadn't hit the ball out of the infield.

The Phenom? While there were no decisions to be made about him, he pulled his first oh-fer in over a week, and the end to his batting streak was ensured by a fuming, frustrating intentional base on balls when Marc Bombard, the Reds' manager, chose to instead take his chances with Lenny Bell, who of course never made it to the plate.

So, what Rick had not been able to do with his bat that night he then did with his hands in the parking lot a short while later when Marty Rivero finally had had enough of his roomie's—

"immature, disorganized, self-centered arrogance and ignorance . . . and a messy slob who thinks everybody should have to pick up behind him just like his damn mama who he has to call before and after every goddam game used to do . . . and be late to his own funeral . . . which would be okay, except he'd probably make me late again, *too*. And I didn't get a gillion dollars to pay all the goddam fines he laughs at!"

—ways, but came out the well-banged-up loser in the shameful punch, slap, and no-holds-barred wrestling, rolling dogfight upon the asphalt out alongside the Dumpster.

Jim Tracy would not learn until the following day that his shortstop, the only Chief who had started every one of the then 74 games played, had been body-slammed out of the starting lineup by his catcher. And even then wouldn't learn the whole truth from our stiff-upper-lip and gentlemen-tell-no-tales-out-of-school "Captain," because at the time and well into the late night he was sequestered in his office with Gordon Goldsberry discussing just who would be out of his lineup permanently, who might be joining that lineup for what would be hoped to be the duration, and the on-again, off-again, quite temporary addition to all of this sudden helter-skelter of one Scott Sanderson, ten-year major league veteran and "star."

While it looked like Mr. Sanderson—who'd vetoed Pittsfield; and Triple A Iowa was off on a cross-country road trip—would now be coming to pitch for the Single A Peoria Chiefs for at least one game on a "rehab assignment" so that it could be determined that he was indeed sufficiently recovered from off-season back surgery to rejoin the staff of the big club, it was still not a certainty as to when and where—or if he would even agree to it.

However, there was an immediate and unanimous agreement that night in Jim Tracy's office about where one "wild, hard, hardheaded" and quite healthy young "thrower" would be going. Which is why John Gardner got the wish he didn't want any more—"Goddam! Can you believe that? He got pissed? Well, I guess he'd gotten a little taste of success, and had gone and convinced himself he belonged here . . . just didn't convince anybody else!"—and was long gone and heading for Geneva the very next evening by the time Brett Robinson had pitched one of his better ballgames of the season for seven and a third innings only to see Jeff Massicotte *and* Fernando Zarranz turn his 5-2 lead over Mr. Mike "He'll pitch in the big leagues next year while the other kid might be pitching softball" Moscrey into a 7-5 loss before either of them could get those other two outs in the eighth inning, and, even though we'd scored four runs in an inning for the first time at home and had gotten eleven hits, the Peoria Chiefs were now 1-and-5 on the second half—exactly where but not "fucking how!" we'd started the first half.

"Damn funny game," Giants' scout Richie Klaus, White Sox's scout Mike Rizzo, Reds' scout, Chet Montgomery, and Bill Haller all agreed as they put away their ring binders and ray guns to head for a motel and another city and we headed toward a clubhouse where we knew not what was going to happen next—only that something was, and that the midsummer "bubble sessions" going on behind Jim Tracy and Rick Kranitz's now almost always closed and locked office door were not over.

While there were few Peoria Chiefs who could pass that closed door without some measures of insecurity, apprehension, or paranoia—who actually was on that midseason bubble list, which is not always administered with the same absolute democracy as during spring training, and how had they done on the third night of Gordon's "I'm tired of this horseshit!" visit?

The Boz, starting at third for the fifth game in a row, had played adequately and sometimes brilliantly in the field, and had gotten two hits and another RBI.

Sergio, starting at shortstop for the banged-up-and-on Marty, had doubled off a fat fastball, walked, scored twice, but his bugaboo, the slider, had produced a wave-and-goodbye strikeout with only one out and a runner at second, and an ass-one-way, head-of-the-bat-another nubbed groundout to second with two aboard and two out in the bottom of the eighth.

Lenny? Ah, Ding Dong. After a batting practice where he'd been so frustrated with the "slop" coming up, off, under, but never out and hard off the bat which had now turned into a loathsome, betraying serpent in his hands instead of the beloved stout club and best friend it had been such a short time before, he'd stepped out of the cage glaring at that bat and had given public voice to the anguish and futility he felt by saying—

"Fuck! Just send me to Geneva where I belong . . . and get it over with!"

—and one of us had again jumped in his face, and Jim Tracy had started to, but had ended up just shaking his big head, his big eyes a mirror to his big breaking heart, and had gone back to just leaning on that cage and staring off into space, muttering and spitting: after *that* BP, Lenny, at first base again, pulled another oh-fer night and saw himself again called back for a pinch hitter in the eighth with two on and one out; and to add further insult to the now much more than just injury to his long-gone confidence, it was a hobbling, .207-hitting Marty Rivero that Trace sent up there to hit for him.

Jerry LaPenta? He sat that one out, his dance card unpunched for the evening.

Eddie Williams? Ditto. It was Davey "Rocket" Crockett that was the racing, diving, flying, wall-crashing patroller of right field again that night.

Elvin Paulino? The same. While only barely on the "bubble," he again had to sit so that Jim Tracy could give Gordon Goldsberry a look at Lenny Bell playing first base.

First thing Friday morning, well before the beginning of the last day of camp, Medallion Day, the next two roster decisions were made public outside those closed doors—and they were both additions, not subtractions.

One was expected, and was the cause for much excitement around the Meinen Field offices and clubhouse that morning. The front offices because of the always welcomed potential for any media hype or box-office boost; the clubhouse for the maybe once-in-a-lifetime novelty it offered to the routine, everyday grind.

The other was quite unexpected by most—however much it might've been foretold or feared by almost as many—but was the cause only for more paperwork in the offices and more than a little bittersweet irony in the clubhouse.

The following night, Saturday, June 25, Scott Sanderson was scheduled to meet us in Clinton, Iowa, and be the Peoria Chiefs' starting pitcher for the second game of a two-game commuter series versus the Giants, and if all went well with the five innings he was scheduled to pitch there, most likely he would pitch for us again five days later at home against the Kenosha Twins and then it would be back up to the big leagues. That same Saturday night, in Winston-Salem, Greg Kallevig would start for the Spirits, then immediately thereafter be sent back down to us.

Scott Sanderson would be pitching down knowing it was just to go up;

Silent Kal would be pitching up knowing it was just to go down. But he *was* coming back to the family at the time we needed him the most.

Along with their medallions, certificates, caps, and T-shirts, many of the youngsters that last morning of camp had wanted some more authentic souvenirs.

About the sixth time that a camper came up to ask Jeff Massicotte for a bat, and he was again having to explain that he was sorry but that since he was a pitcher he didn't have any old bats to give away, one of us who was sitting with "Grandpa" in the corner of the third-base dugout, at the moment not thinking at all about the fact that Jeff had just had his first bad outing since going back to the bullpen a month and a half before—and it was *bad*; facing only five batters in the eighth, he'd walked two, given up RBI singles to two more, and an RBI sacrifice fly to the last—then made what turned out to be a very stupid, insensitive attempt at wit.

"Give 'em your arm, Mass," I said.

The youngster giggled, and then ran off in the direction of Mike Boswell when Jeff pointed and said, "Go ask him . . . he's a hitter. He's got bats."

Then, as another camper was approaching, Jeff had gotten up, said, "The way I threw last night, I *should* give them my arm," and made the long walk to the clubhouse, where, upon his arrival, he proceeded to pick a fight with the water cooler. The water cooler won and Jeff came back out with an ice pack Ace-bandaged around his right hand.

About a dozen or so hours later, Jim Tracy was sitting in the visiting manager's cubbyhole at Riverview Stadium in Clinton, Iowa, allowing himself a moment of jaw-jutting and head-bobbing Shooter yukking.

"Jeez'em'tally . . . hook 'em up any better than these two ballclubs, huh? It's war when we hook up with that bunch!"

A friendly war, yes, but still a war, and we'd won it.

Of course, it being our bosom-buddy marathon partners the Clinton Giants we'd just vanquished, it had taken thirteen innings for the Peoria Chiefs to win their second game of the "second chance."

Billy "Nuke" Mel, without Angie in attendance, and after assuring Trace and Kranny that he and she had indeed "cooled it off some, honest, y'all," had gone nine strong innings and, with a fastball that was often back up into the high 80s, had given up one run on six hits, while striking out eight.

Unfortunately, after the Boz, again playing third, had singled to lead off the second inning, and had then been doubled home by Elvin Paulino, who was playing first while Lenny sat (all thirteen innings, in fact), that was also, except for two fewer whiffs, exactly all we could manage off Giants starter Rod Beck (who went eleven!), and, for the second time on the season, Bill Melvin had had to turn a complete-game no-decision gem of an effort against the Clinton Giants over to a reliever.

And who was that reliever? And why four scoreless, two-hit innings later was he smiling to beat a Mardi Gras marching band?

After two consecutive bad outings out of the bullpen, Mark North had not expected Trace to have enough confidence in him to put him into a 1-1 ballgame—even considering Massicotte's only sore but not really damaged hand. Which was precisely the reason Jim Tracy the Teacher had done it.

And was why, after Rusty Crockett, playing second base that night because Sergio was having to play shortstop in place of the still-banged-up Marty, singled a sharp two-out liner into left field to score Eddie Williams from second in the top of the thirteenth to go ahead 2-1, and the Shooter let Ollie slam his own hammer with a weak groundout and two swinging K's, Jim Tracy went ahead and let himself yuk it up just a little before soon letting the Trace Monster have its so recently more dominant sway and upper hand in the battle for James Edwin Tracy's baseball soul and again started cursing *last* night's game not ten minutes after the one we'd just won was concluded.

"Goddammit!" the Trace Monster said as he spit his dip in one direction and flung his jersey against the locker in the other. "Blowing a fucking lead like that! Oh, goddam . . . I wanna tell ya, I maybe took that loss harder than all of 'em! Jesus, Mary, and Joseph . . . you realize we could be three and four? And if Ollie hadn't rolled up that spinner down in Springfield, we could be four and fucking three! And you know where that would put us, huh?"

It was certainly no secret. At that moment, a 4-and-3 record would've had us in sole possession of third place in the Southern Division, only one game back of the second-place Reds, and only *two* games back of Springfield, who'd gotten off to a fast start on the second half and at 6 and 1 were threatening to make one of their almost annual run-away-from-the-pack-and-hide sprints.

Jim Tracy muttered and cursed until finally he wound down to where it was just under his breath, and then it stopped altogether and there was only silence for a while as he sat there with his head in his hands, motionless, not with the usual head-shaking and sighing and snorting. A long while.

Then he picked his head up and looked right at me and said, "Tomorrow isn't going to be much fun, you know?"

This time we sighed together as he got his answer: "Yeah, I know, and it's gonna hurt."

"Yeah, it is . . . big changes, gentlemen," he said as he went back to staring at the floor. Then, "Lord, Lordy . . . I've got me two ballplayers I gotta talk to . . . two I never ever wanted to have *that* conversation with."

*   *   *

Almost exactly twenty-four hours later, after another 2-1 win over the Clinton Giants, in that same cubbyhole, amid the raucous whooping and hollering occasioned by a sweep, a two-game winning streak, and the prospects of the first real off day of the season on the morrow going on around and about him, Jim Tracy sat rather in sadness, speaking his heart quietly.

. . . "I've got a little bit of hurt in me tonight. He was special to me too, you know?"

A nod, a shrug, a look outside the door where Lenny Bell was dressing to the surreal experience of being the locker-room hero, even as each "atta way t' do it!" was also followed by a goodbye, and then a stare back at the same floor he was, was the only reply the Shooter got. Of course he hadn't expected nor needed one.

"But show me more character than him, huh? Here, I wantcha to see what I wrote in the game report."

He handed over his clipboard, and sure enough, there it was, to be entered officially and forever into the Cubs personnel file:

"Show me more character than Lenny Bell. Knowing he was being sent down in the morning, he chose to play when he didn't have to, then went out and got the game-winning RBI in the clutch!!!"

"Am I right, or what? And could ya write any better script than this tonight?"

Not hardly. Then the Shooter started that slow shaking of that big head and said, "Jesus, Mary, and Joseph . . . what a day this has been! Huh?"

No disagreement there either.

"I mean, this cuts to the quick . . . you know? About all of it . . . maybe even right to the gizzard of that 'What happened to Hoss?' question you're looking to find an answer to. Goddam, I mean, who gives better grist for that fucking wheel than us, huh? Nobody!"

On that day, Saturday, June 25, perhaps nobody indeed.

The bus had rolled late that afternoon. It wasn't because of Rick Wilkins. And nobody else was going to have to pay that dollar-a-minute fine which was the going rate for the contribution to the Shooter's "Boat Fund" when a Peoria Chief was late for the start of any team function. Unless Jim Tracy was going to fine himself. While our skipper does almost nothing in a hurry, he is also almost never ever late for anything. Quite paradoxically, Jim Tracy has almost a fetish about punctuality, organization, and an on-time, methodical attention to detail.

Consequently, for those very reasons, a very harried, very pissy, and also quite melancholy Trace Monster could *almost* forgive himself when he finally climbed aboard and we started that hour-and-three-quarter "commuter" trip to Clinton, Iowa, almost twenty minutes late—after all, he'd just suffered through one hell of a hectic, trying, and disorganized day.

Just the details alone had been enough. On top of his already monstrous load of everyday paperwork, he'd had to coordinate the not at all uncomplicated procedures involved in arranging to have two ballplayers sent down to Charleston, one ballplayer sent up to us from Charleston, one sent back to us from Winston-Salem, all on a weekend, and deal with the still officially only "maybe" of one coming down from Wrigley to join us in Clinton and "maybe or maybe not" be our starting pitcher that night.

But of course there was much more than just detail to all of it.

First he'd had to tell Lenny Bell and Sergio Espinal—separately, of course—that they were being sent down. And why. And then somehow respond to the varying reactions of each ballplayer. And then he had had to ask these two young men who had been with him since the '87 season, if they would go ahead and play for him that night anyway. It would be their choice. They didn't have to. And since Lenny was scheduled to fly out early Sunday morning and Sergio and Dana had a lot of packing and moving details to attend to before their long drive, it would certainly be easier on them if they chose not to. But with Marty still out of the lineup, he really would like for them both to make the trip, and absolutely needed at least one of them to.

"But it's your choice . . . and I'd understand, and nobody could blame you, if you said no."

Since they both had been anticipating the eventuality of this news, and since they both understood, and admired Jim Tracy, there had not been much in the way of the outbursts or embittered "why me?" demands that so often are the stuff of such scenes.

Sergio, smiling and chirping and wisecracking through the tears in his eyes, had finally answered, "Hey, if it's up to me, Trace, you know I wanna play . . . but, like, you know . . . I've gotta talk to my 'boss' about it. But I'll be here when the bus leaves, you can count on it."

And with that pearly smile, and those tears, "Baby" had gone home to tell Mrs. Espinal that they were heading in the wrong direction from the big leagues, but could he play tonight anyway?

Lenny's good-ol'-Texas boy, shit-eatin' wisp of a grin which is almost always there on his face no matter if he's shit-faced or pissed off, had barely flickered, and there were no tears in his eyes, only a suddenly hard, determined look in them, as he'd almost immediately just flicked his hand as if at a fly, and lazily drawled, "Hell . . . let's play ball."

"Goddam . . . that one broke my fucking heart, you know? In now two years at this job . . . that was the hardest! Telling Ding Dong. But he took it like a man, huh?" the Shooter had said after Lenny closed the door. Then he'd put a dip in his mouth, stared at the floor for a moment, and looked up and said, "Goddam . . . that was a big deal! You realize that boy was chiseled in as the starting third baseman at Peoria way back in January? Hell, before then even. Then he was the hottest hitter of the whole damn spring training . . . and for weeks he was our only hitter! I mean, for chrissakes . . . look at this.''

Then Jim Tracy had handed over a copy of the previous Sunday's *Chicago Tribune* sports page that had a sidebar story on the Chiefs which informed its readers that, besides the pitching, Lenny Bell was the ''only bright spot'' down on the Peoria farm.

''Some bright spot, huh? A hero to a goat . . . in a week! Goddam . . . that one hurt.''

''Come on, lemme buy you something, just for old times' sake,'' Lenny laughed and said shortly after leaving Trace's office, motioning toward the soda-vending machine in the mostly empty locker room of the Peoria Chiefs. ''Even if it can't be the real 'real thing'. . .''

''I guess it is only appropriate,'' I said to the strapping, good-timin' young man with whom I'd been sharing more than perhaps at times our fair share of those cups of good cheer on a quite regular and frequent basis for some fifteen weeks in a goodly number of nightclubs, taverns, saloons, and even a run-down pool hall or two stretching from Arizona to Illinois, Indiana, Wisconsin, and Iowa.

And as we clanked those aluminum cans together in toast, I said, ''Aw, what the hell . . . it's nice this time of the year in West Virginia.''

''You ever been there?'' A nod. ''Really . . . what was it like?''

''Uh, that's another story . . . but the mountains and the scenery and all's great.'' There seemed to be no need to delve into the problems one can encounter trying to get a legal drink in far too many of the dry counties in that otherwise often lovely state; he'd find out soon enough.

A sigh, a shrug of the shoulders, a chug of cola, then, ''Aw, fuck it . . . nothin' to it. I never could get my swing back after the injury. I came back when it was still hurting, and that affected it . . . and then when I was healthy, I couldn't find it again.''

Another sigh, a shrug, more cola, and then there came again that hard, determined look in his eyes and he said, ''But, I wantcha to know I'm not down on myself . . . I'm just going to go down there and get it together.''

Amid the emotionalism of that long day, and his efforts to make sure that all of the arrangements for ''my boys going down . . . God love 'em, are done *right,* I owe 'em that''—which was the primary reason we were almost twenty minutes late leaving: he was back and forth on the phone with Brad Mills, the Charleston manager, and Dennis Bastien, the owner of the Charleston Wheelers—the thing that was to him the most secondary of priorities that day was also the thing that was most driving Jim Tracy ''up the fucking walls!''

And that was whether in real *fact* would it be Scott Sanderson, major league All-Star, starting on the mound for the Peoria Chiefs that evening, or Mike Aspray, whose turn in the rotation it was.

Why all the confusion? And why were the words "tentatively," "probably," "he's supposed to" added to any and all of the flurry of communiqués from Wrigley Field to the Chiefs' offices that day? Because the only one who knew for sure whether or not he was going to pitch for Peoria that night was Scott Sanderson.

He didn't have to. He also had the choice of whether or not he wanted to play for Jim Tracy under the banner of the Peoria Chiefs that particular night. In accordance with the rules of the Basic Agreement between the Player's Union and major league baseball, Mr. Sanderson could not be forced to accept any "rehab assignment" at lower than the major league level if he chose not to.

"I don't know, Kranny . . . we know he's already put the kibosh on Pittsfield."

"He'll be there. I don't see where he's really got that much of a choice . . . for that very reason. I mean, he's gotta pitch somewhere. And since he's already used his veto once, pretty soon it gets to be either come . . . or else."

That "or else" was the one option the Chicago Cubs had in this scenario, and of course it was the trump card: if he proved to be too difficult they could reactivate him from off the disabled list and then outright release him, since he himself had said that he was physically sound, or trade him; understanding full well that no other club would assume that salary with all the zeros in it without also wanting to know he was fully recovered from major back surgery by sending him to pitch at least once in their minor league system. So, in reality, Scott Sanderson's choices were only where and when.

"Yeah . . . well, this 'probably' and 'yes, he's *agreed* to do it, so he *should* be there' horseshit is playing hell with my already bad day."

"He'll be there, Trace," Kranny said. "It's perfect for him . . . by agreeing to do it at the last minute, and then choosing to do it in Clinton, Iowa, he's pretty much assured that it won't be as much of a media zoo as otherwise."

"Aw, Christ . . . like this is a distraction I need right now. I got our own ballplayers coming and going like it's Grand Central Station . . . have no idea what that's gonna do for morale . . . I got a shaky starting rotation, a tired bullpen . . . haven't got a clue what my infield's gonna be . . . and I'm maybe just two or three quick wins away from getting smack dab in the middle of this phony fucking half-season pennant hunt . . . which I still think's a crocka shit even as I thank God for it this year!"

"Trace?" interrupted the Kran-dog. "He's going to help with at least two of those problems . . . don'tcha think?"

A beat or two. "Damn, you know he's right." Then, "Aw, Christ, he probably won't even be there anyway . . . and after all this bullshit we been . . ."

"Trace, I'm telling you, he'll be there. Probably come driving up in a chauffeured limousine . . . just in time to warm up . . . trailing his entourage."

"Aw, Jesus, Mary, and Joseph!"

Sergio was there when the bus rolled. But he wasn't on it. With a grim and stern Dana sitting out in the car, he had come to say some goodbyes, clarify his travel orders and expenses, and apologetically explain what we all understood anyway.

Dana, of course, had said no. If they were going to treat "Baby" that way, then she saw no reason why their departure should be a madcap affair, and she ruled that his time would be better spent helping her.

Scott Sanderson was there waiting for us. And he was alone. He'd driven his own modest sedan down from Chicago, had arrived early, and was relaxing his long, tall, very lean body and mind up in the shade of the empty grandstands of Riverview Stadium by his serene lonesome when we'd arrived.

Except for Mario and one book writer who shortly joined him there in his tranquillity—which also seemed to be the only place where there was any breeze to stir the 100-degree-plus air around—the only "media zoo" he'd had to contend with was one local sportswriter and one local radio guy who'd spotted him sitting there and had come down to collect a few politely and patiently delivered quotes and then had gone on about their way.

Even if at the cost of that tranquillity—which all but exudes from the person of the slow-talking, quick-thinking, dark-haired handsome man who stands six-five but is also as thin as a rail—I just had to ask the most obvious but, as of then, unasked question; "Is there pressure for a big-time pitcher to come to this level and try to get hitters out?"

"Yes," he said flat-out, without any hesitation. Then he chuckled just a little, apparently at the look on my face, and went on to say, "I suppose you were expecting another answer. But the truth is, I can go out there and embarrass myself . . . and this is Single A? Sure . . . I'd be more comfortable pitching against major leaguers. If I don't do well, all right . . . they're major league hitters and I'm recovering. But . . . well, let me tell you a story. Back when I was with Montreal, I also had an injury . . . it was the back, but not the same thing . . . and I was sent down to the California League, I think it was Lodi, and I was doing the same thing I'm doing here. I'm pitching, and . . . you know Devon White? Right. So this kid hits a home run off me and I'm watching him jog around the bases . . . and I'm saying, 'Hey' . . . and I had my really good stuff back then . . . and I'm saying, 'Hey, this guy's pretty good! I mean, he's got to be good. Jeez, I hope he's good! He's a Single A ballplayer and he just hit me out of the ballpark?' Well, a year later Devon White was in the major leagues, and boy, did I feel better."

"See . . . you must be a pretty good scout, too."

"Yeah . . . but the trouble was, I wasn't sure!"

And then it was time get on about preparing to play a ballgame.

"Hey, they're short," Lenny Bell said as we walked through the tunnel from the visitor's locker room out toward the ballyard. "They need me . . . I'm even gonna start at third, isn't that kinda funny? But you know what? I'm gonna go out of the Midwest League in a blaze of glory . . . I'm gonna have a good game!"

It was another one of those damn good games the Chiefs seemed to always have with our buddies the Clinton Giants. It was also "a hell of a clinic for my pitchers, huh? Jesus, how can anybody throw a curve that slow . . . and put it and everything else exactly where he wants it every time and at every speed? I mean, I can tell them about how it's supposed to be done, but to see it? That's believing!" So said Rick Kranitz—who, just like the rest of us, had been completely won over by the unpretentious, self-effacing, just-one-of-the-guys, natural, easy charm Scott Sanderson displayed that night when, for five innings, and in four octaves, he had, as the star attraction for a standing-room-only crowd of some 3,600, performed a Mozart aria with the strike zone.

In those five innings, throwing a curveball, slider, fastball, and change-up, which, on ex–Cub infielder and now Pittsburgh Pirates scout Gene Baker's ray gun, had registered from 58 to 63, 73 to 75, 83 to 87, and 78 to 82 miles per hour respectively, he walked no one, went to a 2-1 count only once; and, while there were perhaps more than just a couple future big leaguers in the Giants' lineup that evening, none of those speeds or pitches were sent back hard enough to "hit him out of the ballpark."

There were, however, four would-be-Giants who could now at least be able to forever say that they had once gotten a base hit off a major league pitcher. Even if three of them will have to wait for the passage of time before they become anything but the soft flares they were. Or, as in the words of Gene Baker, "Tomorrow that'll be a line drive . . . and in a few years it'll be off the wall or in the river. They do get longer and louder as time goes by, don't they?"

Unfortunately (well, at least for the moment), the one ball that was hit hard led, somewhat indirectly, to one unearned run being scored. Which was why when Scott Sanderson had finished his allotted five innings and headed for the locker room, he was the pitcher of record on the wrong side of a 1-0 score. And even though it was one of those really good ballgames that you don't see every night, Rick Kranitz and I weren't far behind him.

And was why the pitching coach of the Peoria Chiefs and their resident chronicler were having the game's progress relayed to us through the tunnel by the ever frenetic Stevie Melendez, as Rick Kranitz and his "on loan" pitching star—who was technically also his pupil—critiqued and assessed his game.

"I'm pleased," Scott answered Kranny's first obligatory question as he was draping that long, lanky frame on top of the big wooden Chiefs' traveling dispensary, hardware store, and quartermaster's chest that was crammed into the already cramped locker room so tightly that you got to know anybody trying to get past you perhaps a little more than you would've preferred, peeling off the layers and yards of adhesive tape that bound his long, thin patrician ankles and shins himself instead of sitting back on a commodious trainer's table in a major league locker room having someone else do it for him if he so desired, and was known to leave the proper tip at the end of each series.

"I mean, under the circumstances." A smile and a chuckle, then, "Of course, I wish the other team would've cooperated and not gotten those four hits."

"Typical pitcher . . . first time out and he's upset that anybody hit him at all. But from what you wanted to work on, what do you think?"

"I was wild in the strike zone. I know I didn't walk anybody, but—"

"Big guy . . . you only went to one two-one count."

"Yeah . . . I mean, I don't want to take anything away from those guys in the other dugout . . . but if my location had been as pinpoint as it needs to be, if I'd been able to throw better, hard strikes, those flares would've been broken bats. What did you see?"

"Sure, I saw some of all that . . . but I also think you're maybe being too critical. For the first time back, I'd have to write it up as excellent."

It was just about then that Stevie Melendez ran back to tell us that Rick Wilkins had led off the seventh with another double off the wall.

"Thanks, Stevie . . . maybe, huh?" Kranny said and then continued on with Scott Sanderson. "Really, that's as good as I've seen your curveball. You were changing speeds with it and throwing it for strikes. So, all right, what else about what you wanted to find out tonight? Any pain at all?"

"Yeah . . . that sharp line drive to right field! But, no, felt great . . . no pain at all in my back."

"Good. So what else?"

Before Scott could answer, Stevie came running back and told us that Jerry LaPenta had just singled Wilkins in to tie the game.

"Goddam. . . ? Well, at least you won't get tagged for a loss in A ball to ugly up your stats."

"Yeah, but I gave up a run."

"It was unearned."

"But it was a run . . . and that's something I'm just going to have to think about as I drive back to Chicago replaying every pitch in my mind. Funny, that's when I do my best thinking, behind a wheel."

"So all right . . . what else should you be thinking about as you leave here? And you're not coming back, Scott . . . you don't need another start at this level, and that's how I'm gonna report it."

"Whatever . . . and thanks. But I also didn't throw enough change-ups."

"So what are the things you want to think about and work on between now and your next start?"

"Well, one thing I won't have to think about is that foul ball over the fence." Scott had laughed and then had explained to the book writer. "They'd told me this guy's got a slow bat—they'd pointed him out to me—and I'm thinking, 'If he's got a slow bat, and he pulled my fastball like that? Maybe I'd better stay in the minor leagues!' But when I got back to the dugout, I said, 'That guy's got a slow bat?' And they said, 'No, it was the guy on deck.' Boy, did I feel better! Anyway . . . what I need to work on, Kranny, is better control in the strike zone, get my velocity up a little more . . . and bring my change-up along."

Then came Stevie again. Mike Boswell had grounded out, but he'd managed to advance LaPenta to second.

"You know, this is fun!" Scott Sanderson then said. "I didn't spend much time in the minor leagues. And it's fun playing with these kids . . . their enthusiasm . . ."

Shouted relay this time: "They're walking Elvie . . . gonna pitch to Bell!"

"Ah, shit!" said Kranny. "But look, Scott, I really think it went well. I'll be honest with you, I wasn't expecting anything close to that for your first time back. It was a joy to watch you work . . . I mean that."

And that's when Stevie came a-running and a-hollering at the same time. "He did it! Lenny did it! Clean single to left! We're up two-one!"

"All right!" Scott Sanderson yelped and pumped his fist in the air, as if he were still some high school kid and this was for a state championship. He wanted his team to win. No matter that he was thirty-one years old and already a ten-year major league veteran who was in Clinton, Iowa, pitching a one-time rehab assignment for a Single A ballclub. It was a ballgame, and he wanted to be on the winning side.

Just shortly thereafter, Rusty Crockett came running down the tunnel to get some more bubble gum from his locker before taking the field for the bottom of the seventh. As he passed us going back, Scott Sanderson reached out, stopped him, and then tweaked his shoulder.

"Just wanted to see if you had padding in there," he said to the blushing, grinning, pretty much speechless little professional veteran of exactly seven days.

When the embarrassed but proudly beaming young man had to turn and dash back down the tunnel so he wouldn't be late, Scott called after him, "Hey, kid . . . I like the way you play. Go get 'em, Rusty!"

Then Mr. Sanderson headed toward the showers so that he might get dressed and start that long "thoughtful" drive back to Chicago. And we headed back to watch Mike Aspray finish picking up his fourth win of the season by pitching four innings of two-hit shutout ball; but not before the Kran-dog explained:

"Now, that's the difference between a major league pitcher and a minor leaguer. You understand the kind of control he's talking about? The difference between a flared hit and a broken bat is maybe an inch or less of wood and a mile or two an hour one way or the other. I mean, most *major league* pitchers throw to an area about the size of a small hatbox, but what he's talking about is about the size of a ring box! Now that's concentration . . . and *will*!"

". . . he's just got to go down and get his swing back, that's all." Even though Jim Tracy was of course happy about now being 3 and 5 with that just completed game, and that he had also very much enjoyed the presence of Scott Sanderson (off whom he'd once homered when they were both rookies in the Florida State League) his thoughts were still more on Lenny Bell leaving the family, so he was as yet more melancholy than ebullient as he still sat only half-undressed in his cubbyhole at Riverview Stadium well after most of the other quite exuberant members of the family had already left the clubhouse and were outside by the bus milling about with their women or had already walked on over to the Hardee's just down the street.

But then the Shooter being the Shooter, he'd eventually muttered and mused long enough to cheer himself back up. "Hell . . . Ding Dong's gonna be all right. He proved that tonight. The one tool God can't give a ballplayer is character . . . hell, call it attitude, desire, the ability to take it all and keep coming back, whatever, he's got it. And mark my words, whatever he does in Charleston for the rest of this season . . . Lenny's gonna be back next year—and it won't be here, either . . . it'll be at a higher level . . . and damn! You know something else? We just might be back in this race. We're only four games back of Springfield, we got Kenosha coming down for four at home—and it looks like we've got their number—so you realize we could be going into next weekend's series with Springfield with a real shot of coming out in first place? Jeeze'em'tally . . . figure that, huh? Even though folks would probably think we were plum crazy talking that way . . . hell, we are still a 13-under-.500 ballclub!"

Then the Shooter spit a dip, slapped his leg, and really cackled. "But something tells me not for long! And lemme tell ya something else . . . you're gonna love this third baseman we got coming. He's a 'gamer' if ever there was one. Dick Canan . . . even sounds like what a ballplayer should be called, huh? He looks like a ballplayer, too! You know what I mean? Just got that look. And if he's really healthy like they say? Look out . . . 'cause we just might make us some noise here in this second half . . ."

"Yeah . . . well, why don't you get dressed so maybe we can get home in time to make some fun noises tonight!," said the Kran-dog. "It's Saturday night in P-Town . . . and Trace, we don't have a ballgame tomorrow!"

Perhaps it was crazy, but whatever that optimism was, it was absolutely rampant outside around the bus and down at Hardee's.

As I was helping Mass, Nuke, and Boz off-load the cases of beer that, because of the packaged liquor Sunday blue laws back in Peoria and the fact that we would get back after midnight, one of the wives had been kind enough to go in her car and buy there in Clinton, ensuring that their off day would not be a dry one, Jeff Massicotte stopped in his labors and said:

"I don't know . . . but I think maybe we're on a roll. And if we could get into first place? I know these boys—we could coast!"

"Mass, you tellin' me they could hold it?"

"Bank on it. I played with these boys last year. If we get into first, we'll hold it."

The bus rolled to P-Town, and there was much partying, and at the end of that partying, as we were all finally heading our own way for the morning of our first real off-day of the season, Jim Tracy had shaken that head just as he always does at such moments, and said, "One hell of a day, huh?"

Indeed it had been. Though bone-tired and with a spinning head, I could not drift off to sleep without thinking about. . .

—that last goodbye to Lenny Bell, who would not be having a day off. "Well . . . I won't have much time to savor being the hero. Trace told me that Brad Mills has already penciled me into the lineup for tomorrow . . . I'm hitting clean-up! Drink a few for me, will ya, I'm gonna need it . . . 'cause now I'm supposed to be *the man* down there. Damn funny game . . . huh?" And how some hours thereafter, Jim Tracy, still troubled by that goodbye, so sadly said, "You know, I wasn't in agreement with sending him down. Had real mixed feelings. I know he'd lost his stroke. But he'd *had it* . . . 'course, even then he wasn't hitting the curveball. So . . . I guess it's best for him . . . help him get his confidence back against that pitching down there. But, damn! I worked so *hard* with him, you know that. And I think I was getting through. You see . . . when I look at Lenny I see so much of myself . . . same kinda ballplayer, same kinda tools. *But* because somebody believed in me, and made me believe in myself, I got to play in the big leagues. You understand what I'm saying?"

—what Jim Tracy had said about Sergio going down. "He's getting a little long in the tooth for a utility infielder who's yet to have even one good year. Let's just put it this way, these next two months are *very* important to him . . . and he might just oughta be thinking about that offer to go back and be a coach at Oklahoma State, except Dana wouldn't let him. Nah, they're gonna have to send Serge home . . . and do him a favor."

—what Scott Sanderson had said about Rick Wilkins as a prospect: "I really like him—you know, Jim Sundberg is really high on him. You know how in spring training, when we're all together, you notice some of the young kids, the ones with the tools? But more importantly that hard, determined look and hard-work ethic. Well, Sunny picked out Wilkins. He said he has work ahead of him, a few years maybe, but that he'll be a major leaguer. I told Rick what Sunny had said, and then I added, 'So when the bus rides get long, the road bumpy, just remember that you're going to play in the big leagues.' And right now I think he's already a fine receiver . . . and you can tell he's not afraid to be a leader, to stand out alone. He just doesn't know quite how yet . . . and he's having to learn on the job. That's tough. But he has that look. Rick's going to be one that makes it. Because you can tell he wants it bad enough . . . and that's really what it takes."

—and about Dick Canan, the man who was coming to take Ding Dong's seat at the family table, the twenty-four-year-old with the baseball name and baseball face who would be at third base for us when next we played. And how if anyone should be allowed to come and take Ding Dong's place in our hearts, that it should be this fourth-year pro who would now be making his third return to Peoria. Because comebacks are so much the real stuff of this game of ours; and his, if he did it, would be a splendid one indeed.

After a standout amateur career, Dick had been drafted by the Cubs out of the University of Illinois in only the fourteenth round because his "gamer" style of play had cost him two broken legs—one in multiple places—and much of his speed. But then he'd gone on to have a solid enough rookie season at Wytheville, and was then the starting third baseman on the talent-laden '86 Peoria Chiefs. In that season he had established himself as a bona fide third-base prospect in an organization in need of just such commodities—but with still a few rough edges. So it was decided that he should begin the '87 season again at Peoria, but with the expectation of moving him up shortly thereafter.

Unfortunately it wasn't short enough. Opening Night of the 1987 season, after going 3 for 4, his family had taken him out for a steak dinner to celebrate. During the course of that meal, a most freakish accident had occurred. Reflexively, as some cutlery was about to fall from the table, Dick had reached out to catch it. He did. And what he caught was the wrong end of a steak knife and it severed a large tendon which then rolled up like a spring, sucking the hand and forearm right with it. Surgery was required to reattach the tendon, yet Dick had recovered well enough to return and see some limited service in the latter half of the '87 season. It was also very ineffectual service. Which was directly attributable to the lost time, of course, and he was still considered a real prospect who might perhaps be given the opportunity to begin the '88 season even as high as Double A.

Then, only days before the start of spring training, while Dick had been sitting watching television, methodically squeezing the rubber ball he'd been using all of the off-season to regain the atrophied strength he'd lost, he heard a *snap!* and then saw his arm curl up the same as before. More surgery. More rehab. And he'd missed all of spring training. When well enough, he'd gone down to Mesa with the other walking wounded of extended spring training. Then, with his stock slipping as possibly "damaged goods," he'd been sent to Charleston. Where, in twenty-eight games, he'd hit only .211, but had showed himself to be fully recovered from the injury. So, what the hell, maybe a change of uniforms would be good for both of them, and, since Pete had been asking for him from the moment he'd heard he was available, the decision was made for Peoria and Charleston to switch third basemen. They got a young second-year colt, and we got what in the world of minor league baseball is an aging-fast, twenty-four-year-old saddle horse back to the place where when he'd been a second-year colt; he had played with guys who were now in Triple A and even the big leagues.

Dick Canan had a lot of ground to make up fast.

And if he could do it here and now? Sorry, Ding Dong. See you in spring training. And bring on the "cannon"!

"Jeez'em'fuckin'tally!" By Wednesday, with a seat in "Pete's Perch" a daily prize in a radio station contest, we had our first five-game winning streak of the season, had now beaten our "brother-in-law" Kenosha Twins, the defending league champs and Northern Division first-half winners, 5 out of 5 on the season, and were now 6 and 5 on the "second chance"—and even more exciting?

"Trace . . . Springfield lost . . . we're only three back!"

"No shit? Hey, maybe you'd better just stay up on that roof the whole season, huh boss?"

"Whatever you say, Doc . . . but, how bad's Rusty?"

"At least a slight separation . . . we'll know more tomorrow."

We would indeed. We would learn that in the first inning, on a spectacular, seemingly impossible diving catch for out 2, Rusty Crockett had not only suffered a slight shoulder separation but had "jammed that fucker up pretty good . . . goddam! And he's our pepper pot" and would be out of action "indefinitely."

"But, hey, Mule . . . guys . . . nuh uh, we've come too far to be a one-man team. Haven't we? I mean I've gotta believe that we're now too good of a ballclub to let one rookie midget's going down put us back in the shitter. Nuh huh, all this means is I'll just be wearing out more erasers putting together a lineup. I mean, jeeze'em'fuckin'tally . . . let's just finish sweeping up these brother-in-law Twins of our . . . and then go bite us at least a part of first place out of them Redbirds' ass!"

Now we're talking a real dose of high-octane optimism here. I mean, just for instance, bright and early Thursday morning Pete Vonachen had said:

"Trace is the difference. We all gave up. Even you, admit it. But, he didn't! He's a *teacher* . . . and they're finally starting to learn. . . !"

Peter of Peoria saying that? And *meaning* it with all his heart? I mean, shit fire, save them matches, and get that big net out again. Because how could we lose!

Actually, we had to work pretty hard at it, that's how.

Although at first it looked like we weren't going to have to do a thing to lose except watch Billy "Nuke" Mel—with Angie sitting there right behind home plate—get his suddenly again 83-mile-an-hour fastball hammered. But when he gave up a rocket over the TWA sign in left to lead off the fourth, to make it 4-1 Twins, and immediately thereafter surrendered another base hit that was a single only because it was hit too hard, Jim Tracy stomped out there to the mound, shaking his head and muttering all the way, and unceremoniously dismissed "Lover'fuckin'boy" to go get showered up for "the fucking Black Widow" and brought in Ollie.

And lo and behold if the new Peoria Chiefs don't throw a 4 on the scoreboard themselves in the fifth to take a 5-4 lead that, with Ollie humming along in a shutdown and shutout groove, was stretched to 6-4 by the beginning of the eighth.

When Ollie walked the first man up, Jim Tracy didn't hesitate. He gave Ollie a well-deserved "atta' baby" and the ball to his number-one right-handed setup man, Jeff Massicotte. This one's in the bag, right? First a little of "Grandpa's" two-speeds bender action on them, and then the Z man to close the deal. Wrong. While Jeff bent a nasty enough one in there to get an easy chopper back to him, he also bent his throw to first base way the hell out by the second of the "Cubbyhole" and "Friendly Confines" picnic decks and the runner Ollie had walked now ran all the way around for a run to make it 6-5. And then three singles out of the next five batters later, it was 7-6, the wrong way.

"Tough one to lose," mused a really not very upset Jim Tracy who'd just seen his team score six runs on nine hits." But we can't let Springfield run away with it . . . too easy to do in this split-season crap. I believe I shoulda went to Z when it was still 6-5 . . ."

"Shoulda! Goddam . . . what the fuck you think I was screaming for?"

The Shooter actually laughed and said, "You oughta heard my Mule

. . . never heard him that mad. He's just going crazy in that dugout about Mass. 'Take that son of a bitch out! I'm gonna kill him!,' over and over, up and down the dugout . . . and of course he was right . . ."

"Right? I'm still gonna kill him!"

"Maybe you're wanting to kill the wrong person . . . and the wrong gender," Phil Theobald said.

"Mel really stunk it up, didn't he?"

"Trace . . . that shit's ruined more careers than anything else. But then it serves 'em right . . . if they can't understand," answered Theobald.

"I guess I'm just gonna have to explain it to him a little better this time . . . and not so diplomatically."

That's when Pete Vonachen poked his head into Trace's office and said, "What's this . . . a wake? So we blew one, that's just baseball."

Pete Vonachen saying that?! Of course he then said, "By the way . . . Springfield lost again, guys."

Jim Tracy hadn't been on the bus as it had rolled south that next afternoon for the beginning of the '88 season's most anticipated event, the four-game home-and-away, Fourth of July holiday series with Springfield. Much earlier he had driven north to Rockford to join with all of the other managers in the Midwest League to vote on the players for the All-Star Game to be played July 11 in Clinton, Iowa.

But he'd pushed his van hard and was out of his Sunday-go-to-meeting clothes and in uniform in plenty of time for him to join us and soon be dipping and spitting and leaning on the batting cage as a bustling, bun-tinged, and festive Lanphier Park was already beginning to fill up.

"Well, we got two on the All-Star Team," he said after making us wait some few minutes so he could milk our suspense. "Kal and Z . . . it's the best I could do . . . and let's face it, that's all that really deserved it."

Shortly thereafter, a young man who back in April everyone would've bet good money would be named to his second professional All-Star Team, and who in fact Jim Tracy had thought he might be able to lobby in anyway, stepped out of the cage after a round of BP not quite to his liking, threw his bat, kicked some baseballs, and said in disgust, "I'm nothing but horseshit!"

"Horseshit?" Trace said to Rick Wilkins. "You've been throwing runners out, you've been driving in runs . . . if that's horsehit, give me horseshit. Don't go back to playing 'good' like you were before. Jeez . . . get madder at yourself than you—nobody!"

Then, quietly, in an aside, Jim Tracy said, "You gotta hand it to him. He works hard, and puts all the pressure on himself . . . he *wants* it. And remember . . . you've gotta have a little asshole in you to be obsessed enough to make it to where he wants to go."

That "asshole" had a very good at bat to lead off the fourth inning, fouling off several pitcher's pitches, got deep into the count, and then lined a sharp single the other way, and then, after two polite singles by Pookie and Dick Canan and a walk by Elvin Paulino, Rick Wilkins scored to tie the game at 1-1.

Then, in the sixth inning, his roommate, "the Cap," who has absolutely no asshole in him, after Dick Canan had again singled and Elvie too, hit a three-run homer to left to make it a 4-1 ballgame.

Which, since we had Silent Kal on the mound for his first start since coming back from his all-too-short promotion, was all we needed to spoil the first of the two fireworks shows that Springfield general manager Lee Landers had planned for the series.

Oh my! On my honor—or take that man over there waiting for a bus's word for it—minor leagues or no, we're talking some big-time euphoria and excitement action going on here. Big Crowd! Big Deal! Big win!

On the first of a four-night holiday weekend, some four thousand screaming fans—and, since Springfield is almost exactly halfway between Chicago and St. Louis, one of the oldest, most traditional of heated major league rivalries, not just a few were screaming for us!—saw the Peoria Chiefs, the whipping boys of the first half, knock off the home boys to climb within two games of first place.

And now they had to come to *our* yard for Saturday's and Sunday's games, where there were sure to be a good deal more than four thousand in attendance, and very few of them would have any problem with a dichotomy of loyalty.

While there was much jubilation, rollicking high jinks, and ribald frivolity throughout the family as we ate our concession-stand meal under the grandstands of Lanphier Park that Friday night, there was one Chief who, even though he was going home to more fun for certain than the rest of us, had some measure of apprehension showing through the outward good cheer. Billy "Nuke" Mel motioned one of us aside and whispered in that golly-gee-ma'am manner of his, "Trace just told me he wants to have a meeting with me tomorrow in the office. I mean, I know what it's about . . . and I know we've gotta slow it down . . . but, honest, I've stopped sleeping with her before starts!"

Even though the Peoria Chiefs, and their fans throughout North Central Illinois, awoke that following Saturday morning to the news that Cedar Rapids had also won the night before, and that they were now in first place and we were still actually three games back, from early morning on the Chiefs' offices were like that of an assayer's in a full-blown gold rush.

Extra help had to be called in to handle the demand for tickets. By noon it was a complete sellout, yet still they came and the decision was made to keep selling, but to explain to the purchasers that it would be standing room only and first come, first sit in the bleachers.

Therefore, in a ballpark that officially seats five thousand, there were a

Peoria Chiefs record 6,969 people jammed into Meinen Field that night to see Carl Hamilton, who had now taken over Brett's spot in the rotation, again throw pure "slop" for six precarious innings with that left arm of his that he kept on insisting to an unbelieving Trace and Kranny was "just a little stiff," and the Chiefs went on to lose a 5-4 heartbreaker that wasn't decided until Z hung a change-up in the ninth to that old buddy of mine, Scott Raziano, who had just previously made a game-saving, impossible, over-the-shoulder diving catch of a Mike Boswell looping liner with the bases loaded.

"Jesus, Mary, and Joseph . . . some game, huh? One different bounce here or there and we're maybe working on a sweep. But ya gotta love the way we keep coming back at 'em, don'tcha? But . . . Mule? First it's our starters . . . now it's the bullpen? Jeez'em'fuckin'tally . . . you guys realize if our bullpen, what we thought was our strength, hadda done the job they'd been doing for two and a half months . . . we'd be nine in a row! And if Ollie doesn't roll that fucking spinner, and Mel don't shit all over himself 'cause of the Black Widow . . . we're twelve and two and there would be no pennant race!"

"I'm gonna kill 'em, Trace! I swear I'm gonna. . . !"

"Listen at my Mule here, would ya? Hey, calm down, Kranny. We're all right . . . we're hitting the fucking baseball and scoring runs . . . and we know your guys can pitch. It's all gonna come together."

So did 7,159 Peoria Chiefs fans on Sunday night. While breaking and setting attendance records on consecutive nights is indeed exciting, and is a meritorious achievement for a fine minor league staff, on that night perhaps we would've preferred that about three hundred of them had been anywhere else *but* Meinen Field to watch two teams go at each other with hammer and tongs for nine innings and still be tied 1-1.

You see, if those good folks had maybe gone to the movies or something, then the game would've already been over and we'd have been on our way to Sullivan's and then Spirits and then Sully's, etc., to celebrate instead of still being at Meinen Field with Jeff Massicotte going to the hill in the top of the tenth.

Because, in the seventh inning, after Marty Rivero had singled, Herbie Andrade, getting a start at DH that night, with the hit-and-run on, turned on an inside fastball and hit a shot out into the left-field corner that surely would've rattled around out there long enough for Marty to score and even slow-footed Herbie to have chugged into second with a stand-up double and the game-winning RBI.

But no, that many people have to go somewhere. So the decision was made to rope off the left-field foul territory behind the Chiefs bullpen and put them right where Herbie's now ground-rule double would rattle around among the paying customers as Marty was sent back to third.

All right, so that many people just buy some more beer and settle in for an extended, hotly contested extra-inning affair and squeaker, right? Not on your "I'm gonna kill him!" heart.

The first thing Jeff Massicotte did was surrender a wall-banging double to Chuck Johnson, then he hit Ray Lankford, and allowed an infield single to Dave Payton to load the bases with nobody out. And then who stepped up to the plate? That buddy from back home, Scott Raziano, who just two innings before had driven in the tying run with a single. Well, that goddam buddy of mine hit another bullet single to drive two runs in and Jeff Massicotte out.

Then Ollie came on and gave up three hits wrapped around three Chiefs errors, and a 1-1 tie becomes an 8-1 blowout which made for a most anticlimactic fireworks display that very few members of the family hung around long enough to watch.

We were now 7-and-8, one game under .500 for the second half, twelve under on the season, and, at the moment and more important to many, we were now five games back in the pennant hunt.

"Oh, goddam . . . oh, goddam . . . people on the fucking field!"

"I'm gonna kill all of 'em!"

"Aw, fuck it . . . people on the field or not, we didn't deserve to win it. Not when you leave ten fucking runners on base and score only one run! Goddam . . . have we stopped hitting, too?"

"I'm gonna kill 'em . . . I swear it . . ."

It was during that game that Angie wanted to talk about "the affair." She was now very much aware of the talk, the controversy, but "I'm taking as good a care of him as his mother. I'm running all over buying special vitamins and loading him up with only the healthiest of foods . . . making sure he sleeps better than he did in that apartment. Don't they understand that I love him and wouldn't do anything to hurt his career? That I want to help, not hurt?"

"No," was my honest answer. "They don't."

"I don't know what to do. Trace has him worrying to death about this . . . but still he wants me to come to Quad Cities for his next start . . . and I want to go. He says he feels better when I'm there. What should I do?"

"Go," was again my honest answer. "I do believe in magic, but I don't believe in old wives' tales."

All that next morning and early afternoon, Monday, the Fourth of July, and all the way down to Springfield, Kranny stared holes through the game charts and cursed his bullpen.

"Lord . . . be madder than him? Nobody," Jim Tracy said as he got off the bus at Lanphier Park for the finale of the annual Fourth of July Springfield Series.

"Jeez'em'tally . . . my Mule's pissed, ain't he? The Kran-dog's beside himself . . . he's livid. I wouldn't wanna be the first or the last man out of the bullpen tonight, huh?"

No one had to be. Mike Aspray went nine innings, "pitched" his ass off, gave up four hits, walked one, and lost 1-0.

We'd now lost three in a row, were 7-and-9 on the second half, had dropped into fourth place just behind our next foe, the Quad Cities Angels, were thirteen games under for the year, and had scored one run in the last twenty innings.

"They looked a little lethargic out there tonight, Trace," Kranny said over his chicken strips.

"No shit," Trace said over the cheeseburger he couldn't eat.

Just before we left for the first of two commuters with the Quad Cities Angels, Jim Tracy said, "Good ballclubs, when they hit a stretch with a tired bullpen, or the starting pitching is slumping, find ways to win anyway. We can't seem to do that."

Pookie Bernstine walked into Trace's office with his ribs taped up tight due to a Jeremy Hernandez fastball he'd taken in the ribs the night before and said, "You really need me tonight, Skip?"

Trace put his head in his hands, shook his head hard several times, and then looked up and called for Stevie.

"Can Rusty just DH?"

Stevie Melendez, seeing the almost desperation in Trace's face, moving from one foot to the other, hem-hawed around trying to tell the Trace Monster what was of course the obvious until finally Kranny walked in and heard the gist of the conversation and said, "Trace . . . you're gonna play him? He was only able to swing the bat one-handed yesterday. And you know he's one of those headfirst launchers when he slides."

"Christ . . . you're right, I can't do that. Can't take that chance. Oh, goddam . . . see what this shit's doing to me? What I wouldn't do to get a fucking run, just one fucking run when it means something . . . and that little pepperpot just loves to come up there with the game on the line! And guys . . . this is it, you understand that, huh? These next six games? We have to make a move now, or it's over."

It was a hell of a game—that had been preceded by one of the Trace Monster's locked-door "There's gonna be a lotta pink slips coming!" fire-and-brimstone revival sermons. It had been one of Trace's better ones, and little Rusty, who of course could do nothing to help, had come out looking a little stunned by it all. "Welcome to professional baseball, Davey," I said.

Then, with Angie sitting beside us for moral support, Bill Melvin pitched as well as he had all season for nine innings. His only mistake had been in not walking Bob Rose, the Angels' third baseman, who would be in the Hall of Fame if he only had to play against the Chiefs—six of his then eight home runs on the season had come against the Chiefs, and his batting average against us was somewhere up in the stratosphere. But Mel pitched to him, and sure enough Mr. Rose hit a two-run homer in the second inning.

But that's all they got as Mel's fastball was consistently registering at 88, 89—and even a couple of 90s—on Gene Baker's gun. This was of course of such importance that—much to the relief of Angie—one of my happier duties that night was to report those encouraging speeds to Kranny at different intervals throughout Mel's stint. While Kranny was pleased with those numbers, he still would give that shrug of "Yeah, but I don't know . . . ?" and then look up at Angie and shake his head. Much as Trace was shaking his in the third-base coaching box as our total of five hits through thirteen innings had produced but two runs in the seventh, and one of those had been wild-pitched in.

Then came the bottom of the thirteenth. After escaping a two-on, two-out situation in the frame before, Mass put himself right back into another one by wrapping two walks around a hard line-out to short and a foul-out to first—except this time it was more than just a situation, and in fact more than a pickle and a jam, because it was "that fucking Rose again." He yanked the first pitch past Dick Canan at third so hard that there was going to be a play at the plate. Gator, if he could get a good jump and a good throw, could get the runner. He got the first two but they weren't quite good enough and Wiley Lee was well past the plate when Wilkins's catch and swipe-back tag found a knee—and "Grandpa," who'd had the composure, or the muscle memory, to run and set himself in position behind the plate to back up the throw, sank to one knee, put his head in his hands, and started crying; and we're not talking just that moist glistening in saddened eyes.

At first none of the Chiefs noticed him as they were leaving the field in that sick moment of instant defeat. But then Billy Mel did. He was the first to reach the sobbing youth and kneel down beside him and put his arm about those heaving shoulders. Then Mike Aspray came and picked him up to his feet. But could get him to walk only as far as a metal folding chair beside the dugout. There he sat hunched over and cried by himself until well after the grounds crew had pulled the bases and dragged the infield.

"What's wrong with that kid?" Mike Feder, the Quad Cities general manager, a man who has spent most of his adult life in the business of baseball, asked. "You can't take a loss like that. What's he crying for? Jesus . . . he's supposed to be a professional."

"He's just having a little confidence problem," I answered after returning from a visit down to that banged-up chair and crushed young man who hadn't even been able to look up when he'd been told, "But, Mass, you threw the ball well," but instead had just continued sobbing into his hands.

"Must be a pretty big one," Feder said.

"Yeah . . . I guess it kinda is, Mike," was all I said, seeing no reason to explain Jeff Massicotte's not-so-little confidence problem.

That of course is not the case here. What I didn't tell Mike Feder is that Jeff Massicotte's father had been a ballplayer. He, like Jeff, had experienced immediate, brilliant minor league success. And then, when he'd struggled, facing a dose of adversity, he'd had a nervous breakdown. Soon after he had dropped out of baseball, and out of the lives of his wife and young son.

Fear of Success syndrome is what that type of behavioral pattern has been so often and erroneously labeled. What it is in this case, as in so many others, is just the opposite: fear of failure *after* having success. Since natural talent, when it is bestowed by the gods, is such an inexplicable, intangible, randomly dispensed "gift" that one never asked for, and one never understands why he was "chosen" to possess it, those who are "touched" by it never know when it is just going to disappear and prove to the world what they themselves had feared all along—that it really wasn't there to begin with; and that is called the Impostor Syndrome.

Richie Zisk has said that throughout his long and successful career, he'd often wondered, "Do I really belong up here? I mean, why me? Out of the millions of boys who also played this game, why me?"

Jim Colborn has said that he had felt it in each of the 301 games he pitched in the big leagues, even the night he threw his no-hitter, and throughout the season when he won 20 games. And that it was only later, after retiring as a player and becoming a coach, that he understood the problem and that it was widespread. "If someone had been able to make me believe and accept that I did belong, that 'hey, I'm a big leaguer, I'm one of the best just by sake of being here . . . and I have a right to be here,' there's no telling what else I might've accomplished in my career."

So, not only was Jeff Massicotte dealing with the Fear of Failure After Success and the Impostor Syndrome, he was also living with the fear of "father like son"—and just when would he also "go crazy too"?

Now you know, Mike Feder, why a professional baseball player held up your postgame stadium shutdown routine by sitting there on your field crying long after you would've liked to turn the lights out.

On Wednesday, back in John O'Donnell Stadium, while the Chiefs were limbering up, Jim Tracy sat in the dugout and turned to Greg Kallevig, that evening's starting pitcher, who was sitting quietly at the other end of the bench, and said, "You give up a run and you're off the team."

Kal just smiled and went back to his quiet meditation. And the getting-daily-more-alarmingly-dejected Jim Tracy went back to staring out at a world he could no longer make any sense of, and musing.

"I quit too soon," he said. "These two years of managing have taught me the real value of a man who can go up there and drive in that run when you need it."

Then a long silence, before; "Hell, I could still be in the big leagues doing what Jerry Mumphrey's doing . . . he's older than me and coming off the bench when they need a stick, and he ain't doing it, but making tons . . . and I can still hit!" A long pause again, then, "But I gave it up because my standards were too high. I couldn't run or do the things like I used to . . . but I was wrong. You need that man who knows how to use this when it's nut-cutting time." Then he got up and started hefting the bat in his hands, "Yep . . . I quit too soon . . ."

Then he went on and took some more serious batting practice with his now again punchless Chiefs.

Then Silent Kal went out to the mound, pitched nine innings, gave up five hits, and that one run—on a suicide squeeze! And Kal came within a microsecond of getting him with a perfect flip and a bang-bang play at the plate—and the Peoria Chiefs lost 1-0.

We'd now lost five in a row and had scored only three runs in the last forty-three innings. That monster had us by the ass again.

Jim Tracy threw his clipboard across the bus that night. Mario said that in the now two years he'd worked with him, the Trace Monster had never done that. He also didn't get off the bus when we stopped at Hardee's to eat.

The doom and gloom had settled back in and it was worse than it had ever been before. Through all of the other, Jim Tracy had always been able to move back and forth between the Shooter and the Trace Monster. Not any longer. Never had anyone seen him this dejected. Everything is negative.

"LaPenta has quit . . . he's given up, and we know it. He's just playing out the string.

"I stood up for Boz this year, I won't be able to do it again. He's probably played himself right out of a career. But at least he got his chance . . . and I gave it to him!

"All this talk of Stevie Hill coming! Who loves him more than me? Nobody. But can he turn this team around? He's not an impact player. What's he gonna do? But Pete's pushing it and pushing it . . . fuck it . . . and oh, goddam!

"What can I do? Somebody tell me, please. I've got five guaranteed outs in my lineup! This guy tonight will probably punch out ten!"

Then we made the ride to Clinton, Iowa, and lost 2-1 in eleven innings. It was Carl Hamilton's start. With the score 0-0 in the top of the third, Carl made one pitch to the first batter up, Dickens Benoit, and then jumped and grabbed his left elbow with a look of anguish and great pain on his face and then walked off the mound for the last time of the 1988 season.

Then, the eleventh, Gabby struck out the lead-off hitter only to see him standing on base when Herbie dropped and then couldn't find strike three. Two outs, an intentional walk, and a wild pitch later, that runner was at third and Mr. Benoit singled again, and there was that sick moment of instant defeat.

Ah, but there had been one moment when you could actually feel the electricity in the air, when the look on the Peoria Chiefs' faces had momentarily lost that defeated, lifeless pallor. It came in the ninth, when, with two out and Warren Arrington at second representing the go-ahead run, we saw Rusty Crockett replacing Elvin Paulino in the on-deck circle. We knew he still couldn't raise his arm above his head for the pain, but still there was that feeling that somehow, someway he would get the job done. And he did, at least his half of it. In his first at bat since the injury, "Davey, Davey Crockett," on the first pitch, lined a single toward the left-center gap; with Gator's speed surely this was that "one fucking run when we need it!" But then Gator made a wide turn at third and then stumbled and fell and then was out by an umpire's eyeblink.

At another Hardee's the Trace Monster stayed on the bus again, and Kranny was starting to worry about him.

"Did Trace get off the bus? Damn . . . we need to get him away from this shit. Maybe the All-Star break . . ."

Then he looked around the fast-food restaurant at Peoria Chiefs who were smiling and laughing and flirting with the local girls.

"Look at 'em . . . laughing and joking. Well, they'd better do it now, because they won't be next year . . . they'll be out of baseball!"

Then a few halfhearted bites later, the Kran-dog said, "This is the most frustrating year I've spent in baseball. If you're getting blown out, your ass kicked . . . that's one thing. But to always be in a ballgame night after night and still lose . . . that's slow death."

Then the subject turned to one of the young men who was not smiling and laughing, the young man who always set the correct example, our Captain, who was also now becoming very much a part of the problem— his now thirty-six errors on the season were mounting in such a fashion as to cause serious concern.

"He's tired, Kranny . . . it's wearing him down," I said. "Plus we know he's out of position, he's a natural third baseman . . . but then how can you project him at third, he won't hit enough . . ."

"He doesn't project at all!" Kranny said as if I were crazy. "He's gone, he's out of baseball soon. Most of these kids are! Besides pitching, you and I both know there are only two real prospects on this team . . . Wilkins and Canan. Rusty? He's gonna have to fight that size stigma his whole career . . . but prospect or not, we need him back."

"No shit."

"And maybe he can play short . . . if we get Steve Hill?"

Then he said, "These goddam hitters we've got make it tough to file a report. Every pitcher we face, we make him look like a world-beater . . . how do you evaluate him? And when we beat one, you know he's no prospect! Can't be any good if we hit him!"

And then the bus rolled west toward home with Jim Tracy muttering to himself over and over again, all the way in:

"I can't believe it . . . I just fucking can't believe it . . . eleven years of baseball and I've never seen anything like this . . . I just can't believe it . . . eleven years! Nothing like this . . ."

Friday afternoon we made that ride back to Clinton and got blown out 7-3, which was actually worse than it sounds. It was over. We were out of it. There would be no pennant race for the Peoria Chiefs in 1988.

We were lifeless. Joyless. Punchless. Rusty had not played.

We were a "national-fucking-disaster zone!"

So Jim Tracy locked the visitors' clubhouse doors and gave by far and away his single best "Pink slips are coming and you'll all be selling fucking shoes!" revival service of the season, and then we went to Hardee's and ate while the Trace Monster again sat in the bus by himself, and Rick Kranitz actually looked out at that bus in the parking lot and said, "I think it's time we start keeping all sharp objects away from Trace . . . and you probably think I'm kidding!"

Then that bus rolled back to P-Town and when we got there we heard the message that Frank Castillo was finally and definitely coming; in fact that he would be arriving on Monday.

The Trace Monster said, "Great . . . just what the fuck we need, another pitcher that's gonna throw a shutout and lose one to nothing in thirteen innings!" And then he said it was time to do a little drinking.

After the first drink he suddenly announced: "Rusty Crockett is the best *ballplayer* on this team!" He repeated it periodically throughout the night, often adding, "The kid's a throwback to another generation of ballplayers . . . he sits beside me every night, listening . . . wanting to learn everything he can!"

Then after he'd nursed and stared and muttered at that drink at Spirits long enough, we went to Sully's and Kranny talked about how Jerry La-Penta had been limping all over Hardee's making sure that everyone knew that that spill he'd taken rounding the bag at first had given him "a deep thigh bruise . . . son of a bitch hurts, bad! I don't know . . ."

"Yeah . . . I caught his show. You watch, that's gonna give him an excuse to be out a week, ten days, whatever. He's ready to quit and that's a good excuse for him."

"Trace . . . with Rusty still out, and now Jerry . . . ?"

"What the hell . . . we'll just play short."

"Yeah . . . but we can't play that short. Only twelve position players, and two of them down? And the one ya got left is a backup catcher? Kinda limits your options, huh?"

"Yeah . . . like to zero!" he agreed.

"I'm gonna ask Billy again about activating myself." He looked up from staring at that glass. Then, as if he was still trying to make rational to himself that fuzzy dichotomy between winning and development, he tried it out on us.

"It's a teaching tool, ain't it? I've gotta show 'em how the game is played, don't I? What's wrong with it . . . it's still teaching . . . just show and tell, right?"

"Trace . . . it's the ultimate teaching tool."

On Saturday afternoon, Rusty talked his way into the lineup as the DH for that night's game with the visiting Burlington Braves.

"I can swing, Trace . . . and I promise I won't slide headfirst. Come on . . . please?"

It did not take much persuading. After enough of the requisite cautionary I-don't-knows, head-shakings, jaw-rubbings, and a reflective spit of dip or two, the Shooter soon enough capitulated, tore up the lineup card he'd been working on, got out another one, and wrote in Rusty Crockett's name as the DH. Batting in the three hole!

Then, just about an hour and a half later, with the "Davey Crockett" theme song being played over the PA, Rusty walked up to the plate and, with one out, promptly poked a single to left, moving Phil Hannon to third. Then only minutes after that—and a Dick Canan smash that ate up the second baseman, and a Wilkins double—the Peoria Chiefs had a 3-0 lead. Which became a 6-0 lead in the fifth when Rusty sacrifice-bunted Phil to third and Dick Canan drove him across with a sacrifice fly to the warning track in left.

The visibly recharged and almost instantaneously rejuvenated Peoria Chiefs had a 6-0 lead! And they'd done it all with their bats! A veritable explosion of textbook hitting and run production!

The beneficiary of this explosion? One very stunned by the largess— but thrilled indeed—Mike Aspray. And what did he do with this seeming miracle? He took a no-hitter one out into the eighth!

But after that only one hit in the eighth had managed to score, and with the no-hitter or the shutout no longer an issue, Jim Tracy blessed Mike's gem of an effort, gave him an honored seat in the dugout, and sent Ollie out to mop up a 6-1 lead in the ninth: which, after three hits and two errors, became a 6-5 nail-biter for Z to save by striking out the last batter with some high, hard inside heat with the tying and winning runs aboard.

But we'd won. On Rusty's first game back as a starter. During the nine games he'd been out, we had gone 1 and 8. Rusty hadn't won that game by himself, of course. Somehow that spark had ignited almost everyone. Only two Chiefs batters had pulled oh-fers that night, Marty Rivero and Mike Boswell. And with Boz's oh-fer he stretched his slump to 0 for 30.

Of course it also would've been rude of us to lose that game, with the Peoria Chiefs Boosters Club throwing us their monthly barbecue out on the picnic deck after the game and all. But the steaks were great. Jim

Tracy yukked until our sides hurt, then he let it be known that the un-written rule that Spirits was a "management-only bar" was in abeyance for that evening and, after chowing hearty with many thanks, we all—en masse and happily so again—went partying.

With all the talk on Rusty—and aside from Jim Tracy's bit that night of periodically looking at Mike Aspray with that goofy Shooter grin and saying, "You're released . . . you gave up a hit," his other most repeated refrain had been "Rusty Crockett is the best hitter on this team"—Mike Boswell had seen fit to point out to several of us that maybe this Crockett thing was perhaps just a bit of a want-it-to-be-so-so-it-is phenomenon, and that it was also certainly premature:

"He hasn't been here long enough for everybody to be saying, 'He can *play!*'"

"Yeah . . .", Mike Aspray had agreed; but then added, "But when he's in the lineup, we win . . . you've gotta look at the truth."

On Sunday evening, our last game before the two-day All-Star Game break, we went over to Burlington, Iowa, where for six innings Billy Mel just flat-out mowed like he can when he's on, shutting out the Braves on three hits. But then from the very first pitch he threw in the seventh it was obvious that it was gone, vanished, poof: there was nothing on the ball and no spring at all in his legs.

That first pitch had been a ball. After three more, Al Martin was on first base. He was soon at third when Brian Hunter singled hard up the middle. And then they were both in the dugout when John Mitchell knocked the living hell out of an 83-mile-an-hour poop-chuter for a three-run homer and we blew a two-run lead and had to ride back to Peoria anticipating the wonders of two days without Chiefs baseball with the bitter taste of a 4-2 loss and the fact that we were going into the All-Star break seventeen games under .500 in our mouths.

"It's not the fucking," Jim Tracy said. "But . . . it's the totality of the thing . . . the affair itself. Ya know, just all the shit that goes on when you're having a goddam full-bore love affair. Your eating and sleeping habits change . . . you're out doing things together . . . the flush-of-love things . . . going places. And if you're not fucking, you're up late talking. It's gotta take something out of ya . . . and we're seeing it! Christ . . . it's there. It's a fact. He ain't the same pitcher he was before this woman . . . and goddam, that boy has the arm to maybe pitch in the big leagues? And he's gonna piss that away because of some woman fifteen years older than him . . . who's just gonna break his heart when she's done playing with her stud toy! And I just gotta watch it happen? Not fucking likely I'm goin' to."

After he'd chewed on the continuing saga of Nuke and the Black

Widow sufficiently, Jim Tracy got quiet for a few moments and then said, "Kranny . . . I'm gonna call a full-squad workout Tuesday night."

"Jesus, Trace . . . I thought we were gonna try to relax some on this break? Goddammit, you need it! And as for me . . . well, damn, whaddaya know . . . I feel the sniffles coming on, think I just might be sick in bed Tuesday night."

"You'll be there . . . and every other son of a bitch will too. Because, Mule, I've had just about all of this losing shit I can take. It's about to end, or I will . . . and you know goddam sure I'm not going nowhere!"

After the All-Star Game, when with ringing, spinning heads the adults eventually got back to Peoria at some still vague time the following morning we found that we had *two* new pitchers waiting for us instead of only the one long-awaited Frank Castillo.

It seems that just that past Sunday, out of a tryout camp, Cubs scout Ron Hollingsworth had signed up one Dean Edward Schulmeister II, a twenty-four-year-old right-handed pitcher who up until that moment had been pitching for a local semipro team somewhere down by his hometown of Staunton, Illinois. Not knowing what else to do with him at the moment, the Cubs had simply told him to report to the nearest place— Peoria.

Of course no one had thought to call the Chiefs' offices to inform Jim Tracy of that piece of news until early that Tuesday morning—when he was still in Clinton, Iowa, or someplace in between.

Which was why when Jim Tracy did arrive and found that this big, absolutely farm-fresh-green, not-so-kid kid—who'd been golly-shucksing and gawking around all morning and midday wearing a mix-and-match hodgepodge uniform of his semipro team and asking of everyone who walked by, "Is that the *coach*?" but was in fact at the moment of Trace's arrival out in the parking lot working underneath the jalopy he'd driven up in—had been assigned to his roster, one very bewildered Trace Monster muttered and spit and shook and rubbed and pondered upon the question of "Just what in the devil's crooked tail do they think I'm going to do with twelve pitchers?"

"Obviously nothing, Trace . . . we can't carry twelve pitchers. They know that . . . so there's got to be more moves coming," Rick Kranitz said. "And going," he added not a little ominously.

"Yeah . . ."

"And how's that gonna look? That'd really be horseshit . . . a slap in somebody's face! To send somebody down and bring in some yahoo out of a tryout camp? What does that tell your other kids in the organization? And we don't have anybody that deserves to go down . . . maybe Mass, but they'd never do it."

"Yeah . . ." Jim Tracy agreed and picked up the phone to call Bill Harford to find out "just what the fuck's goin' on around here!"

It was a long phone call. It raged pretty much in confusion and bewilderment on the Peoria end of the line for a time. Then it subsided into
ifs and ands and buts and maybes for a while, before it had finally quasi-
and-semi-settled upon the facts that: we really didn't know yet if Carl
could pitch again, that Frank Castillo probably shouldn't start for at least
ten days, only throwing on the side to make sure he was all right, and
that since Schulmeister was greener than green and a totally unknown
quantity, we actually only had nine pitchers effectively; and what the hell,
that made about as much sense as anything else, so why not?

Then not too long after that, with Jim Tracy saying, "Well, let's go find
out what this 'Roy Hobbs' has got"—which of course was the nickname
that the Shooter had immediately tagged Dean Edward Schulmeister II
with—we went on out to the field for a full-squad workout less than a
dozen hours before we were to leave for a four-day road trip into South
Bend and then Kenosha.

Strangely enough there was almost no grumbling about having to work
out on the night of the last off day of the 1988 season, and what little
there was, was only of the ritual good-natured kind that the situation was
ripe for.

Jim Tracy stood behind the bullpen mounds and watched "Roy Hobbs"
throw for a while and then stepped back a pace or two and said, "Pretty
decent fastball . . . slider . . . hell, I probably would've signed him myself. He's got enough that he deserves a shot at playing some pro ball.
But . . . what I'm going to do with him? I ain't got a clue," he added
before calling out, "Hey, Schulmeister? Hey, Roy Hobbs . . . ya got a
pretty good arm there."

When Frank Castillo started throwing, Jim Tracy watched that compact, fluid, consistent, methodical delivery pop deceptively explosive and
deadly accurate fastball after fastball after snap dragon slider everyplace
that Rick Wilkins placed his mitt. Then he stepped back again and said,
"My, oh my! Hmmm! Does he look good? And I do have a clue how I'm
gonna use him, just as soon as they let me . . . and from the way he looks
to me, maybe sooner. Welcome back the El Paso Buzz Saw, huh?" Then
he called out, "Hey, Frank . . . you throw like an old woman!"

Then Jim Tracy walked slowly toward the batting cage, stopping and
turning every now and then to look and wonder at what he was going to
do with all of the now two full dozen Peoria Chiefs spread across Meinen
Field. The two dozen that would be twenty-five tomorrow.

Something else had been finally and completely confirmed during that
phone call, but was yet a secret to those two dozen who were already
antsy enough with all the comings—and potential *goings*. And they
would find out soon enough anyway. Because our new second baseman
was meeting us in South Bend on the morrow.

"At least we're gonna lead the league in midgets," the Trace Monster
said shortly after finding out that five-foot-seven Stevie Hill was indeed

returning to the scene of his greatest glory as a professional baseball player.

It had taken him a little over three months to do it but in the end Pete Vonachen had gotten his way again. No matter that it was only the most logical and best available move the Cubs could make at the time, to Pete Vonachen it was perceived as another victory justly earned.

Of course, to the Shooter, it also meant that in all probability, Bill Harford would not now let him activate himself.

CHAPTER

9

JUST SHORTLY AFTER Fernando Zarranz had turned a hard and nasty comebacker into a game-ending 1-6-3 double play to notch his fourteenth "zave" and the Peoria Chiefs had headed toward that most commodious visitors' clubhouse carrying a 7-6 blowout-turned-nail-biting win and a two-game sweep of the South Bend White Sox with them, a beaming Jim Tracy was standing at the backstop netting looking up at the legendary "super scout," Brandon Davis, the Cubs' National Scouting Supervisor, who'd called him over from the home-plate box-seat section of the raised grandstands to apologize.

"Sorry, Trace," Brandy said. "But it was just such a high school draft this year . . . I wished we could've helped you more."

"Hey . . . I don't want that," Jim Tracy interjected quickly, obviously both embarrassed and thrilled at the notion of Brandon Davis believing an apology to him was even necessary.

"I don't need that, Brandy . . . I don't . . . I want exactly what I've got. I'm happy with what I'm doing. All I want to do . . . in the month and a half left, is to make this a better ballclub than what it is now . . . and I'll be satisfied. You don't need to apologize to me."

He absolutely meant it. It wasn't organizational lip service. Jim Tracy, the teacher and the field general, had what he believed was exactly the right challenge—and now the right pupils and troops to meet it—for which he lives.

And a challenge is exactly what it was—or more simply just "the Bet" as it would come to be more colloquially and cryptically referred to among the family in the weeks to come.

You see, Jim Tracy had done something else besides just wondering what in the devil he was going to do with "Roy Hobbs" that Tuesday night of the off-day workout.

As soon as everybody was limbered up, he had called all of the old and

259

new members of the family together down around the left-field foul line, told them to "take a knee, gentlemen," and made one of his longer and most effective speeches of the season. It really wasn't even a speech, and it wasn't another fire-and-brimstone revival service either. The Shooter had just talked quietly from the heart.

"Guys . . . I've had to lock that clubhouse door and ream your asses out pretty good these past few days, haven't I? And then on Saturday night, I bent our rules a little, and we all partied pretty good too, right? And the partying was a lot more fun than the ass chewings, huh?"

There he had paused long enough to elicit nods and grunts of agreement before continuing.

"And now we've had a couple of days off after playing ninety-one ballgames . . . ninety-one ballgames where we didn't have much to party about. Hey, it's a fact . . . we stunk it up . . . you blew the first half, and now the middle. And there's not a damn thing that can be done about it. It's history. But you know what? One of the great things about this game . . . and life, for that matter . . . is that nobody remembers beginnings and middles . . . only endings. That's what counts . . . it is what *you* will remember about this season. What you will have to take home and live with over the winter . . . and maybe for some of you, it is all you will have to remember and live with for the rest of your lives after baseball . . . the ending of this season."

He'd paused again to give that thought emphasis and time to sink in.

"Gentlemen . . . there are only forty-nine games left in this season, and right now you are a ballclub seventeen games under .500. You have the respect of no one. You've been written off as losers by everybody . . . those folks in the seats, those folks up at Wrigley. And even by yourselves . . . some of you. Is that what you want to live with? Not even respecting yourself? Nuh-uh . . . I think I know youse guys better than that. You've got more pride than that. So that's why when you walk into the clubhouse tonight after this workout you are going to see two big numbers written on the blackboard . . . forty-nine and thirty-three. Why? Because I'm going right at that pride I still believe you have in you . . . and I'm throwing a challenge at you. Me to you. My pride to yours. Let's call it a bet. You want to party like we did Saturday night? Make the rest of this season one helluva party on, and off, the field? Something to really remember? Something to prove to all those folks that they're wrong . . . that we're not just that one horseshit ballclub that once played in Peoria? Then you give me all you've got and end this season as a winner and not a loser. Gentlemen, the bet is for you to end this season a .500 club. To do that . . . you're going to have to win at least thirty-three of the forty-nine games left. Sounds impossible? Not to me. Show me something, gentlemen. Let's find out what's really in you. And *you're* gonna know exactly what that is, every day. Because every day it's going to be staring you in the face . . . in every clubhouse . . . every day either one or both of those numbers is going to be changed and posted as big as day. Gentlemen . . . you have no control over the first one. But the second one? That's all yours . . . and every time it doesn't change along with the other one, we're going to know exactly how much pride we've got . . . and how much fun we're *not* gonna have! All right . . . let's get to work."

And so it began.

That second number changed the very next night.

After Stevie Melendez and Lee Kline had taken that big bus from the Days Inn motel hard by that famous golden dome to go to the South Bend airport to pick up Stevie Hill, our fire-hydrant short and stocky, pugnacious, sardonic, long-wavy-black-haired, and fiery-eyed new second baseman; and then some hours later, after Rick Wilkins and Marty Rivero had missed that bus by exactly one minute, and Jim Tracy had said, "They know the rules—hit it, Lee," and it had again rolled out of the motel parking lot, and Rick and Marty had had to fork out cabfare plus the fine for the eight minutes they were late getting to Stanley Coveleski stadium, Silent Kal had gone to the mound and left no doubt as to exactly how much pride he had by needing only seventy-five pitches—only sixteen of which were called balls!—to shut out the South Benders for nine innings on five hits.

But then, of course, shutouts—even as masterful as that one was—do not win ballgames. However, a shutout plus nine runs on twelve hits by your guys will do the trick every time!

"Jeez'em'tally, Mule . . . you think they're not trying to tell me something? I mean, what have we got here, huh?" Jim Tracy had said more than a few times that night as he came back to the dugout with his arm tired from waving runners in, but his big heart soaring.

"We murderlized 'em!" he said when it was over and he was in that penthouse that does service as the visiting manager's private office, dressing room, and shower, as almost a block away, in a visitors' clubhouse about as big as some small towns—and surely better-equipped than most—Stevie Melendez was erasing some numbers and writing new ones.

"That's one," the Shooter had said when the bus had pulled back into that Days Inn parking lot. And what had made that "That's one" game even sweeter?

Gordon Goldsberry had driven down from Chicago to be there for it. And that frown he'd worn on his face when he arrived—and carried with him through batting practice as he discussed and speculated with Trace and Kranny upon just what all the comings and goings since last we'd seen him nineteen days before might've wrought—was gone and had been replaced by more than just a cautious smile by the time he waved goodbye as we headed toward the motel and he for home.

"It is good to see him smiling again, huh, Mule?"

"What a question," Kranny said and then added, "You too, big guy."

"Oh, yeah. . . !"

So big was Jim Tracy's smile, and so happy and tranquil was his heart, that the next night, even as he was watching Eduardo Caballero contort himself through the process of perhaps blowing a 7-1 lead in the sixth inning, he not only made Greg Kallevig smile, but he actually made Silent Kal laugh out loud for the one and only time any of us could remember. At about the seventieth-pitch mark, after yet again watching Eduardo do his ritual two-handed skull crush and crotch pull, the Shooter said, "You know, if he does it that many times . . . that's gotta constitute playing with yourself, right? And if he does it a hundred and twenty times . . . isn't that jerking off?"

The Trace Monster did not let Eduardo get to that moment of self-rapture. In the seventh, with the score still 7-3, but two aboard and only one out, he sent Eduardo to the showers where perhaps he could finish what he'd started in private and comfort and brought in Brett Robinson. Then, three batters and only one more out later, with the score 7-6, he sent Brett to chaperon Eduardo and brought in Gabby.

And then, of course, five outs later, the Z Man turned that hard come-backer into the game-ending double play that sent all of the rest of some very happy Chiefs into that "major-fucking-league!" clubhouse and Trace to the backstop fence to tell Brandon Davis to waste no tears or worries on their account, but thank you very much for caring all the same.

"That's two," Jim Tracy had shaken his head and looked up and said more than just a couple of times as he of course took his now quite merry, yet still ever so slow time getting out of uniform and into the shower before we could go eat and get out onto the road and head back up into that fair state of Wisconsin.

"Trace . . . you can't use Brett in short relief," the Kran-dog said as we'd waited. "He needs to start an inning . . . long man is how we're going to have to use him."

"He's right, you know . . . what would I do without my Mule? We're a team, him and me . . . we're a package . . . after this year, anybody who wants me at any level from here to the big leagues also gets him . . . and I want you to write that down, ya hear me? Put that in that tape recorder, Yo . . . or you're off the team." Jim Tracy had yukked and spit and bobbed that big old wonderful head which was such a joy to see back to its old Shooter self.

"Yeah, well you're on my Christmas-card list, too," the Kran-dog dead-panned to put a stop to all that gushiness and to get on with some real business at hand. "Speaking of team . . . is Carl on vacation?"

"What'd he do today?"

"Plenty. Picked up a ball, made a couple of short tosses, said his arm didn't feel 'sound,' and then went hard back to working on a suntan he doesn't need."

"Mule . . . you know, that's a bit of a touchy subject."

"No shit."

"And we're not going to solve it . . . that's over our heads."

"Yep. Just thought I should keep you up to date."

"Yeah. Well, tell me some good news on Frank Castillo."

"Looking good, Trace. He threw eight minutes yesterday, and twelve today . . . we're following the schedule Colby set . . . but damned if he doesn't look like he's gonna be ready long before then."

"Gotta follow orders, Mule . . . but, hmm hmmm! Get him in the rotation? Oh, Lordy . . . huh?"

Jim Tracy savored that thought, and what it could mean for "the Bet," in head-shaking silence for a moment or two before finally—and again—saying, "That's two."

Then he stood up, slipped out of his last undergarment, headed for the shower, and said, "Let's go to Kenosha, guys!"

There is a special bond between the Chiefs and the "'Peoria' of the Northern Division" of the Midwest League; and it's not just that Kenosha Twins president and general manager Bob Lee is as committed to running a "new minors" operation as professionally for both fan and ballplayer as is Pete Vonachen—albeit without all the bombast and "meddling beyond his province."

Kenosha, Wisconsin, which is almost a suburb of Chicago, is also a Cubs town. So much so that when the Chiefs visit there, it's kind of like old home week, because much of Bob Lee's staff take their annual snowbird vacations to Mesa, Arizona, and spend every day of it at Fitch Park and HoHoKam with their beloved Cubs. For those three to six weeks, they are very much a part of the family. Therefore, whenever the Chiefs visit Kenosha, they are greeted, treated, and dined as family. Oh, we might have more extracurricular, after-hours fun on the road in Waterloo, or Cedar Rapids, but nowhere else is the game itself more enjoyable.

Even when our "brother-in-law" Twins, with '87's first-round pick, the still-teenage Willie Banks, on the mound throwing consistently in the mid-90s and *higher*—but a bit more accurately since last we'd seen and beaten him twice—got to Mike Aspray for three unearned runs courtesy of seven hits and three errors (two by the Captain) and we got five hits (one of them by Stevie Hill, his first back as a Chief) and one run off young Mr. Flame-Throwing Willie for the first loss since "the Bet."

And even the next night when Billy "Nuke" Mel got shelled and was gone after only four innings and Jim Tracy sent "Roy Hobbs" into a 6-1 blowout for his first professional outing, only to get three outs on his first three professional pitches, and then get tattooed in his next two dozen or so to make it a 9-1 laugher as the fog rolled in off Lake Michigan; Jim Tracy and I went into the Twins' locker room to jaw a bit on Twins manager Ron Gardenhire's smoked trout and actually laugh and joke, even though with those two losses we were right back to seventeen games under .500—but with now only forty-five games to go.

Yet so pleasant was our short stay, as we were leaving that Twins happy locker room for the somewhat grimmer "iron lung" and the long, quiet ride home, I said to Jim Tracy, "These folks are just so nice up here, huh?"

"Yeah . . . ya gotta love 'em, don'tcha?"

"Trace . . . just think, what if we *could* make the play-offs and come up here and have a real Fall Classic with these people? It can still happen . . . can't it?"

For a brief moment that thought rippled across the Shooter's face and danced in his eyes. But then, Jim Tracy, who only two weeks before would have yukked an exuberant, expletory affirmative along with a couple of good one-liners at such a question, caught himself, shook those ripples and sparkles away, and quietly answered a foolish dreamer's stupid query.

"No, pal . . . it can't happen. You don't climb over the backs of four teams . . . four ballclubs don't just all of a sudden fold."

When everyone was back on the bus, Jim Tracy also quietly addressed his crestfallen troops.

"Last night we gave away a ballgame to a good ballclub. Tonight? Well . . . I don't wanna talk about it, and I don't think Nuke wants to hear about it . . . huh, Mel? But I bet you wanna *think* about it, don'tcha? But . . . youse guys? The bet's still on . . . you've just got four less games to do it in. So I suggest you all get some sleep after we stop and eat . . . instead of playing cards . . . 'cause the game number's gonna change five times in four days . . . twice tomorrow . . . so we've either got a chance to pick up some ground real fast, or lose it just as fast. But why don't we just go home and whup Wausau's ass? How about it? Hit it, Lee."

A short time later, over a table of gut-bomb fast-food tacos and burritos, Jim Tracy said, "Kranny, we've gotta stop the bleeding. I wanna flip-flop the way we had it figured. Let's throw Kal the first game tomorrow and Mass the second one. You got any problem with that?"

"Nope."

Then Jim Tracy turned to Stevie Melendez and asked, "When's Crockett gonna be ready to go both ways?"

"When do you need him?"

"Yesterday. Gordon called, guys . . . appears he's seeing the same thing we are. Marty's errors are starting to show him something. Mainly that he's not the shortstop we thought he was. And let's face it . . . he's disappointed all of us . . . he's not the shortstop we thought we saw in Instructional League or spring training."

"Or last year at Geneva, Trace," Stevie said.

"Whatever. Gordon's anxious to see what Davey can do with the job . . . so when can we do it?"

"He'd tell you tomorrow."

"What do you tell me?"

"It's just pain . . . and that's going to be there awhile. But medically? The doctor said he probably can't do it any more damage . . . so, you want him, you got him."

"I want him . . . and we need him."

"We're just a bad ballclub," Pete Vonachen said to Phil Theobald a little after noon on Sunday as Phil, after dropping off his Chiefs Chatter program inserts, popped into the big office to get the early scoop on exactly what Pete had planned for his entrance back into the ballpark now that the suspension was over. "Now it's just a matter of how far we sink."

"Hey . . . I called it twenty-three under from the get-go, right? You wanna double the bet?"

"What bet?"

"My Jack Daniels to your VO?"

"I bet you that?"

"No . . . 'cause ya chickened out . . . but the offer's still good."

"Go on, Theobald . . . go flirt with Rose or something. I got me a show to get ready for . . . and I don't need to buy you any more of that rock-gut whiskey you drink."

It was a grand entrance indeed that Pete Vonachen made at a little before six o'clock that Sunday evening of July 21 to mark the end of his suspension as he wowed and oohed his audience of almost four thousand by arriving in a real paddy wagon, led by real motorcycle cops, and then, as this procession with blaring sirens finally wound its way to home plate, the real sheriff of Peoria County, George Shaddid, opened the back of that paddy wagon and removed his "prisoner" wearing real handcuffs and dressed in a real county prison orange jumpsuit.

After the sheriff unlocked the handcuffs and Pete peeled off the prison garb to reveal the tuxedo he was wearing underneath, he stepped to the microphone at home plate and delivered one of his better ad-lib "speech" performances. It brought the house down. So much so that in all of the razzmatazz and vaudeville atmosphere that had the fans buzzing for the next five hours, very few people even noticed, nor much cared, that the Peoria Chiefs made that right-side number decrease by two in one night.

Kal "stopped the bleeding" in the first one by going the seven-inning distance allowing but one run on four hits, and the Chiefs won the third game since "the Bet" 5-1. Jeff Massicotte needed a little help from Gabby and Z to win his first start since the days of the "Train Wreck" period. But then not really all that much help was required—not when your hitters explode and hand you an 11-4 laugher on a twelve-hit, seven-inning platter.

"Jesus, Trace . . . Dick went and had himself a week in one day, huh?"

"Week? He had himself a month!"

Indeed he had. With two doubles in the first game, and two more in the second, Dick Canan had gone 4 for 7 with *seven RBI,* to more than triple his run production of three in the first three weeks he'd been back.

"But what about that Crockett, huh?" Jim Tracy then said. And would say again and again to anyone who popped into his office that night.

What about Davey? With a great deal more pain in that right shoulder than he would admit to to all but a few of the family, he had started the first game at shortstop and, in the fourth inning, with the bases loaded and the game still much in doubt, he had sucked up that pain and completed an inning-ending, slow-developing 3-6-1 double play by cutting loose with a do-or-die bullet peg, and strike to first base to nip the runner and the Wausau Timbers' last threat of the night.

In the second game, he had started in right field, chased and dived and caught everything that came anywhere even remotely within his reach, and he had also singled in one run, smashed a liner over the center fielder's head, one-hopping the wall, for a triple and two more RBI.

"What about that Crockett, huh? Little sumbitch . . . he's just a winner, that's all!"

"He's not hot, he's unconscious!" Mick Kelleher said the next night, as he was now with us again and a part of the celebration in Trace's office after Dick Canan had gone 3 for 4 with two more RBI that had done more than a little to ensure that Brett Robinson—now back into the rotation with Carl still on "vacation"—while not really sharp would even his record at 6 and 6, and Z would be able to notch his fifteenth "zave," when the Chiefs outslugged the Timbers thirteen hits to eight for a 7-5 victory and the "That's five!" win since "the Bet" and now three in a row.

"He's on a tear . . . no doubt about it . . . we knew it was only time in coming . . . and he sure picked a good time to do it, huh?" the Shooter yukked and then looked at his pitching coach, who had shown up that afternoon sans his mustache. "Don't ever grow it back, ya hear? Or you're off the team!"

"What a question. Hell, next time I'll shave my nuts!"

"Hey, guys . . . but what about that Crockett, huh?" Jim Tracy then again had reason to ask after Rusty, playing right field that night, had also gone 3 for 4 with two RBI.

"We told you he could play," the Killer answered.

"Yeah . . . but you didn't tell me he was a win magnet! When that midget's in the lineup? We don't lose . . . !"

*   *   *

"That's six!" Jim Tracy said the next night, right before he again yukked and spit and beamed and said, "Jesus, Mary, and Joseph . . . what about that Crockett, huh? I mean, goddam . . . and it doesn't matter where you play him!"

It hadn't that Tuesday night of July 19, when, back at shortstop, Rusty's two-out, two-RBI piss-cutter past third had been the key hit in the five-run sixth inning that had given a dominant, then shaky Eduardo Caballero a 5-3 victory for his fifth win on the year (5 and 9) and Z the opportunity to collect his sixteenth "zave."

Rusty also had not had to kiss the pig that night; but instead one Heather Zenk, Miss Heart of Illinois Queen, whose kiss had been the award, and the squealing baby porker the booby prize, in a musical-chairs "Kiss the Pig" contest and promotion for the Heart of Illinois State Fair that was also going on that week in Peoria. When there was only one chair left out of the seven, Rusty, our towheaded, every mother's favorite son, had gone for it with the same quickness he does a baseball, and gotten it.

He also had gotten a date with heavenly Heather when his shyness had occasioned him to only be able to blush and give her a peck on the cheek instead of the big bussing that his teammates were screaming for; and the beauty queen had been so intrigued by that very shyness that she had sent one of her entourage over to give Rusty her phone number with the message that a call and a date would be welcomed.

We got something almost as nice—and in the cases of some members of the family, perhaps every bit as nice. We went out en masse and partied like there was no tomorrow in celebration of the fact that we were now 6 and 2 since the All-Star break, had "climbed over the back" of Waterloo, and were now in fourth place in the Southern Division—but ever so much sweeter to a crooning, dancing-by-himself Shooter that night was the fact that we were now only thirteen games under .500 on the year!

But there was a tomorrow. The hundredth game of the 1988 Peoria Chiefs season. And communal hangovers not withstanding, we "won that fucker, too!"

It wasn't, however, quite as easy. It was also just a bit more worrisome, because after that night of partying, Z had left Spirits with the "Peacock Lady," and had shown up the next day with a great deal of pain in his right shoulder, and wasn't available for his "hammer" role.

"I must've slept on it wrong, Trace," Fernando had said. While when he'd said it, it might've been momentarily hilarious to all of the family—including Jim Tracy—who of course knew with whom he'd "slept on it wrong," it really was no laughing matter. The pain was severe. And Z was scared.

"It hurts, man. Goddam . . . it's like nothing I've ever felt before . . .

and there's no explanation for it, you know what I mean? It could be my career here, bro!"

"Hey . . . calm down, Z. It's probably nothing, all right?" Stevie Melendez had said. "We'll do a little ice, heat, and whirlpool today . . . and if it's still there tomorrow, we'll get it checked out by the doctor."

"Yeah, man . . . but what if Trace needs me tonight? Shit . . . we've got something going here, you know?"

While it would have been more comforting to know that Z was available out there in the bullpen, Mike Aspray mitigated that some by simply taking his hangover to the mound and throwing nine innings of five-hit, one-run ball. Which was just enough, as Wilkie—who had started the season too young to drink legally and then never really partied with the family anyway—after two strikeouts in his first two at bats had worked a fine-looking pitcher by the name of Burnau for a one-out walk in the seventh of a 0-0 ballgame; Stevie Hill—who parties hard and had left Spirits with *two* lovelies—still had had enough vigor left in him to get his job done and moved Wilkie to second with a tough-to-handle groundout to the right side; Gator Arrington—who the last time we'd seen him that early morning had been hanging out of Jeff Reeser's car throwing up and completely oblivious to even where and who he was—had looked through his bleary eyes, seen a pitch to his liking, and spanked a sharp single through the left side to score Wilkins on a bang-bang play at the plate; and then the Captain—who parties only in moderation and was back in the lineup at shortstop with Rusty playing right field—with his true love Stephanie visiting from California there to see it, doubled down the third-base line to drive in Gator with what turned out to be the game-winning RBI to complete a five-game sweep of the Wausau Timbers.

"That's seven!"

Along with his tiny "training" glove, Mick Kelleher, on this visit, had brought along a Ping-Pong paddle with the handle cut off and finger straps fitted to the back with which he first demonstrated some fine "picking" with himself, and then put it into the hands of Rusty and Marty for them to give it a try during morning workouts that week.

During one such session on the morning of July 21, he'd also talked about Rusty Crockett the "suspect prospect" and his chances of making the big leagues.

"Sure a kid like that has all the deck stacked against him because of his size . . . but he can make it, why not? He has speed . . . I really like his hands, great hands, good arm . . . instincts for the game you can't teach. He's a *baseball* player. So, yeah . . . why not?"

Just before the bus rolled that Thursday afternoon for a commuter with the Burlington Braves, Pete Vonachen said to Jim Tracy, "Good luck, Doc . . . you know if you win tonight we'll be back to .500."

"Oh no we won't . . . eleven under, Boss."

"Yeah, well . . . that's your arithmetic."

"Yep . . . and the only one that matters—*overall*!"

There was one piece of arithmetic, however, that was beyond dispute when Lee Kline steered the "iron lung" off the University Street ramp and headed us west on I-74 that afternoon—there were now twenty-four Chiefs instead of twenty-five on that bus. Dean Edward "Roy Hobbs" Schulmeister II would, in just a few hours, be a member of the Wytheville Cubs family, and not ours.

"I think I can go tonight, Trace . . . if you need me," a quickly re-covered and much relieved Z Man said as he came into the dugout after warm-ups.

"Good," Jim Tracy answered. "'Cause I've gotta get you twenty saves before the end of this month . . . and twenty-five, maybe thirty, before this year's out. And you know why?"

"Yeah . . . you want me to break the Otter's record."

"Fuck the Otter . . . it's because I want you at Double A next year. You've earned it, son."

"Appreciate that . . . Skip. That means a lot coming from you. But . . . really, I'm ready if you need me."

"Hey . . . with loverboy Nuke going tonight, it might just be bullpen by committee, so you keep 'em on their toes down there, and I'll getcha when I need you," Jim Tracy yukked and Z nodded knowingly.

About three and a half hours later, Jim Tracy, sitting in the rathole that serves as a cubbyhole in Community Field, was still yukking, but also shaking his head in joyous disbelief, as he repeated several refrains over and over again:

"That's eight!"

"Jeez'em'tally . . . we didn't murderlize 'em, we buried 'em too, huh? Goddam! What have we got here, guys?

"What about that Crockett, huh? If he ain't a *ballplayer* I'm an Ayrab!"

"Good Lord a'mighty . . . somebody throw some ice water on Dick, that boy's on fire!"

"Hey . . . is Mel trying to tell us something or not?"

No. Z had definitely not been needed that night. Which was why out in the parking lot, as Jim Tracy kept on yukking for some time still over *that* win, Billy "Nuke" Mel was also repeating a refrain of his own:

"God . . . is it good to be back on track! Oh . . . you don't how good it feels . . . I'm back!" Not only had he won only his second start since May 30, mowing like the Mel of old, he'd pitched a complete game, had given up but six hits, walked no one, struck out eight, and allowed only one run—and it was unearned.

Of course, Mel actually could've gone ahead and stunk up the joint if he'd wanted to and still would've won that ballgame. I mean, you've got to work real hard to lose on a night when your guys put fourteen runs on the board on fourteen hits; on a night when your midget shortstop, with a shoulder so sore you see him wince on every throw he makes, is ranging from the hole behind third to the hole back of second, making acrobatic snares and gunning runners out while falling down, twisting in the air, or standing flat-footed, and also drives in two runs and scores two more himself; on a night when your vacuum-cleaner third baseman continues his torrid hitting to the tune of another three-hit, three-RBI game; and you know you can't lose when your manager plays a hunch because a ballplayer's girlfriend is visiting and plays a .202-hitting shortstop—who from that night on had lost his job for the season to the midget—as your DH, and all that the Captain would do was wallop two doubles to the wall in the left-field corner good enough for three RBI! All of which was why Jim Tracy had so many refrains to yuk that night that it took him so long to dress we were so hungry that we pigged out at an imitation Cajun greasy spoon as if it was K-Paul's in the French Quarter.

If there had been any discordant note at all struck that night, it had not come from a ballplayer; but did in fact come from a member of the extended family, albeit the most controversial one.

"Him?" Angie had said when it had been suggested yet again that she was just having a "summer fling" and would in the end just "break poor, innocent Mel's heart." "Everybody is worried about him . . . but it's me! He's a kid who's moving up and going on in a month—and I'm thirty-five! And I'm in love. So who's going to get their heart broken in that little scenario? Not too hard to figure out, right?"

Indeed not, Angie. And give 'em hell.

"That's eight!" Jim Tracy said once more when we arrived back at Meinen field and he himself went to the blackboard to do the erasing and put up the new equation that now read: 39-25. Then we went partying. And, among other things, talked some baseball.

"There are three dimensions to a ballclub," the Killer said that night. "In the first half this team had excellent pitching, spotty defense . . . adequate at times, but erratic . . . and no hitting at all. Now we've got good—and getting excellent again—pitching, much better than adequate defense with the addition of Crockett, Canan, and Hill . . . and a little hitting. If we'd had this combination from the beginning, with just the hitting we're getting now"—team BA .222—"it would've been an altogether different season. Because you can win with good pitching, excellent defense, and only a little hitting. But you must have two of the three . . . you can't have one and a half."

"Whatcha trying to do, Killer . . . get in the book? Stop making speeches and buy me a beer," the Kran-dog said. "Oh, and you can't leave . . . you're our charm! We haven't lost since you got here!"

"Hey . . . you think I wouldn't want to cancel all my trips and stay here with you guys? This is fun! But I don't think Billy would go for it.

Besides, you don't need me. Yep . . . you guys have gotten this team straightened out. I don't think Chicago's going to be worrying with this club anymore."

Jim Tracy went to the blackboard himself again the next night, Friday, July 22, when Burlington came commuting to us and Greg Kallevig pitched another complete game and the Chiefs won a 4-3 come-from-behind nut-cutter in the bottom of the ninth after Silent Kal's only mistake of the night had been to deliver up a three-run dinger in the eighth.

How did we do it? Well, first it helped that Rick Sweet, the Braves manager, for some silly, strategic reason having to do with perhaps some overworked and clichéd baseball "percentages," took Mike Stanton—a 90-plus-throwing left-hander, and another Midwest League pitcher who would be in the big leagues within a year—out in the eighth inning, off whom we'd managed to get but two unearned runs on only three hits during his impressive stay on the hill.

Then . . . "a little hitting." In the ninth, Rusty, who'd come up from Mesa with a Richie Zisk scouting report which read in part, "Finds a way to get on, and then starts shit," hit a sharp ground ball straight to the third baseman for what looked to be nothing but a routine 5-3 putout. That was until Rick Berg, a catcher playing third that night, bobbled the ball just slightly, but just slightly enough for "Rocket Crockett" to beat the throw for an E5 to go along with the two hits and one RBI (on another perfectly executed safety squeeze) he'd already chalked up for the evening's work. Then Dick Canan doubled with Rusty holding wisely at third. Stevie Hill walked to load the bases. Rick Wilkins then hit a long, loud sacrifice fly to right field. And up stepped the Captain, who, with Stephanie still so pretty and demure up in the stands, was DH'ing again that night because Jim Tracy had figured that one good hunch might as well be milked for all that was in it. He had figured right. While it wasn't pretty, the soft single Marty Rivero looped over a drawn-in infield was certainly effective enough for the Peoria Chiefs' first seven-game winning streak since the first week of June *1987*.

We were now 9 and 2 since the All-Star break, 17 and 16 on the "second chance," 45 and 56 on the "real fucking season," and of course, most importantly—

"That's nine!"

On Saturday night, with 5,370 in attendance, Frank Castillo made his first start of the season, and although as planned he only pitched the first two innings, the El Paso Buzz Saw would be tagged with only his second loss in professional baseball when, during the first inning, being just a little nervous at not only his season debut but all those screaming Peorians, he walked the first batter, got a popped-up infield fly-out from the second, hit "that fucking Bob Rose again," and then surrendered his first hit of the season, an RBI double, and the Angels had a one-run lead—which on that night turned out to be all they needed, even though it wasn't all they got.

Frank quickly enough regained his inscrutable composure and retired the next four hitters he faced, two by strikeouts, and then turned the ball over to Brett Robinson, who then pitched four shutout innings until he and Jeff Massicotte combined to give up three runs in the seventh before Grandpa then retired all six batters he faced in the eighth and ninth, five by strikeouts.

But we lost 4-0 when all we could manage off big, hard-throwing Roberto Hernandez, the Angel's first-round pick in '86, was seven scattered singles as he pitched a complete-game shutout—the ninth time on the season the Peoria Chiefs had been shut out.

But then turnabouts are only fair play, so on Sunday night, with but 2,444 in attendance for what was quite ironically "Feed the Hungry Night" at Meinen Field (a can of food was the price for a general-admission seat; a corporate sponsor was paying the real box-office freight), Eduardo Caballero, pitching like that gun was in his hands and not at his head, threw a complete-game, nine-strikeout, two-hit shutout and we got eleven hits and won 5-0.

The game-winning RBI had come early and was only appropriate in how it occurred. Rusty Crockett, batting in the lead-off spot that night, singled to begin our half of the first frame, and then two outs later, Dick Canan singled to drive him in.

Appropriate? Well, some hours before the start of that game, we had received a communiqué from the Howe Sports Bureau announcing that Dick Canan had been named Player of the Week for the Midwest League!

You want to know what hot is? Look at these numbers for eight games in seven days: twenty-nine at bats; eight runs; thirteen hits; six doubles; eleven RBI; .448 batting average; and a slugging percentage of .655.

"That's ten," Jim Tracy said not quite as exuberantly as before; and it was Stevie Melendez who did the arithmetic on the blackboard. Jim Tracy also said a couple of other things that night as he was dressing and we were waiting.

"Looks like our boy Wilkie's hit himself a slump here, huh? And . . . at a bad time, too . . . going into Springfield? And he hasn't exactly had a lotta success down there . . ."

"No shit!" more than one of us replied.

"Yeah . . . but guys . . . we're gonna need a big game or two out of him if we're really gonna do us some damage down there and maybe get back into this thing."

Then a few musings yet only a stirrup removed later, Jim Tracy said; "Hey . . . tell me something, is Gator not the most improved ballplayer on this team, huh? I mean . . . real quietly he's gone and made himself into about the most valuable player on this team over the long haul. And jeez'em'tally, you remember back in April and May we were talking about how that buddy of yours that signed him must've scouted him with his eyes closed?"

That weekend also produced some more roster arithmetic along with the minus-1-plus-1 blackboard computation. We were now back to twenty-three active players. Carl Hamilton had gone up to Chicago to be examined by the Cubs' doctors. Their diagnosis was that the bone chips in his left elbow they could not find during arthroscopic surgery back during the winter were in fact not chips but a bone spur. They scheduled him for surgery on that coming Wednesday. While his doctor did not agree with that diagnosis, and there would, over the next couple of weeks, be a great deal of controversy as Carl would first use the excuse of his girlfriend wrecking his car to miss that scheduled surgery, then hide out God knows where for a while as his lawyer began legal action against the Cubs for their having reassigned his contract to Peoria at a time when he was both officially "medically unsound" *and* on the forty-man major league roster, which "was clearly in violation of the Basic Agreement," according to him and his attorney, the upshot of it all as far as we were concerned was that he would not pitch for the Peoria Chiefs anymore that season and had left the family.

While we had lost a player, something else had returned: a touch of pennant fever. Development and pride aside, play-off and pennant dreams do die hard, even in the minor leagues, and have a way of resurrecting as miraculous as any Phoenix.

About midmorning of Monday, July 25, Jim Tracy looked up from his paperwork, stared at the season schedule tacked on the pegboard above his desk for more than a moment, then sighed and said, "No way around it . . . we need a sweep if we're to have any shot at all. We don't play those guys again after tomorrow . . . and the only time we're going to see Cedar Rapids again is the last two games of the season up at their orchard. Let's hope it's for something, and the only way we can maybe make that happen is to take these two tonight and tomorrow . . . hmm-hhmmm!"

Then, just a little before seven o'clock that evening, Bill Melvin, with a hot dog in one hand and his clipboard in the other, settled into his seat behind home plate in Lanphier Park and said, "We've gotta win these two . . . this is our season."

Almost five hours later, standing at the then all but deserted concession counter under the third-base grandstands, Jim Tracy shook his head after staring at the uneaten steak sandwich in his big hand and said; "You just can't play any better than that." Nope. Not unless you play exactly like that *plus* not have Chuck Johnson jar the ball loose from Rick Wilkins's mitt in a collision at the plate in the bottom of the twelfth inning. Because, after three hours and forty-six minutes of gut-check, incredibly *good* baseball, that ball trickling out of Wilkie's mitt after he'd just played perhaps his finest offensive game of the season was what it all came down to and was why Jim Tracy had croaked those words with a dry, empty mouth, instead of yukking them in between greasy, beaming mouthfuls of grilled steak, onions, and green peppers.

What a game. In the first inning Dick Canan singled to drive in Phil Hannon and the Chiefs led 1-0. In the third inning, after two infield singles, Ray Lankford went the other way with a Mike Aspray slider for a double past the bag at first and the Cardinals led 2-1. In the fourth inning Ed Fulton sent one of Mike's change-ups out of the yard, and the Redbirds led 3-1. In the fifth inning, Rick Wilkins got his second hit of the night, except this one went quick, hard, and far over the wall in right center for a solo dinger and the score was 3-2.

With one out in the seventh inning, after Rick's homer had long since chased Cardinals starter Rob Glisson, the Phenom hit a Mark Grater spinner over Ray Lankford's head in center for a triple—and that, folks, ain't easy to do. The next batter due up was Marty Rivero. But then, for the only time on the season, we would see our Captain lose his composure, say "Shit!" loud enough to be heard in the cheap seats, and then throw his helmet and bat in disgust when Jim Tracy, figuring that the baseball percentages outweighed the hunch and magic of Stephanie still sitting up in those box seats watching, called Marty back and sent up to the plate a much happier Jerry LaPenta now that his Mary was in for a visit also. (Believe me, Jim Tracy misses little and figured that hunch factor into his percentages, too.)

Jerry "Pizza Man" LaPenta delivered. A hard one-hopper through the right side scored Rick to tie the ballgame. Elvin Paulino then lunged into a 4-3 roller for out two but good enough to advance Jerry to second. Then Cardinals manager Mark DeJohn made a mistake—he intentionally walked Phil Hannon to pitch to Midget Number One. For that insult, and because he couldn't get at DeJohn, Warren Arrington, on a 2-2 fastball, almost took Grater's head off with a screaming liner to plate LaPenta for the go-ahead run; however, after the bad-hop relay had eluded cut-off man Scott Raziano, Phil Hannon eventually ended up being the victim of one very goofy 8-to-5-to-1-to-2 putout as he too tried to score. The inning ended with Jim Tracy arguing and tobacco-splattering the call just long enough to make his point, but not to get tossed—he didn't want to leave this ballgame; we hadn't brought along any walkie-talkies, and the clubhouses at Lanphier Park aren't even in hand-signaling distance from either dugout.

They immediately answered back with a lead-off double by Bernard Gilkey and a sacrifice bunt by Lankford to end Aspray's six and a third innings of yeoman duty on the night. Gabby Rodriguez then struck out

Johnson, but wasn't so fortunate with Rod Brewer, whose twisting chopper rolled up Dick Canan's arm for an infield single that scored Gilkey and knotted the affair at 4-4.

Which is where it stood for four and a half more innings as first Frank Castillo and then Jeff Massicotte shut them out on one hit, and two more of their pitchers did the same on three scattered singles (one by Canan, his third on the night, and another by LaPenta, who was getting mellower and happier by the day if not the minute).

Then came the bottom of the twelfth. Massicotte was lucky for the first out when Ray Lankford's shot to end it then and there was thwarted by Gator leaping and catching it high up against the wall in left. Jeff was then quite unlucky as Chuck Johnson barely looped a single beyond Stevie Hill's diving glove. Luck had nothing to do with Rod Brewer's double into the right-center gap; but Gator's speed and accurate arm had a lot to do with Johnson having to hold at third.

In comes the Z Man. In comes the drawn-in infield with that sick moment of instant defeat only ninety feet away. And up steps our old buddy and now nemesis Scott Raziano.

He hit it hard, and he hit it nasty. But Rusty dived, snared it, and came up throwing hard, low, and in time right into Rick's mitt as he braced himself for the collision with the charging Johnson and the sure putout that would perhaps have meant that we'd be able to throw Pookie, Dick, Rusty, and maybe Rick at them in the top of the thirteenth. But then that ball was slowly spinning in the dirt and there would be no sweep.

At about twenty minutes after seven o'clock the next evening, with the bases loaded and nobody out in the bottom of the first, Angie said, "Oh no . . . this is terrible! What's wrong?"

"Go get a beer and calm down," she was told.

Two Cardinals batters later, after Polly had come home with a hard two-hopper and Rusty had turned a sparkling 6-4-3 double play to let Billy "Nuke" Mel escape the two-hit, one-walk jam that he'd immediately put himself into without giving up a run, and Angie had gone for that beer, Brandon Davis, who had scouted Bill Melvin in both high school and junior college, said, "That's what I wanted to see . . . he was choking off that curveball then, and while he's improved it some, he's still doing it. And I've been telling them to teach that boy a slider for three years. I had hoped they would have done it by now. That's the problem . . . not all this other malarkey about that woman everbody's so worried about. There's nothing wrong with his velocity. He just needs to forget that curveball . . . or else just show it every now and again, but not for a strike . . . which he can't do often enough anyway."

Still rolling that curveball, always behind in the count and then having to come with his fastball, Bill Melvin, after giving up five more hits, but fortunately only two runs, was gone and out from under the scrutiny of a man he knew well and much admired after only three and two-thirds innings of the start that followed his "I'm back!" one.

Fortunately only two runs? Absolutely. Because even though the Cardinals would tie the match 3-3 in the seventh with an Alex Ojea solo homer off Ollie North, Jim Tracy, with one out in the top of the ninth, would call our Captain back for a pinch hitter for the very last time of the 1988 season, and "Pizza Man" would deliver again as he drove Dick Canan in from third with a sacrifice fly to deep center field, which, after Z had held them scoreless in their last licks for his seventeenth save, would be the game-winning RBI in a 4-3 Chiefs win, our eleventh in the fifteen games since "the Bet."

And while there was joy in that, there was also sadness, poignancy, and extreme frustration; and not only in the fact that the sweep we had needed we had not gotten, yet had come so close to in two nights of hard-fought baseball.

There was much sadness and poignancy in watching Marty Rivero walk back to the dugout without any of the histrionics of the night before, but rather in the stoic, resigned manner of a young man who knows that his dream is passing him by.

There was extreme frustration as, later that night, much distraught over the fact that not only had he had another "Stunk it up! I was totally horseshit!" performance, but that Brandon Davis had been there to see it, Bill Melvin went back to his apartment and tried to drown his sorrows alone with a few too many beers. Then, wanting no longer to be alone with it, but too drunk to drive, he called Angie to please come and pick him up. But she too had tried to ease her pain for him with too much to drink and was in no condition to drive herself. So Nuke went out into the night and jogged the several miles to her house so that his misery could be comforted if not forgotten.

Jim Tracy had for some time been wanting to get Rusty to back off from the plate some. But since he is always reluctant to tinker with a ballplayer's stance until he's absolutely sure that it is in the best interest of the ballplayer and not just some theory, and also until the ballplayer is beginning to show evidence that what he's doing isn't going to work over the long haul, he had left well enough alone until he thought the time was right.

But now that Rusty had gone hitless in his last eleven at bats, and was asking for help, the Shooter spent Wednesday morning's workout giving it.

"How've they been getting you out? In here, right? But they're not jamming you, you're jamming yourself. Your natural move is to dive into the ball . . . with that shoulder tucked in and attacking the ball . . . and that's good, I don't want you to stop that. But up here, and especially as you get into higher baseball, the pitchers are gonna spot that and all you're going to see is shit in on your hands . . . and they're not going to be balls but strikes on the corner and you're gonna be fisting, and flaring or breaking bats on balls you should be driving, right? So, it's simple. Back off the plate to about here . . . you've still got plate coverage, 'cause that's where your natural swing takes you . . . but now you've got the whole plate to work with instead of only the half you've been using . . . right? Let's try it."

And he did, happily. If Rusty is anything, he is coachable.

That afternoon, Wednesday, July 27, between batting practice and the start of the first of a two-game home series with the Burlington Braves, Jim Tracy had another talk with his ballclub. And it wasn't a sermon, or a speech, but, just like the night he'd first laid out the "challenge," it was indeed just a quiet talk.

He did not speak of the what-could-have-beens of the Springfield series. And there was no mention of play-off hopes, or pennant races. He spoke about arithmetic.

"Gentlemen . . . we put us on a pretty good run since the last time we had one of these talks . . . you took yourself a pretty good bite out of those numbers up there, didn't you?," he asked rhetorically as he pointed at the number on the right side of the blackboard, the number that was now 22 instead of the 33 it had been exactly fourteen days and fifteen games before.

"But, gentlemen . . . it doesn't take a rocket scientist to look at *that* number," and there he had pointed at the 34 on the left side of the blackboard, "and figure that if it isn't going to run out before the other one . . . we can't go keep winning one, losing one, winning one, then losing another like we've been doing the past four or five days. Yeah, sure that's playing .500 baseball . . . except you're just pissing into the wind, right? In fact, right now you're eleven under, just exactly where we were at the end of the first half . . . and that ain't .500!"

A long pause as he let that sink in until even Rick Wilkins looked at the board and nodded his head.

Then, "So, we can't be *splitting* too many more series . . . especially with ballclubs we know we're better than, like the two we've got coming up here the rest of this week! Right? Okay, then . . . let's go get us four quick ones, and then we've got a score to settle next week with them Appletons. No more fucking splits, right? Save them for the really good ballclubs we've gotta play next month."

So spake Jim Tracy. So what do we do?

That night Kal went to the hill and protected an early 1-0 lead by scattering five singles and one double over eight and two-thirds innings only to lose 2-1 on two errors and a single off of the Z Man in the top of the ninth.

Of course, the fact that big Mike Stanton was Kal's dueling mate had a little something to do with our fifth loss since the All-Star break. He went the full nine innings and throttled us good and tight on six hits. And *us* is a bit of a misnomer. Because if it hadn't been for Rusty, he'd have thrown a complete-game, two-hit shutout. After the Bat Doctor Number Two's session that morning, Midget Number Two had his first four-hit night in professional baseball and also drove in the only run.

Then the next night, the day after the "no more fucking splits" talk? With 5,500 laughing and screaming in the stands at the antics of Max Patkin, "the Clown Prince of Baseball," who was in for his annual visit to Peoria, Frank Castillo, not at all nervous any longer, struck out five of the first seven batters he faced (the first four in order) and then went on to finish his scheduled four-inning stint in shutout fashion before letting Brett Robinson and Gabby Rodriguez get in on the fun for a win and a save respectively.

Fun? Absolutely. That game was never in doubt from the time Rick Wilkins's mom got to her seat just in time to watch Rick's seventh home run on the season get up and fly over the scoreboard in right center in the bottom of the first for the Chiefs' first run. The quite attractive and always bubbling Pat Wilkins also saw Rick double off the wall in the third and hit a long sacrifice fly in the fifth.

Of course, she also saw some other Chiefs have fun that night. She saw Rusty Crockett go 3 for 4 (seven hits in two nights!), and she also saw "we've got the best midget in baseball!" let a relay on a force at second get by him and then kick off into left field well behind third, where Dick Canan picked it up and threw it back to Rusty who then outraced one very surprised runner for the tag-out at third. She saw Gator steal three bases and get an RBI liner to boot. And she saw a now quite contented Jerry LaPenta go 2 for 3 with yet another RBI.

In sum, what she saw was a 5-2 win for a split with the Burlington Braves that, while it reduced that right-side number by one, also reduced that left-side number by two; and left us still eleven games under .500.

Then the next night, with the Wilkins caravaning with us for a commuter to Quad Cities, she saw her son go 1 for 4 and not be the story. That night, Friday, July 29, the story was how Rick Kranitz had finally figured out how to motivate Eduardo Caballero through one of his typical mid-innings fall-apart acts.

The Panamanian Devil was perfect through the first four innings—as in twelve batters faced, twelve batters out (even Mr. Bob Rose, twice). Then, when the first man up in the fifth blooped a single to shallow left to break up his premature gem, and after he'd stomped and contorted and cursed the heavens for his bad fortune and grooved one to the next hitter for an RBI triple and then walked the following one on four pitches, Rick Kranitz went out to the mound and said, "I'm gonna kick your fucking ass all over this ballpark unless you get this man out!"

Now that he understood! He immediately stopped his shenanigans, struck out the next two hitters, and got the third on an infield pop-up; and then continued on to retire only one over the minimum in the sixth, seventh, and eighth, before Jim Tracy tipped his cap in honor of his eight-inning, three-hit performance and let Jeff Massicotte get in a little work pitching the ninth, since we by that time had a 5-1 lead that would soon be a 5-1 win.

"We are now a good ballclub" was the first thing Trace said in his cubbyhole after that game.

The next thing he said now that his team had again put together back-to-back wins was: "That's thirteen!"

But then almost exactly twenty-four hours later, Saturday, July 30, and sitting in the same cubbyhole in John O'Donnell Stadium, after Mike Aspray had pitched a complete-game five-hitter only to lose 2-1, Jim Tracy didn't feel like saying much of anything except for various repetitions of "Goddammit . . . I told him! You saw me . . . I even had him step out the box to come let me tell him again . . . I said, 'Rusty . . . all this Buckles has is that rinky-dink knuckle curve, but if you let him get ahead of you in the count, he'll hurt you with it, so jump on him early'! So what's the little sumbitch do. . . ?"

What had the "best *ballplayer* on this team" done to get his biggest booster so mad at him? In the top of the ninth, with two out and the bases loaded, Rusty had taken two mediocre fastballs down the middle of the plate to get behind 0-2, and then sure enough had come that knuckle curve low and away, and Rusty, having to protect the plate, had swung and missed at a pitch too close to take but too nasty to hit, to end the game.

So upset was the Trace Monster that when he finally got on the bus he had roared, "Somebody remind Crockett that this is where that fucking monster bit us in the ass again . . . right here with these sons of bitches in Quad Cities! And I don't want to see any of *you* sons of bitches after one-thirty in any barroom . . . if I do it's your ass!"

For the first time since the All-Star break, Jim Tracy did not get off the bus when we stopped to eat.

With the Appleton Foxes coming in for a four-game series, Jim Tracy did not have to say much at all to get his Chiefies pumped for their arrival. As in "Remember the Alamo," all he had to say was "You guys that were there tell the new guys what happened up there in the cold and snow of April. Remember that doubleheader they made us play when it was too cold for Eskimos? Well, now we've got 'em in our yard . . . and it ain't cold out there now . . . so let's go make it even hotter for 'em!"

There was another reason for the family to be even more pumped up— the ever frenetic and never repressible Jimmy Piersall had arrived that Sunday morning.

Oh, and for even further incentive, and certainly much interest, the umpires for the series would be none other than Mark Widlowski and Rich Roder, who were making their first visit back to Meinen Field since Pete Vonachen had made his now nationally infamous visit onto the playing field.

So, with all of the above for interest, incentive, drama, and comedy, how could the first game of the "Remember Appleton Series," Sunday, July 31, not have been one hell of a fun, exasperating, crazy, hilarious, thrilling, and in the end triumphant night?

What a question.

The fun had started even well before the match commenced, when Widlowski and Roder went into the umpires' dressing room and found bouquets of flowers, a tongue-in-cheek note of welcome, and Hershey chocolate kisses waiting for them courtesy of Pete Vonachen.

The exasperation started early also—with the second Appleton batter lining one of Billy "Nuke" Mel's behind-in-the-count, hard but grooved fastballs into right field for a single, the first of the ten hits which led to the seven runs he would allow in the five and two-thirds innings Jim Tracy left him out there on the hill to twist in the wind.

And the wind was the crazy part of it all. On a day that, like all the others for what seemed like weeks, saw temperatures once again above the 100-degree mark, just as the game started, a swirling windstorm came out of nowhere, and before it vanished in the sixth inning just as quickly as it had appeared, it threatened to blow down not only the scoreboard but the some 5,100 people in attendance right along with it.

The hilarity also came early and continued throughout Mel's nightmarish stint. Like all good humor it came out of seriousness and at the expense of another's sufferings.

"Damn!" Pete Vonachen said up in the press box where all who were allowed had gone to escape the gale-force winds. "That boy was one of our real assets in the beginning when we didn't have too many of those. Now he's a liability . . . son of a bitch is hurting us, not helping us. And it's all because of that broad!"

"Just going to have to send that boy to Charleston to break up this romance," Phil Theobald said. "Be the best thing for him . . . plus he deserves to be in Charleston."

"Bullshit!" Jimmy Piersall answered the owner and sportswriter. "Yeah, we've been hearing all this stuff about Mel and this woman up in Chicago, too. But lemme tell you something. I'd rather have my ballplayers fucking any day over all the drugs and rock-and-roll shit that's messing up the rest of this country! Getting laid ain't gonna take nothing out of a ballplayer . . . son of a bitch just isn't getting the job done! There's something else wrong . . . 'cause I'm gonna tell you something. You show me a man who can come more than one time a night and I can find you a fucking liar!"

You tell 'em, Jimmy. Because at the time I was laughing too hard to be of much help to you in explaining the real facts of life and baseball and sex to a couple of guys who hadn't noticed what Kranny and Terry Tripp and Gene Baker and Art Stewart and Don Welke and countless other scouts had already finally figured out about "Nuke's problem."

In Kranny's words, "It's location and command . . . he's not getting his change-up and curveball over for strikes. And even though his velocity is back up to what it was, he can't be a one-pitch pitcher. He's throwing eighty-seven, eighty-eight-plus . . . but even Single A hitters are going to hit that hard if that's all they're looking for."

Which was exactly what the Appleton Foxes were doing at the moment. But then so were the Chiefies. And of course that was the real fun, along with the thrill and triumph of that night when Pookie, pinch-hitting for Eddie Williams in the bottom of the tenth, drove in Gator with a sacrifice fly after midget number one had led off the frame with a double for the Chiefs' fourteenth hit of the night, and Polly had bunted him to third with the fifteenth hit, and the good guys won 8-7.

"Whew!" a yukking-again Shooter had said before adding, "But . . . that's fourteen."

On Monday night, August 1, after Silent Kal had methodically gone about running his record to 11-4 by allowing one run on five hits, and Dick Canan had had his fourth three-hit night in the fifteen days since he'd exploded in the doubleheader sweep of Wausau, and with those three hits had joined Rusty Crockett as the only Chief hitting over .300, and Pookie, in a getting-rarer-and-rarer start, had also gone 3 for 4 with two runs scored, and the Chiefs won 5-1 on a night when the temperature was still 104 degrees just before game time, a very yukking, playful Shooter just said, "That's fifteen!" and got dressed faster than usual and we went partying just a little; after all it was a Monday night.

Trace was in such good spirits that, with the heat again forecast to be upward of the 100-degree mark, he had made the "call" for six o'clock on Tuesday instead of the usual four o'clock for home games that start at seven-thirty, forgoing batting practice. However, from the way we hit that night, one would've thought we'd been out there at the cage all day long.

With Frank Castillo now allowed to pitch until he showed any signs of tiring, or until the seventh inning, whichever came first, which meant that he would get an opportunity to notch a win for the first time since he'd pitched and won in the New York–Penn League Championship series almost a year before, the Chiefs wasted little time giving him some run support. After he'd pitched a scoreless first inning, Rusty Crockett, who was now settled into the lead-off spot in the order, walked and then stole second (the first of three stolen bases he would get on the evening), Phil Hannon singled, and then Rick Wilkins hit a ball over the center-field wall that somehow ended up being caught and brought back into the field of play by a did-he-really-do-that? leap and catch by Foxes centerfielder Darren Watkins and was but a sacrifice fly scoring Rusty instead of the sure three-run dinger that God had intended it to be, and then Dick Canan drove in Phil Hannon with a groundout. Those two runs would be all Frank needed—but would not be all he would get.

Frank Castillo had his first win. The Peoria Chiefs were now 24 and 20 on the second half, 53 and 60 for the season—seven games under .500. *And 16 and 6 since the All-Star break.* "That's sixteen!" We partied hearty that night indeed.

It was about midafternoon on Wednesday, August 3, the last day of the Appleton series, and Jim Tracy was sitting at his desk working on his report recommending candidates for the Arizona Instructional League for the coming fall.

The subject being bandied about among the members of the family— albeit not hotly contested since it was a choice between two positives— had eventually been meandered around to: who had had the most impact upon our turnaround, Dick Canan or Rusty Crockett?

It really wasn't a debate. Jim Tracy didn't know himself. But he did like to muse upon it, which was what he was doing as he put down his pencil, leaned back in his chair, and started talking about Dick Canan.

". . . that boy needs to be at Double A next year. He's too good for this league. He's a pro in every sense of the word. You never see him 'umpiring,' throwing a bat, a helmet . . . just pure professionalism. And if he'd done nothing else, that attitude alone has influenced this ballclub. He leads by example and I can see it working . . . 'course he also can *play,* he's a bona fide prospect again."

But then, after writing a little more, he again leaned back and said, "But then . . . jeez'em'tally, it's just a plain fact . . . hell, you're the one that pointed it out . . . we've won twenty-five out of the thirty-one games that Rusty's been in the starting lineup going both ways . . . and that's nothing short of outright amazing. And it's a fact, I don't care where I'm managing, A, Double A, Triple A, or the major leagues, I want a player like Rusty."

Just thinking about those numbers then got Jim Tracy to musing upon some other ones since he was still all aglow and very much pumped over the last three wins.

"I know we're eight games back, and that's a long way to go. But, dammit . . . we're on some kind of a roll here. This is a *good* baseball team now, that's playing good baseball . . . so why not? I mean, the fact is . . . it's possible. Springfield's still faltering a bit. So, are we in a pennant race? Even though it's probably just a faint hope . . . I've gotta believe we are, and we sure as hell have to play like we're in one . . . but, dammit, it's possible . . . hey, didn't we always say we could win if this team could just hit .230? Well, we're hittin' .229."

*　　*　　*

Just a few hours later, Jim Tracy said to his ballclub, "Let's go out there and get this sweep. Those bastards did it to us when we were down and miserable and freezing. Let's return the favor . . . and then go up there to Beloit and knock another bunch of those numbers off the blackboard!"

Then Eduardo Caballero, who just that weekend had been named by the Howe Sports Bureau as Pitcher of the Week for the Midwest League, went out and spotted the Foxes four runs on six hits in the first inning, and that was it as we got blown out 6-1.

"Aaaa . . . what the hell, you're gonna have ballgames like that. Nothing you can do about it. We sure as hell knew we weren't going to go twenty-nine and oh for the month of August, I mean this ain't high school!" Jim Tracy said in his office afterward. Then he studied the schedule on the pegboard for a moment or two and added, "But with what we've got coming up down the stretch, we're gonna have to take at least three out of these four with Beloit . . . if we're gonna make a run at this thing, huh?"

Angie had been there with us in the family's section of box scats behind home plate that last night of the Appleton series, but she had not been her usual vivacious self, and while she looked as beautiful as always, dressed to her finest, you could see the pain in her eyes and the brave but wan smile she tried her best to show for as long as she could before getting up and leaving after the third inning.

I was surprised—but ever more proud for her—that she'd even shown up at all. Because Bill Melvin had finally succumbed to the pressures coming at him from without, and his own desperate frustration from within.

"You know I broke it off with her," he'd said during batting practice, as we had gone into the dugout and then had lingered over the water cooler to escape the heat for as long as we could get away with. "She took it hard, too. I mean bad. She was crying and everything. I felt like a dog . . . felt really bad . . . aw, man, like a heel . . . I was about to cry too. But I just had to do it . . . my career has to come first."

"Do yourself a favor, Mel . . . tell her you take it all back and learn yourself another variety of a breaker."

"Hey, you know Kranny told me that's what they want me to do at Instructional League! They want me to learn a slider. I mean if I get invited, you know. And I told her we could still be friends and all. But I had to do it, there's just being too much said . . . it's just causing too many problems, you know . . . and something's *wrong,* 'cause I was really horseshit last night! And I've just gotta turn it around."

CHAPTER 10

BARELY ABOVE A hoarse, croaked whisper, Jim Tracy said, "What happened between Peoria and Beloit, Yo? You were back there watching from that special vantage point. Are they that good? Or have we suddenly gotten that bad?"

"Trace, we ran into some pretty damn fine pitchers, a fucking covey of 'em. I ain't real sure you'da been able to hit a couple of 'em."

"Yeah . . . that's what it looked like from the dugout . . . and that's what Colbie said. But you know our hitters, he watches pitchers."

"Trace . . . we also fell back into an old habit I thought we'd broken for good."

"I know . . . taking strikes! Jesus . . . when you're always hitting behind in the count, particularly against pitchers with breaking balls like these guys they've been running out at us these past three nights, you're at their mercy . . . and this is what happens!"

What had happened was thirty-four strikeouts in three games—sixteen of which set one Midwest League record and tied another—and of course, counting the last of the Appleton series, a four-game losing streak, our first in almost a month.

From that "special vantage point" (Pohlman Field has a special row of theater seats down on field level, below the box seats, and right behind the plate, which is reserved for scouts, visiting officials of the parent major league clubs, and other dignitaries) on Thursday night, August 4, Colbie and I—

—in between his cogent and quite academically metaphysical dissertations on the art of pitching as it relates to all of life in an almost Zen spirituality which a goodly part of the time only he understands (and not even he some of the time); and his fretting and saber-rattling about the "bean counters" who are now so much more in control of the baseball operations of the Cubs, and how their penny-pinching ways were about to

284

come to a head with the "baseball men" at the conclave scheduled for August 14 and 15 in Winston-Salem to not only select the invitees to Instructional League, but to also decide if the Cubs should cut back from fielding the two teams in that league that they had under Dallas's reign and that most of the "baseball men" in the organization still wanted and were prepared to go down fighting for—

Saw one Leonardo Perez, still only twenty-one years old but already a veteran of three seasons in the Triple A–equivalent Mexican League, wax our asses with a 90-mile-an-hour fastball and several different, but all nasty, breaking balls, to the befuddling melody of four hits—and two of those were bunts—for a complete-game, seven-strikeout, 5-2 win (and believe me, it really wasn't that close; the two runs were gifts) on a night when Mike Aspray wasn't "Hard Luck" Mike but instead was hit hard and often.

Then on Friday night we saw Bill Melvin pitch almost as well as he had at any time of the season, going the route on only three hits but getting beat 3-0 when one of those hits came after two questionable walks, and the other was a solo home run.

But then if he hadn't given up those runs perhaps we'd still be out there—because we wouldn't have done diddly-squat against the Brewers that night if we'd stayed out there until you read this." Not against the two guys named Chris Johnson and Mark Chapman that Mel dueled. Oh, Johnson perhaps, we were so suddenly and inexplicably lifeless and lethargic that we'd made a just-a-little-bit-better-than-average "prospect" look like a world-beater for the six shutout three-hit, seven-strikeout innings Gomer Hodge let him work before bringing in his "secret weapon" Mark Chapman so he could collect his nineteenth save. All he did was strike out the first Chief he faced, have his shortstop boot Gator's nubbed roller for an E6, then proceed to strike out the next eight Chiefs in order! In other words, all of the last nine outs were recorded by strikeouts, wrapped around an error, and that had never been done before in the forty-eight-year history of the Midwest League.

Then on Saturday night, we had us a look at a rookie by the name of Mike Ignasiak, who'd just been drafted and signed out of the University of Michigan—where he'd been on the same pitching staff as Jim Abbott, the one-armed phenom who at that very moment was starring on the U.S. Olympic Team and would jump right into the big leagues the following season without pitching a day in the minors. Must've been one hell of a staff! Because all this kid did was throw a mean split-finger diver that was the best any of us had seen in this league and strike out the first six Chiefs he faced! Which, added to the eight consecutive strikeouts to end the game the night before, tied a Midwest League record.

But eventually we nicked away at him and a reliever for three runs on eight hits. Unfortunately, Silent Kal did not have one of his better nights and Jim Tracy, by his own admission, and to his night-and-day-long "Be more pissed at yourself than him? Nofuckingbody!" chagrin, had let Kal go "one more batter, and I knew it at the time, fuck me!" too long in the eighth and they scored two and we lost 4-3.

What had happened between Peoria and Beloit? What can make a team on fire and cocky and confident that they can beat anyone they face suddenly, literally overnight, and quite visibly, go into the baffling malaise that enveloped us for most of those first three days in Beloit?

There are no single and absolute answers. Perhaps it was just time for it. Only so long can just emotion and motivation carry a ballclub before that very emotion and motivation hits overload and the circuit breaker trips and, almost as a defense mechanism, shuts the unit down for a spell of what looks to be a breakdown but is in fact a necessary time of reflection and regrouping.

Certainly, to a man, we were tired. Except maybe only in war is there anything like the daily grind of battle, win, lose, sleep, eat what you can and on the run, and then do it again under the pressure of constant evaluation over the course of 140 games in 143 days. And to this constant, in the case of the Beloit collapse, we must add several variables. It certainly had something to do with the bleakness of the worst motel on the Midwest League circuit, the Plantation Motor Inn, whose bleakness was made even more manifest by the fact that it was far on the outskirts of town without a decent restaurant or lounge anywhere close by that stayed open past nine.

And certainly the fact that almost all of the talk among the ballplayers was the speculation of who would be invited to Instructional League, and that everybody knew Trace had already turned in his recommendations but no one knew who they were, and that Jim Colborn, a man who would have no small say in who would get those much coveted invitations, was traveling with us, had more than a little to do with it.

And surely it did not boost morale when, on our second day there, Jim Colborn asked Mario and me to leave the bus and gave this winning ballclub a major league tongue-lashing on what to them and to Jim Tracy was the least of their priorities—adherence to a dress code—just prior to the game which would result in a sixteen-strikeout, goose-egg whitewashing.

And it didn't help that our "star" catcher, with his parents still traveling with us, had gone into a 2-for-16 slump and was also now in open, shouting rebellion with the entire pitching staff about his "stupid, flat-out ignorant, mule-headed and self-serving" calling of pitches.

And perhaps the tone was set when our two spark plugs, Crockett and Canan, made two errors in the first inning of the first game, which led directly to a run and a lead we never caught up to; and the fact that they too stopped hitting, although unlike most everyone else they did not stop hustling. And surely the pitching we ran into *was*, on that weekend anyway, truly brilliant.

All of the above played its part. And also in all fairness we must note that in the third game, most of the lethargy and lack of aggression had vanished and we really should have won that ballgame except for a finally less than superlative effort by Greg Kallevig.

And it was no coincidence that we in fact played well and aggressively and matched them hit for hit in that third game, but just lost it because that's how baseball is some nights when one hit at the wrong time means the difference between winning and losing. It was no coincidence because Jim Tracy, understanding all of the factors above, never stopped motivating and teaching. After the second loss, even though he knew that those two losses, in all probability, ended any real chance at a play-off spot, Jim Tracy made another speech; and, even though we lost again that next night, we lost playing mostly good baseball and it would be the last such speech he would have to make for the season.

"You've worked too hard and come too far in the past three and a half weeks to fuck it up now. Somewhere between here and Peoria you lost something. For two nights you've looked like you're just going through the motions. This isn't the team these guys have been reading about these past few weeks. This is a team that if they get a run or two on you, they think you're going to roll over and play dead . . . because that's what you've done. I'ma tell you what they think now, they think you're horseshit. Gentlemen, we have twenty-four games left. And if you wanna do something you can be proud of, coming from as far back as we were, prove something to yourselves . . . not to me, but to yourselves? Then we've gotta win seventeen of twenty-four. Now, tomorrow, and the next day we can kick some ass and go back to Peoria just like we came in . . . nothing really lost toward our goal. Or . . . you can just play out the string! Now, I want youse to think about it. Are you gonna do something to make yourself proud, prove something to a lotta people . . . or stay horseshit?"

On Sunday afternoon, the day of the annual Beloit Brewers Booster Club picnic, just shortly after we'd heard a Brewer player walk by the batting cage and say, "Let's go, guys . . . whip these sons of bitches again and go have a picnic," Frank Castillo took the mound, went seven innings for the first time, struck out ten, gave up only four hits and two cheap runs, and, although Z made it interesting by giving up a run in the ninth and then loading the bases before collecting his eighteenth "zave" and preserving Frank's second win, we whipped those sons of bitches asses 5-3, and then went to their picnic, ate everything in sight, and headed for P-Town saying, "That's seventeen!"

And who had caught that day and driven in the insurance run to seal the affair while Mr. All-Sullen sat the bench?

The young man who the day before had hung a sign up in the dugout that said, "Herbie is alive." Trace liked that spunk and gall and took heed of the message and played Herberto Andrade.

*   *   *

On Monday, August 8, while I was up at Wrigley Field to attend the first-ever night game to be played in that grand old ballpark—which of course would not be the "official" first-ever night game when the heavens opened up and washed away the festive event in the bottom of the fourth; but good god Bacchus did we and Scott Nelson and others have a ball anyway—the Peoria Chiefs, in the only game that I would miss on the season, beat the visiting Waterloo Indians 11-9 in what Jim Tracy said "jeeze'em'tally . . . and I'm not shitting you . . . had to've been the ugliest baseball game I've ever seen."

It seems Eduardo Caballero didn't even give Kranny time to give him his motivational "kick your ass" pep talk when he was gone after getting only four outs while giving up five runs on five hits. But with the Indians not able to throw strikes or catch a baseball, and Rusty Crockett and Eddie Williams seemingly having a penchant for hitting doubles that night with the bases loaded, we'd outslugged them just long enough until the same rains that had washed away the game up in Chicago ended the affair in Peoria after six and a half innings.

Somewhat timely too had that rain been—because while Brett Robinson and then Jeff Massicotte were throwing strikes, the Indians kept hitting them harder and harder and we were having a bit of trouble catching the damn ball ourselves. But all's well that ends well.

Which of course was why the first words Jim Tracy said upon the return of the "bigwigging it, huh" resident scribe were:

"That's eighteen!" Then he added, "No matter what it looked like, when it was over we had more on our board than they did on theirs . . . and that's all that counts, huh?"

What a question.

There also were a couple or three other things our lingering in Chicago had meant that we needed to be caught up on upon our return.

The first was a phone call that Jim Tracy had received early that very morning from Bill Harford, but that he would only hint at while steadfastly also keeping it a secret.

"Hey . . . I know it can't be bad news. I was just with Billy, and his very words to me were, 'No more concerns over that ballclub, huh? Trace has gotten them right on track.'"

"Did he say that, really?"

"Verbatim. So what's the news he gave you?"

"Mum's the word. Just wait and find out."

Whatever. Then Bill Melvin couldn't wait to let me know that "hey . . . me and Angie are semi-back-together. But it's not going to be like before. She feels a lot better about it, though. She came to the game last night. We're gonna date and still see each other and all . . . just not like it used to be, that's all. I thought that'd make you happy."

It did. What happened next out on the field during warm-ups, however, did not. Jeff Massicotte came storming past, tears in his eyes and murder in his voice when he was asked, "What the hell's wrong with you?"

"I'm just sick of these people fucking with me!"

Then he stormed on toward the dumpster carrying what looked to be a torn-up placard and a stake broken into several pieces.

Baseball humor and pranks can be rough at times. Jeff had been getting hit hard and with some regularity of late. He'd been hit hard again the night before; one particular shot had been a screaming-meemie right back into center field for a run-scoring base hit. Therefore, with Z of course as the mastermind and Marty the artist, a bull's-eye target had been manufactured, attached to a stake, and planted right behind second base for Jeff to see as soon as he came out for batting practice.

Actually, it was funny. But then not everyone knew exactly what demons "Grandpa" was struggling with; and his reaction to what was just a practical joke had not been appreciated by the pranksters—and Jeff's relationship with his fellow pitchers and his attitude about the game and life and the meaning of it all deteriorated from that time on.

Good Lord, do I still shudder to think that we had actually thought of returning to Chicago for what was to be the first "official" night game at Wrigley and then would've missed the second game of the Waterloo series, Tuesday, August 9.

And it wasn't just that the always welcome Tony Franklin had arrived for another of his roving visits. Of course his company was much enjoyed as we sat and chatted with the always present scouts, and the distaff members of the family, and watched Mike Aspray look particularly sharp with all of his "dancing pus" as he struck out the first two Indian batters to begin the match by hitting spots within spots at all of the various slow speeds that Mike throws his repertoire of fastball, change-up, slider, and curve—none of which he throws any harder than 81 to 83 miles an hour, tops.

We were used to seeing Mike do this. Perhaps the strikeouts were a bit unusual, especially when his whiff total reached six through the first four innings. But still, we were much more excited about the four runs we exploded for in the bottom of the fourth, led by little Stevie Hill's first homer of the year, a two-run blast to left. After all, the Indians were one of the better-hitting clubs in our circuit, and an early four-run lead on them with Mike pitching looked to be a lock—and an absolute godsend to Aspray, whose 7-and-14 record (the most losses ever by a Peoria Chiefs pitcher) but exemplary 2.95 ERA were almost solely due to the fact that we had scored two or fewer runs for him in seventeen of his then twenty-three starts on the season.

But then, as he set them down in order in the fifth, including yet another strikeout, and ditto in the sixth after we'd scored again to make it 5-0 Chiefs, one of us had torn his eyes and heart away from flirting with one Peggy Jean Duggan, one of the prettier, newer members of the extended family, scratched his head while perusing his scorebook, and remarked to Tony and the scouts, "Hey, guys . . . you realize that not only has he got a no-no working, he ain't walked a batter . . . in fact they ain't put anybody on base period?"

"Jesus . . . you're right!"

So our attention was now totally on the ballgame; the ladies could go unadmired and unattended for a while, thank you, please.

Then came the seventh inning: a foul-out to first; can of bean shit to shallow center field; and a little pop-up to second: 1-2-3.

By this time the 2,600 folks in attendance that night had begun to catch on too, and there was less bustle and chatter in the stands as somewhat of a hush fell over the crowd when Mike went back to the hill in the eighth.

Of course, we had seen Mike go this route before. Twice, in fact, Mike had taken no-hitters into the eighth inning, only to see them get away from him against Kenosha and Burlington. So, while my heart was pumping, I was already prepared to see this one go the way of the other two.

But Scott Khoury, one of the league's leading hitters for average and power (.296, 17 HR), who always seemed to murder us, led off the inning with a 4-3 roller to second; Sean Baron struck out for Mike's ninth K of the night; and Rick Faulkner tapped out 1-3.

Now we had something here. Even the Chiefs hitters were affected by it, as they almost seemed in a rush to get out themselves so that the real event could continue and were gone 1-2-3 in our half of the eighth.

There was almost a total hush as the tension and thrill of the moment gripped everyone as Mike walked to the mound to start his warm-up tosses. No-hitters are rare enough, but perfect games are somewhat like hen's teeth!

So, when Mike struck out Scott Mackie, the first batter in the ninth, that crowd and even the "baseball men" stood up as one and the only noise you could hear came from the cars passing on I-74 immediately behind and down the slope from Meinen Field.

Then, with Pete Kuld now at the plate, the tension and pressure began to get to both Mike and plate umpire Mike Everett. Mike missed outside, but close on the first pitch, and it was called a ball. The next pitch was closer still, well in on the black, but Everett, surely due to his own nerves, squeezed Mike and called that one a ball, too. Oops! Mike was behind in the count 2-0 for the first time that evening. Then two quick strikes, the first one called, the second one swinging. And damned if Everett didn't then let his nerves really get the better of him and squeeze the plate on a fastball on the inner third and right at the knees which he hesitated on and then called ball three.

Mike stepped off the rubber for only a moment, took a deep breath, and then toed it and fired his best fastball just a little over the belt buckle and well below the letters—but Everett, and probably rightly so, this ain't playground ball, called it ball four.

A gasp, and then a sigh went through the crowd as Kuld trotted to first and the perfect game was not history. But Mike, in the heat of the moment, was confused, because, as he would later say maybe a hundred times during the second-best party night we would have on the season, "Somehow I just went blank, I thought I'd lost my no-hitter. Stupid, huh? But that was my first thought."

It was still one of his thoughts as he threw the next four pitches not anywhere even close and walked Todd Butler. But then Kranny ran out and helped him collect those thoughts, by reminding him, "Hey, they haven't hit you yet," and he then threw six strikes in a row, whiffing Ramon Bautista with the third (eleven strikeouts for Mike Aspray!) and got T. J. Gamba to pop up weakly to Polly at first . . . and then all heaven and hell broke loose.

Mike was mobbed by his teammates. Then after they all ran off to the clubhouse to prepare for the moment when Mike would walk in there, he was mobbed by fans. He had to sign so many autographs that we didn't think he was ever going to get into that locker room. But he did. And he was hit with shaving cream, doused in cola, thrown into the showers all the while yelling, "Not my hat, guys! Not my hat . . . you're all going to have to buy me a hat!" He was also crying, partly from joy, but mainly because of the cola and shaving cream getting into his contact lenses.

Someone else was crying, but it was quietly, and while they also were partly tears of joy, they were mostly quiet tears of the Shooter's big heart bursting with pride. Only during the initial moments of the raucous, customary clubhouse reception had Jim Tracy participated. Then he had gone into his office and had just sat quietly, caring not that we saw those tears in his eyes, as he just kept shaking that big head and repeated over and over again, "I'm so proud of that boy . . . how could it have happened to a better man, huh? I'm just so proud of that boy . . . here we don't give him any support all year long . . . never complained, huh . . . oh, God, guys, I'm just so proud of that boy."

And he would repeat it over and over again, well into the wee hours of the morning as we en masse descended upon Spirits downtown and partied like we'd never done before.

"That boy 'pitched' a no-hitter . . . he didn't 'throw' one!" Kranny said loud and often.

And ever-mild-mannered Mike, even as he was getting as hammered as the rest of us, had this to say when asked about Everett "squeezing" him: "Yeah . . . on a couple he did, but you've gotta remember, he was as nervous as I was."

"Aaaa . . . you weren't nervous, were ya, Mike?"

"Joe . . . after I got that first batter out in the ninth, you don't know how nervous I was!"

Nobody said "That's nineteen!" that night. For that night, "the Bet" was not the story.

And even as he partied and drank a little more than he usually does, Jim Tracy would not reveal the secret that had come by way of a phone call that morning from Bill Harford.

He would, however, have to reveal it that following morning. He couldn't hold it back. After all, Mike Aspray's and Marty Rivero's travel schedules had to be arranged.

Yepper, on the day that Mike Aspray was to throw the first no-hitter of both his amateur and professional career, he had already been summoned "up."

The "up" is in quotation marks because he was going to Winston-Salem, which is very definitely *up* and a promotion in the Chicago Cubs scheme of things. It is, however, definitely not "up" to Pete Vonachen, who, while nothing like the ones he'd thrown before, threw a plenty good enough hissy-fit as soon as he heard about it.

"End of conversation!" he barked and then huffed away when I forgetfully, quite innocently, used the word "up" in regards to the rather incredible events of those couple of days.

And while his provincialism might sound petty, there was more to it than just his notion that there was no difference in the quality of play between the Midwest League and the Carolina League. You see, Winston-Salem was very much still in a pennant race. And since August 15— the last day that player moves could be made at that level for the purposes of "pennant drives"—was fast approaching, we had for some time been wondering when they would take at least one or more of our pitchers as we had already watched the Cubs begin the "stacking" process by moving two of my own back-home boys, Mike Tullier and Jimmy Bullinger, down from Double A Pittsfield.

That was what stuck in Pete's craw. "Are we not fighting for something? The attendance race, and 'the Bet'? Isn't what we're trying to do just as important and meaningful? And what are they sending us to replace my no-hitter pitcher? Here, look at these stats . . . they're sending us Winston-Salem's rejects!"

There was no need to look in the book. James "the Animal" Matas, a hell of a fun guy and free spirit, did not have impressive numbers for the limited service he'd been allowed during the past four months of the season at Winston-Salem.

Pete was livid, and would remain so for days.

On the other hand, Mike Aspray was ecstatic. While he had mixed emotions about picking up and moving with only three weeks left in the season—to just pack up and go across country and say goodbye to friends, and place, and the feelings he had for this team and what Jim Tracy was trying to accomplish would not be easy—still, "Hey, they're in a real pennant race! And it's one step up the ladder! Hell yes I'm happy!"

For Marty Rivero it was only a change of scenery, but while he knew he was going to Winston-Salem only as a backup, at least he might get *some* playing time. Since Jim Tracy had called him back for a pinch hitter in Springfield almost two and a half weeks before, our Captain had appeared in only one game.

While there is never any "blood on the floor" when a member of the family is called "up," those two fine young men who had been with us from the first morning of spring training would be sorely missed. And not just because—in Mike's case—we would be losing their efforts on the field, but because we were losing two of the rocks upon which this family had first been built and then maintained and stabilized through the hardest of times.

"Pitcher" Mike, and our Captain.

Those were two tough goodbyes to say. Particularly Marty's, whose goodbye handshake was accompanied by the words, "I'll see you in spring training . . . if I'm there."

Since they were not scheduled to fly away from the family until early Thursday morning, August 11, at least they got to hear "That's twenty!" and be on hand when Trace again did the honors at the blackboard.

That afternoon, as we were again escaping the heat by watching the end of batting practice from the dugout, Mel said, "You know . . . I've never felt better. Really, this is the best and most confident I've felt in so long I can't remember. You know what I mean . . . that feeling you get?"

"That's great, Mel . . . but look . . . if a chink hit or an error or something happens, forget it. Just focus on that mitt, and hit your spots . . . and pitch your game, not Wilkie's . . . because he doesn't get that W or L, only you. Shake him off all night long if you have to."

"Jeeze . . . you sound just like you're my daddy, and that's a compliment."

It was taken as such, and therefore made it even more meaningful to watch Billy "Nuke" Mel throw a complete-game, five-hit shutout as we got eleven hits and spanked and then whitewashed the Indians again 6-0.

"Jeez'em'tally . . . a no-hitter, and then a complete-game shutout? Those guys over there in the other room gotta be wondering what hit 'em and if they're ever gonna stomp that plate again, huh? And with Kal going tomorrow night . . . smell us a sweep here, guys!"

After the debacle of the first three days in Beloit, we were now 28 and 24 on the second half, 20 and 10 since the All-Star break, and 57 and 64 on the season—*seven games under .500*. We had come a long way. But those blackboard figures read 19 and 13.

In other words, to meet our "challenge" we would have to win thirteen of the nineteen games left.

Unfortunately, after Silent Kal gave up only five hits, but we could manage only three, and the Indians avoided the broom 2-1 by virtue of Kal's own error, there were only eighteen games left for us to win thirteen of.

"Hmmm! Them's some tough odds, huh?" I observed.

"I wouldn't wanna bet 'em."

"No shit . . . Trace, that's playing .720 baseball!"

"Well . . . we pretty much knew it was going to be impossible. But then I reckon that's what a lotta folks must've said about climbing Mount Everest . . . until that dude what's-his-name went and did it, huh?"

The ever methodical Jim Tracy, who sleeps little if at all anyway during the season—except for the catnaps he takes on the big sofa in Pete's office—had stayed up most of Thursday night and Friday morning catching up on his paperwork; and when that was done he had then made himself a small chart that he could carry in his pocket which detailed exactly what we would have to do in the eighteen remaining games if we were going to "climb that mountain."

When we came in that Friday morning of August 12 and aroused him from his fitful slumber on that sofa, and after he'd gotten a cup of coffee in him and a doughnut or two, he proceeded to run down his chart for us.

"We've gotta take these next two in Quad Cities . . . split the two up at Waterloo . . . two from Clinton, or at worst split . . . then split the four with Rockford, and sweep Burlington for two . . . three out of four with Madison . . . and then split the last two at Cedar Rapids . . . and we're there, guys!"

"Got it all figured out, huh, Doc?" Pete said with a wink at the rest of us.

"Yep . . . but these next four days are the key, we've gotta take three of the four to get on the track."

A few hours later the bus rolled for a commuter match with the Quad Cities Angels and, after Frank Castillo went eight innings, gave up but four hits, struck out eight, and allowed only one run—largely due to the fact that when he got into trouble in the third, Gator went up high against the wall and quite incredibly came down with the third out to strand runners at first and third—while the Chiefs got eight hits, two of them in the fifth inning when we scored the only three runs we would need to get Frank his third win and Z his nineteenth save by virtue of three walks, a passed ball, two errors, and a double crushed into the left-field corner by Dick Canan, Jim Tracy would say, "That was a big one, we did what we had to do, and we're on that track, guys!" and then get dressed in almost record time and we would be rolling back to P-Town quickly so that we could get to Spirits for the always big Friday-night happenings there that by this time had become a ritual event in the life of the family.

"That's twenty-one."

We would be "right on track" again the next evening when the bus had rolled back to Quad Cities, but it wasn't a commuter because as soon as we'd won probably the single craziest baseball game of the season—excluding Pete's "incident," of course—we would be heading for Waterloo, Iowa.

For starters, Jim Tracy ran Z's "dick into the dirt" beforehand, along with the fifty-dollar fine he'd imposed when Z, knowing full well the risk he was taking, had gotten a phone call from "the Peacock Lady" asking him to meet her at Sully's, and then did—*well* after the one-thirty curfew hour that Trace is somewhat lenient about as long as they are attempting to get out and home by that time. What Fernando had gambled on was that Trace and the rest of the quartet of "adult" members of the family would not be out that late and if we were that surely we would be at Spirits. He'd gambled wrong and gotten caught.

"I hope she was worth it?" Trace said as the tongue-dragging, exhausted Z was finally told he could stop running.

"What a question" was Z's panting but self-satisfied answer.

But then Z got ten dollars promptly reduced from that fine when, about the fourth inning, he alerted Trace to the fact that Mike Boswell's parents were here for their second visit all the way from Florida and had yet to see their son play an inning of baseball.

Trace then immediately inserted the Boz in as the DH to replace Jerry LaPenta, who under the circumstances was more than happy to oblige willingly and graciously for the cause.

The Boz promptly walked and scored in his first at bat, got on by an E6 in his next, and then hit a moon shot over the left-field wall for a two-RBI dinger that then made the score *15-0* Chiefs in the top of the ninth.

That is no misprint above. And I did say this was one crazy game, right? The Chiefs did more than just explode that Saturday night of August 13, they went atomic. On an evening when the Angels couldn't catch it (four errors, two passed balls) or throw it (eight bases on balls, two wild pitches), the Chiefs collected fifteen hits, four of which were doubles, one triple, and two homers (Wilkins had hit his eighth).

The Angels also couldn't hit it. So, after Eduardo had held them scoreless through six, and with the score then ten for the good guys, Jim Tracy decided to let his bullpen get some work and commenced to running each of them out there for an inning apiece, Brett the seventh, Ollie the eighth, and Mass the ninth. That's when the fireworks started.

Literally. And I don't just mean on the field, I mean the World War II–type fireworks which erupted directly behind center field and started bursting all around and about the night sky just as Jeff threw the first pitch in the bottom of the ninth.

Just a little background information is needed before we go any further. It seems that the City of Davenport, Iowa, was having a big arts-and-crafts festival down on the riverfront and directly behind the ballpark which included a 10K road race and, for the finale, a ten-thousand-dollar fireworks display. Now, the lady who was in charge of this event had planned for this fireworks display to start at precisely nine-fifteen. To accommodate her, Mike Feder, the Quad Cities general manager, had moved the start of the game to six-thirty, figuring that while it might be cutting it close, a professional baseball game should be completed by then. Well, not a fifteen-run affair such as that one. So, as the deadline approached, this lady was calling a beleaguered Mike Feder every five minutes, demanding that if the game wasn't over by nine-fifteen, then it should be halted and the lights turned out so the show could begin.

Mike Feder, a professional baseball man of excellent reputation, tried explaining to this lady that you just do not stop a professional baseball game for such reasons, and that *he* couldn't do it anyway even if it was proper—only the umpires can stop a game once it begins. And "I'm not about to go down there and ask them to, ma'am . . . they'd laugh me out of baseball!" So a compromise of sorts was reached: she would hold off until exactly nine-thirty, but "not a second longer."

That would've worked just fine except that Eddie Rodriguez, the Angels' manager, decided that with the game out of hand anyway, he wasn't going to use up another pitcher, so he brought his right fielder Bill Robinson, Jr. (yes, the son of the former big leaguer), to pitch the top of the ninth. So of course we commenced to hitting him pretty hard—when he threw strikes—for four more runs and a whole lot more time.

So, bang! That lady was good for her word and off went the fireworks and off went the Angels hitters who seemed not to be bothered at all by the truly spectacular pyrotechnics exploding behind and above Jeff Massicotte's head, as those he didn't walk started hitting rockets in syncopated time with the ones going off overhead. Of the seven batters Trace let him face, he walked four, the other three tattooed him, and all scored.

While this was going on, one of us who is quite fond of the real person Jeff Massicotte is when he has those diamond and ghost demons at bay went more than just a little bit screaming berserk as all of the people who suddenly started streaming into the stadium just to see the fireworks were hollering for either the lights to be turned out "now!" or for that "busher!" on the mound to be taken out so this game could end and they could better enjoy the spectacle in the sky.

Jim Tracy soon obliged and brought in Gabby, who, while he too quickly gave up a couple of bazooka rounds for yet an eighth run to be added to Jeff's ballooning-by-the-minute ERA, eventually got a double play and a fly-out to end the game 15-8.

However, one of us was so outraged at the seeming cosmic conspiracy of it all, he was still hollering at everybody in sight—while at the same time Rick Kranitz was resorting to physical violence, and it was not directed at the folks in the stands but rather at Jeff Massicotte, whom he'd commenced to throw against the wall in the tunnel below.

And as it turns out, Kranny was right, and I must now confess to the city of Davenport, Iowa, that I was dead wrong!

Because what we didn't know, but would find out very shortly thereafter in another goddam Hardee's before we headed for Waterloo, was that Jeff had been bitching and moaning all night long out in the bullpen about how he had been misused all year long, about how they had "fucked up" his career, and that furthermore he was "too good" to have to come in to pitch in such a ridiculous mop-up role, and that that was why he went out there and in Kranny's words "just gave it up . . . and then wanted to give me some shit with his mouth and then the fucker came at me! Horseshit son of a bitch."

Whew . . . whatever . . . and "That's twenty-two!"

And we're off to Waterloo, "right on track, guys," as Jim Tracy said, looking at his little pocket chart.

"Now, all we have to do is split with those Indians, and the plan's working fine," he added.

Split hell, how about a sweep?

The only thing that could make a visit by the Chiefs to "groupie capital" of the Midwest League, to the Holiday Inn with the best lunch buffet in the Midwest League, to Spinner McGee's, the best nightclub (outside of Peoria) in the Midwest League, to Municipal Stadium, the second coziest ballpark in the Midwest League, better would be to go into the home of the Waterloo Indians and mess up Jim Tracy's chart with a +1 by sweeping two. Which is just what we did.

And the very best part of it all was that the first one was a day game, Sunday, August 14. Which meant that after James "the Animal" Matas, throwing gas, picked up a 3-zip win, we had a whole night to be real "citizens" in a place where that can be a lot of fun.

The only problem was that it was a Sunday night, which meant that while we had as much fun as we could, we mostly talked baseball. And the "adult" quartet did their talking over a fine Chinese dinner in a real restaurant in a leisurely and civilized manner just like real people for a change, which is a *very* big deal in the minor leagues. It was of course a happy meal since we were now 23 and 11 since "the Bet," 31 and 25 on the "second chance," 60 and 65 on the season, *five games under .500,* and only a half game out of second place! While we talked about everything and anything having to do with baseball and what we'd been through and how far we'd come, much of the talk eventually and inevitably kept coming back to familiar themes.

"No doubt that Rusty, Dick, and Stevie were what we needed to turn it around . . . but the truth is, ever since I took that whip-handle bat away from him, Gator has been the most valuable player on this team."

No disagreement there. "Trace . . . of the guys that have been here from the getty up, he's leading the pack. Christ, he's hitting .257 . . . to come from .180 to there during the middle of a season and playing every day? That's damn near amazing!"

We also talked about Rusty's continuing slump, and Wilkie's possibly just ended one.

"They're both doing the same thing wrong . . . not rolling that shoulder. Rusty wants to learn, and he's listening, and trying and the truth is, guys . . . he's still hurting bad and won't admit it. But Wilkie won't listen for shit. And did ya notice that right after his folks arrived and he hit that dinger, his slump started? What'd he do, drop twenty points on his average?"

"Uh . . . actually only seventeen . . . but who's counting?"

"Yeah . . . but then just as soon as his parents went home, he's starting to hit the ball again. Tells us something, huh?"

Again no disagreement, the phenomenon too obvious to all.

Then Trace said, "Kinda funny how all those E's on the scoreboard have evaporated since Marty started sitting and then left, huh? Strange thing . . . at times he'd make those spectacular plays and you'd think he was one of the best you ever saw . . . hell, he dazzled us, huh? Even the so-called experts . . . but, damn, hit him one that was routine? Boot city. If he had time to think, he had time to doubt, and he'd think wrong."

"God forgive us, Marty, you were one of our favorite people, but you're going to be a better graphic artist than an infielder," the Kran-dog said.

Then Mario asked, "Hey . . . what is this? We keep getting messages from Zisk saying he's coming . . . and then nothing?"

"Hell . . . he keeps trying to come, but they keep rerouting him away from us. They say we don't need him anymore . . . that we're healthy and well and on the right track . . . they ain't worried about us anymore! Ain't that a kick in the ass . . . huh? We were dead and dying again just a month ago . . . and now we're heroes!"

Yepper, and it was even more of a kick in anywhere but the ass when the next time we sat down for dinner it was at another goddam burger joint just before the bus was to roll back to Peoria—but we didn't mind at all. We had just finished a 10-3 "flat-out old-fashioned ass-whupping" of the once-mighty Indians who had so tormented us months back during the horrors of the "train wreck" period.

And Billy "Nuke" Mel had his second win in a row. Again he hadn't had command of the strike zone, and hadn't been really sharp with any of his stuff, but he had battled, and "pitched" his way through seven innings giving up but three hits and two runs, and all in all Kranny and Trace were more than pleased with his performance. Although it hadn't started out that way.

When Mel walked the first two batters he faced, Trace kicked the top step of the dugout and barked, "Goddammit!" loud enough to be heard by everyone in the yard and most especially Bill Melvin out on the mound. Which might've been the reason he then settled down and went to work, winning even though he didn't have much.

Of course, even if he hadn't pitched his way out of it, it probably wouldn't have mattered. Because as Jim Tracy kept saying all night long, "Jeez'em'tally . . . that wasn't an ass-whupping, Kranny . . . that was an *assault*! I'm telling you, an assault! We dented up those walls some plenty tonight, huh? Never seen anything like it! Damned assault . . . knock that wall down!"

With the double tall outfield wall in that cozy bandbox which is Municipal Stadium, we didn't get any of our fourteen hits to go over it, but almost every one was off that wall. While only five were for extra bases, it wasn't because they weren't hit hard enough—doubles and triples were only singles because they would bang off that wall and bounce back almost to the infield.

"Just an assault! Huh?"

But then Jim Tracy spoke the next-most-popular refrain of that night, which actually was far more the story than even the win, and would still be talked about long after that game had been forgotten.

Hollering down to the other end of the several tables we'd pulled together in the McDonald's we'd eaten in that night—eating communally again now that we were a happy family and did not have to segregate ballplayers from the "adults"—Trace said, "Hey, Nuke . . . the wife came up, huh? She made it just in time for your first pitch, huh, Nuke? Which car did she bring? Which . . . the family car? Or did she bring the Winnebago?"

Bill, not at all any longer embarrassed or shy about "the affair" now that Angie had sophisticated most of the innocent country boy out of him, laughed and proudly said, "Nah . . . she brought the Jag."

Indeed she had. It is a little better than a four-hour drive from Peoria to Waterloo; Angie had made it in exactly three and had arrived, looking her usual stunning self in a white and frilly sun dress, just before Mel threw his first pitch. She had sat and worried and fretted or rejoiced and cheered over every pitch he threw. Then came that scene at the backstop that told so much in so few words.

When the game was over she stood and waited at the railing down front in the box-seat section behind home plate where we always sat. Finally, Bill, who had not gone to the showers after his seven innings but had stayed in uniform in the dugout, stopped milling about in the high-fiving and then equipment-gathering that goes on after a win and came over to acknowledge her presence.

There was such reticence but also almost a practiced nonchalance to his greeting and then nothing else for a quite awkward moment until she finally just had to come out and bravely ask, "Should I wait . . . I mean wait around or something?"

"No . . . we're going to be a while, we've got to shower . . . and then go eat."

"Should I wait up for you?"

"Nah . . . I'm going to be busy . . . and I gotta get some sleep."

"How about tomorrow?"

"Nah, I've got a busy day tomorrow . . . I'll call you sometime," he answered as he started walking away. But then he turned back, put his hand between the netting, and offered her a handshake. And that's exactly what it was, just a quick shake of her hand as he said, "I really want to thank you for coming all the way up here to see me pitch . . . I really appreciate it."

Then, blinking back tears, this lady they called the Black Widow had the courage and strength to quite sincerely and without mockery say, "Isn't he a gentleman?"

Yes, Bill Melvin is and always will be a gentleman. But he is not innocent any longer. He has learned the duplicity of this world. While bowing to the pressures that the affair had occasioned, he also was taking full benefit of and much pride in keeping her on a string, knowing full well that she would be there to reel in again with her mansion and her cars and charms whenever he was in need of them. But then it also must be understood that in only a few short weeks he would be leaving and going on with his career and his life and it would all soon be but a memory of a "summer-when-I-was-young." And she would be going on thirty-six. The lady he had been so enraptured over. So dizzyingly moonstruck over. Fuck. Go get 'em, *Nuke*.

And what the hell does anything really mean anyway? After all—

"That's twenty-four!" And we've got a two-day date with the Clinton Giants to get home to.

As that bus rolled south and then east, I reflected upon a conversation with the now so different, and, they say, the "old," Jerry LaPenta. This intelligent, serious man had finally wanted to talk.

". . . it's every day, if you have a bad day you're afraid they're going to release you or send you down. If you have a good day, you worry about whether you can do it again the next day. Because every day it's 'what have you done for me today?' There is no seniority or tenure or the Players' Union or that inertia factor of once in the major leagues you're a major leaguer and that alone will get you chance after chance. But not here, it's what can you do for us today and, in someone's opinion, will you someday be able to do it at the major league level . . . or are they just wasting their time, effort, and money to keep you around? So, every day you have to go out and perform . . . and you're tired, or you're banged up . . . knowing that at any moment they can send you here, there . . . anywhere . . . and your only choice is to do it or give up your dream . . .

"Yeah . . . I was a real Bitter Bob, because I'd gotten off to a good start at Pittsfield . . . and hey, that's Double A and I'd gotten there fast, only a season and a half and I was there. But then I hit a slump, and Pete's crying to get me back . . . and so I'm expendable and handy because I'm not hitting well . . . but yet they made it seem like I was the guy that had to come in and save the day. I felt all the pressure was on me . . . and on top of that I was bitter, I didn't want to be here . . . so the two combined was a horrible feeling . . . I thought, 'Hey, I should be able to come back down and just tear up this pitching, I'm a Double A hitter!' So I kept going to the plate trying to get back to Pittsfield on one swing . . . but, damn, the pitching wasn't any easier, I didn't see any difference between the pitching here and in Double A, some a lot better. But finally I guess I just accepted the fact . . . and relaxed some, and said, 'Hey, you're here . . . make the most out of it, at least you're playing ball and there's that chance.' So I feel good now, I'm playing regularly, and I'm hitting . . . my goal is to get my average up to .250 . . . and hope for the best next year. I mean, most guys back home would give their right nut to be doing what I'm doing . . . so why not just enjoy it for as long as it lasts."

Well, it certainly lasted longer than our four-game winning streak. Kal didn't have it, the Giants hit him hard and early, and he was gone after only five and a third, his earliest exit on the season; we didn't hit and lost 5-1. But no one took it badly.

"Hey, it's one of those nights in baseball when you just don't have it," Jim Tracy said. "Maybe the heat . . . whatever . . . but you just play horseshit and lifeless. But nothing's hurt . . . hell, we're still one to the good on my chart, right?"

Right. But something was hurt. It was Jeff Massicotte's right shoulder. He had gone up to Chicago that day and the Cubs' doctors had diagnosed it as tendinitis. Rest and no throwing for two weeks was the prescription. Which meant that "Grandpa," while he would still stay a member of the family for the duration, had thrown his last pitch for the 1988 Peoria Chiefs.

"Whupped 'em every which way but loose! Huh? And we beat their best," Jim Tracy said after Frank Castillo had gone seven innings, giving up only four singles and one earned run, and struck out eight; Gabby had been touched a bit for three hits, but only one run, and got two more strikeouts, and the Chief's batters had chased Rod Beck, now the 11-and-5 ace of the Giants staff, after four innings with four runs on seven hits, and then continued hammering their top long man Mark Dewey (second only to Kal for the league's best ERA, 1.60) and three more relievers that Bill Evers, Trace's first professional roommate, ran out there that Wednesday night of August 17, for a total of fifteen hits and an 8-2 laugher.

And it was a laugher, because the Famous Chicken was on hand to strut his antics and the ballplayers and crowd had a ball—the Chiefs' ballplayers at any rate.

Yet, while "That's twenty-five!" and the fact that at 62-66 on the season we were now only four games under .500, and that the Chicken had been there for it, were certainly fun and wonderful and exciting, none of it was the real story of that night and the next day.

The story was the real story that had to do with why all of us were there to begin with, and why we had been there all season, and why it had all been going on for years and would go on for years to come, the real story of minor league baseball, the one and only reason for its existence—"prospects" and "suspects" and "roster fillers"; in other words, player development. Or in the terms of the real world, asset development.

Brandon Davis had arrived that day, directly from the big meeting down in Winston-Salem. It had been intense, but the "baseball men" had won—this time.

"Though don't look for two teams in the Instructional League next year," Brandon said. "And the truth is, there really weren't enough prospects for two teams this year. But with so many injuries throughout the organization this season, big club on down, there are a lot of people who need some work . . . so we decided that this year we'd go ahead and have the two teams."

Therefore, on the morrow, there would be some fifty-plus ballplayers throughout the Cubs organization who would have every reason to believe that they were "prospects," and some hundred-plus who would have good reason to fear that they were "suspects"—Instructional League invites would officially be extended.

While there are various reasons that a real prospect might not be invited to Instructional League—chief of which would perhaps be too many innings already pitched, or that the prospect had already expressed a desire not to attend for personal reasons (family, college)—and that for public consumption and dissemination, and particularly in the Cubs organization, where it is strictly enforced policy, *every* ballplayer in the system is said to be a prospect, the real truth, and how it is perceived by the ballplayers themselves—is that if you are not invited to Instructional League or arrangements are not made for you to play winter ball in one of the Latin leagues, then you ain't no prospect, you are a suspect, or even worse, a "roster filler."

Prospect? Suspect? Roster filler?

Perhaps Brandon expressed the very essence of what it's all about that very night.

"There has to be somebody for the prospects to play with, there sure aren't enough of them to play by themselves."

There is, of course, one problem with that simplification of the most fundamental of professional baseball's truisms, which is also its most perplexing enigma—and that was best expressed by one Richie Zisk, during spring training and at several times since:

"Ah . . . but who really knows who those prospects are? Who knows which ones are going to make it? We know they're out there . . . but which ones are they? After all, some scout somewhere thought he saw enough potential in each of these kids to project that he had the tools to maybe make it to the big leagues, right? Oh, sure, some are projected more 'equal' than others . . . and a higher dollar value is placed on this one or that one . . . the higher draft choices . . . but once we get 'em all out there and they start playing, it's all a crap shoot . . . and it's all up to them. There are too many Pete Roses and Bruce Sutters in baseball to prove that prospects too often become busts and that more than a few suspects are destined for Cooperstown and a lot of opinions were just that . . . opinions . . . but then what the hell, the numbers tell us that about ninety-five percent of all our opinions are wrong anyway, right?"

Brandon Davis the scout has a succinct and most revealing answer to that also: "Our mistakes become the roster fillers."

"Damn crazy business, isn't it?" is how Richie always sums it up.

But what are the thoughts about all this from the man who in the Cubs organization has the only opinion that really counts—Mr. Jim Frey?

"You have all different types of prospects. When these boys are signed, they're signed at different levels. As free agents they're drafted on tools . . . and they put a dollar figure on trying to sign them out of high school or college, and that usually represents the level to which you think a player is a major league player. Could he make the major leagues? Would he be a regular on a second-division club? Would he be a good regular on a winning club? Could he help a team win a championship? In general, those are the ways that they try to evaluate players as free agents. And then, like in all sports, you have surprises. Players get bigger . . . some get bigger, some get stronger . . . and some people seem to have a better instinct for the game, are able to learn quicker. Some fellows level off . . . some guys you sign at twenty or twenty-one don't get better, don't get stronger, don't seem to have instinct.

"Now, after they're signed . . . in terms of numbers of prospects, that varies from one period to another. Organizations go through periods when they're strong in pitching, strong in position players. You might go to camp one year and list thirty as major league prospects. You might go to camp five years later and list only fifteen . . . and then three years later list forty. The scouting department becomes so important in getting the right kind of people into an organization, so that your hope always is that some of these fringe players—which of course is the biggest part of an organization—go beyond what you expected when you signed them. They just become bigger and better than people thought they might be.

"When they talk about a young kid going to the big leagues, there wouldn't be a question in most people's minds, or an argument about his future ability. The only question would be how would he react to adversity. If you take a kid to the big leagues—and anybody can go two for thirty—but how would he react? And would it have a long adverse effect on him? Psychologically, not physically. And would that adversity set him farther back than he might be if he'd played at a level where he could have success? That's the point of view of giving guys success at every step of the way before they get to the major leagues. And the old idea used to be that a guy would play maybe five to six hundred games *at least* before he really started to feel comfortable and knew what he was doing . . . so that going to the major leagues is just another step. Now, with so many kids playing college ball, and coming into pro ball older, and with so many fewer minor league clubs, the tendency is to rush them along . . . or out . . . faster. But you have to watch the individual. Some guys can go after two years, we've seen guys go after one year . . . some other players with equal ability, but not the same makeup, it takes four, five, six years . . . or of course never.

"I guess you can use any group of words for it . . . but the way I say it is that some people seem to have the instinct for our business and some don't. And they can have equal ability. But it's the ability to learn, to adjust . . . I think the ability to adjust on a regular basis is the key. Some guys just never quite get the feel of it. Some other players with lesser ability do have the feel for it. And that's why these managers and instructors in the minor leagues are so important. It's no special trick to grade tools. I don't think you have to be a baseball man to grade tools . . . you have to be a baseball man to understand the makeup of ballplayers and what it takes, that special something inside, whether it's intellect for the game, not academic intellect, but intellect for the game, instinct, character for the game, all those things . . . desire, competitiveness, all of these words that everybody uses . . . whatever it is—but the managers and coaches that are with these guys for five, six months understand it. The rest of us just see the tools, and we have to go by the gut feeling that these people give us.

"When I talk to scouts, I try to talk to them about first grading the tools . . . and that shouldn't take very long . . . and then spending a lot of time on trying to determine to what extent this guy really wants to be a baseball player. What is he willing to sacrifice? To what extent is he willing to work and grind it out and develop himself both physically and mentally for the game? I think these are the qualities that, if you're a good scout, you just have a feel for and recognize. If you're not a good scout, you keep signing guys with good arms and good legs who never become big leaguers. And I've tried to stress with our people that we want to just as importantly grade the makeup of a player as his physical ability. I'm taking for granted that we're going to sign players with tools. I want the other part."

We wanted at those "fucking Rockheads!"

One hundred and seventeen days "After Rockford," 117 days since the season-long highwater mark of two games under .500, we would now not only have the opportunity for a long-overdue payback, but we would also have the opportunity—in what would be sweet poetic justice indeed—to wash over that so dubious highwater mark against those very same Rockheads. We were four under, and they would be in *our* yard for four games.

However, it would have to wait a day, and be even more poetic and cosmic in its potential justice, when, only moments before Eduardo Caballero was to take the hill, the rains came, and came in bucketloads, and Pete Vonachen had no choice but to announce, "Doubleheader tomorrow," and we had an unscheduled night off to be citizens.

While we hated doubleheaders with a practiced passion, perhaps it was just as well we didn't play that Thursday night, August 18. Because while there were nine very happy Chiefs that day, there were at least three rather important ones who were not.

Bill Melvin, Frank Castillo, Jeff Massicotte, Eduardo Caballero, Gabby Rodriguez, Fernando Zarranz, Rick Wilkins, Dick Canan, and Rusty Crockett all received invitations to the Arizona Instructional League, where they would get to spend two sun-drenched, laid-back months in Mesa, Arizona, playing only day games where no one really cares who wins or not and every Sunday is an off day. It is heaven. It is fun. And for two more months you get expenses, a room, and meal money to play baseball instead of having to go home and look for a job. Conspicuously not invited was our "Soul Patrol" outfield.

Pookie Bernstine was pissed. Not only had Gator, Phil, and Fast Eddie not been invited, neither had he; and only two weeks before, up in Beloit, Jim Colborn had indicated that he indeed wanted him to go to Instructional League as a coach so that he might better learn his new profession. That, however, Pookie would take up with Bill Harford. But none of our outfielders? Particularly Warren Arrington?

"Trace . . . not even Gator?"

Jim Tracy, who, with only two weeks left in the season, was still doing what he loves best—teaching—and had Rusty, Rick, and the Boz at the batting cage for an early-work session of BP, answered Pookie with a tight jaw and strained voice: "They said they weren't needed . . . said they had enough outfielders."

The truth was, Trace had lobbied hard for Gator, and was as disappointed as Pookie and Gator himself. Plus *he* had not been invited; which was all for the best because he really needed to be with his family. But still it would've been nice to be asked before declining.

The further truth is that Jim Tracy was also thrilled that, from a team that everyone had written off only a month and a half back, nine *had* been invited. Plus, as he also said a little later, "Other than Gator, they took everyone who deserved to go. And Kal? He's been to Instructs before. And he's thrown a lot of innings, plus he wanted to get back home for school."

Then a little later, with the season winding down, and because the day of Instructs invites reminded him that this was not just a game but indeed a hard, cold business, Jim Tracy wanted to spend some time in his office talking about Mike Boswell, and by proxy all the thousands just like him who have come before and will come again.

"You know . . . Boz has as much power as anyone on this team . . . if it's a fastball, not a curve . . . but what if we give up on him and then that light pops on in his head . . . but it's too late, he's gone and out of baseball . . . or someone else has taken a shot at him and he's in another uniform when it happens? That's why I'm still fighting for him, why I'm still trying to teach and work with him . . . even though we know it's going to take more than just me to save his career, and that probably he'll be one of the first to be released this next spring, if not sooner. Yet, it's such a minor adjustment . . . though so hard to make . . . but if he just waits back a little . . . and he doesn't have to hit that breaker for a home run . . . or even hit it hard . . . just chink it, or flare it off . . . but show them you're not a dead out on the curveball . . . then you'll see your fair share of fastballs you can hit hard. No, I can't give up on that boy . . . and I'll keep working with him right up to the second he gets that tap on the shoulder . . . and they send him home."

That day of the Instructs invites was a day of reflection about the "business" of baseball not only for Jim Tracy, but for many of the Chiefs as well. And even with a gift night off, instead of partying hard, some of them were in the mood to sit and talk quietly in Sullivan's over a few beers.

Jeff Massicotte was still bitter but philosophical about the "experiment," and said with only a little rancor, but mostly just a newfound determination, "It lost me a whole year . . . and almost everybody was against it. But the head few won out, and stupid me, I went along with it. But no more! That's it. If this has taught me one thing, it's taught me that we're all in this business for ourselves . . . we're independent contractors . . . and sometimes you have to say no to these people. They have plans for you . . . they're deciding your career. But if you don't speak up for yourself, some of the things they decide will ruin your career. I wished I'd stood up this spring."

That's when feisty little Stevie Hill said, "Hey, that's why I'm here and Marty's in Winston-Salem. Because of their needs, they were making me play third base. Christ, I've got no future as a third baseman . . . the only shot I've got is at second, and I told 'em that!"

Then Z said, "Hey, you better believe you're in this business for yourself . . . that's why you always see me going up and shaking scouts' hands and introducing myself . . . being superpolite, man. Because you know this 'Boys Who Would Be Cubs' thing? It's boys who would be any fucking major league team! Hey, man . . . I know I've opened some eyes this year . . . but I also know my rep, man . . . you know . . . what they think about the way I'm just Z the goof-off . . . that they're not gonna give me a real shot and I know it. But I know I'm a prospect. And listen up, dudes . . . it don't matter which uniform you're wearing . . . getting to the bigs is all that matters! I wished like hell they'd trade me . . . so, bro, always be nice to scouts, and hustle like hell when you know they're watching . . . because we ain't Cubs, we're ballplayers, that's our business . . . that's all we have to sell."

And then Jeff Massicotte said to me, "Hey, you're tired . . . worn out . . . and just wanna go home, don'tcha? Live like a human being again, if just for a little while, right? And haven't you felt like they've used you for their purposes, even though you don't even work for them?"

Yes. Very, very yes was the answer.

"So now you know how we feel."

". . . I said, 'Why can't a kid stay another year at the same level, what's wrong with that?' And Billy says, 'You've gotta reward him, don'tcha ya?' So I said, 'You wanna reward him? Give him a raise and tell him he's got a job next year!' "

Even though Brandy Davis had told this story in reference to his belief that Rusty Crockett should be sent back to Peoria the following year so he could "solidify his success," and even though neither Trace nor I happened to agree with the Superscout's assessment of that particular piece of player development opinion, we laughed pretty good anyway because we could both picture the look that must've come over Dollar Bill Harford's face when he heard that line.

Then a little later, Jim Tracy the motivator, with just a little of his buffoonery, made us all a family again, prospects, suspects, and roster fillers.

And of course he did not have to rah-rah any Chiefs for the games to be played against "those fucking Rockheads"—even the new guys knew by rote the "Fuck Rockford" tales of thievery, deception, bitter cold, and woe.

Then we went out and swept a doubleheader from the team that everybody in the Midwest League—in only their first year of operation—had already learned to hate. On top of the fact that we just didn't like them, we also took no small satisfaction in the fact that we quite soundly and handily put a double-dip spanking on the first-place team in the Northern Division.

In the first one, Eduardo went the seven-inning route, as Gator and Rusty drove in and scored all of the runs we needed for a 3-1 win, and the Panamanian Devil's second W after the two terrible outings he'd had immediately after winning Pitcher of the Week honors—which his team-mates felt was only proper justice, since he'd been strutting around with a bit too much of a big head there for a week or so, but then got real humble, real quick.

In the second one, James Matas was the beneficiary of a five-run first inning with Rusty and Gator and Canan doing the hitting and Wilkie and Hannon doing the RBI'ing. However, "the Animal" wasn't really sharp and it took some fan'dazzle defense behind him and Gabby's coming on to get a quite nifty and somewhat rare but fun-to-watch 4-6-5 double play with two on and one out in the sixth, and then needing only six more pitches to get the last four outs in a 6-1 Chiefs victory, for Matas's second win in as many starts since the "Winston-Salem reject" had joined the family and Gabby's fourth save on the season.

Then we said, "That's twenty-six and twenty-seven!" Jim Tracy got dressed in a new record time. We pigged out at the summer's last Boost-ers Club's dinner for the family out on the "Friendly Confines" picnic den. Then we went and had the third-best party night of the season. We were *two games under .500*. It might've taken 118 days "After Rockford" to get back to that mark, but when the time came, we did the paybacking all at once, and were still +1 on Jim Tracy's chart.

And we still would be the next night. But it damn sure was a lot harder to do. In fact, it took thirteen innings to win 2-1—with all of the runs coming in the thirteenth inning as Z got a "zin" instead of a "zave."

Brandon Davis (who has a personal policy—for the purpose of "main-taining strict objectivity"—of never entering a clubhouse) told me, "You go tell Trace he just plain outmanaged Alan Bannister" (the Rockford skipper; and yes, the former big leaguer).

And I replied, "Brandy . . . I will. But you know what? There are at least a dozen wins we wouldn't have except for Jim Tracy's outmanaging somebody. But this *was* a special one."

With that "That's twenty-eight!" victory we were only *one game* under .500 with nine games left to play and still one to the good on Trace's chart.

That victory also put us into second place in the Southern Division. However, with Springfield still eight games ahead, we weren't playing for place, we were playing for pride and the "impossible challenge."

We could reach it on the morrow—which would be sweet indeed if we could, because Richie Zisk would be there to see it. Finally, they were letting the Bat Doctor come for sure.

*   *   *

There was one race that we were winning handily. It was now all but a certainty that half of Pete Vonachen's dream for 1988 would come true; 4,819 paying customers had been at Meinen Field that night, bringing the then season total attendance to 190,488. With still five home dates left, last year's Midwest League record of 195,832 was a cinch to be broken.

We were winning, Pete knew he was going to break another record that only a couple of months ago he was sure couldn't be done with his "bunch of donkeys" team, so all was well with our world . . . and tomorrow night? Well, tomorrow night it should get even better, and what a party that would be when we finally reached "the top of that fucking mountain, huh guys? And to do it against those sons of bitches . . . with a sweep . . . ah, paybacks are a bitch!"

Is three-fourths of a payback still a bitch? If not, it'll just do, because, on the morrow, we were back to being two games away from our so-elusive goal, while Pete Vonachen was 2,481 butts-in-the-seats closer to his.

Because that's how many people, plus Richie Zisk—when he wasn't running popcorn down to the guys in the bullpen—who sat there that almost balmy night and watched Greg Kallevig lower his already league-leading ERA from 1.43 to 1.35, but yet see his record go to 11-8 with his fourth loss in a row, even as he pitched perhaps his best game of the season.

All Silent Kal did was go nine innings, give up only three paltry singles, strike out ten (Kal!?), get eleven groundouts, and lose 2-1 on two first-inning errors by the first-scason-pro, tired, hurting, still slumping Rusty Crockett (down to .259), and one error in the seventh by the tired, veteran, seasoned Phil Hannon (the only Chief who had started 131 of the then 132 games played), when we could manage only two hits off the Expos' long, tall, hard-throwing but wild Nate Minchey.

"Hey . . . nothing to it . . . sure it's tough to lose one like that, especially to those guys . . . but, no harm's done. We said we needed three of these . . . and we got 'em. Hey . . . we're still plus one in my book, right?"

"Yeah . . . but that means we do it in *Burlington*? Lot of thrill in that, huh?"

No. There is never any thrill in a visit to Community Field. But then, because we never quite made it to Burlington, Iowa, that Monday evening of August 22, there was a hell of a thrill for somebody which put any thrill we might've had on that gravel pit diamond to shame.

While we never looked forward to going to Burlington, that afternoon we just flat didn't want to go period. It had nothing to do with it being the pits of the Midwest League. It had to do with the fact that the drought in the Midwest League had ended with a vengeance and it was raining cats and dogs along with our curses at Burlington general manager Paul Marshall as we sat around the Meinen Field offices for four hours waiting for him to only accept the obvious and bang that night's game.

As much as we hated doubleheaders, we hated a long drive in a pouring rain and thunderstorm only to have to then turn around and come back even more. And there was no doubt in anyone's mind, including the National Weather Service, that that was precisely what we would do if Paul Marshall kept insisting that possibly God would intervene at the last moment and suddenly disperse the solid block of violently inclement weather that had settled over parts of three states for at least the duration of that day and night.

But then Mr. Marshall had the Famous Chicken scheduled for that evening, so he was going to give God every chance up until the last second to perform this miracle. Which is why, after all those hours of just hanging around, and maybe two dozen phone calls back and forth, his final indecision was for us to get on the bus and drive to Monmouth, Illinois—which is well more than two-thirds of the damn way anyway—and then stop and call to see if the rain that was dumping buckets on the field at the moment was still doing so after we'd made the little better than an hour drive for "fucking nothing!"

So we did. When Stevie Melendez, Richie Zisk, and I sloshed our way into a mom-and-pop convenience store—Stevie to make the call, Richie and I for some refreshments for the drive back—Paul Marshall told Stevie that the miracle hadn't occurred, sorry, doubleheader tomorrow. And we're bitter.

The next morning, however, and forever since then, those of us with any humanity in us at all were eternally grateful for Paul Marshall's obstinate stupidity. Because if he had not had us make that drive, then Brett Robinson would not have been driving on that lonely stretch of country road, heading for home, at just the right moment and just the right place to pull an elderly gentleman out of a flipped-over and burning automobile and save his life.

Richie Zisk has no fondness for the "iron lung," so we were again rental-carring it behind the bus as we drove back to Burlington for the doubleheader the next day, Tuesday, August 23.

"You know, Richie . . . doubleheaders have a nasty habit of getting split."

"Dammit . . . there you go, you put the jinx on us. Now if we do split it's all your fault."

A little further on, Richie, speaking about Eduardo Caballero, who would be pitching the second game that evening, said, "You know, that boy's never pitched a good game that I've seen. I know he's good . . . I just haven't seen it. And I've got to go by what I see."

"Now who's putting the gris-gris on us. If he loses, I'm gonna tell him what you said . . . and that it's all your doings."

Then, maybe two hours later, as Frank Castillo was walking off the mound toward the dugout after pitching his third perfect inning, Richie said, "I'm going to call it now . . . he's going to throw a no-hitter. You wanna bet?"

"Jesus, Richie . . . you just spoke the worst whammy in baseball!"

"Oh, I did, didn't I . . . but he's still going to do it."

Then, three innings later, with two out in the sixth, with the Chiefs up 1-0 benefit of a Wilkie double and a Dick Canan single, and Frank still not having allowed a Burlington Braves hitter to leave the batter's box in any direction other than the dugout, Jerald Frost, the Braves' shortstop and nine-hole hitter, catching us all napping and concealing his intentions until the last second, took a running step for first base while he dropped the bat head and dragged a sweetheart of a base hit with him.

Almost in the same breath, and certainly in tandem, we both yelped, "You son of a bitch!"

Then also in tandem, and only a sigh and a couple more curses later, we said, "Hey . . . it's legal . . . it's baseball, and it's a close game." Of course one of us also added, "Yeah . . . but fuck him anyway."

Which must've been exactly inscrutable Frank's attitude about the matter, because he simply dismissed that cheaply broken-up perfect game like it hadn't happened at all and proceeded to retire the next four hitters in order while Rusty drove in Polly from third with a sacrifice fly and we win 2-0 on a one-hit shutout for Frank's fifth win in a row since he'd been allowed to pitch enough innings to get one, and our twenty-ninth win in the forty-one games since "the Bet."

But then, a little less than two hours later, it was twenty-nine wins in forty-two games as Eduardo Caballero, erratic as always, struck out six Braves to set a new Peoria Chiefs strikeout record with his 155th whiff on the season, but also gave up seven hits and three runs in five and two-thirds innings while their guy, Brian Cummings, shut us out on four hits and seven strikeouts.

Oops! Since Trace had those two down on his little pocket chart as a sweep, there went our +1 cushion, and we're heading back to P-Town still two under with only six games left on the left side of that blackboard.

"Maybe you and I should get out of the predicting business," Richie said after the first mile or two of the drive back.

Then, while we talked about many things—Richie Zisk is a man who is as fond of talking politics, literature, cinema, philosophy, and particularly world history, especially anything written by the late great Barbara Tuchman, as he is of baseball—we eventually got around to talking about the little guy that was becoming dear and near to the hearts of any number of us—Russell Dee Crockett.

"I love him. Here's a kid that just because of his size has been told he can't play at every level since he started playground ball. And at every level he's proved he could. We need to do the same thing with him—let him play until he hits the wall. He's a great athlete, we know that . . . so just let him go to each level and see if he can do it there. If we're going to carry people like Bell and Espinal and the Boz, think we shouldn't give Rusty all the rope he needs? To either make it or hang himself with it . . . let him prove that he can or can't play at every level."

The Bat Doctor also put his teaching where his heart was. The next morning he had Rusty in the batting cage. A little adjustment here, a little adjustment there . . . and a lot of the Bat Doctor Philosophy. Rusty soaked it up like a sponge, listening, smiling, nodding, and adjusting.

"It's a chess game. The pitcher does certain things and you have to adjust. A pitcher's getting you out a certain way? You make an adjustment at the plate, a correction, and start beating him at his own game. Now the pitcher has to make an adjustment because you've adjusted . . . and it goes back and forth. It's the hitters who don't make adjustments that you see struggle at the plate, have very short careers, or never make it to the big leagues . . . yeah, thatababy . . . see what you did with that pitch? Freeze it, remember it . . . so when the situation comes again, you'll know the adjustment you have to make."

And it certainly didn't take long to have an effect. And it certainly couldn't have come at a better time for "Davey, Davey Crockett" to break out of his slump—a night when breaking or tying records was the order of the day.

Just a little after seven o'clock, Wednesday, August 24, as soon as Mike Nelson and Bob "Crowd Control" Strunk were certain that enough of the 2,983 who would attend that first of the four-game series with the Madison Muskies had passed through the blue-and-white-canopied turnstiles to break the attendance record, Pete Vonachen stood by the gate and searched the oncoming stream of ticket-holders until he found just the right All-American-looking couple and then, with television crews rolling tape, and print media photogs snapping film, surprised all hell out of them by announcing that they were *the* record breakers, ushered them down onto the field, showered them with gifts and lifetime passes to all future Chiefs games, made a speech, and then led them up to sit in the big leather chairs he'd expropriated from his office for the occasion. Then we played some baseball.

"The Animal" Matas, starting his third game since being shipped down to take no-longer-"Hard Luck" Mike's seat at the family's dinner table, made quick work of the Muskies in the first, setting them down and out and back to the dugout in order.

Rusty, leading off the bottom of the frame, sent the first pitch he saw, a slider away, over the second baseman's head for a single to break out of an 0-for-17 slump. Then, with the count 2-1 on Gator—who Jim Tracy had finally moved permanently up into the two-hole spot some two weeks prior—Rusty stole second, and was then in the dugout with the first run of the night when Gator also went the other way for a double into the right-field corner. Pookie drove him in with a single to right; and the Chiefs had a 2-0 lead for "the Animal" when he went back out to the hill.

James knew what to do with it. He allowed a lead-off single and then nothing more until his shoulder suddenly tightened up and "hurt like hell" and he had to come out with two outs in the sixth and surrender the ball over to "Hero" Brett Robinson, who, by that time, had a 3-0 lead to protect after the second of the three hits Rusty would get that evening had been a hard liner into left center to drive in Phil Hannon.

I suppose after saving a man's life by kicking out the rear window and pulling him from a burning, about-to-explode automobile, saving a 3-0 lead is but a cakewalk. Which is exactly what Brett made it look like, as he pitched as brilliantly as he had at any time on the season and retired the next seven men in order, and it certainly appeared that he would be able to do the same in the ninth.

But then Jim Tracy wanted Z to get his twentieth "zave" to tie Brian Otten's Peoria Chiefs record for saves; the Z Man did precisely that with a 1-2-3 ninth, and the Chiefs won 3-0, and we were back to one game under .500. And Pete Vonachen had his record.

He was as tired, if not more so, than the rest of us; he had been suffering from manic stress, exhaustion, high blood pressure, and a nagging, nasty respiratory infection that just wouldn't seem to go away—all of which had landed him in a hospital even though he'd managed to keep it a secret from most everyone—but on that night, through his fatigue and illness, as he sat reflecting quietly for a few moments in his office after that game was over, there was great peace and joy and pride shining on that jowl-jiggling face.

He spoke about what a real achievement that second consecutive record-breaking attendance actually was. Particularly considering how horribly we had played for so long. Plus the worst and longest heat wave and drought in the Midwest since the 1930s—"Hotter than a fresh-fucked fox in a forest fire . . . but still they came out."

Then he said, "Look . . . in this book thing? I wantcha to give all the credit to my guys, the staff . . . they did it. They do it all. Seriously. Except wastebaskets. That they don't do. I have to empty the goddam wastebaskets. But that's all I'm good for."

Then he leaned back, rubbed his hand over that balding pate, and added, "As for me? Just tell 'em I'm *gunpowder-mean*. That's my contribution."

About three-thirty on the afternoon of Thursday, August 25, Billy "Nuke" Mel wheels in, parks Angie's Corvette, and starts walking in that loping, gangling style of his toward the clubhouse.

"What's this?" I ask, with a knowing grin and sardonic inflection.

"Aaa . . . we just had to switch cars for the day," he answers sheepishly while trying to make it sound flippant.

"*Riiight,* Mel," as we continue on into the clubhouse to prepare for what just might be the Night.

Then, just a little after seven o'clock, when Mike Nelson and Bob Strunk are certain that enough of the 5,355 ticket-holders who would attend the second game of the Madison series have passed through the turnstiles to make the Peoria Chiefs the only franchise in the forty-eight-year history of the Midwest League to draw 200,000 *paid* Midwestern butts into seats to see a baseball game, Pete Vonachen again stands by the gate searching a sea of faces lined up far beyond that canopied entrance until he again finds just the right couple—this time with a small child, "Oh, that's perfect, press'll love that"—to again surprise the living daylights out of by announcing them as that night's record-breakers, and then bestowing upon them even more of the royal treatment than the couple the night before received.

Then, just a couple of minutes after seven-thirty, as Bill Melvin is making his last few warm-up tosses, Angie, perhaps smarting from the so-public on-again, off-again yo-yo Mel has her on, and wanting us to know that she still has her man-child, somewhat boastfully announces to Rene, Silent Kal's fiancée, and Peggy Jean, now *the* classiest member of the family, "Oh, I just know he's going to have a good game tonight . . . I gave him *two* rubdowns this afternoon."

The demure Rene and always proper Peggy Jean exchange raised-eyebrow looks as I chuckle and turn my attention to home plate and watch Billy "Nuke" Mel walk Darren Lewis for the first of the several Muskies baserunners he will allow on the evening as again he's struggling to find command of his breaking ball, and now also location with his hard-enough but errant "heater."

Just shortly after that, as he continues to pitch behind in the count as his defense extracts him from jam after pickle time and again, I say, purely in jest, and only for the fun of it, "Two rubdowns, Angie? One is therapeutic . . . but I think two is maybe having fun."

She laughs. But then about an hour later, Jim Tracy, not laughing one bit, and without even a hint of a smile on his face, goes out with the hook in the top of the fifth and yo-yos Mel to the dugout with the Chiefs down 2-0 with two on and no outs, and brings in Brett, who promptly gets a strikeout and a double-play bouncer to end the inning. Nuke, in his four innings plus three batters, had given up four hits and three walks, but oh so fortunately only those two runs. Fortunately, because "Hero" Brett, who has really been on a yo-yo all season—in the rotation, out of the rotation—is masterful yet again until Gabby comes on in the eighth to hold a Chiefs 3-2 lead for one inning until it's time for the Z Man and his hammer.

Whoa . . . a 3-2 Chiefs lead? In the eighth inning of *the game?* Yepper.

And was it ever poetic justice how we scored those three runs against the ballclub that, back in the second week of May, the last time we had seen them, had been the team that had sent us plunging into that lowest of the low monster-jerkings, that "There's gonna be blood on the floor!" period of utter futility when we scored only twelve runs in nine games—we *bunted* the sons of bitches to *their* utter futility, and befuddled distraction.

After getting five hits off their starter, Pat Wernig, all for naught through six, even letting him wiggle out of a bases-loaded jam in the fifth, in our half of the seventh, Phil Hannon, batting in the eight-hole now since Rusty and Gator have taken over the first and second spots in the batting order, leads off and drops a beauty of a bunt down the third-base line with the Midwest League's All-Star third baseman, Scott Brosius, playing deep, almost on the grass behind third. Not even a play.

Hey, if it works once? And Brosius ain't moved in a step? Dink—Polly does the same; again not even a play, and Polly runs about like he drinks, all in one place, forever, and hard.

Now you think Brosius might've caught on by now, and moved in at least a step or two—particularly when he sees this little midget step up to the batter's box. Nope. So Rusty pushes another one at him! This time at least he comes up with it and tries to make a throw—too late, of course. Three bunt base hits and we've got bases loaded with *no* outs. We would have one in just a few minutes, however, as soon as Madison manager Jim Nettles (yes, the brother of Graig Nettles, and an ex–big leaguer himself) replaces Wernig with one Bob Stocker, who promptly strikes out Gator.

Then comes the play that was the real key to that most unusual rally. Pookie, hitting third that night in a rare start, bounces a three-hopper to second baseman Marteese Robinson, who, instead of flipping to his short-stop for the routine double play, tries to tag Rusty as he's racing by. Big mistake. Not only can Rusty run, he has that "instinct" Jim Frey talks so much about. A little stutter step, a bit of a twist, and no tag. So now Mr. Robinson decides maybe he'd best go to first and get the sure out. But Pookie, who knows this game, and knows only one way to play it, is flying down the first-base line, not at all content with just the RBI he's collected.

"He got no fucking body! No fucking body, Richie!" I'm hollering in tandem with the Bat Doctor.

So the bases are still loaded, but it's quickly two down when Dick fouls out to third. Then comes *the hit.* Midget Number Three, the .195-batting Stevie Hill, yanks a bullet deep into the hole at short, Chris Gust manages to glove it, but there's no play on Stevie, because while he might look like a fire hydrant, he runs like a wildfire. There is also no play at second with Pookie hauling his still-can-play ass; but Mr. Gust, just to look like he's hustling I suppose, makes the throw anyway—right into and beyond the shitter and two runs score. Wilkie then strikes out, stranding Pookie and Stevie. But it's 3-2 Chiefs.

And then soon it's "Zave time," blares Eddie Hammond, the PA announcer. It is also time for Scott Brosius to atone for those three bunts. And he does with a sharp liner to left for a single off a Z fastball that's lost a foot or more of its oomph over the course of a long season. So the tying run is aboard and it's gut-check time.

Whatever else Fernando Zarranz might have inside that strange-bird soul of his, he most assuredly has enough guts that he could donate a pound or two for transplanting and still have more than enough left. So he reaches down inside those innards, and into his repertoire of pitches besides the fastball, and gets the next batter to foul out to first. The next he teases with the off-speed stuff and then has just enough left to slip a hammer by for a swinging K and out two.

Then comes *the play.* Matt Siuda spanks a one-hop screamer definitely heading for center field, where it would most likely leave runners at first and third. Except it never gets there. There was only one play on that ball, and there was only one man anywhere close enough to take a stab at making it. Fernando Zarranz, off-balance, and with his natural delivery carrying him toward the first-base line, reaches back behind him with his bare hand, the hand that had just delivered that pitch, snares that so-threatening missile, flips to first for the out—and then tumultuous pandemonium!

The emotion of that moment cannot be captured in any words I know. It can only be remembered.

Of course, Jim Tracy had words to express his emotions. While there was raucous whooping and hollering going on all about and around us out in the clubhouse, and with a steady stream of well-wishers and backslappers popping in and out of his office, Jim Tracy, Richie Zisk, and I sat with tears in our eyes as the Shooter, slowly shaking that big head, said over and over again, "We climbed that mountain, guys . . . huh? How far we came . . . but we climbed that mountain . . . we did it, didn't we?"

Richie Zisk said, "This is better than a championship. It's nothing to run out in front and hide . . . but to do what this team did? That eruption out on the mound? That was their championship. And they did it for pride . . . and for that man right there . . . knowing they had nothing to win but mediocrity . . . unh-unh, that's not mediocrity. Thirty-one and fourteen since the All-Star break? Right now this is the best team in this league . . . and that's what the other managers are saying! And you did it, Trace."

"And my Mule . . . couldn't've done it without my Mule . . ."

"Yeah . . . and your Mule . . . hey, where is your Mule?"

"Right here!" Kranny said as he came through the door, having spent some time high-jinking with "the best fucking pitching staff in this league! The best fucking pitching staff I've had in five years of coaching! Fucking A!"

"They're the ones that got us here."

"We did it, Trace! We fucking did it!" The Kran-dog was pumped.

But then, of course, Jim Tracy snorted back the teary sniffles, shook his head hard, and said, "Not yet we haven't. We've still got four to go . . . and we could slide right back down that mountain."

And so we did.

As 4,586 folks came out for Fan Appreciation Night, Friday, August 26, Silent Kal went nine innings again, gave up eight hits, one of them a three-run dong in the fifth inning; their man, Greg Ferguson, a junk-baller, also went the distance, but gave up only one hit, and we lost 3-0 for Kal's fifth loss in a row. One under again. But that wasn't the story that day.

"I'm numb, man . . . you know, bro . . . Trips! Can you dig it?"

What a question.

Fernando Zarranz had been called up to Triple A Iowa, he would leave in the morning. But that wasn't all of the story either.

While we were fighting just to get to a .500 record, Iowa was driving for a pennant in the American Association. They were three games back, and had a crucial three-game series coming up that weekend with Denver. They had to take at least two out of the three if they were going to go down to the wire and perhaps into the play-offs. If they did, and with the September 1 call-ups to the big club coming—the date when all major league clubs are allowed to expand their roster and take a look at some of their better prospects under big league conditions—Pookie Bernstine and Rick Wilkins were also going to Des Moines immediately after our last game in Cedar Rapids.

Pookie's reaction to that news wasn't surprising, since he was not only bitter about not being invited to Instructional League, he was also still bitter about the fact that first the Cubs had said they "no longer saw a future for him as big league player" and had then granted him his release when he'd asked for it because he had already negotiated a deal to be picked up by the Giants and continue his playing career with their Triple A club, and then the Cubs, making full use of the ol'-boy network, had let the Giants know that what they were really trying to do was to get Pookie to stay in their organization for grooming as a coach. Of course, the Giants had obliged, and when Pookie went to them with proof of his release, he was told that there was no longer a spot for him and the deal was off. So Pookie's only choice after sitting at home for a month was to accept the Cubs offer to come to Peoria as a player/coach, only to do a lot more playing than coaching for most of the season. And now, when they needed an experienced Band-Aid for a pennant race at Triple A, they wanted him to be a player again?

"Crazy business, huh?" I said to Pookie that morning as all this news was being phoned back and forth between Chicago and Peoria.

"No, it's a fucked-up business!"

Rick Wilkins, of course, took the possibility of his jumping all the way to Triple A—even if it was for only a week or so—right in stride, with no excitement, as if it were only his due. That view was not shared by his manager, Jim Tracy.

During a speculative jawboning that very morning between Trace, Kranny, and Richie, as to what level each of our Chiefs should perhaps spend the 1989 season, the subject of Rick's future came up in due course, and Jim Tracy said, "He needs to be at Winston-Salem next year . . . and that's all. Hell, they wanted to send him to Double A a couple of weeks ago. But I just flat told them he wasn't ready yet."

That surprised Richie Zisk, and a discussion then ensued as to how Trace and Richie each viewed Rick Wilkins as a prospect. Both agreed that he would be a major league player. They disagreed, however, on what kind of a major league player he would be, and on how fast he would get there.

"He's a long ways away," Jim Tracy said. "And I don't think he's going to be the offensive player, the impact player with power up there, as some people think."

"I think he will," Richie said. "He's got that short, compact swing . . . it's almost textbook form. Quick bat, Trace? And I don't understand what you guys mean when you say he's too young to play higher ball right now. Hell, he's twenty-one!"

That's when Rick's immature behavior throughout the season was explained to Richie. "Yeah . . . he's twenty-one chronologically, but he's about *maybe* eighteen up here," Kranny said.

"He hasn't cut that umbilical cord, Richie . . . and if he pulls the same shit he's done here up at dubs or trips, those guys'll eat his lunch," Jim Tracy said. "He's just not ready . . . and Richie, our Phenom hasn't been all that phenomenal of late. He still can't hit lefties with any regularity . . . he's still taking too many pitches . . . and he doesn't want to learn, he fights every instruction you try to give him."

"Yeah . . . and he can't call a game for shit. My pitchers don't trust him as far as they can throw him . . . which is about exactly what they'd like to do to him . . . and he's still boxing too many balls in the dirt."

"Hey . . . you guys are the ones that should know . . . but, hey? He's got that one thing you need most . . . he wants it, believes he's going to make it, and he'd spit in even God's eye if He stood in his way."

"Yep . . . but he's not ready yet."

There was one reaction to the news of that morning which had been both surprising and perplexing. Pete Vonachen had always maintained that he was only too happy when one of his Chiefs was "really called up." Well, there's only one more "up" after Triple A. But. . . ?

"What?" was Pete's response when I, thinking that it was great news, and that surely he would already have known about the phone call that

had come that morning, quite innocently brought up the subject of Z's good fortune.

John, Jeff, and Mike had purposely avoided telling him about Z's call-up until just the right moment, like when perhaps he'd had a VO or something and was in a particularly good mood; or until they *had* to tell him.

"Pissed?" he said when questioned about his reaction. "That ain't the half of it." Then he stormed into the front offices and all hell broke loose. So Pete had shown his true colors.

Whatever. He ranted. We lost. And then we went and partied pretty damn good anyway in honor of Fernando's call to the land of the three A's.

The drought in the Midwest was definitely over. It rained like a monsoon all day that Saturday, August 27, and it appeared to be impossible that the last home game, Awards Night, would be played at all.

But Peter of Peoria doesn't have much brook with the impossible, and that game couldn't be made up. It was an important game. For one thing it would've played hell with Jim Tracy's arithmetic; we damn sure didn't want to go up to Cedar Rapids still one game under with a record of 68-69. Sure, a two-game sweep against the powerful Reds would give us a record of 70 and 69, one game over .500; but a split would leave us, forever and ever amen, a "loser" at 69 and 70.

Further developments over the past twenty-four hours had made even a split appear more than just a bit iffy; and a sweep all but a miracle. We'd lost the services of two more pitchers. Greg Kallevig was being sent home two days early for registration at South Dakota State University, and James Matas was off to Chicago to have his injured shoulder examined. Although Kal's loss at the time did not appear quite so serious, since he'd just pitched a complete game the night before and would only be available, if at all, for maybe an out or two if we needed it out of the bullpen; the loss of "the Animal" was serious indeed, since he'd been scheduled to pitch the last game against Cedar Rapids.

We were down to six pitchers. And with Frank Castillo going to the hill that night—if Peter of Peoria had his way with God and the torrential rains slowed to at least only a shower—we would effectively be going to Cedar Rapids with actually only five available pitchers, none of whom were either "stoppers" or "closers."

You can only play and win or lose them one at a time, however. And after a lengthy rain delay, and the tarp was finally pulled, we had a damn important one to win or lose that night in front of 1,401 soggy but loyal fans who had come out for what was "goodbye night" between the family and the stalwart few who had stood with us throughout.

But before Frank threw his first pitch, there was the matter of some awards to be presented. As is customary in such a situation, there was some kind of an award for almost everybody. But there were two or three that were most coveted.

And, with each of us "adults" who had been with the family for the duration at home and on the road, plus Phil Theobald and Pete and his staff, having one equal vote, I think we surely surprised some folks, even as we in the end opted for a bit of hair-splitting compromising.

One of the more prestigious awards was academic and required no vote. Dick Canan won the Batting Title with his .286 average. After several ballots, and some of us changing our votes on each one, it was finally agreed that one honor should be shared: Warren Arrington and Greg Kallevig were co-MVP.

Since a number of us had voted in enough strength to make it a toss-up as to whether or not Greg Kallevig or Fernando Zarranz should share the MVP award with Gator, we really split hairs and, while it might seem odd that a pitcher who was a co-MVP should not also win Pitcher of the Year, it was the only route we could take and still live with ourselves; so the Z Man, though not there to receive it, was awarded Pitcher of the Year.

Of the lesser awards, one must be mentioned here. Because how often does it happen that the Most Improved Player of the Year also wins Most Valuable Player? Not often. But Warren "Gator" Arrington did. Midget number one. Who for two months we "experts" had been all but convinced was overmatched in this league. And Earl Winn, the scout who signed Gator, and who of course was the person that had started us on this journey so long before, should be—and was—mighty proud of that fact.

Then we played baseball. Naturally, with the sudden scarcity of pitchers, we were hoping for an early blowout so we could get Frank off the hill in time that he might be able to come back in relief if we needed him in Cedar Rapids.

The El Paso Buzz Saw certainly did his part. And it did turn out to be a 5-0 laugher. Just not soon enough. Frank had to go nine innings and throw a three-hit, ten-strikeout shutout for his sixth win of the year. And while there was not the spontaneous eruption of emotion on the field and in the stands as there had been two nights before when we'd "climbed that mountain!" the first time, there would be, commencing about an hour later and lasting until just before dawn and just a little before that bus rolled for Cedar Rapids, the single best party night of the season.

It was indeed that strange kind of outpouring of joy, triumph, release, relief, uncensored candor, and celebratory melancholia which sometimes happens when times of great communal import and struggle are finally and victoriously at an end: the thing that brought them together over; the last battle won, the war at an end; the final curtain down to thunderous applause, the play they said couldn't be produced done. It was over. We did it. Someday we'll meet again.

For Johnny Buts, the Greeser, Big Nellie, Dogs, the Rose of California, Dawn, Holly, Mom and Pop, and the hundreds and thousands of others who were Peoria Chiefs baseball that winter, spring, and summer of 1988, it was over. Us? We still had two more ballgames to play. And, much as it had all begun those four and a half months before, it would be just the family alone, banded together on foreign soil, although no longer besieged by doubt from within or without.

There were actually three things the Chiefs had left to play for in Cedar Rapids, Iowa. First and foremost "the Bet," of course. And since "second place" has a far better ring to the ear and ego than does "third place," and since Cedar Rapids had a second-half record of 39-28 and ours was 39-29, by virtue of that one fewer loss in one less number of games played, the Reds were eight and a half games back of Springfield, the Chiefs nine, so there was that. The third thing, while even more esoteric, had perhaps as much if not more importance within that insular world which is professional baseball, and was certainly a much truer measure of player development than either of the other two. The Cedar Rapids Reds had a league-leading team ERA of 2.83. The Peoria Chiefs' ERA was 2.84, one one-hundredth of a percentage point behind. And let me assure you that that one one-hundredth of a percentage point was damn important to the Kran-dog.

We did not have those three reasons for very long. On the early evening of Sunday, August 28, after exactly two and a third innings, the last of the three was no more. That's how long it took Eduardo Caballero to give up five runs, all earned, on six hits—two of them moon shots over the Marlboro Man high above the rightfield wall—three walks, and one hit-by-pitch.

So into the breach came "Hero" Brett Robinson to try and hold it all together long enough for the Chiefs' batters to pick up the pieces and come back from a 5-1 deficit (Jerry LaPenta had also taken a howitzer shot over that Marlboro Man). And hold them he did, pitching masterfully yet again, giving up one hit and no runs for the next three and two-thirds innings as we tried to peck back and made it 5-2.

But then, after the first Reds batter in the seventh, we no longer much cared about reason number two. Not after a fine-looking ballplayer and definite prospect for the big leagues by the name of Reggie Jefferson smashed a wicked one-hop comebacker full into the mouth of Brett Robinson.

It was an ugly and terrifying scene. Brett's first instinct was to look for the ball and the runner even as his hand went to his face to try and hold in whatever was still left of his mouth. He took two dazed steps forward and sank to his knees, motionless. Then followed twenty minutes of horror as he knelt like that as two trainers, two managers, two coaches, two umpires, a policeman, and most of the Chiefs huddled around him while also searching the ground for the missing pieces of Brett's mouth.

Finally an ambulance arrived and the paramedics took him away.

Then, of course, the game went on. And while it seems so trivial and petty even now to remark upon it, the game went on in much the same fashion as it had begun. Only now it was Gabby Rodriguez who was getting shelled. He almost doubled the earned runs he'd allowed in a season's worth of relief work as he and we lost 10-2.

One game under .500. Again. But . . .

For once there would be no wait for Jim Tracy to dress and rehash a ballgame play by play. The moment the last out was made, Trace threw on his street clothes and jumped into Reds trainer Sandy Krum's car so he could get to the hospital to see about his injured pitcher.

While Jim Tracy and Sandy Krum would get to the hospital, it was not as soon as they had thought. They made one unscheduled stop first—and for the second time in the span of less than a week, Brett Robinson would be at least partially responsible for another human being remaining among the living for yet a while longer.

You see, if Jim Tracy and Sandy Krum had not been racing through the deserted downtown section of Cedar Rapids at that late hour of a Sunday night to get to the hospital, then they would not have been there only seconds after fifteen-year-old Steve Tamayo took a spill on his skateboard, striking his head hard on the pavement.

When Trace and Sandy reached him he was unconscious, his body twitching spasmodically. Only seconds thereafter, with Jim Tracy cradling that young head away from the vomit, the twitching stopped, his eyes rolled back into their sockets, his breath ceased, and Sandy could find no pulse.

"He just checked out . . . he was dead . . . right there in my lap!" Jim Tracy would tell us later when he finally got to the motel.

But no, while the doctors would later say he was within maybe a minute of being brain-dead, Sandy Krum, a trained CPR instructor, who had never actually had to apply his training in anything but practice, went to work, and with Jim Tracy's assistance, pumped and breathed life back into that young boy.

Sandy Krum would receive a National Red Cross and a Presidential commendation for his action. And Jim Tracy had an experience he hoped never to have to repeat. But he was so awed, grateful, and pumped-up by having been a part of such an experience that he would stay up all that night and, in ever-more increasing awe, and wonder, and the sudden mix of humility and vulnerability which comes when we are brushed by the utter, random fragility of it all, told and retold and relived and reenacted the story.

In the light of a new day, the last that the family would be together, the horror and wonder of that night, while still a part of the talk of that last breakfast and lunch, subsided and the reason that we were there again took its dominant place: baseball, "the Bet," and our last and final opportunity for the 1988 Peoria Chiefs to be remembered not as losers.

This was easier to do when we saw that the actual damage to our stricken "Hero" was not as severe as first thought. Yes, his lower lip had been cut straight through and many stitches had been necessary to put most of the remaining flesh back in place and together; but most of the teeth that he had not been able to feel in his mouth as he knelt inside that huddle were in fact still in his mouth, they had just been shoved in and up flat against the roof of his palate. He would need much dental work to repair and crown the teeth that had been broken and chipped off, and he would be eating gingerly for a while, but he was down for breakfast, joking and smiling as best he could through a face swollen as large as the grapefruit Mario had in front of him, and proudly showing off the baseball that had done the damage—with the teeth marks clearly visible.

"That's what gloves are for, Brett . . . but no, you've been on such a roll lately you wanted to show us that you could catch that mother with your teeth!" was an oft-repeated refrain that day.

But with the medical atrocities over and done with and all ended well, Jim Tracy and Rick Kranitz had two matters of baseball import to attend to for the balance of that last day of the 1988 season, Monday, August 29.

The first was the most time-consuming. It is Cubs policy that players "shouldn't be left in the dark" about what have or have not been their achievements or progress over the course of the season, what future in the organization at that moment they are perceived to have, and what areas of their game they need to work on over the winter.

While this is Cubs policy, it is usually handled perfunctorily, quickly, and with clichés. Not so with Jim Tracy. Which was why it took most of the day, as one by one each Chief had his full, private, candid, and most personal session.

The other matter, of course, was how in the hell were we going to beat those son of a bitches and climb that mountain to stay when we were now down to five pitchers?

Which was effectively only three, since there was no way Jim Tracy was going to take the risk of perhaps blowing out the arm of one of the organization's brightest pitching prospects, Frank Castillo, who had just gone nine innings less than forty-eight hours before; plus no way was he going to let the Reds have another opportunity to shell Eduardo, even in relief, and even though he'd gone only two and a third—but *long*—innings in that drubbing the night past. That left him Mark North, Bill Melvin, and Gabby Rodriguez.

Mel had not started on three days' rest all season, and had been anything but effective in his last start on Thursday last. Plus, right during one of those debriefing sessions, Angie, not getting an answer when she'd called Mel's room, had the motel operator ring Trace's number, and she

then asked the Chiefs' manager, on the single most important and pri-
oritized day of the season, to please find Bill and have him return her call
collect. Trace *did*—he stuck his head out the door and cackled loud
enough for the whole wing to hear, "Somebody tell Nuke to call the wife
. . . on her nickel!" Later Billy Mel would let it be known that the message was that she would be waiting for him in the Jaguar back at Meinen
Field wearing a mink coat and nothing else; and while that became the
joke of the day, it also gave Jim Tracy reason to have more than a little
doubt as to where Mel's thoughts might be that night if he went to the
mound. Gabby had to be held in relief, his role all year, plus he had been
absolutely stinko in his stint with the Reds' bombers after Brett had gone
down. So there really was no choice. Stout-hearted Ollie would get his
third start of the year, in the single most important game of the year.

"Give me all you've got, for as long as you've got, and then it's Mel
and Gabby behind you," Jim Tracy said to the big, clean-living, soft-
spoken, articulate college graduate and Alabama squire. Then we went
and played some baseball.

For the Cedar Rapids Reds it is a meaningless game, its only purpose
to set up their pitching rotation for the Play-off Series with Springfield.
So Marc Bombard elects to have Mike Moscrey, who would be his starter
in the first play-off game, throw the first two innings and then use a suc-
cession of relievers thereafter.

It is everything but meaningless to us and we waste little time in letting
them know it. Rusty surprises the Reds immediately by pushing a sweet
rolling bunt up the first-base line; clean one-bagger and no chance to get
"Rocket" Crockett. But Mr. Moscrey feels like throwing it anyway, so he
does and Rusty is on second when big-league-bound Moscrey throws it in
the shitter. A passed ball while Gator strikes out puts Rusty on third.
Pookie battles Moscrey for a walk. Dick Canan knows his job and scores
Rusty with a fielder's-choice groundout deep enough to avoid the double
play. Wilkie strikes out. But it's 1-0 for the guys on a mission.

Ramon Sambo, the Reds' DH and lead-off hitter, almost twenty-six
years old, but already in his seventh year of pro ball and still in Single A
baseball because he has only one and a half tools, he can just often
enough make contact and he has world-class speed, hits a two-hopper
hard back up the box. But Rusty goes well behind the bag at second,
gloves it, whirls, and guns it to Polly at first in time. But Sambo is safe on
an E3 when Marc Widlowski (yes, the one and only), umpiring the bases
that night, says Polly was juggling the ball and not in full possession of
same when Sambo came streaking by.

Mr. Sambo, who had scored his hundredth run of the season the night
prior, and wanted badly to get his ninety-eighth, ninety-ninth, and one-
hundredth stolen base on the year for a Midwest League record, and had
quite vocally bragged that he was going to be the only "100-100 man" in

the history of the league, and that he was going to do it against us—which, of course, was the only club he *could* do it against—promptly decides to challenge Rick's arm and takes off; and Wilkie has him dead to dumb-ass rights! Except that Widlowski sees a balk by Ollie that not even God saw, so he's on second—sans stolen bases, however—with nobody out. Then Ollie gets Greg Lonigro to fly out to Pookie in right; and Sambo isn't so dumb that he's going to try and advance on the Pook Monster's arm. Jeff Forney, the Reds' left fielder, is gone on a swinging K for out two. But then, with switch hitter Reggie Jefferson up at the plate and shielding Rick, Sambo gets a running jump and steals third for his ninety-eighth stolen base. And then Mr. Jefferson, a hitter with power and average (.286, 18 HR), drops a lovely bunt down the third-base line good for an RBI and a base hit. Ollie then whiffs third baseman Chris Lombardozzi for out three. One hit, no earned run, but the score is 1-1.

It stays 1-1 until the top of the third, when two Reds errors and an RBI bloop single by Wilkie just over a drawn-in infield makes it 3-1 for the guys on a crusade.

With Ollie rolling on—but not "rolling spinners"—the score stays 3-1 in the bottom of the third, when, after getting safely to first on a fielder's choice, Ramon Sambo goes for number 99 and Wilkie guns him down like he's a milk wagon, not even close.

In their half of the fifth, Rusty boots a lead-off ground ball; the ever dangerous Steve Davis doubles into the right-field corner, but Pookie comes up running and gunning and runners hold at second and third, nobody out; Rich "I wouldn't let referee a Spanish dogfight!" Roder squeezes Ollie tighter than Roder's asshole on two sweetheart curveballs that are strikes and always will be strikes except he calls them balls, and right fielder Norm Brock nubs a 4-3 roller for an RBI; Roder squeezes Ollie again and gives second baseman Scott Sellner a gimme ticket to first, and it's first and third with one out; Sambo gets hold of a fastball and sends it just deep enough to center field for a sacrifice fly; and Ollie gets Lonigro to do the same for out three. We've got a 3-3 ballgame.

Not for long, however. After Steve Davis makes a shoe-top diving catch of a Stevie Hill blooper to short center field, and then makes a truly spectacular back-to-the-plate, sprinting, over-the-shoulder grab of a smash off the bat of the Boz, Phil Hannon works a walk off the second of the scrubeenie relievers that Marc Bombard must have thought he could get away with. Polly triples off the wall to plate Phil. Rusty K's on a good breaking ball down and away. But it's 4-3 for the guys on a do-or-die Pride's Last Charge.

It's soon enough 4-4 when Ollie gives up a single to Mike Malinak (in for Reggie Jefferson at first, only one of the mistakes Manager of the Year in the Midwest League Marc Bombard would make that night) only to catch him leaning toward second and picks him clean for out two. Lombardozzi walks, and Tony Defrancesco, a reserve catcher, replacing power-hitting starter Pete Beeler (as Marc Bombard digs himself deeper into a hole with his bench), doubles in Lombardozzi. Ollie then strikes out the next batter. But the match is knotted.

Ollie has done what Jim Tracy had asked of him; giving all he had for six innings, which were almost exactly one-tenth as many innings as he has pitched all year. Earl Winn has every reason to be proud of another one of the back-home, God's-Country boys he's signed. Just one of those four runs was earned.

So in comes Billy "Nuke" Mel, for his only appearance out of any bullpen in two years, to win or lose the most important game he would pitch in that season. "Pitch" he does. Through the seventh, eighth, ninth, and tenth he shuts the Reds down and out as he faces only two men over the minimum, and erases the only small jam he gets into by picking Steve Davis's pocket clean at second after a two-out walk and single in the ninth.

The tenth? The last game for the '88 Chiefs is to be decided in extra innings? On the road where "the home team always has the advantage because they have six outs to work with and the visitors only three"?

Yes. Marc Bombard, apparently deciding he wants to win this ballgame after all, in the eighth inning ran his ace right-handed reliever Milt Hill in, and that better-than-fair-looking prospect shuts us down and out completely—almost to perfection; and the only reason that doesn't happen is that Stevie Hill outruns a dropped third strike in the eighth.

In the eleventh Bombard, apparently now deciding that, with the play-offs, perhaps his ace closer had best not pitch a fourth inning, runs another pretty decent right-hander by the name of Bruce Colson out to start his warm-up tosses—which is when we learn via the press box that Denver has made a clean sweep of it with our 3A brothers down the interstate in Des Moines. Wilkie and Pookie won't be going to "Trips" after all.

The first batter Mr. Colson has to face is the .207-hitting Stevie Hill—who is hitting .208 after his first swing off young Mr. Colson is a seed through the hole at shortstop. Mr. Colson, seeming not to like that bit of effrontery, immediately tries to pick Stevie off first and throws the ball well beyond the shitter and Stevie is soon standing on third laughing at him. Trace then sends Jerry LaPenta up to pinch-hit for the Boz. "Pizza Man" works the count hard and hangs tough, but ends his last at bat of the season with a swinging K at a fastball cross-firing up and in.

Phil Hannon just knows Trace is going to put on the safety squeeze. But he doesn't get the sign. So, thinking surely he must've misread them, Phil calls time and trots down to the third-base coaching box to make sure that everybody's working with the same set of flashes and wipes and pats tonight. Trace *hadn't* put it on—not yet, not on the first pitch. But then he damn sure likes the look in Phil's eyes when he makes the suggestion. He likes it all the more when Phil trots back and drags a beauty with him on his way to first as Stevie scores and Phil has himself the last base hit he will get on the year. Polly skies to left. Rusty to short. But it's 5-4 for the guys on top of that hold-it-or-die higher and holy ground.

And out lopes Mel to try and keep us there as perhaps that Chalice will finally be ours to fill with twelve-year-old scotch and toast the top of that mountain in style.

It looks like we just might get to do that when Mike Malinak rolls out to Rusty for a quick 6-3 assist and putout which brings us within two outs of that pinnacle we've had in our sights for so long.

Ah . . . but then Mr. Lombardozzi breaks his bat on one of Mel's heaters in on the hands and beats out an infield roller for a base hit. Up steps Mr. Defrancesco. Mel saws *his* bat off at the handle, only to see that goddam ball go trickling and twisting treacherously down the third-base line. Is this going to be it? Two on, only one out, and Steve "Kills the Chiefs" Davis waiting on deck to do it again? Not on Dick Canan's charging-one-hand-pick-up-and-gun-that-sucker-across-the-diamond gamer's heart!

But of course Mr. Lombardozzi is now at second. And Mr. Davis is walking to the plate. Jim Tracy doesn't hesitate. That ball hasn't even been relayed back to Mel before Trace is on his way to the mound and pointing for Gabby.

This is the moment the Shooter has been waiting for. He knew it would have to happen as he watched Marc Bombard steadily unload his gun over the course of the game. He knows that of the three right-handed hitters left on the bench, only Doug Eastman could strike any fear in a pitcher's heart; but he also knows Bombard won't use him now with Steve Davis at the plate, and have no bullets at all left in his revolver. He knows Bombard will not counter, and will let lefty Davis hit against lefty Rodriguez.

Jim Tracy knows the situation, and he knows his man. Remember all that paperwork? While Steve Davis hits left-handers just about as well as right-handers—*he doesn't hit Gabby.* Just the night before, while Davis had helped to bury us with one of those homers over the Marlboro Man, and even though the rest of the Reds had continued to hammer Gabby the same way they had Eduardo, Steve Davis had not. Of the only five outs Gabby had been able to get, two had been made by Davis.

It's all come down to one moment, 140 ballgames minus one out— which is at the plate. Will we be losers after all that struggle?

Gabby's loose. He's on the rubber. He checks Lombardozzi at second. Then that swayed-back and glove-and-ball-swooping, high-leg kick motion so similar to Steve Carlton's. And it's a big breaker. A pretty breaker. So pretty Steve Davis just has to watch it go by. 0-1.

Back on the rubber. Check the runner. The kick. Fastball just outside. Davis doesn't nibble. 1-1.

The rubber. The runner. The kick. Big breaker. Prettier than the first. Davis again savors the beauty of it. But that's all. 1-2.

Davis shifts his feet just slightly in relation to the plate. His hands inch up higher from the knob of the bat. He's adjusting. He's a smart hitter. He's looking for Gabby to come back with that fastball away and he's going to slap it to left field and we play on . . . ?

Gabby shakes Rick off. Another set of signs. Another shake, but then a nod . . . it's all a decoy maybe?

Nope. Here comes that big north-to-south sweeping yakker. Davis picks up the rotation and instinctively stops the already-forward-going weight shift, and brings his hands back to wait just a split-second longer, just like you're supposed to when you're fooled with two strikes and all you're looking for is a piece so maybe you'll get a chance to swing again.

Steve Davis's next swing in competition would come in the play-offs—because, at ten-six on the night of August 29, when *that* swing found only air, Gabby Rodriguez jumped twisting and high up into that cool Indian-summer night and came back down into the arms of his riotous and jubilant teammates. Not far behind them came Jim Tracy and Rick Kranitz.

It was laughing, crying, hugging, pounding, screaming, howling, chanting bedlam—in a vacuum. Because some 3,700 people in Veterans Memorial Stadium looked on in bemused, befuddled, cynical wonder at why in the world nineteen baseball players, a manager, a pitching coach, a bus driver, a radio play-by-play man, and a book writer were crying and laughing and hollering, "We did it! We did it!" much in the fashion one would see at the end of a seven-game World Series.

How could they know that to us that precise 70-and-70 sublime mediocrity *was* a World Series and serious victory? We would not let them wonder long.

Soon we were in the clubhouse. Ice buckets and Gatorade were dumped over heads and people were thrown into showers and people were hugging and pounding and crying and howling and chanting all the more.

"We did it!"

"We did it!"

"Trace . . . Trace . . . we did it!"

A soaking-wet, crying, grinning, head-shaking Shooter, sitting on a stool after having been the first victim of the various dousings, croaked in a hoarse, cracking, choked-back, and whispered voice, "Yeah . . . we did . . . didn't we, Yo? We climbed that mountain to stay . . . so far . . . so far . . . we came . . . this . . . *this* is my greatest moment in baseball . . . to see what those kids did . . . with nothing . . . and from nowhere . . . for nothing . . . but themselves . . ."

And then eventually, at just a little after midnight, in a McDonald's in Cedar Rapids, Iowa, as now with burgers and fries and chicken strips and colas and milkshakes we were celebrating and mourning the simultaneous occasion of that final redemptive victory, that so-long-dreaded fortieth anniversary of the birth of one us, and the fact that Pete Vonachen had sold the goddam ballclub "in our absence!"

Pete had called Jim Tracy just shortly before we left the motel with the news. He had not wanted Trace to have to read it plastered over the front page of the *Journal Star* upon our arrival back in Peoria not long before the coming dawn. But the Shooter had not wanted to tell his ballclub or the other "adults" of the family the news that would stun all of us who thought we knew Pete Vonachen so well.

Trace had waited until we'd won and had some time to celebrate before dropping that bombshell.

"Well . . . that explains one thing," I said. "Now we know why this year was so important to him . . . why he acted the way he did."

"Yeah . . . I guess it does . . . when you add it all up . . . it makes sense . . . but why announce it now? His timing is just a bit piss-poor, huh?"

What a question. Even in our finest hour, Peter of Peoria had found a way to upstage us. It was a city in shock, caring nothing about the wondrous achievement of the family, that we'd all but snuck back into unnoticed that Tuesday morning of August 30.

So as Trace and Kranny and Mario and Phil Theobald and I kept that predawn coffee-and-doughnuts-and-all-morning vigil and reminiscent gabfest, first waiting to, and then saying, our goodbyes to the intermittent stream of Chiefs who came back to the clubhouse before being ferried to the airport, we time and again interrupted our retelling of high tales and low jinks to stare at or reread the lead, front-page headline and story that Phil had written himself, wondering why and to whom the ballclub had been sold.

As was all of Peoria, the Cubs, and the Chicago media, who were calling us to find out what we knew. Which was nothing. We, who had lived and worked and played and fought with Pete Vonachen for so long, knew only what the rest of Peoria would wake up to find splashed in six-column-headline boldness, as they choked over their first cup of coffee and never even got to the season's shortest Chiefs game story detailing ever so briefly our biggest win, written and included almost as an afterthought, because of course Phil had a much larger story that his editors were pushing him hard to investigate and report—who was this "Unidentified Chicagoan," this "successful Chicago-area businessman" who had purchased "majority control" of the Peoria Chiefs?

We, like the rest, had to wait in the whirling "cloud" that engulfed and buffeted us until the full-blown show-biz press conference which was held at home plate of Meinen Field the following Wednesday morning to find out that Clarence Krusinski, that "prominent real estate developer down from Chicago . . . might just want to do some developing around here. Peoria needs some apartment complexes," was now the boss of "the most successful franchise in the forty-eight-year history of the Midwest League."

Yes, that same Clarence Krusinski that Pete had introduced us to some two and a half months before on that late afternoon of June 14 when he'd admonished us, "So, be on your best behavior, right, boys?" and then that night had gone out onto the field and hit an umpire.

Jim Tracy stood at the far right end of the line of dignitaries which flanked the buntinged table where the newsmakers and their children sat in their glory and made speeches and answered the questions of the horde of media present.

No questions were asked of, nor barely even any remarks made to, the big man with the big heart who had, by sheer will, pride, love, and caring, accomplished the "impossible" all of those media-types had been both heralding and doubting so prolifically only three days before by making *winners* and *believers* of a .231-hitting Single A baseball team which was already being forgotten.

And that big man, as he stood there and tried his best to smile as the window dressing he was that morning of August 31, said, in that low Shooter croak and head-shaking whisper:

"Hey . . . it's all right. We know what we did . . . and that's all that counts. Isn't it?"

EXTRA INNINGS

The "Adults"

ON OCTOBER 29, the last weekend of the '88 Arizona Instructional League, one year to the day after Dallas Green's exit, Jim Frey fired Gordon Goldsberry and three of his scouts. Shortly thereafter, Gordon accepted the position of Special Consultant to Roland Hemond, General Manager of the Baltimore Orioles.

On that same October weekend, Bill Harford and Tony Franklin agreed to disagree on Tony's future with the Cubs organization and that he would not be offered, nor would he accept, a contract for 1989. "The Professor" subsequently signed on with the White Sox and managed Sarasota into the Florida State League playoffs.

What had been unofficial during Instructional League, was made official that same weekend: Richie Zisk was promoted to Coordinator of Minor League Instruction in conjunction with his duties as Minor League Hitting Instructor. James Colborn returned to the position of Minor League Pitching Coordinator for the 1989 season. For 1990, Colbie has accepted a quite lucrative offer to do his coaching in the Japanese major leagues.

In mid-November, after Jim Tracy had sent his contract back unsigned, and was in the midst of trying to negotiate a modest raise out of Bill Harford, the Cincinnati Reds sought permission to approach him with an offer of their own. Whereupon the Shooter soon got a bit more of a raise and promotion than he'd expected when he was named to manage Chattanooga of the Double A Southern League. Unfortunately, with a young team made up mostly from the '88 Cedar Rapids ballclub, and with the parent organization pulling up most of his best prospects while the others were spending time on the disabled list, the '89 Lookouts struggled to a record of 58-81. The Trace Monster is determined to improve on that as he returns to Chattanooga for the 1990 season.

When the Peoria Chiefs elected to go with a more powerful radio station, Mario Impemba went down to Atlanta for the Winter Meetings in early December and returned as the new play-by-play announcer for the Quad Cities Angels.

By the time of the Winter Meetings, the Cubs had hired Dick Balderson as Director of Scouting; the minor league department and the scouting department became separate entities. Earl Winn was promoted from territorial scout to Central Area Supervisor.

In early January, Brandon Davis was relieved of his duties as National Scouting Supervisor. He then chose to sit out 1989 courtesy of the Tribune Company, as the Cubs honored the last year of his contract.

To mitigate the heartbreak of a divorce, the Cubs arranged for Rick Kranitz to spend his winter as the pitching coach for Caimanes in the Dominican Winter League. He then returned to Peoria for the '89 season to be Brad Mill's "Mule," and the coach of a pitching staff whose 2.69 ERA was the third best in all of minor league baseball. The Kran-dog will be the pitching coach at Double A Charlotte of the Southern League for 1990 (the Cubs vacated Pittsfield at the conclusion of the 1988 season).

And Pete Vonachen sold his cake and got to eat it too. While he pocketed a cool million dollars profit on the sale of a franchise for which he'd paid $125,000 in 1983, he also made sure nothing would really change by hand-picking the new majority owner, and then negotiating a deal that would keep him as chairman of the board with a minority interest, and John Butler as general manager, also with minority ownership. Then, while John settled into the big paneled office along with all of the everyday headaches, "the boss" still made speeches selling Chiefs, came down to Arizona for his annual spring training lobbying trip, and was Mr. Showman on hand as Peoria broke yet another attendance record by drawing 225,757 into Meinen Field while the Chiefs missed the playoffs by three percentage points because of two less games that Cedar Rapids couldn't play in the first half, even though their overall record of 80-59 was third best in the Midwest League and better than both Rockford and Springfield who did make the playoffs.

The Ballplayers

Herbie Andrade: shared catching duties at Charleston; hit .159 with 176 at bats. Released, January 3, 1990.

Warren Arrington: returned to Peoria; struggled, shared playing time in a five-man outfield, and hit .221. Released, December 8, 1989.

Lenny Bell: starting first baseman at Winston-Salem. Had by far his best pro season, leading that club in average, .271; hits, 119; RBI's, 68; and was second in home runs, 9. Is expected to be the starting first baseman at Double A Charlotte for the 1990 season.

Pookie Bernstine: full-time outfield instructor; however, was not offered contract for 1990.

Mike Boswell: released, March 25, 1989.

Dick Canan: had fine Instructional League, his .327 average was fourth best on the two Cubs teams; but struggled at Winston-Salem from early on and ended up sharing playing time at third base. Hit .246 on season. His gamesmanship, versatility of being able to play third and short, and the fact that he's an "organizational" baseball man the Cubs want in their system, however, have him already penciled into the Double A Charlotte roster.

Rusty Crockett: aggravated shoulder injury cut short his participation in Instructional League. Was starting second baseman at Winston-Salem. Got off to terrible start with the bat; hitting below .200 fully halfway into the season. Then got hot enough to finish the year batting .241, third on the club in hits, 109; led in at bats, 452, and stolen bases, 22. Cubs still high on "Davey"; is expected to be starting second baseman at Double A Charlotte.

Sergio Espinal: released, March 25, 1989.

Phil Hannon: starting centerfielder at Winston-Salem. While Jimmy Piersall still says he's the "best defensive centerfielder in the system," Phil's .233 batting average didn't erase his biggest question mark. He is, however, chiseled in as the starting center fielder at Double A Charlotte.

Steve Hill: released, April 1, 1989; one of the last cuts before breaking camp. However, on next to the last day of camp, after Stevie was already back home with shattered dreams in San Diego, the Seattle Mariners called Bill Harford and asked him to recommend one of the Cubs' recently released infielders. Bill recommended Hill. Stevie was immediately signed and went on to be the starting third baseman for the San Bernardino Spirits of the California League. On a prospect-laden club, he hit a solid .280 and was among the team leaders in several offensive categories.

Jerry LaPenta: released, March 25, 1989.

Elvin Paulino: returned to Peoria where he led the club in average, .295, and RBI's, 72; was second in hits, 122, and home runs, 8. Polly is young, and still very much a prospect; was invited to '89 Instructional League. It was discovered he'd played the previous two seasons with a separated shoulder, which he was popping back in himself rather than telling anyone for fear surgery would prevent him from playing winter ball back home—which he counts on to support his family. He's now had the surgery and his next stop will be Winston-Salem.

Marty Rivero: utility infielder at Winston-Salem; hit .200 with 145 at bats. Released, September 15, 1989.

Jossy Rosario: split playing time at shortstop, Charleston. Hit .194 with 319 at bats. Still young, with excellent athletic skills. Will have to start hitting soon, however; in all likelihood that opportunity will come at Peoria in 1990.

Bob Strickland: left-handed platoon DH at Winston-Salem; hit .250 with 260 at bats. Released, December 8, 1989.

Horace Tucker: released just shortly after being sent back to extended spring training from Peoria in May 1988.

Rick Wilkins: had great Instructional League, hitting .338. In April, in their "The Best of '89" issue, *Baseball America* ranked him as the fifth best catching prospect in all of the minor leagues after Rick had had the third best caught-stealing-against percentage, .427, in the minors, and was first in total caught-stealing with 73 while at Peoria. That publication also rated him the fourth best prospect in the Cubs organization overall, ahead of catcher Joe Girardi, who at that time was already playing in the big leagues, and catcher Kelly Mann, who soon would be (but with Atlanta). As the starting catcher at Winston-Salem, Wilkie hit .249, led the club in home runs, 12, and was second in RBI's, 54. Was named to the Carolina League All-Star Team. Voted "Best Defensive Catcher in Carolina League" by the respective managers. And was the only catcher in the league to be ranked by Baseball America as a "Top 10 Prospect" of that circuit. He was again invited to Instructional League before the Cubs then sent him to play for Zulia in the Venezuelan Winter League. Prior to the Winter Meetings in Nashville, Rick was placed on the forty-man roster and will report to big league camp in February 1990. Barring trades and injuries, he is expected to start the season at Double A Charlotte— and possibly end it higher still.

Eddie Williams: returned to Peoria as everyday rightfielder; hit .244 batting exclusively from the left side as the attempt to make him a switch-hitter was abandoned. Fast Eddie had 14 stolen bases. Both of those numbers need substantial improvement for Eddie to be considered the prospect he was when drafted in the third round; will get that opportunity at Winston-Salem, 1990.

Mike Aspray: 8-15, with an ERA of 3.86 in the starting rotation at Winston-Salem. His ten complete games was third highest in minor leagues. Is expected to make rotation at Double A Charlotte with a good spring training.

Eduardo Caballero: 5-6, with an ERA of 3.65 in seventeen starts in twenty-three appearances at Winston-Salem. Arm problems limited him to 111 innings. When he was healthy, he was still erratic as attested by 117 hits given up, but 75 strikeouts with only 38 walks. Ticketed for another season in Carolina League.

Frank Castillo: in March '89, *Baseball America* ranked him as the fifth best prospect in the Cubs organization overall, and the second ranked pitcher. Began season in starting rotation at Winston-Salem where his 9-6 record, ERA of 2.51, and 114 strikeouts in 129 innings pitched with only 24 walks, and 8 complete games, earned him a spot on the Carolina League All-Star team, plus a promotion to Double A. At Charlotte, in ten starts, Frank posted a record of 3-4, with an ERA of 3.84. His total of twelve complete games was the best in the minor leagues. The Cubs placed him with the Zulia Winter League team, and also on their forty-man roster. He too will report to spring training with the big league club in February 1990. It is expected that he will begin the season at Triple A Iowa, and possibly pitch in the major leagues before season's end.

John Gardner: used both as a starter and out of the bullpen at Charleston, he surely pitched his way back to at least Peoria for the 1990 season with a record of 3-4, ERA of 2.51, only 72 hits in 103 innings pitched and 84 strikeouts; of course he walked 69.

John Green: in an "accommodation deal" shortly after Dallas Green dared to match egos with George Steinbrenner, his son was traded to the Yankees for a nonprospect outfielder who was then promptly released by the Cubs in spring training. Mr. Greenjeans, on the other hand, opened the season with Fort Lauderdale of the "high" Class A Florida State League and pitched well enough to get himself promoted to Double A Albany of the Eastern League. There he posted the not-at-all shabby numbers of 2-1, three saves, an ERA of 2.68 over forty innings pitched in twenty appearances, and got in on all the fun as Albany made a mockery of that circuit (92-48!) on their way to the playoffs and then a championship ring.

Carl Hamilton: after finally agreeing to surgery on his elbow, he was left unprotected by the Cubs, and the Orioles took him in the minor league draft at the Winter Meetings in December 1988. With his shoulder then hurting him, he threw one inning in spring training and was released.

Greg Kallevig: in a full-season stint at Double A Charlotte, pitching mostly out of the starting rotation, he went 7-10 with an ERA of 3.61. Kal will be given every chance to make the Triple A roster in spring training. If he doesn't, age and the numbers game will have him decidedly "on the bubble"; the Cubs left him protected only at the Double A level for the Winter Meetings and there were no takers.

Jeff Massicotte: returned to Peoria, where he was the long man out of the bullpen and a spot starter. Grandpa put together a solid enough season statistically, going 3-3, with an ERA of 2.82 in ninety-three innings pitched, striking out sixty-nine. The Cubs felt that those numbers were deceiving, however, and that now in two years he has not come close to fulfilling the promise of his rookie season. Is "on the bubble" for spring training 1990.

James Matas: released, March 23, 1989.

Bill Melvin: even though he hung around Peoria for several days after the season, and returned there for another visit after making some progress learning a slider at Instructional League, in the end, "Nuke" jilted "the Black Widow" instead of the other way around. Without "Angie," Billy Mel spent the season in the starting rotation at Winston-Salem going 6-9, with an ERA of 4.69, mostly due to the fact that he again had trouble with the strike zone, walking 81 in 127 innings, and then giving up 140 hits as he all-too-often was forced to groove one behind in the count. But the Cubs are still high on that "live" arm, invited him back to Instructional League, and protected him at the Triple A level for the Winter Meetings. Pretty good chance though that he'll be at Winston-Salem again for the start of the 1990 season.

Mark North: on March 29, 1989, just as his name was on the wrong side of the "bubble list" board, the Minnesota Twins came calling and traded a Triple A outfielder to get him. The Cubs eventually released the outfielder; but all Ollie did was take the Twins ladder three rungs in one season. Starting the year back in the Midwest League at Kenosha, he was soon at Visalia of the California League, and then on to Double A Orlando of the Southern League, where he held his own as a starter going 2-1, with an ERA of 3.55, in five starts down the stretch and into the league playoffs.

Brett Robinson: returned to Peoria and had an outstanding season as a starter on a staff of "Aces"; 15-9, ERA of 2.79, and 160 strikeouts in 187 innings. Was invited to '89 Instructional League. Robbie and family should be inquiring after housing in the Charlotte area, as he will be given every opportunity in spring training to compete for a starting spot on the Double A staff.

Gabby Rodriguez: spent the season at Winston-Salem doing pretty much the same thing he did at Peoria in '88, left-hand setup man, posting a record of 4-3, with an ERA of 2.00, 2 saves, and sixty strikeouts in sixty-eight innings, but with forty walks. Was invited back to Instructional League. Experienced some aggravation of the shoulder problem that had occasioned major surgery during his college career. However, the Cubs remain high on Gabby's arm—if low on his wardrobe and lifestyle—and he could make more than one move in 1990.

Scott Sanderson: big leagues. A member of the '89 National League East Champion Chicago Cubs. Subsequently signed as a free agent by the World Champion Oakland A's.

Dean Edward Schulmeister, II: released, March 25, 1989.

Fernando Zarranz: after an excellent Instructional League, he joined Kranny at Caimanes of the Dominican Winter League, where he pitched well at times but developed a problem with the strike zone and a sore arm. The soreness was still there by spring training and the frustration of it simmered the "Z" in him until it finally brought forth an extreme episode of "That Fucking Idiot," a petulant, vulgar, loud, and embarrassingly public confrontation with Bill Harford on the next-to-last day of camp over a matter as inconsequential as beer not being served at the annual barbecue the Maricopa Inn throws for all the Cub minor leaguers who are their guests for any number of weeks during each year. Although he was assigned to the Double A Charlotte roster, he spent much of the early weeks of the '89 season at extended spring training. When he did pitch at Charlotte, he was markedly ineffective: 0-2, ERA of 11.70, ten innings pitched, thirteen hits, fourteen walks, and seven strikeouts. Those numbers got him a ticket back to Peoria, which improved his attitude not at all, and his numbers only somewhat as he sulked and stomped his way around to the tune of a 0-1 record, ERA of 4.50, two saves in seven appearances, giving up twelve hits in ten innings. But his arm was now sound, and he'd found the strike zone, as attested by only two walks and fourteen strikeouts. He then finished the season at Winston-Salem, pitching as the Z Man we know and love: 4-3, 1.70 ERA, nineteen appearances, forty-eight innings pitched, twenty-seven hits, fourteen walks, and forty-two strikeouts. Fernando's future is uncertain; while pitching through an injury will almost always buy you another year—at what level? Bill Harford holds no grudges, but Z has yet to demonstrate any effectiveness beyond Single A ball; age and the numbers game mean that the right Z Man had best show up for spring training and then make some progress quickly in this, his season "on the bubble."

The Organization

The move toward fiscal economy within the minor league department continued. After the 1989 season, the two-year experiment of a third full-season Class A club ended when the Cubs terminated their affiliation with Charleston. They also fielded only one team in the '89 Arizona Instructional League.

However, any debate over the effectiveness of the scouting and farm system that was in place when Jim Frey took over must be summarily dismissed by the fact that no less than five homegrown rookies stepped right up and joined with ten other recent grow-your-own young veterans already there to be major contributors in the 1989 Chicago Cubs winning the National League East crown. Two of those five, Jerome Walton and Dwight Smith, finished one-two in balloting for the National League Rookie of the Year. Also, two of the five made the jump straight from Double A, Walton and Joe Girardi. Indeed, Don Zimmer and his Kiddy Corps gave America quite a thrill this past summer and fall of '89.

But, wouldn't you know it, that downhome "Hoss," Will Clark, hitting 'em even farther than he used to against my O. Perry Walker Chargers, almost single-handedly made sure that when this book is published it would *not* be about the farm system of the defending 1989 World Champions.

Final Stats, 1988

PLAYER	AVG	G	AB	R	H	2B	3B	HR	RBI	BB	SO	SB	CS	SLG	OBP	E
Andrade	.163	29	80	5	13	3	0	0	3	7	28	0	3	.200	.227	3
Arrington	.252	133	488	73	123	20	11	2	41	41	114	46	6	.350	.315	11
Bell	.245	64	245	20	60	9	1	1	19	12	65	2	2	.302	.280	16
(Charleston)	.199	54	196	11	39	9	2	2	19	12	44	0	2	.296	.254	18
# Bernstine	.250	63	204	19	51	8	3	0	22	12	30	11	2	.319	.293	2
Boswell	.175	72	200	17	35	7	1	3	18	16	61	4	3	.265	.241	13
Canan	.287	63	230	32	66	12	1	0	35	19	45	0	3	.348	.351	18
Crockett	.243	63	239	33	58	3	1	1	30	14	32	18	6	.276	.305	19
Espinal	.209	53	163	20	34	7	1	3	17	22	55	4	3	.319	.305	3
(Charleston)	.194	44	129	15	25	4	0	0	5	17	23	3	0	.225	.289	8
# Hannon	.237	139	562	61	133	20	4	1	49	27	98	33	19	.292	.277	7
Hill	.208	47	168	15	35	7	1	1	15	15	26	9	4	.280	.282	3
(Winston-Salem)	.250	78	272	35	68	9	4	1	22	31	37	9	4	.318	.332	17
* LaPenta	.225	79	218	27	49	8	0	4	26	38	47	5	3	.317	.345	4
(Pittsfield)	.205	27	73	4	15	3	0	1	7	8	15	1	0	.288	.293	1
* Paulino	.233	122	404	44	94	19	5	2	40	48	71	3	3	.319	.325	16
Rivero	.209	101	374	36	78	14	1	5	30	15	80	4	1	.291	.244	42
(Winston-Salem)	.190	18	58	9	11	2	0	0	3	1	11	0	0	.197	.203	3
Rosario	.188	56	181	12	34	5	0	0	15	11	24	3	1	.215	.234	15
(Charleston)	.189	44	148	12	28	4	0	0	9	5	20	2	2	.216	.228	6
* Strickland	.236	26	72	8	17	2	2	2	11	9	23	1	0	.403	.317	0
(Charleston)	.245	27	98	6	24	5	0	2	12	6	19	0	1	.357	.288	0
(Pittsfield)	.207	41	82	8	17	3	0	1	14	7	16	0	0	.280	.272	5
Tucker	.200	6	10	0	2	0	0	0	0	0	4	0	0	.200	.273	1
* Wilkins	.243	137	490	54	119	30	1	8	63	67	113	4	6	.357	.337	19
# Williams	.223	111	323	43	72	12	1	0	24	35	82	23	12	.266	.319	6

TEAM TOTALS

	AVG		AB	R	H	2B	3B	HR	RBI	BB	SO	SB		SLG	OBP	E
Peoria Only	.231		4652		1073	34		458		997		77		.307		213
				519		186	33		408		170				.300	

PITCHER	W-L	ERA	G	GS	CG	SHO	SV	IP	H	R	ER	HR	HB	BB	SO	WP
Aspray	8-14	2.80	25	24	7	1	0	180.0	149	73	56	10	5	45	116	3
(Winston-Salem)	2-0	2.28	4	4	2	0	0	28.0	24	9	7	0	1	12	15	3
Caballero	9-12	3.73	28	28	3	2	0	166.1	155	82	69	16	3	50	158	6
Castillo	6-1	0.71	9	8	2	2	0	51.0	25	5	4	1	1	8	58	0
Gardner	2-0	5.65	7	1	0	0	0	14.1	13	10	9	0	0	11	18	4
Green	0-1	2.18	13	0	0	0	0	20.2	21	9	5	2	2	6	20	1
(Pittsfield)	0-3	5.16	11	2	0	0	0	16.1	19	14	10	2	0	10	6	1
(Winston-Salem)	5-2	3.49	27	0	0	0	9	56.2	55	24	22	4	6	18	43	3
* Hamilton	0-1	3.57	4	4	0	0	0	17.2	22	7	7	1	0	7	10	1
Kallevig	11-9	1.44	29	18	8	1	0	175.1	132	38	28	5	8	29	80	6
(Winston-Salem)	0-3	5.26	4	4	1	0	0	26.2	32	19	15	4	1	8	12	0
Massicotte	8-12	5.63	41	7	0	0	1	80.0	84	66	50	1	8	51	74	4
Matas	3-0	0.50	3	3	0	0	0	18.0	8	1	1	0	0	9	19	0
(Winston-Salem)	1-4	5.37	26	3	0	0	2	60.0	55	43	36	4	5	43	59	7
Melvin	8-9	3.54	28	27	3	2	0	180.2	151	80	71	11	4	70	134	7
* North	2-0	3.07	32	3	0	0	0	73.1	67	40	25	9	4	30	68	4
Robinson	9-6	3.64	30	16	0	0	0	131.0	135	66	53	7	1	48	94	4
* Rodriguez	2-2	1.51	53	0	0	0	5	83.1	57	23	14	0	1	33	62	8
Sanderson	0-0	0.00	1	1	0	0	0	5.0	4	1	0	0	0	0	3	0
Schulmeister	0-0	7.71	1	0	0	0	0	2.1	3	2	2	0	1	2	0	0
Zarranz	3-3	1.15	46	0	0	0	21	55.0	42	10	7	1	0	9	59	0
(Iowa)	1-0	9.64	3	0	0	0	0	5.0	8	6	5	1	0	2	7	0

TEAM TOTALS

	W-L	ERA	G			SHO		IP		R		HR		BB		WP
Peoria Only	70	2.88	140			8		1254.0		513		64		408		48
	70					23	27		1068		401		37		973	

Note: * denotes left-handed batter or pitcher
 # denotes switch hitter

ACKNOWLEDGMENTS

AFTER TWO WINTERS, two spring trainings, a season, an instructional league, and almost eighteen months on the road in about half that many states, the author is endebted to literally hundreds of people, in and out of baseball. Alas, they are so numerous, yet all so important, that we dare not even attempt to list them here for fear that we leave some-one out.

In that spirit then: thank you—each of you. You know what you did, and so do we. And that's all that matters, isn't it?

INDEX